PENGUIN BOOKS

SHOWTIME

'Leahy's book is an excellent mixture of political history and compelling narrative. At times, it is truly like a thriller, where we anxiously read on to see what happens next, even though, unfortunately, we know what happens next' Eamon Delaney, *Irish Times*

'I really loved Pat Leahy's *Showtime* . . . It's a very easy accessible book, and a fascinating insight into our version of a fun-sized Roman Empire, and all the follies that go with it. The books I read have to be engaging from the get-go – and the appeal of *Showtime* was that it was done with almost a breathless excitement. As a political anorak, I loved all the intrigue and shenanigans between Bertie and his minders. It was *Yes Minister* meets *House of Cards*' Ryan Tubridy, RTÉ

'The premise behind Leahy's book is spot-on. "*Showtime* politics as ruled by the electoral cycle and everything – politics, economics, government personnel and coalition choices – were subjected to the overwhelming imperative of maintaining power," he writes. And yet this is not a cranky rant about Fianna Fáil shenanigans, or another angry (and wearying) diatribe about how Ahern got us all into this mess . . . Not only is Leahy's account written well, and studded with fascinating anecdotes, it is immensely wise in its analysis and insight. This is easily the best book about Irish politics produced in the period that Leahy has covered' *Sunday Times*

'Easily the most elegantly written of the political books on the market this year. I don't agree with his angle on Bertie Ahern, but he writes with brio and balance' Eoghan Harris, *Sunday Independent*

D1341222

ABOUT THE AUTHOR

Pat Leahy is the political editor of *The Sunday Business Post*, and is a regular contributor to radio and television programmes. He has a degree in law from UCD and was a Reuters fellow at Oxford University in 2001. He is a native of Clonmel, Co. Tipperary, and now lives in Ranelagh, Dublin, with his wife Nicola MacKenzie and two children, Elizabeth and Hugh. *Showtime* is his first book.

Showtime

The Inside Story of Fianna Fáil in Power

PAT LEAHY

PENGUIN BOOKS

PENGUIN BOOKS

Published by the Penguin Group
Penguin Books Ltd, 80 Strand, London WC2R ORL, England
Penguin Group (USA), Inc., 375 Hudson Street, New York, New York 10014, USA
Penguin Group (Canada), 90 Eglinton Avenue East, Suite 700, Toronto, Ontario, Canada M4P 2Y3
(a division of Pearson Penguin Canada Inc.)
Penguin Ireland, 25 St Stephen's Green, Dublin 2, Ireland
(a division of Penguin Books Ltd)
Penguin Group (Australia), 250 Camberwell Road, Camberwell, Victoria 3124, Australia
(a division of Pearson Australia Group Pty Ltd)
Penguin Books India Pvt Ltd, 11 Community Centre, Panchsheel Park,
New Delhi – 110 017, India
Penguin Group (NZ), 67 Apollo Drive, Rosedale, North Shore 0632, New Zealand
(a division of Pearson New Zealand Ltd)
Penguin Books (South Africa) (Pty) Ltd, 24 Sturdee Avenue, Rosebank, Johannesburg 2196,
South Africa

Penguin Books Ltd, Registered Offices: 80 Strand, London WC2R ORL, England

www.penguin.com

First published by Penguin Ireland 2009
Published in Penguin Books 2010
1

Copyright © Pat Leahy, 2009

The moral right of the author has been asserted

Printed in Great Britain by Clays Ltd, St Ives plc

A CIP catalogue record for this book is available from the British Library

ISBN: 978–1–844–88225–0

www.greenpenguin.co.uk

Penguin Books is committed to a sustainable future
for our business, our readers and our planet.
The book in your hands is made from paper
certified by the Forest Stewardship Council.

For my mother and my father

Contents

Introduction

'How's the hard-workin' Chancellor?'

The aides to the Taoiseach listening in on the call with the Chancellor of the Federal German Republic, Gerhard Schroeder, allowed themselves a smile. They were used to this mix of barroom familiarity and international diplomacy as the President of the European Council sought to push his agenda of compromise and incremental progress. The nudging towards a deal, the frequently expressed understanding of the other's predicament, the sympathizing that, sure, if only the rest of them would listen to your sensible arguments, Gerhard (or Tony, or Silvio, or whoever) – all that would come a little later. It was usually effective.

In the six months of Ireland's EU presidency in 2004, it was brilliantly effective, as Bertie Ahern steered an increasingly diverse European Union to a treaty that admitted the former Soviet satellites of Eastern and Central Europe, cementing them into the political and economic norms of the West. At home, he had presided over an economy that was the envy of the world. And he continued to shepherd an historic peace process in Northern Ireland towards a reluctant conclusion. Gathering in Dublin, Ahern's European counterparts must have envied him. He was the most successful political leader in Europe. And he showed no sign of decline; days or maybe even hours after this call and hundreds like it, Ahern would be on the streets of his Dublin constituency, knocking on doors, greeting people in the street with his familiar 'How's the hard-workin' man?'

The great resuscitation of Fianna Fáil under Ahern, and his journey to the summit of Irish and European politics, had been a long and sometimes unlikely road. When he assumed the leadership of his party in 1994, it was distressed and divided, riven by years of fraternal strife. Moreover, it was about to be cast into the darkness of opposition, from which there might well have been no escape for a decade. Under Ahern's leadership, the party was united and transformed into an election-winning machine. His embrace of coalition transformed Fianna Fáil from a party with all of the power for most of the time into a party with most of the power all of the time. With the Progressive Democrats, the party presided over an economic boom that transformed Ireland, bettering the lives of millions of her citizens. The settlement of the Northern Irish conflict healed the island's open sore. Ahern's governments resolved the two great failures of the independent Irish state: economic failure and Northern conflict.

But by the time Ahern took his deserved European plaudits, the model constructed by this political Midas was in trouble. Promises made at the previous election were unfulfilled, and the electorate was angry. Only weeks after the call with the German Chancellor, Ahern was to suffer what was then the worst defeat that a sitting Taoiseach ever experienced in the 2004 local and European elections. These defeats would have a profound effect on Ahern's administration, not by changing the system, which sought to placate as many people as possible, but by reinforcing it to the exclusion of much else – including, as events would transpire, sound economic management.

When PJ Mara fired the starting pistol for the 2002 general election campaign, he declared it was 'Showtime!' He could have been summing up Fianna Fáil's approach to winning, using and keeping power.

Showtime politics was ruled by the electoral cycle and where everything – policy, economics, government personnel and coalition choices – was subjected to the overwhelming imperative of maintaining power. It was the retention of political power above all else to which Bertie Ahern's Fianna Fáil was dedicated.

The electoral imperative expressed itself in a chronic short-termism when governing, and an almost manic desire to cultivate, carefully and individually, a myriad of constituencies – ranging from school action groups to powerful public-sector unions, from builders to hospital consultants. 'Politics is keeping enough people happy at the right time and taking the shit for the rest of the time,' one of the most senior figures in Ahern's administration told me later. But for all the economic and political successes of the government, it never articulated a vision of what it was all for.

Nor, it should be said, did Fianna Fáil's opposition offer anything of substance or distinctive appeal. The outstanding performance of the Irish economy was not matched by a politics of equal calibre. Lacking any central defining purpose, the mass appeal of Ahern's Fianna Fáil could be sustained only by greater largesse: extra spending, bigger promises, more Showtime. Its denouement would come with a spectacular economic crash which will partly define the legacy of the Ahern years. The problem wasn't Showtime election campaigns: it was Showtime government.

By the time the full extent of the economic crash had become evident, Ahern had departed his office, finally beaten by an inquiry that seemed to have little relevance to its original purpose, but to which he had been unable to answer satisfactorily basic questions about his own financial dealings. When he was subjected to an investigation whose workings were often questionable and which sometimes struggled to justify itself, Ahern's apparent defence was not that he shouldn't have accepted money from private sources while a public officer-holder but that it was unfair that he had been caught.

This is not a book about Bertie Ahern, though he is, unquestionably, its central character. I have not attempted a portrait of the former Taoiseach, though some assessment of his character is inevitable. Other characters occupy pivotal positions, too: Charlie McCreevy, the most influential finance minister in Irish history; PJ Mara, a political veteran of the Haughey era who ran the most modern election campaigns in Irish history; Mary Harney; and then, circulating like planets around the sun of political power, a host of ministers, TDs, advisers, spin doctors and officials. This book is the story of how their feuds, fears, compromises and sometimes dazzling successes made Irish politics for a decade and a half a time of very great achievement, but also of great mistakes. Václav Havel's characterization of politics as 'not only . . . the art of the possible, especially if this means the art of speculation, calculation, intrigue, secret deals and pragmatic manoeuvring, but . . . the art of the impossible, namely the art of improving ourselves and the world' was lived out by Fianna Fáil in these tumultuous years.

I had been idly considering the idea for a book about Bertie Ahern's leadership of Fianna Fáil for almost a year before I received a call from Michael McLoughlin at Penguin in February 2008. Michael displayed great enthusiasm about the project from the start, reinforcing my view that while there were good reasons not to write the book – a day job, a forthcoming baby – there were also good reasons for going ahead with it.

I was conscious that the real story of the extraordinary recent period in Irish politics had not so far been told in any satisfactory detail. Moreover, the demands of daily and weekly journalism are such that any sort of coherent narrative of a government's term of office tends to get lost in the demands for headlines and copy. The nature of journalism is that it concentrates on the story of the day or the week, and then moves on. I was attracted by the prospect of going beyond those constraints. I was encouraged by officials and politicians, who saw merit in the idea of trying to record an account of the time that went beyond the already published versions or the authorized ones surely to come. The more I discovered about the inner workings of Ahern's administration, the more I discovered that journalists – myself included – got some things right, and some things very wrong.

I have not tried to construct a day-by-day account of the period, or to record all, or even most, of the actions of Bertie Ahern's governments. Rather I have sought to relate in as much detail as possible the course of events and episodes which I believe to be significant or illuminating of the true nature of the Ahern governments. On Northern Ireland, given the wealth of published material already in circulation, I have confined myself to an account of how the peace process affected southern politics.

At the beginning of the project, I decided to conduct all interviews on an off-the-record basis. Some readers might find this frustrating, others unsatisfactory. It is a price I believe is justified to encourage candour and truthfulness from politicians and their aides and officials. Journalists are constantly amazed that politicians with whom they have had revealing and entertaining private conversations can go on to be stilted and dull when interviewed for broadcast media or where they expect to be quoted by name. Politicians and those who work for them are franker and fairer, more revealing and better value in private. Speaking to them on an off-the-record basis simply recognizes this fact. Anyway, there already exists much printed and broadcast material which records their attributed thoughts.

I have quoted conversations between people where I have a reliable record of what passed between them from the principals, from people who were present or from people to whom they related the exchange afterwards. A small number come from contemporaneously published accounts. Many of them are, I am afraid, replete with profanity. That is how it is. Politicians, like journalists perhaps, tend to swear quite a lot.

I am enormously grateful to the very many people who spoke to me in the preparation of this book. I am grateful not just for their time and their co-operation but for their trust. Many spoke to me not just to record their own involvement in the events described, but from a genuine feeling that it was a story that deserved to be told. This book is the product of almost a hundred interviews, but also of many more conversations with people at every level of politics. Often, I am sure, I trespassed on people's patience and goodwill, and on the tolerance of their assistants and staff. They all have my thanks.

I have been blessed with an understanding editor at *The Sunday Business Post*, who has tolerated occasional absences from combat duty in the preparation of this work. Cliff Taylor continues to provide me with the very great benefit of his knowledge of economics and government finances; he also read drafts of chapters and provided helpful suggestions. I am grateful to him and to all my colleagues at the newspaper for constant good humour and stimulation. Simon Carswell, Paul Farrell and Roddy O'Sullivan brought their skills and knowledge to bear on the drafts of chapters, as did my colleague Gavin Daly. My sister Caitriona Leahy read chapters and made suggestions, and was a constant encouragement when spirits and energy flagged. My father, Seamus Leahy, brought his wit and wisdom and his demands for clarity of expression, well known to many generations of Rockwell College students, to several chapters. Remaining errors, needless to say, are mine alone. Stephen and Barbara MacKenzie and Naomi Kidney provided a priceless quiet space for writing. When it was done, Patricia Deevy, my editor at Penguin, wrestled with the manuscript – and sometimes with its author – to improve it.

My wife, Nicola, encouraged the book from the outset, and acted as a sounding board for ideas and a critic of first resort. Her help throughout was tireless and selfless, and she assumed almost entirely to herself the burdens of first one, then two, wonderful but demanding small children. Without her, this book, and very much else, would not have been possible.

Pat Leahy
June 2009

1. Ambition Fulfilled, Plans Thwarted

It was early December 1994, and the tail end of a North Atlantic storm was blowing its last gasps when the early morning peace was broken in several households across the sleeping city of Dublin. Noisy telephones rang to convey shock news: there would be no deal. Bertie Ahern would not become Taoiseach later that day. The revival of the collapsed Fianna Fáil–Labour coalition government, under the new leader of Fianna Fáil, was cancelled. Dramatically reversing his earlier intention, the Labour leader, Dick Spring, had decided definitively that he would not re-enter government with Fianna Fáil, and had communicated his decision to the new leader of that party in a 2.00 a.m. phone call. Ahern himself has said that his reaction to this news was to fall back on his pillow and say, 'Hell!' Other reactions were somewhat stronger. Chris Wall, a doughty constituency lieutenant of Ahern who would often provide a link between his St Luke's base and the national party apparatus, rang PJ Mara, Charles Haughey's urbane right-hand man, who had returned to the centre of power with Ahern's election as leader. 'The fucking thing is gone!' Wall spluttered. 'This thing is gone!' 'What thing? What?' answered a confused and sleepy Mara. 'Don't fucking ask me! It's just gone!' Ahern himself was more direct in his explanation to his long-time adviser Paddy Duffy. 'Guess what?' he asked. 'Springer's after pulling the fucking plug!'

Ahern and a few Fianna Fáil ministers had spent three weeks painfully putting back together the pieces of the broken arrangement between Labour and Fianna Fáil, with one important piece of the jigsaw left out: Albert Reynolds. Reynolds' resignation had been the price of keeping alive any chance of saving the coalition government. He could not survive following Labour's withdrawal

...ber in protest at attorney general
...nt as President of the High Court.
...pushed through by Reynolds over
...made just as his office's delay in extradit-
...t was coming to light. It soon emerged
...diting the priest, Fr Brendan Smyth, was not
...han's office. Nonetheless, Reynolds defended
...t stoutly in the Dáil in a disastrous performance
tha... ...ately to cost him his job.

Tao... ...n in two coalition governments, Reynolds was, by his
own admission, a doer, a man of quick action, a risk taker. 'If
you are not a risk taker you will not achieve anything. The easiest
way in life is not to be a risk taker,' he told the Dáil in his final
statement as Taoiseach. He had wrested the leadership of the
party from the epochal figure of Charles Haughey and sacked
every Haughey supporter in the government, bar one – Bertie
Ahern. Within months, he had effectively blown up his own
government in his evidence at the Tribunal of Inquiry into the
Beef Industry, the judicial inquiry set up to examine alleged
malpractice in Ireland's massive beef industry, and which centred
in part on government export guarantees to the huge Goodman
group. Despite a final report that was considered to be equivocal
by many, the lengthy judicial process lobbed a number of grenades
into public life and politics. One of them was when Reynolds
accused his then coalition partner, the Progressive Democrat
leader Des O'Malley, of being 'dishonest' in his evidence. The
ensuing election in November 1992 was a disaster for the party,
but Reynolds snatched victory from the jaws of defeat by persuading the Labour Party to join an historic coalition. Now, after
two years, that shaky partnership had come to a sticky end –
for Reynolds. Ruairi Quinn's crass but celebrated demand for
Reynolds' head was met ultimately by the willingness of the
Taoiseach's colleagues to offer it up on a plate. Until the telephones rang that morning, Ahern and the rest of his ministers
believed that the prompt sacrifice of Reynolds would be enough
to relaunch the coalition.

Later, Reynolds would come to believe that Ahern had had a hand in his downfall. During the Dáil debate that would prove fatal to Reynolds, his finance minister sat beside him with a briefing note that might have prevented his disastrous performance, and never passed it to him. But Reynolds had already been briefed on the content of the note, as had other ministers.

With twenty-five years of bitter division in the party, of heaves and plots and coups as a background, Ahern was highly sensitive to the suspicion that he might have had a part in Reynolds' spectacular fall. On the evening of Spring's declaration that Labour would leave the government, he had met Noel Dempsey, the government chief whip and an important early supporter of Reynolds in his campaign to replace Haughey, as Dempsey walked away from the Taoiseach's office. Ahern was on his way in. He immediately assured Dempsey that he was coming over to pledge his support to Reynolds. It was a message to Reynolds' 'country 'n' western' supporters: there's no heave on here.

But Dempsey knew the game was up for Reynolds. His political sense told him the situation was bad and the longer he looked at the situation the worse it got. He went on a tour of the bars and the restaurants to take the pulse not just of where the Labour Party TDs were but, crucially, also of the mood in the Fianna Fáil parliamentary party. It wasn't pretty. After about an hour and a half spent talking in corners with his party colleagues, Dempsey glumly returned to Reynolds' office. The Taoiseach was alone, and gloomy.

'Well, what do you think?' Reynolds asked.

'Ah, you did the best you could today,' Dempsey replied carefully.

'No,' said Reynolds, 'generally – what do you think?'

Dempsey knew what he was asking, and he didn't relish giving the answer. You have the numbers to survive as leader, he told him. You could stay. But it will be a death by a thousand cuts. It will be like Haughey's end.

'Are you advising me I should go?' asked Reynolds forlornly. Dempsey had been instrumental in Reynolds' accession to the leadership, and the young Meath TD had been rewarded with the pivotal and important position of chief whip.

'No,' said Dempsey. 'I'm just telling you as I see it.'

I'll have to think about it, said Reynolds. I'll have to discuss it with Kathleen. I don't want to cause a general election. Dempsey swallowed hard and told him he didn't have to cause an election. If he did go, another government could be formed. Or the present one could continue.

Check that out, will you? Reynolds said. But Dempsey knew he was gone. Reynolds would announce his decision to resign as Taoiseach the following morning. Dempsey left the Taoiseach's office, walking slowly and sadly down the long corridor. He looked up and saw Ahern.

'What do you think?' Ahern asked.

'I don't know,' said Dempsey guardedly. 'But there's an awful lot of negativity about.'

Ahern knew what he was thinking. 'I was only coming over to tell him that as long as he wants to stay he has my support . . .'

Dempsey believed him. 'Go over and tell him anyway. He'll appreciate it.'

OK, said Ahern. Dempsey caught him. 'But look – if he goes, and I think he'll go, and if he does, I'm supporting you. I can't say it publicly, but I'll vote for you.'

Ahern believed him, too. The bandwagon was already beginning to roll. As with everything else in that extraordinary week in Irish politics, it would move quickly.

Ahern's culpability, if any, in Reynolds' tragedy has never really been established, and he has repeatedly denied any deliberate action or inaction on his part. Certainly he was the beneficiary of Reynolds' chaotic fall. But Albert's demise was Albert's fault. His press secretary, Sean Duignan, wrote simply: 'Albert gambled and lost. We finally got caught.' Albert, of course, was a gambler; his successor most assuredly was not.

Ahern's supporters, which numbered younger TDs such as Micheál Martin and Síle de Valera as well as the dispossessed former allies of Charles Haughey, were marshalling their forces.

The chieftains of the ultra-loyal and highly effective constituency operation that Ahern had built in Dublin Central drew up the lists of the parliamentary party. Ray Burke counted heads; PJ Mara arrived in St Luke's and began to run a media campaign as well as directing the lobbying of individual TDs.

The Reynolds allies were distressed and dispersed following the fall of their champion, immediately disadvantaging their presumed candidate, Maire Geoghegan-Quinn. She needed a delay to gather her forces; Ahern wanted a quick contest to press home his advantage. The atmosphere was febrile, hysterical even. 'Sure we didn't know what a paedophile was,' recalled one. With Leinster House in a ferment, Ahern's lieutenants were confident that they could get the parliamentary party to agree to an immediate vote. But first they had to make sure that Reynolds did actually go.

Despite his decision to resign as Taoiseach, Albert seemed to be having second thoughts by the time the parliamentary party met, hinting to the meeting that he might be prepared to stay on as party leader if the party asked him. Some of Ahern's supporters were unnerved. 'You could see it in his face,' one of them thought. 'He was hoping a few of them might say, "Don't go, Albert, don't go!"' They stayed silent, and the moment passed. The king was dead, and he would not be disinterred. All that remained was to choose a new one.

In fact, most of the parliamentary party had already psychologically moved on from Albert; politics is the most unsentimental of professions. Many of his former supporters, discerning the likelihood – inevitability to some – of an Ahern succession, had moved to reconcile themselves to that reality, attempting to curry favour or to reassure Ahern that their loyalty was to whatever leader the party chose. Those on the Haughey wing of the party were determined that there would be no reprieve for their tormentor. Between those who were genuinely committed to Ahern, and those who were desperate to be seen backing the winner, his numbers looked good to the headquarters in St Luke's. Moreover, the feeling began to emerge among TDs that if Reynolds could be shunted out quickly, and a new leader installed, it might be possible to complete the whole wheeze without having a general election, just as Dempsey had privately suggested. Several TDs approached Ahern with this course of action in mind.

'TDs are like headless chickens in a crisis,' one minister at the time said in reflection. But they all have sharp antennae for self-preservation. For many of them, Ahern's obvious caution and his determination to avoid conflict was very attractive. They were heartily sick of the crisis-a-week feeling around the last few months of the Reynolds government. 'If you keep making decisions on the day, then what happened to Albert will eventually happen to you,' said one.

There was another consideration working in Ahern's favour among the middle ground of the party. Unless you were a member of Geoghegan-Quinn's tight group of loyalists, there was, says one TD, 'quite literally no one else'. The previous contenders for the leadership against Reynolds, Mary O'Rourke and Michael Woods, weren't in any position to challenge; of the Reynolds-led country 'n' western wing, only Maire Geoghegan-Quinn had the stature. And she didn't have the numbers.

It quickly became clear to Geoghegan-Quinn that she didn't have the numbers, or anything remotely near the numbers. Some of the Reynolds supporters whom she regarded as naturally in her camp she discovered to her horror were committed to support-ing Ahern. Noel Dempsey, perceived as a country 'n' westerner, though he was really more of an impatient anti-Haugheyite by the end of the Boss's rule, was regarded as a natural supporter of hers; but she got a shock when she called him to solicit his support.

'Look, as chief whip I can't take any public position,' he told her. 'But I'll be honest with you – I'm voting for Bertie.'

Geoghegan-Quinn let loose a string of invective, threats and accusations against Dempsey – and Ahern. But Dempsey wasn't playing ball.

Ahern was in the driving seat, but some supporters worried that his campaign was rather flat. Bearing the scars of not just the leadership election but the many heaves against Charles Haughey, when he and his fellow lieutenants had to fight hand to hand in the parliamentary party for votes, Mara felt Ahern wasn't sufficiently engaged in his own campaign. He was a bit 'semi-detached', he told friends at the time. Mara devoted himself full-time to the task. Others remember that Ahern was strangely reticent. Brian Cowen, a fierce Reynolds loyalist, was one of the last people he spoke to. The Offaly deputy told people, 'I don't really know the man.' Nonetheless, Ahern's numbers were irre-sistible. The combination of the Haughey faction, those demoted or ignored by Reynolds and those in the middle ground who could see that he was going to win was irresistible. It was, in the words of one of the organizers, 'a bit of a shoo-in in the end'.

Geoghegan-Quinn's supporters were led by Charlie McCreevy. When Ahern called him to solicit his support before the parliamentary party meeting – at which stage it was obvious that the leadership was Ahern's – McCreevy said, No, I'm going to nominate Maire Geoghegan-Quinn. 'That's OK, sure, not to worry,' Ahern replied amicably. The exchange was courteous and brief. Ahern knew McCreevy was a Geoghegan-Quinn supporter, but he was interested to see if McCreevy would jump ship. Like Ahern himself in 1992, Geoghegan-Quinn was the representative of the outgoing power bloc; like Ahern, she didn't push it all the way. 'We knew she wouldn't get it,' recalls one prominent supporter. When the parliamentary party met to elect its new leader, McCreevy nominated Geoghegan-Quinn, and then she withdrew.

McCreevy wasn't just sticking with Geoghegan-Quinn out of characteristic cussedness or tribal loyalty to the Reynolds wing (many of whom, seeing the way the numbers were swinging, had made their peace with Bertie): he believed that she would make a better Taoiseach than Ahern. In fact, he told friends subsequently, he just never thought that Bertie Ahern could become Taoiseach. He thought about the role of prime minister – representing the country, leading the government – and he couldn't see Bertie doing it. He respected the younger man's political and organizational skills, but he didn't see him as a national leader. He would change his mind, and joke about how wrong he had been; but not immediately.

Unlike McCreevy, there were many who thought that a young metropolitan leader was a brilliant recipe for the party – and there were those who didn't share the Kildareman's elevated view of Geoghegan-Quinn. Haughey, they remembered, had been free enough in sharing his opinion of her. After dropping her from the 1982 cabinet he told one of his lieutenants that he thought she was lazy. The description was repeated to wavering members of the parliamentary party. Haughey was profligate with such dismissals, and there were few even of his intimates who didn't feel the lash of his tongue at some stage.

Whatever Haughey's abuse a decade previously, Geoghegan-Quinn's claims were not illusory. She was a politician of long experience and considerable ability, having been first promoted to cabinet rank at the age of twenty-nine by Charles Haughey, the first woman to attain such office in the history of the state. Granted, Haughey later discarded her, but she grew into one of the more formidable forces in the party, displaying courage when telling Haughey in 1991 that the people of Galway West never wanted to see his face on a poster again, and strategic nous when she allied herself with Reynolds. Her return to cabinet in 1992 was the reward for her judgement, and she was a key pillar of the country 'n' western set. As minister for justice she was a cabinet heavyweight and close to Reynolds throughout his endeavours on the North, and she had displayed a willingness to upset people in her own party with her decriminalization of homosexual acts in 1994. As a potential leader, she ticked most of the boxes.

Later, when she had retired from politics and Ahern nominated her for a prestigious and lucrative post at the European Court of Auditors, some of her former colleagues believed that Ahern was even still wary of her, and had given her the job to 'get her off the pitch'. One minister subsequently explained to me: 'She was six foot tall, she spoke Irish non-stop, she was from the West of

Ireland. I'd say Bertie didn't want six-foot amazons from the West of Ireland causing bother for him!' 'She was a cut above the rest, in her own mind anyway,' says one Ahern supporter. 'But loads of the parliamentary party disliked her intensely.' Another was more generous. 'Some of us had time for her, but she didn't have what Bertie had,' he said.

By any standards, it was a poor campaign. Geoghegan-Quinn didn't even approach some TDs who she thought were natural Ahern supporters, or hostile to her. This was a mistake – politicians are always open to making deals, even with those they dislike, so long as they can protect their own interests. A broader effort by Geoghegan-Quinn probably wouldn't have been successful; in any case, it never manifested itself.

There were other differences between the two campaigns. Geoghegan-Quinn had a group of supporters who were devoted to her, but there was another equally numerous group who disliked her intensely. 'A lot of us just didn't like her,' recalled one TD who later went on to serve in cabinet. Ahern didn't really have the same sort of polarizing effect. He had a few very strong supporters, certainly, but there was nobody who really disliked him. Unlike his main rival, he wasn't the potential saviour or the possible ruination of the party. He was just . . . Bertie.

The parliamentary party met for the decisive meeting on a Saturday morning, 19 November, just two days after Reynolds' resignation. Having been proposed by McCreevy, Geoghegan-Quinn withdrew, leaving Ahern as the only nominee for the post of president of Fianna Fáil. At forty-three years of age, he was the party's youngest ever leader.

'I will be a consensus leader,' he told a press conference in the Burlington Hotel immediately after his election, 'because that's what Fianna Fáil needs . . . We've had twenty-five years of heaves and counter-heaves, of hassles and controversies. We've recovered from all of them, but we've lost focus at times, and we've lost market share with the electorate.'

'All one big happy family again?' a reporter asked one minister.

'For the moment,' was the deeply equivocal reply. Whatever Ahern said about healing the wounds of past heaves and uniting the party, there was no doubt about what most people in the party thought: the Haughey wing was back in charge. That's certainly what Haughey loyalists such as Burke and Mara thought. The journalist Olivia O'Leary met Ray Burke, bounding up the stairs that led to the Dáil chamber the day Reynolds made his resignation speech. 'The praetorian guard is changing!' he beamed at her. The truth would turn out to be a little different.

But not yet. For many of those on the Haughey wing in the party, Ahern was righting the wrong of two years previously when he had belatedly pulled out of the contest with Reynolds. That episode had given many TDs and party figures their first real experience of Bertie Ahern in a situation where he was forced into tough decisions. Some of them emerged as losers; not Ahern.

Reynolds had played a bold hand in November 1991, challenging Haughey's leadership from within the cabinet and being sacked for his effrontery. Though his country 'n' western alliance lost the showdown at the parliamentary party then, Haughey's days were numbered. 'Albert won the leadership that day,' one of his lieutenants told me. He just had to wait a little longer. Haughey being beset by scandal involving the murky areas where business and politics sometimes intersect, his TDs were impatient for his departure, his ministers jostling for preservation. Reynolds worked the parliamentary party after his departure from cabinet in anticipation of a second round. It came quicker than anyone expected. Haughey's former ally and minister for justice during the phone-tapping scandal of 1982, Sean Doherty, broke his decade-long silence on the controversy and announced that Haughey had not only authorized the surveillance of journalists' telephones: he had personally requested and reviewed the transcripts of their conversations. The revelation that the Haughey government had tapped the phones of journalists – ostensibly because of concerns about cabinet secrecy – had caused a political storm when it was revealed by the succeeding Fine Gael

administration in 1982, and established an important legal precedent when the journalists involved, Geraldine Kennedy and
Bruce Arnold, successfully sued the state. Ten years after
shouldering the blame for the episode, Doherty wasn't exactly a
credible witness. But he was more credible than Haughey, the
Progressive Democrats concluded. 'Are the Irish people more
entitled to believe me, who has been consistent in everything I
have said about this affair from the beginning, or someone who
has been inconsistent and by his own words untruthful on
countless occasions with regard to it?' Haughey pleaded. It was no
use; the game was finally up.

Already mobilized for battle, the Reynolds camp made their
preparations. His lieutenants – Padraig Flynn, Geoghegan-Quinn
and McCreevy prominent among them – were sure they had a
comfortable majority, whether Ahern threw his hat into the ring
or not. Reynolds was a natural campaigner, a backslapper, a doer
of deals, and he had calculated, cajoled and promised his way
through enough TDs to win him the leadership by the time
Haughey went. The simple key to it was patronage: he promised
to reward his supporters and punish his enemies. By his own
admission, he was straightforward like that. Ahern bided his time.

The Haughey wing was now desperate for Ahern to stand.
Even from Kinsealy, the signals were clear. Citing a conversation
with Haughey, a friend of the departing Taoiseach told the *Irish
Times* that he was critical of Ahern's indecisiveness. 'What the hell
is going on with this man from Drumcondra? I'm not very
impressed to know he's going back to Drumcondra to consult
with his gang. It's not what you'd expect from a future taoiseach,'
the paper quoted Haughey as saying. Other, anonymous, TDs
complained that Ahern's indecisiveness had diminished him.
Chris Wall told the makers of the Mint Productions documentary
on Ahern broadcast on RTÉ in late 2008 that Ahern was ahead,
that he would have won. Ahern himself just acknowledged that
they had 'counted heads'.

Then, with days to go to the leadership election, the *Irish Times*
headlined Ahern's entry to the race at last: 'Ahern expected to

enter race today'. Ahern himself had given the paper to understand that he was running, telling its finance editor in the course
of a post-budget interview that he was 'canvassing as if I was in
the race in the normal way'. It was a classic Ahern answer to a
straight question. The ordinary sense of the words conveyed to
any reasonable listener that he would be a candidate for the
leadership. However, he had left himself enough wriggle room
to get out of it – he hadn't, after all, said that he would definitely
be a candidate; he had just used words to convey that impression.
But if he chose to change his mind, well, then he couldn't
actually be accused of having said that he would. Get it? It was
more than just political-speak: it was a special type of political-
speak. It was Bertie-speak. He was even doing this with TDs he
canvassed, refusing to give them a firm promise that he would
actually run. One TD complained to the Ahern camp, 'How can
I give a guarantee to a man who has not given *me* a firm guarantee
he is running?'

Ahern went on to claim that he would have the support of
the majority of the cabinet if he ran. Well, of course he would.
If Reynolds became Taoiseach, it would cost them their jobs.

A few hours after the *Irish Times* headline heralding his
campaign appeared on the streets, Ahern was out of the race,
declaring his support for Reynolds. Some of Reynolds' supporters
believed it was the declaration of support for Reynolds by the
Tánaiste, John Wilson, that appears to have pushed him over
the edge. Reynolds' lieutenants had deliberately held Wilson's
endorsement back, and released it on Saturday 1 February on the
last weekend of campaigning for the leadership. Wilson's statement of support was released at midday; by 1.30 p.m., Ahern
had announced he too would support Reynolds. The more
likely trigger was a meeting between Reynolds and Ahern at the
Berkeley Court Hotel that morning. Reynolds would not stay
too long, he told the younger man. Ahern later told people he
imagined that Reynolds would last perhaps until the end of the
decade – an eternity in politics. More importantly, Reynolds
conveyed to Ahern what he already knew: Albert would win, and

he would be vindictive in victory. Better to wait, better to wait.

An *Irish Times* editorial admonished Ahern, wondering at 'the disquieting image of a man who has not thought matters through'. No. If anything, he had spent too much time thinking things through. It was a habit that was to become familiar.

Could Ahern have won had he contested the leadership in 1992? It's an unanswerable question. Several of his loyalists believe he would have; the Reynolds camp is adamant: no way. The most likely answer seems to be that if he had been sure he was going to win, he would have stood; without being sure, he was content to become the heir apparent.

Ahern's decision not to run infuriated many of the Haughey loyalists in the cabinet, who had believed that he would be their standard bearer against Reynolds. They were left with the certainty of a Reynolds leadership – having rebuffed his approaches – and the deleterious consequences of what that would mean for them. Many would later bitterly observe that Ahern had made his peace with Reynolds and retained his cabinet seat. It was a signal from which the parliamentary party took different lessons. Among the lessons they learned was that even by the standards of politics, Ahern's principal loyalty was to himself.

Bertie Ahern's election to the leadership of Fianna Fáil in November 1994 was a departure for the party in a number of ways. He was the youngest leader in the party's history. He was a Dublin TD at a time when the party's vote in the electorally all-important capital city was under pressure. And he was – and this was shocking to some people in a country where divorce was still prohibited by the constitution – separated from his wife and in a relationship with another woman. He moved to neutralize the issue immediately.

The banks of microphones were arrayed across the table in the Burlington Hotel and the Dictaphones clustered around them. The Fianna Fáil press office had received instructions from a new master – PJ Mara – about this event and they were sharp and to the point. It was the first encounter between the media and the new leader of Fianna Fáil and some very important things were going to be said.

Ahern's personal circumstances had been an issue when he chose not to contest the leadership against Reynolds in 1992; in 1994, he was persuaded to confront it head on. At the Burlington press conference he chose to take an early question from Paddy Clancy, a tabloid journalist of the old school, then working for the Irish edition of the *Sun*. Was Ahern's appointment as leader of Fianna Fáil and possible appointment as Taoiseach evidence of an 'enlightened attitude' in the party, given that he was separated from his wife? The Fianna Fáilers present hissed and booed; some looked as though they would throw the tabloid hack out. Ahern knew it was coming, and silenced the crowd. 'I do think it's an enlightened view and I'm very conscious of the support I receive from every constituency throughout the country. Unfortunately, I think it is generally known, I am separated from my wife Miriam, we now live apart and I'm glad of the understanding of the party and of my colleagues.'

It was an important moment for him, and for his partner, Celia Larkin. But there was another message in his comment too: the apologetic tone, the name-checking of his wife without any mention of Larkin, the humble gratitude for the forgiveness of his sins by the party — all these would continue to be part of his public attitudes to his private life. Larkin's status as the other woman was not about to change.

Ahern sought to address the marital issue because he believed it had the potential to damage him politically. In fact, he believed it had damaged him already. Some of Ahern's intimates claimed that his reason for not standing in 1992 was related to a number of comments made by both Reynolds and his campaign team about his marital situation in the course of the weeks and months before the leadership election. Some of them claim it still. And though Ahern publicly maintained to the media that questions about his private life didn't cause him to withdraw from the race, clearly some of his closest supporters and those with a claim to know his mind didn't agree, and they put it about with some enthusiasm.

The North Tipperary TD, Michael Smith, came in for particular opprobrium for his comments to the local newspaper in 1992, when he observed that Albert Reynolds was the 'envy of other politicians in terms of his family life'. Smith's comments weren't entirely innocent, but did they merit the focus that Ahern's people subsequently put on them? Reynolds himself had made a far more pointed attempt to focus on Ahern's private life a few days earlier when he told the *Irish Independent* that while Ahern's 'marital separation was not something he felt he should discuss', he offered as an 'afterthought' that people would 'want to know where the Taoiseach is living'.

Ahern chose to ignore this remark and focus on the milder comments made by Smith. But then he didn't want to fall out with Reynolds. Perhaps because he knew the older man was going to be Taoiseach.

Smith's relations with Ahern's Drumcondra pals were never mended. As late as 2008 Paddy Duffy told the makers of the documentary series about Ahern that 'people in Tipperary' chose to direct attention to Ahern's marital situation, and Ahern himself also gave the programme to understand that he was still angry about the Smith intervention. However, while his own relations with Smith weren't especially cordial, they were businesslike and – from the point of view of both men – entirely productive. Though Ahern left Smith out of his first cabinet, he assured him privately that 'You'll be first in', and he kept his word, promoting him to cabinet in the autumn of 1997 after Ray Burke resigned. He stayed there until his exit in 2004. If Ahern really bore the grudge about Smith's intervention and believed it had cost him the leadership in 1992, he managed to get over it. In the light of history, it seems more likely that it was a useful excuse for quitting a race he wasn't going to win anyway.

Ahern's election as leader also brought his 'Drumcondra mafia' into the national spotlight. This was the 'gang' in Drumcondra that Haughey had so derided. In fact, they were one of the most effective constituency operations in the country. In the two decades before he became leader, Ahern had assembled a remarkable local political machine that supported and sustained him as he made his way up the ladder of national politics. They had ruthlessly supplanted the existing Fianna Fáil organization in the inner suburbs of north Dublin – 'We stood on their fucking heads,' one later claimed – and replaced it with an organization that was completely controlled by Ahern. They were uncompromisingly loyal to him, and he to them. 'You could insult Bertie Ahern to his face. You could insult his family. You could say anything about him. But the one thing you couldn't do was say anything about or do anything to his constituency,' says a close ministerial associate. On one occasion he gave party general secretary Pat Farrell, with whom he had just returned from a trip down the country, a tour of parts of the Dublin Central constituency. He showed him where the boundaries ran, pointing out that this side of the street was in Dublin North West, but here it's still Dublin Central. Who was here for him, who covered there. It was as though he was caressing it, or showing a garden he had planted.

The seeds were planted in the mid-1970s, when Ahern became active in the local Fianna Fáil organization. He was one of a number of politically minded young men and women, ambitious for themselves, impatient with their country's politics. Another, Paddy Duffy, had joined Fianna Fáil in Finglas, where he was a teacher in the De La Salle brothers' primary school, in 1975. At his second meeting he found himself sitting beside a well-built, slightly unkempt individual who introduced himself as Bertie Ahern. Duffy was a blow-in; Ahern, sprung of solid republican stock, had been steeped in the local organization since his schooldays. The more Duffy got to know the organization, the more he realized that this Ahern was the coming man. He became one of the cadre of intensely loyal supporters who were coalescing around him in the bearpit of local Fianna Fáil politics. The national school teacher became the wordsmith, drafting leaflets and, after Ahern's election in 1977, assisting him with occasional Dáil contributions. But mostly Duffy's compositions were leaflets to be distributed locally, extolling the tireless efforts of the local representative to fix footpaths and other important matters. The Christmas circular; the Easter message. Political communications followed an ecclesiastical calendar in those days – two decades later, as Ahern prepared his acceptance speeches as the new leader of Fianna Fáil, Duffy was still tap-tapping beside him at his word processor.

Just like Duffy, many of Ahern's closest associates when he became leader had been with him since the days they tramped around Dublin Central. They were Ahern supporters above all else. 'We weren't even really Fianna Fáilers – we were Bertie people,' one of them told me. 'Our people weren't traditional party people. They came in on a personal basis.' When Haughey summoned Paddy Duffy to Kinsealy on a snow-bound morning in February 1982 and asked him to join his election staff in Mount Street, Duffy deferred to what Ahern might say. Ahern said: 'The fucker!' Duffy heard no more of moving to Mount Street.

They built his organization street by street, selecting street representatives, ward bosses and so on, each feeding information upwards and distributing patronage and favours down. By the time of the 1982 general election, just five years after his arrival in the Dáil, he had a military system installed in the constituency. Lists were compiled of every street, and details and timetables for the first, second and third canvass; on the morning of the election, every house received a leaflet drop – 'As you go to the polls today . . .' The milk run, as his supporters called it, started at 3.00 a.m. and finished at 7.00 a.m. Like a football team that has been through gruelling pre-season training – and several were members of the same football team – the early experiences bonded them tightly together.

There were hardened constituency scrappers like Chris Wall and Tony Kett, Paddy Reilly and Dermot Carew, councillors Paul Kiely and Tom Stafford and machine operators like Cyprian Brady. Many were to achieve public office, either elective or appointed, because of their association with Ahern. Similarly businessmen like Joe Burke, Dave McKenna and Tim Collins flourished as their champion ascended the political ladder. Several were appointed to state boards.

And then there was Des Richardson, brought in by Ahern as party fundraiser, and who would be the subject of considerable controversy when it emerged that he had private business arrangements with companies that had business with Fianna Fáil, or had lobbied Ahern for favours. As well as fundraising for the national party, he fundraised for Ahern's constituency operations. And, it later emerged, for Ahern personally. Sceptics would wonder if he managed to maintain the Chinese walls between all these roles.

The Drumcondra boys (and they were almost all boys) had little time for the political professionals that necessarily surrounded Ahern the higher he rose. 'There's a lot of money around this fuckin' table,' growled Chris Wall at one election strategy meeting in 2002. 'A lot of fuckin' money.' The Drumcondra boys called them 'the hired help'. They believed that the hired help was loyal not to Bertie but to themselves and the party. The hired help had little regard for most of the 'mafia' and sometimes referred to them disparagingly as 'the bungalows' – that is, they had nothing upstairs.

Many Fianna Fáilers scoffed at the 'mafia' tag. If the Drumcondra boys saw themselves as a mafia, it was in the image of Don Corleone and his mob bosses: tough but fair, ruthless but also looking out for the little guy. Others saw them more in the mould of Tony Soprano's goonish henchmen.

Much later, when several of the group co-operated in the 2008 television documentary on Ahern, they were widely perceived as macho, clannish and devoted to their gang and its leader. Suddenly, the mafia tag didn't seem so far-fetched.

At the centre of the web was Ahern: enigmatic, cautious, watchful. His colleagues in the parliamentary party, who had elected him by acclamation, didn't really know him.

'His popularity both inside and outside the party is undeniable,' wrote the political journalist and author Stephen Collins. 'He has a compulsion to shake hands and treat every day as if he was in the middle of an election campaign, but he wears a mask that has proved impenetrable to most of his colleagues in the Dáil. None of his colleagues is really sure whether he is possessed of all the deviousness and cunning attributed to him by Haughey or whether he simply suffers from chronic indecision disguised as political shrewdness.'

What did he believe in? What was his political philosophy? In what direction would he lead the party? What would his policies be? Would he be imperious, like Haughey? Or impetuous, like Reynolds?

Actually, as one attested, his colleagues 'didn't really give a shit about any of that'. They just wanted to know: can he get us back into government?

Spring's telephone call in the blustery early hours of Tuesday 6 December had now confirmed that, whatever the future, Ahern would not be leading his colleagues back to government that morning. He and his party had demonstrated that they were prepared to do anything to stay in government, but still Labour had left him at the altar. To him and to Fianna Fáil, Labour's abandonment couldn't be explained by their professed reasons. There must be something else at work.

The first inkling that there might be a problem had been the previous day, Monday, when Noel Dempsey, who had been a key figure in negotiating the new deal with Labour, received a telephone call from his private office whilst in his car driving to Dublin. Brendan Howlin and Ruairi Quinn were there, and they had a problem. When he walked into his office, the two Labour men were waiting for him. One of them thrust that morning's *Irish Times* at him. Read that, they said.

Dempsey read it. 'What's the problem?'

No, read it again, said Howlin. This changes everything.

Nothing had changed, and everything had changed. Geraldine Kennedy's story in the *Irish Times* that day revealed that Reynolds had asked Whelehan to resign before he expressed complete confidence in him in the Dáil. An interesting nugget, but not perhaps entirely amazing given what had transpired in the preceding weeks and, more importantly, it was concerned with the behaviour of the now departed Reynolds, not the new regime. But it was what followed this in the story that was apparently disturbing the Labour men. Kennedy reported that the Fianna Fáil ministers had been told and understood about the Duggan case – a previous case in which the extradition of a Catholic cleric had been delayed for several months – before Harry Whelehan had been sworn in as a judge, and before Reynolds had defended his appointment in the Dáil.

Yeah, thought Dempsey. So what?

The paper had repeatedly reported that Fianna Fáil ministers knew of the Duggan case before Whelehan's swearing in and Reynolds' Dáil defence of him. When the controversy first broke, the paper reported on 17 November: 'Remarks of the Minister for Justice Mrs Geoghegan-Quinn last night may have hurt the chances of other Fianna Fáil ministers becoming Taoiseach. She declared that she and other Fianna Fáil ministers knew of the Duggan extradition case in advance of the Taoiseach's speech last Tuesday. This may cause Labour to have second thoughts about a renewed coalition with Fianna Fáil.'

The newspaper repeated this fact and observation on its front page the following day, again on the following day ('FF ministers still have questions to answer') and also in the editorial of that day, 19 November. It featured on the front page on Monday 21 November and again and again in the many news reports of the following weeks which attempted to explain the convoluted saga to a justifiably confused public. The editorial of 2 December complained: 'No adequate explanation has been advanced to explain why the Dáil was not informed that a previous case had been considered ... on November 15 when this information had been made available to ministers one day earlier.' In other words, the fact that the Fianna Fáil ministers – including Ahern – knew about the Duggan case had been advertised for weeks. Dempsey didn't understand what the problem was.

Previously, Kennedy had reported that Fianna Fáil ministers had told her that Whelehan had been asked to resign on Monday

14 November, because of the threat to the peace process; now she was saying that was untrue. She had been misled, and her story made that clear. It also made clear that Fianna Fáil ministers had not just known about the Duggan case: they had known about the significance of the case – that's why the attorney general had been dispatched to seek Whelehan's resignation. Maybe it was a nuanced difference – between knowing about something and *really* knowing about it – that would make all the difference in the world.

In his memoir *Snakes and Ladders*, Fergus Finlay recalls: 'We had believed until that moment that only Albert Reynolds knew about the Duggan case on Monday, and therefore what happened on the Tuesday was down to him alone. Now ... it seemed that other members of the government knew about the Duggan case on the Monday and were to some degree complicit in what happened in the Dáil on the Tuesday.' It's difficult to understand how the Labour men could have believed this, unless they weren't reading the *Irish Times*. Nonetheless, the men stuck to their guns: this changes everything.

This is rubbish, thought Dempsey. They couldn't be serious. What's really going on?

In one sense, Spring was simply being consistent, if belatedly so. If he had insisted on the resignation of Reynolds because he knew about the Duggan case before he told the Dáil what an excellent judge Harry Whelehan would make, then he couldn't in all consistency enter government with ministers who had supported Reynolds in his position, who had been complicit in the appointment and defence of Whelehan. Applying the same judgement to Ahern as he had to Reynolds meant that the game with Fianna Fáil was up.

But what was really going on was that Spring's calculations had changed. He now believed that the adverse consequences of forming another government with Fianna Fáil would outweigh its benefits. Besides, he now believed that he couldn't trust Fianna Fáil, Reynolds or no Reynolds. He was confirmed in this conclusion by two important developments. The first was the growing media climate against a renewal of the Fianna Fáil–Labour alliance. Though a continuation of the coalition was the clear preference of the public expressed in an MRBI opinion poll, Labour was shipping increasing criticism for contemplating a return to office under Ahern. The *Irish Times* in particular – to which Labour, even more than politicians of other parties, paid attention and occasionally obeisance – found Labour's willingness to re-enter government with Fianna Fáil evidence of a thirst for office at any cost, exactly the charge it regularly levelled against Fianna Fáil. It was even the charge that Labour levelled against Fianna Fáil. 'They are prepared to sacrifice anything to be in power,' one senior Labour figure was reported as saying. Fergus Finlay, Spring's most important adviser, didn't believe that Spring wanted power at any price, and was deeply suspicious of a new arrangement with Fianna Fáil. He had scribbled a tearful resignation note when the first resuscitation of the coalition was attempted three weeks previously, telling Spring that he could not support a renewal of the government. The relationship between Spring and Finlay was always very clear: Finlay advised, Spring decided. But no one was more influential with the Labour leader.

There was another important development: two by-elections in Cork in November, resulting in victories for Fine Gael and the small left-wing party (and rival for the Labour vote) led by Prionsias De Rossa, Democratic Left. The Dáil arithmetic had changed slightly, emphasizing and strengthening another path of escape for Spring which did not necessitate a general election. He could form a coalition with Fine Gael and the Democratic Left – eighty-five Dáil votes would give him a bare two-vote majority. It would be a government in which Labour ministers would enjoy even greater clout than they had with Fianna Fáil. The embattled Fine Gael leader, John Bruton, once opposed to the involvement of the Democratic Left in a 'Rainbow' administration, was now growing desperate for government at almost any price. That price might include a rotating Taoiseach or, if not, a Labour finance minister. Labour would remain in government, stronger than ever, and it would be free of the taint of Fianna Fáil. The party could complete its programme for government, continue with the peace process (in which Spring would now be the commanding voice) and face the electorate in two years' time with the benefits of a growing economy behind it. To Spring and some of his advisers, it was an idea whose time had come. They also knew that, despite the disappointing by-election results, Labour was operating from a position of national political strength. The recent MRBI/*Irish Times* poll had indicated that, at 22 per cent, support for the party was running ahead even of its 1992 level of 19 per cent. (It has passed into Labour history that the party's poll ratings and political support never recovered from the decision to enter government with Fianna Fáil in 1992. This is demonstrably false.)

In the event, an election wasn't necessary. Reynolds did not ask the President to dissolve the Dáil – probably because Fianna Fáil had never been in a weaker position to contest an election – and when the Dáil met to elect a taoiseach on 15 December, John Bruton, the accidental Taoiseach, was elected by 85 votes to 74. Ahern's speech to the Dáil was warmly complimentary about the new Taoiseach, and he managed, characteristically, to conceal much of the rage he still felt inwardly at the Labour Party for their last-minute betrayal. Few of his colleagues managed the same feat. They were incensed at what they regarded as Labour's super-ciliousness, furious at their superiority. One senior Labour figure had told a newspaper just days earlier: 'They [Fianna Fáil] just don't know the difference between right and wrong. They are like bold children . . . they just don't know the difference. That is why it is so important that they are watched carefully in government. They have to be saved from themselves. And the public has to be protected.' It was driving Fianna Fáil TDs crazy. But most of all, they were angry because they were out of government. The bitterness poured out of their Dáil speeches that day. 'We deserve better,' thundered Cowen – 'We certainly deserve better than the farce that took place here last week . . . We deserve better from those who conspired to organize a witch-hunt against my party in the past three weeks and from those who agree to take decisions on a certain basis and do not follow them through.'

The Labour benches grinned back with that special smile government deputies reserve for the impotent rage of opposition. It says: 'Say what you like; we're over here, and you're over there.' Fianna Fáil tended to be good at giving that; not so good at taking it.

The bitter break between Labour and Fianna Fáil would turn out to be a watershed in Irish political history. It pushed the larger party into the embrace of the Progressive Democrats, so reorienting the party's economic policy rightwards, even as most of its leading figures freely admitted they were closer to Labour on policy. Ultimately, it gave Ireland a decade and more of tax-cutting, pro-business, free-market governments when it could as easily have had centre-left, Fianna Fáil–Labour coalitions. Spring and his kitchen cabinet told each other and their party that their stance was on a matter of principle, though the evidence suggests it was more a matter of politics. Either way, it would prove to be an expensive decision.

2. Consolidation and Preparation

In the middle of the long winter of 1994–5, Bertie Ahern assumed the leadership of a fractured, damaged, disillusioned Fianna Fáil party. Its senior figures were in a state oscillating somewhere between bitterness and denial over their sudden defenestration from government; the organization was ragged and confused. Ahern had the job he had coveted and for which he had planned, but the road back to power was uncertain and unlikely.

The fall from office was agonizingly drawn out over a period of weeks, and then brutally sudden in the end, and the immediate consequences of the loss of political office for Fianna Fáil were obvious and painful. Ministers who had enjoyed their roles at the head of entire departments, with hundreds of staff to do their bidding and the gratifying knowledge of their own power that spurs all politicians, were suddenly bereft of not just the trappings but that sense of worth and status that office brings to those who spend their lives pursuing it. The trauma of being so violently ejected from government scarred the party and its senior members. Some former ministers went to the pub; some just went home; some lost interest in politics; some vowed revenge. 'In hindsight, I think some of them actually needed therapy,' one senior party figure told me.

Fianna Fáil was in crisis and it extended through all levels of the party. Headquarters reported that active membership had declined precipitously and the number of cumainn or local branches actually engaged in political activity had fallen to less than half the 3,000 it had been. This was mostly because the top level of the party had spent much of the previous two decades engaged in a civil war with itself; those times that weren't marked by open conflict were characterized by scheming and plotting. The party had become consumed with its own power struggles; it was rotting from the centre out. The spectre of Fianna Fáil at war with itself was sometimes compelling for those on the outside, but it was corrosive for the party. Among voters whose ancestral ties to both big parties were loosening, and who despaired of a model of politics that so clearly venerated the personal advancement of individual politicians above the national interest, it was repellent.

The signs of what this was doing electorally to the party were pretty clear: the Fianna Fáil vote had plummeted by five points in the disastrous election of 1992, from 44 to 39 per cent, Fianna Fáil's lowest share of the vote since 1948. And following the acrimonious break-up of the first two coalition governments that the party had ever been part of, a view was taking hold well beyond the political commentariat that Fianna Fáil was simply incapable of working with another party. 'They [the public] believed that Fianna Fáil just couldn't get on with anyone,' says one senior figure of the time. 'We would have been left in the position where the largest party would have been permanently out of government.' As leading Fianna Fáilers surveyed the wreckage in the early months of 1995, they were not just faced with the reality of being out of government: they were facing the likelihood of being out of government for a very long time.

There was another legacy of the split with Labour, too: an abiding and deep-rooted bitterness, both on a corporate and personal level, towards the party that many saw as Fianna Fáil's most obvious and natural coalition partner. Fianna Fáil believed there was more than just political calculation to Labour's decision. They could, to a point, live with that. But the 1994 split, many believed, arose from a sort of cultural antipathy towards Fianna Fáil. They looked at how, when the frantic efforts were being made to mend the Spring–Reynolds coalition, Labour insisted that Albert Reynolds abase himself in the Dáil, pleading how Labour had been right about the appointment of Harry Whelehan, and how he should have listened to them. To the likes of McCreevy, Geoghegan-Quinn and many others, it was degrading. They felt that Labour didn't just want to win politically: they felt that Spring and the others wanted Fianna Fáil to admit to Labour's moral superiority.

They felt that Spring had succumbed to an element within the Labour Party which viewed Fianna Fáil as amoral mucksavages led by gombeen men who exercised a sort of electoral voodoo over the non-*Irish-Times*-reading sections of the population. They knew that many in Labour had never accepted the coalition deal with Fianna Fáil and they suspected that these sinister forces had worked on the inside to bring down the government.

Fianna Fáil laid much of the blame at the door of Dick Spring's advisers and most of that on the head of Fergus Finlay, the *éminence grise* who was Spring's most important and influential counsellor. Finlay was one of the most consummate backroom operators in the history of Irish politics, and an important figure in the election of Mary Robinson as President in 1990 and the subsequent rise of the Labour Party in the early 1990s. He was a political strategist, a policy wonk and a highly effective briefer of journalists. He was wary of Labour's coalition with Fianna Fáil in 1992, and Fianna Fáil believed he was instrumental in the falling apart of that government in 1994.

'Obviously, Mr Finlay had decided ahead of the Labour ministers and even of the Tánaiste, that the government was doomed. All that remained to be done was to rationalize this in a suitable tone of high moral indignation,' Ahern told the Dáil in a 1995 debate on the fall of the coalition. Reminded by the chair of the precedent under which third parties are not criticized or attacked in the Dáil, Ahern responded: 'I am being very restrained in talking about this individual.'

There was little Fianna Fáil didn't believe Finlay was capable of. Even his impressive beard counted against him; they took it as evidence of untrustworthiness, revolutionary intentions or hidden agendas. One of Ahern's closest aides at the time says simply, 'Bertie believed Finlay was Rasputin.'

To this day, it's hard to find anyone in Fianna Fáil who will say a good word about Finlay. At all levels, right to the very top, Fianna Fáil was to retain a grudge against the Labour Party for what they believed Spring and his lieutenants did to them in those confused few days in November 1994. They would neither forgive nor forget. A decade and a half later, some nurture it still.

Months after the events of November 1994, in that same debate on the fall of the government, Ahern said, 'For many years, the enemies and rivals of Fianna Fáil, inside and outside the Dáil, have been vainly on the look-out for a major scandal that would confirm their prejudices and suspicions and prove their case about the political culture of Fianna Fáil, to use another expression of Deputy Rabbitte's.' It was an accurate summary of Fianna Fáil's sense of itself and of the wider politics at the time. They're all out to get us. Trouble was, they *had* got them.

The bleakness of the prospect of opposition hit Ahern early that January. In the first week, his belongings and personal files were removed from the minister's office in the Department of Finance and brought to an office on the fifth floor of the Leinster House annexe. When Mary O'Rourke went into his office, workmen from the Office of Public Works were hammering and sawing. It was like a building site. 'I suppose this is going to be our lot for a while,' she said. It was like a desert up there, thought Paddy Duffy when he arrived in the first day. Duffy went in to Ahern's office and found him sitting on a box, glumly leafing through his papers. He looked up in resignation when Duffy came in. 'It's no fun being in opposition,' Ahern said. 'Let's get the fuck out here as quick as we can.'

Ahern's accession to the leadership was not unexpected, but he did not gain – nor did he expect – the loyalty and fealty of his parliamentary party immediately. That would take patience and politics and patronage. It would also take success. Ahern knew that he had to deliver power back to the party. No Irish political party – and few in the world – is as singularly devoted to the acquisition and retention of power as Fianna Fáil. That's one reason why they have held it for so long: they want it more than the others. They will do anything and say anything and promise anything and, in the end, concede anything to secure it. 'They're

fucking dilletantes!' one senior figure gloated at Fine Gael's
expense following the 2002 rout. 'They don't have the hunger!'
Fianna Fáil, he said, always has the hunger. At the beginning of
1995 there were, at most, just under three years before a general
election had to be held. Ahern had to win it. If he lost the election, he would not survive for a further four or five years in
opposition. He would get one shot at it, and one shot only.

Ahern's first public job was to choose a front bench. In fact, he
had made many of his selections prior to his expected but un-
realized appointment as Taoiseach a few weeks previously. His
principal objective was to forge a coalition between the Reynolds
and the Haughey wings. He did this because he wanted to, but
also because he had to. This meant giving several positions to
prominent Reynolds supporters, most notably Charlie McCreevy.

The appointment of McCreevy to the finance brief was to be
one of the most important decisions he was ever to make. Though
they came from the opposing Haugheyite and country 'n' western
wings of the party, and had been on opposite sides of the Haughey
heaves in the 1980s, Ahern and McCreevy had become friendly
when they served at cabinet together in the governments led
by Albert Reynolds. McCreevy was particularly supportive of
Ahern's firm line on public spending at cabinet and frequently
spoke up in support of the finance minister – an unusual position
from a social welfare minister, which portfolio McCreevy held
in the first government led by Reynolds from February 1992 to
November of that year.

Despite McCreevy's failure to support him for the leadership,
Ahern wanted him as finance spokesman. The appointment
caught many by surprise – it 'confounded all predictions', recorded Maol Muire Tynan of the *Irish Times* – but not McCreevy
himself. Despite his lack of support for Ahern, the pair had
maintained close contact since the leadership election, particularly
as McCreevy attempted to put the Fianna Fáil–Labour coalition
back together. In fact, when that deal appeared to be done,
McCreevy suspected that he might be made minister for finance.
On the night before the new Fianna Fáil–Labour government

under Ahern was supposed to take office, Albert Reynolds had told McCreevy that he would be finance minister. 'He doesn't have anyone else,' Reynolds told him. 'It has to be an existing member of the cabinet, it has to be a Fianna Fáiler. It has to be you. There's nobody else.' McCreevy could see the logic, though he wasn't confident.

If Ahern's front bench was a careful mixture of the two wings of the party, a signal of his intention to heal the rifts of twenty-five years, it was also an acknowledgement of the relative weakness of his position. McCreevy's appointment as finance spokesman nodded to both realities: not only was he a Reynolds man but, unusually in a finance spokesman, he was no threat to Ahern's leadership. McCreevy knew he would never be Taoiseach, and he didn't want to spend his period as finance spokesman or minister for finance trying to become Taoiseach. When Ahern rang him the two men discussed related matters; Ahern muttered that McCreevy would be on the front bench, and talked about the economy. 'Yeah, yeah, you'll be grand,' Ahern told him. 'Right, grand, right,' he replied. But McCreevy wasn't quite sure what job he was being asked to do. He wasn't certain until later, when he and Michael Smith were chatting in an office in Leinster House. Noel Dempsey walked in and said, 'So you're finance.'

How do you know? asked McCreevy. 'I've seen the typed list for the press release,' Dempsey replied. 'OK,' said McCreevy. So this is how it was going to be.

The rest of the front bench was a cautious mixture of Haughey loyalists like Ray Burke and Mary O'Rourke and the Reynolds people: Joe Walsh, Brian Cowen, Geoghegan-Quinn, Noel Dempsey, even Michael Smith. No previous cabinet members were dropped. There was also a scattering of younger TDs like Micheál Martin and John O'Donoghue, and others like Síle de Valera who could be loosely described as Ahern supporters. But the simple act of appointing Reynolds supporters could hardly eliminate the deep-rooted divisions, the suspicions and the incessant plotting from the parliamentary party overnight. Many of them were to circle each other warily for a long time to come.

Besides, Ahern's authority over his front bench was questionable, to say the least. The Haughey–Reynolds divisions remained barely submerged, and though Ahern relied on some of them, such as McCreevy, he didn't fully trust them. Most politicians are habitually paranoid about their seats and, for those who have them, their jobs. In a pretty Darwinian profession, much of this insecurity is entirely warranted. Ahern believed that the country 'n' western gang would take the opportunity to depose him if he gave them one, and replace him with Geoghegan-Quinn. Amazingly, Ahern allowed most of their offices to be near one another – Reynolds', Geoghegan-Quinn's and McCreevy's offices were all within whispering distance. As Ahern supporters saw it, they were forever in and out of each other's rooms; often, when one of Ahern's staff arrived, all conversation would stop.

Ahern was habitually concerned to know what they were doing and saying. Many of them gathered in an area of the Leinster House self-service restaurant that he christened 'Nuts' Corner'; he would tell his staff to go on scouting missions to see who was talking to whom in the bar, and who was whispering in Nuts' Corner.

Geoghegan-Quinn was the obvious alternative leader, and she knew it. She would 'flounce in and out of Bertie's office', remembers one staffer, announcing, 'I need to see the leader!' She entertained the denizens of Nuts' Corner with colourful critiques of Ahern: his appearance, his emollient style, his unwillingness to make decisions or alienate anyone. She took particular delight in annoying Mary O'Rourke, the deputy leader. 'Oh, she was a menace,' remembers one of Ahern's then staff.

Ahern's people complained about her, but conceded that she could be highly effective. She struck up a productive relationship with Positive Action, the lobby group for women who had been infected with hepatitis C from poisoned blood transfusions, and inflicted terrible political damage on the Rainbow government on the issue, and particularly on the health minister, Michael Noonan. On one occasion, the women staged a walk-out from the visitors' gallery in the Dáil when Noonan was speaking. It was enormously damaging, and the hepatitis C scandal was to come back to haunt Noonan when he fought the 2002 general election as Fine Gael leader.

By then, of course, Geoghegan-Quinn was long gone. Opposition politics can be a thankless grind, and she always faced a battle to be re-elected in Galway West. Headquarters, with its eye on a seat gain in the constituency, was troubled by what it thought was a lack of activity and determined that a shock might be necessary: she was shown a doctored poll result that suggested she was faced with the loss of her seat. 'It might get her off her arse,' party staffers told one another. To hell with it all, she thought when she saw it. I'm done with this. When the *Sunday Independent* published a story about her son's expulsion from school, she announced she was quitting politics for good. Few at the top of Fianna Fáil believed that was her reason. But what of it? She was gone and that was it. A major threat to Ahern had disappeared.

If Geoghegan-Quinn was perceived as the most likely alternative leader, some of her lieutenants were less than reliable. Brian Cowen seemed to his colleagues more interested in social-izing and diverting himself by going to the races and GAA matches and functions than doing serious work that would get the party elected. After one visit to the Irish Farmers' Association headquarters, the IFA leadership complained to Ahern about Cowen's uninterested performance. On another occasion, also reported to Ahern, a staff member had to wake him in his hotel room in Brussels before a scheduled *Morning Ireland* appearance. The staffer later regaled colleagues with descriptions of entering Cowen's room and finding the agriculture spokesman still asleep amid the detritus minutes before a scheduled appearance on the most-listened-to radio programme in the country.

Ahern didn't really know what to make of Noel Dempsey. Many of the Reynolds allies blamed him for pushing Albert into the hardline stance that ultimately led to his destruction, and he took the removal from office deeply personally. His office wasn't near theirs and he didn't fraternize with them much. Geoghegan-

Quinn thought he was treacherous for failing to support her. But he wasn't one of Ahern's intimates by any reckoning. Before Ahern's first ard-fheis as leader, Dempsey called at his office and gave him a good-luck card. Ahern could hardly have been more dumbstruck if Dempsey had tried to hug him. A staff member who was next into the room to see Ahern remembers him being 'completely flummoxed'. Should he display the card, for everyone to see? Should he put it away? 'Noel was in touch with his feminine side, I think. Bertie most assuredly was not,' the staff member told me.

In truth, most of the conspiring that was being done by the country 'n' westerners was pretty idle stuff, born of the frustration and boredom of opposition. Even the most wild-eyed conspirator knew (well, most of them did) that the party couldn't just dump Ahern. They muttered that Ahern couldn't make decisions, and was leading them nowhere. But there was little appetite for another bloodbath in the party. Not so soon, anyway.

Front-benchers were told that they were expected to put together policy documents on their areas, which would form the basis of the manifesto for the general election. Ahern exhorted them to reach out to experts and interest groups from beyond the party, not just to get the assistance of their input but to signal that Fianna Fáil was looking outwards and was receptive to ideas. He wanted a policy renewal to be at the heart of resuscitating the party, he told aides and colleagues. But he was also embarking on a sort of meta-canvass, looking for votes in places where Fianna Fáil had never sought them before. It didn't matter to Ahern whether they were party supporters or not – in fact, better in some cases that they weren't. At one stage, even the environmental group Greenpeace – not normally associated with the party, then or since – addressed a party meeting on environmental policy.

The policy groups not alone gave people something to do in opposition but provided the opportunity for front-bench spokesmen and women to attain if not a deep expertise, then at least a comfortable familiarity with policy in their areas – something that would pay off in media and Dáil appearances. Later, Ahern would meet Paddy Duffy and press officer Marty Whelan regularly to review the performance of his various spokesmen, giving the two advisers a valuable influence on his perception of the would-be ministers – something that subsequently annoyed many of them.

Some party staffers, though, thought that many of the front-benchers didn't really know what was going on in the policy groups. 'And most of them couldn't care less,' reflected one. Nonetheless, Ahern kept a close eye on them, and insisted that they keep producing initiatives that would interest the media and give the party 'hits'. The policy groups also presented a fund-raising opportunity; the process of gathering views and informa-tion from interested parties put many of them on the party's radar for the first time. They would be invited to lunches and launches and, along the way, tapped for a contribution by Des Richardson, whom Ahern had introduced to take charge of party fundraising.

Ahern had also brought in Padraic White, the former head of the Industrial Development Authority, to co-ordinate the work of the policy groups – to his staff's eventual annoyance. They took the view that it was difficult to get a broad range of action-able stuff out of White and several found him 'obsessed with the issues of ageing and the grey vote'. One frustrated staffer asked one of Ahern's closest advisers about the best way to deal with White, wondering how tight he was with Ahern. 'Ignore him,' was the reply.

The 1990s were the time when advisers became political stars in the Irish firmament for the first time; the system of special advisers and programme managers instituted by the Labour Party and followed by Fianna Fáil in 1992 was to bring a new dimension to politics, as a predominantly younger, non-traditional and media-savvy cadre of political operatives appeared. Some of the more senior advisers wielded as much power as many ministers. Through 1995 and 1996, Ahern also assembled a backroom staff, which was to have a significant influence over his leadership.

His first outside hire after he became leader back in late 1994 was – incongruously – an *Irish Times* journalist. Jackie Gallagher was the newspaper's industry correspondent and so their paths had crossed previously. But Gallagher didn't know Ahern well, and was surprised to have got the call. Gallagher jumped at the chance, and was pleased to learn that he was going to be paid considerably better in his new job. Ahern always tried to ensure that anyone joining his staff received a 10 per cent pay increase on their previous salary, on the basis that they would be working at least 10 per cent harder, he reckoned. This practice, once it became known, led to some later hires exaggerating their pre-government salaries. Gallagher went on to become one of Ahern's closest advisers until he left in late 1998 for a career in public relations.

In opposition, Paddy Duffy, Ahern's old friend from Drumcondra, was Ahern's 'chef de cabinet' – not, joked the staff, a title chosen by the boss himself. He retained his responsibility for a great part of Ahern's communications.

Mandy Johnston and Marty Whelan were the dominant figures in the party's press office. In opposition, the press office is much more important than it is in government, when ministers all have their own press offices. Johnston and Whelan were famously rivals – for the ear of the leader, for allies in the broader apparatus, for supporters in the media. Many of their ongoing battles were played out in the pages of *Phoenix* magazine, which each side appeared to brief to its own ends.

Gerry Hickey, who had worked for Ahern in the Department of Finance, was also brought in, although Ahern was typically evasive when announcing his appointment to the staff, suggesting to one that he was being brought in temporarily. After a promotion from the Department of Finance to the Department of the Marine, Hickey had left the civil service to join the ferry company Irish Continental Group. Now politics beckoned. He was an habitué of Doheny & Nesbitt's, the Baggot Street pub much favoured by the politicians, their hangers-on and journalists. Far from being a stop-gap appointment, he went on to become one of Ahern's closest advisers for more than a decade.

Of all the advisers, none brought more to the table in terms of stature, clout and experience than Martin Mansergh, the Oxford-educated, Protestant, republican Tipperaryman who had become an integral if unusual part of Fianna Fáil's backroom team.

Ahern was the third leader of Fianna Fáil to whom Martin Mansergh had brought his formidable intellectual skills to assist. A former career civil servant, Mansergh joined Charles Haughey's staff and stayed with Albert Reynolds when Haughey was forced out. Mansergh's secret contacts with Sinn Féin had formed part of the genesis of the peace process.

Ahern and Mansergh knew one another, but not well. More than a decade previously, Ahern had recommended a constituent of his, Evelyn Egar, for a job as Mansergh's secretary. The arrangement endured – Egar worked with Mansergh for fifteen years.

Around the time Ahern became leader, Mansergh was attending a meeting of the Forum for Peace and Reconciliation at Dublin Castle, when he fell into conversation with Ahern, who asked him if he would stay on to work in his office. Mansergh agreed immediately. Later, he was leaving Government Buildings to catch a train to Belfast, when Frank Murray, the secretary to the government, came running after him. 'I just barely restrained John Bruton from walking into your office,' he said. 'He wants you to stay on as adviser on Northern Ireland.' Mansergh agreed to think about it, but he was never in doubt about his response. Though originally a civil servant, he was by now a Fianna Fáil man, and when Fianna Fáil left government, he left too.

Mansergh's reluctance to serve a Fine Gael taoiseach spoke of a wider belief in Fianna Fáil that the peace process was a Fianna Fáil project, and that Fine Gael was culturally and politically unsuited to dealing with republicans and with the British government on behalf of nationalists north and south. That view wasn't confined to Fianna Fáil. David Trimble's adviser Stephen King observed a 'slight snobbery within Fianna Fáil ... that they knew how to handle republicanism, and that Bruton and Fine Gael were just not really from the right mindset to really deal with the peace process,' he told Mansergh's biographer, Kevin Rafter. It was more than a slight snobbery: it was a full-blown prejudice. (It was echoed in Sinn Féin: when Fianna Fáil left office in 1994, Sinn Féin felt there was an immediate change of gear in Dublin's engagement with the progress towards inclusive talks.)

What Mansergh brought to Ahern's team was a depth of knowledge about the North, an issue which few of his other recruits – whose political abilities and understanding of the media were to prove invaluable – had a grounding in, or a natural feel for. Few of them had either the traditional Fianna Fáil 'fourth green field' attitude to the North or the belief that there was any political payback from investing time and energy and political capital in the quagmire. 'He really believed all the stuff about a united Ireland,' one of his closest advisers told me, with genuine surprise. But then many political professionals are surprised when they learn that politicians believe in anything. Like many of their generation, Ahern's younger aides had grown up when the only news they heard from Northern Ireland was of shooting and bombing and sectarian strife. They knew that Ahern was committed to engaging with the Northern issue perhaps above all else and they worked assiduously to his agenda. But they just didn't care that much about it. And they couldn't see the electoral payback – they could only see Sinn Féin eating into their electoral base.

'There's not a single vote in all this, you know,' a government adviser told me in later years after one of the many Northern stalemates had been moved on another few centimetres.

'Ah, come on, there must be some votes in it,' I ventured.

'Well, there's not enough to justify the Bert spending all his fucking time on it,' was the reply. Some of Tony Blair's aides said much the same about him.

Yet the commitment to the Northern question was there from the moment Ahern became party leader and remained unwavering throughout his career as Taoiseach. In one sense, he was the epitome of the Fianna Fáil republican. His father was a teenage member of the IRA in Cork during the War of Independence and Ahern grew up in a strongly republican household where the view of the North had not changed since de Valera's constitutional insistence that the 'reintegration of the national territory' was 'pending' in 1937. Ahern often wondered subsequently what his father would have made of his accommodations of unionism and his closeness to the British. His 2008 claims that he nearly joined the IRA in the 1970s seem extravagant, though they are an indication of the extent of his traditional republicanism. He had a detailed knowledge of local combat engagements in Drumcondra and beyond between the IRA and the British Forces during the War of Independence, the sort of things that boys suck up from their elders and remember for ever. 'It was personal in his family, almost visceral,' recalled one of his staff.

Though Mansergh was the pivotal figure in Northern policy, his role also extended to general research and speechwriting. He had edited a book of Haughey's speeches, entitled *Spirit of the Nation*. He had a high regard for Ahern, but he realized he wouldn't be editing a book of his new boss's speeches.

Mansergh's verbosity became a joke among some of the staff, though it genuinely irritated others, who felt that he simply ignored Ahern's oratorical weakness when he wrote, and Paddy Duffy felt that he had a better grasp of his leader's demotic distinctiveness. Ray Burke used to call him 'Dr Mengele' to his face, though it never really caught on. Ahern himself valued Mansergh enormously, though he was sometimes exasperated by him. At one meeting of advisers, Ahern complained directly to the Oxford scholar, 'There's a sentence in my speech that's fourteen lines long!' The others made Mansergh read the offending excerpt, and were vocally gratified when he stumbled over several passages.

Despite his political nous and his sharp intellect, an apparent other-worldliness was often evident. On another occasion during a meeting, when a mobile phone's ringtone sounded near him (it was admittedly a time when mobile phone ownership, if no longer exotic, was hardly commonplace), Mansergh picked up a television remote control and began to speak in a rising tone into it – 'Hello? Hello? HELLO?'

Probably more important than any of the paid staff that Ahern assembled was the return of PJ Mara, Haughey's former press secretary, to the very centre of political decision-making.

Mara had suggested himself for the position of director of elections because he had seen the role messed up in the past by politicians whose real concerns centred on their own constituency. Chatting to Ray Burke one day about the post, Mara told him, 'The worst thing [Ahern] could do would be to have one of you guys running the election campaign. You're too concerned with your own constituency, too concerned with your own pals and you just can't focus on the job.'

'Well, who would you think, then?' Burke replied.

'I'll do it if you want.'

In fact, Mara's combination of natural ebullience, political skill and deep knowledge of how both Fianna Fáil backroom politics and media dynamics worked were to make him an enormous success in the job. And, of course, though he had made plenty of money as a lobbyist while Fine Gael were in government, it wouldn't do his business any harm to have a Fianna Fáiler in the Taoiseach's office – especially a Fianna Fáiler who owed him a debt of gratitude. Over the years, he has often been accused of a conflict of interest (including by the present writer) between his roles as a vital cog in the Fianna Fáil election machine and a corporate adviser and lobbyist for commercial interests, and though no individual instance where Mara abused his access has ever been chronicled, it's sometimes difficult to see where Mara the lobbyist stops and Mara the political operative begins. But ultimately he has spent most of his adult life working for Fianna Fáil because he is, first and foremost, a party man. He is a Fianna Fáil chauvinist to his core, wherever that is.

Mara was to fulfil the role of director of elections for each of Bertie Ahern's three triumphs, and he was another of Ahern's

most important appointments ever. Would Ahern have won in
1997 without Mara? Perhaps. But he would not have won without someone doing the jobs that Mara took on. And the chance
of anyone else doing them – certainly of a single person doing
them – was tiny.

But if the parliamentary party needed work, the organization
was badly in need of some tender loving care, too. Ahern was
well acquainted with Pat Farrell, the party's general secretary,
though the two men were hardly friends. They were to agree
very quickly on some basic but far-reaching conclusions about
the state of the party, and the improvements needed if a repeat of
the disastrous 1992 election was to be avoided.

Ahern had been treasurer of the party, but he kept his distance
from the headquarters operation. 'He kept his distance all right,'
remembers one headquarters staffer. 'He seemed to us to be
moving pretty inexorably towards the leadership, but he didn't
have all that much to do with headquarters. He had his own
set-up, his own support group independent of the party and outside the party.' He was emphatically not a headquarters insider;
the centre of his political universe was Drumcondra, not Mount
Street. Conversely, Farrell was never pulled into that political
circle. Ahern liked to keep things compartmentalized.

Farrell met Ahern shortly after he became leader. The atmosphere wasn't unfriendly, but it wasn't excessively cordial either.
Farrell had been brought in by Haughey after the departure from
the general secretary's office of Frank Wall, who had held the job
for twelve years. Farrell was hardly six months in the job when
Haughey was finally taken down and Albert Reynolds became
leader. He was distrusted by the Reynolds camp as Haughey's
man, and now he feared Ahern's guys would pigeon-hole him
as Reynolds' man.

In fact, though he was suspected by some of the Ahernites of
being Albert's man, Farrell never achieved the sort of ease with
Reynolds that he subsequently did with Ahern. The Reynolds
years, of course, were a bumpy ride for everyone concerned;
Reynolds' impetuosity and his 'I'm the leader and now you'll

do what I say' approach didn't sit well with Farrell's more methodical, managerial approach.

To those who thought he was too close to Reynolds, Farrell recalled one national executive meeting where disciplinary action against a member was being dealt with, and Farrell's slow and overtly procedurally correct approach began to irk Reynolds. The weight of the evidence was against the member; however, Farrell insisted that the charge against the member be set out, and both sides of the argument be rehearsed in equal detail. Reynolds became increasingly agitated, wanting to cut short the discussion. Farrell tried to tell him that they had to follow correct legal procedures, which had been advised by senior counsel David Byrne, whom he had consulted and who was on hand in another office. Reynolds suddenly barked, loud enough to be heard by those near by: 'If you don't wrap this up I'll take your head and your fucking legal adviser's head OFF!'

Farrell knew that Ahern's leadership style would be different, and that he had still to prove himself as a successful general secretary. But he also knew that Ahern was being advised to put his own man in the job. When they met in early January, Farrell told the new leader that he would go if Ahern felt he needed a new general secretary. 'I can make this easy for you if you want. I can resign. But I'd love to work with you on this,' Farrell told him.

Ahern had offered a listening ear to those who had counselled Farrell's removal, but he wanted someone who could start work immediately on renewing the party. He couldn't afford the time it would take for a new general secretary to get to know the party properly. Besides, he had a high regard for Farrell, and didn't believe that he was responsible for the debacle of 1992. 'Of course you'll stay, Pat,' Ahern replied.

The two men soon agreed that the party organization was on the floor, and in need of complete rejuvenation. With the number of active cumainn having fallen from about three thousand to less than half that, the scale of the job was enormous. Ahern and Farrell planned a rapid tour of the constituency organizations. For several months, Ahern criss-crossed the country intermittently, often in the company of Farrell. They shook thousands of hands, ate a lot of bad food and felt the pulse of the organization.

Of all the organizational changes effected at this time none was more difficult, more important nor had more far-reaching consequences than the revolution in how the party picked its candidates for the general election. More than anything else, the changes effected in this area helped Ahern win power in 1997 when the odds seemed stacked against him.

In another life, Charlie McCreevy could have been a bookie, not an accountant turned politician. His hail-fellow-well-met persona is not so much an act as a side of his personality that he chooses to emphasize to mask a cool and calculating – albeit sometimes prone to a diverting hubris – intelligence. He has an instant command of numbers that would have made him a rich man at the track-side, or on the trading floor. For years, McCreevy had been friendly with Sean Donnelly, a Dublin Corporation engineer whose real talent lay in political polling. Donnelly had done some private polling for McCreevy in Kildare before previous elections, and the TD trusted his friend's methods completely. The complex mathematics of Irish elections had long been a source of study and fascination for them both, and the subject of many conversations.

They concluded that it was a mathematical fact that Fianna Fáil could win elections on a much lower share of the vote than had been habitual under Charles Haughey. In other words, Haughey should never have lost an election. Fianna Fáil was wasting thousands and thousands of votes on candidates who would never be elected: on the third and fourth candidates in three-seaters, where the task should have been to win two seats, and so on. A successful new approach depended on running the right numbers of candidates in the right parts of the constituency, and splitting the party vote evenly between them.

McCreevy and PJ Mara had also discussed this on several occasions. Mara had watched his previous boss repeatedly achieve

45 per cent plus in elections, only to fail to win overall majorities on each occasion. Haughey's polarizing character was no doubt a significant factor in this trend; however, on the bare mathematics of the process, Mara had always believed, Fianna Fáil was throwing away seats by running too many candidates in many constituencies. Under a factionalized party, it was impossible to fix this structural flaw. Now, with Ahern in the leader's office, they saw the chance to actually do something about it. It would mean the imposition of a discipline that the party hadn't known in recent decades, and an extension of central power that it had never seen. It would mean taking the power to decide conventions from the local party barons and assuming it to the centre. They could do it not because Ahern was a strong leader – he wasn't, yet – but because they could see that he could become one.

As the Fine Gael–Labour–Democratic Left Rainbow government bedded down and the economy continued to improve, it became clear that winning the next election was going to be an uphill struggle. Managing the Fianna Fáil vote more efficiently, the two believed, could level the playing pitch somewhat, and cutting the numbers of candidates would become key to the new electoral strategy. They spoke to Farrell about imposing strict discipline on party tickets. They found they were preaching to the converted; but he warned that it could be done only with the full backing of the leader.

But rather than approach Ahern directly with such a radical – and, in its application, potentially troublesome – proposal, the two determined to work through Chris Wall, one of Ahern's most loyal and trusted pals from the Drumcondra gang. Wall was the only one of that gang with whom party headquarters really achieved a level of comfort over the years. 'We'll bring Donnelly in and we'll bring Chris Wall,' McCreevy told Mara. 'If we can convince Chris Wall we can convince the Bert.'

The crucial meeting was in Mara's house on Wellington Road in Dublin 4. Donnelly's job was to supply hard numbers in support of the proposition, so he produced a set of graphs and tables that showed that with the share of the vote that he won in every general election, Haughey should never have been out of power. Fianna Fáil could win a general election with a lot fewer votes than they had always thought. Mara was also convinced of something else: that the opportunity to win a general election – even with Donnelly's magic formulas – mightn't extend beyond the next one if they didn't do it then. He came to believe that almost nothing was more important.

Under the high ceilings and amid the tastefully restored Georgian features of Mara's townhouse, McCreevy and his host, supported by Donnelly's numbers, explained the radical proposal to exert greater central control over constituency operations than had ever been attempted in the party's history. Wall was walking around the room. 'Jaysus,' he reflected, 'that'll never work in Dublin.'

But Mara and McCreevy kept hammering away at the idea. The main point of argument in their favour was the extraordinary mess that the party had been making of elections in the past.

'Jesus, 1992 was a disaster,' remembers one protagonist. 'Candidates were just thrown on tickets overnight – conventions were called after the election was announced. So we were determined to have candidates in place long before an election was called.'

The candidate strategy that obtained until then was described by Farrell to his reluctant colleagues as 'Throw the four of them at it and let the best man jump the ditch.' He told them about one instance in a local election where Fianna Fáil ran nine candidates for a town council election, where it had previously held four seats. None of them managed to take a seat. That result was freaky, but it underlined how congested tickets wasted votes.

Having run their electoral ju-ju past Chris Wall, Mara took it to Ahern. He was circumspect, but not hostile. The logic, he could see, was unanswerable. Ahern knew that there would be opposition to the plan in the parliamentary party and in the organization. Politicians had all come up through the 'let them at it' approach and they all had a fear of having bright young fellas imposed on them in their own constituency. The existing system gave them a measure of control many would resent giving up. Ahern could see that he would have to fight it every inch of the way with the politicians, so better to get someone to do it on his behalf. 'Well,' Ahern told Mara carefully, 'you had better take it up with MacSharry's committee.' Former finance minister Ray MacSharry headed a committee on electoral strategy and candidate selection. It was a parry by Ahern that would become a characteristic response to a difficult decision.

MacSharry's committee had existed before the new strategy was conceived, but it played an important role once the decision was taken to rigorously control selection and candidate numbers.

Mara was co-opted on to the committee, and attended his first meeting for a discussion on the constituency of Cork North Central, then a five-seater where Fianna Fáil had managed only one out of five seats in 1992, and had ambitions for at least one more. The candidates discussed were Billy Kelleher, Noel O'Flynn and Danny Wallace. Three candidates would give them the optimum chance of three seats. Gene Fitzgerald, an old party grandee who sat on the committee, interjected. 'I don't know, I don't know, I think we might need a fourth candidate . . .' Other views around the table were sympathetic.

'For fuck's sake,' Mara waded in, 'You guys need to rethink this whole thing . . .' The lecture went on for some time – possibly longer than was necessary, thought some around the table. But when it became clear through MacSharry in subsequent meetings that the party leader was supportive of the strategy, the point hit home.

In the event, Fianna Fáil ran three candidates and won three seats in North Central. The party improved its share of the vote from 1992 certainly; but the real difference was splitting the vote equally among the three candidates. In 1992, the party won 28 per cent of the vote in the constituency, which translated into just one seat. In 1997, it won 36 per cent, which brought in three seats. Without those two extra seats or the others like them, there would have been no Ahern government.

The most important function of the MacSharry committee was that it gave Mara and Farrell cover to impose the will of headquarters on an often recalcitrant and rebellious organization. Ahern watched and approved, though he often seemed to be listening sympathetically to the many complaints about the committee's decisions on his travels. 'The notion that headquarters would do anything without the leader's approval in this regard is absurd,' one senior figure told me. Another elaborated: 'He'd be listening to the organization complaining about HQ and saying, "Jaze, that's terrible, that's terrible." And he'd be telling us: keep doing what you have to do.'

The programme of constituency management was tough going, but it was being pushed through, albeit usually against significant local opposition. Some of the opposition was overt; some of it was procedural; some of it was amateurish; some of it was almost comic. But the more constituencies Farrell and the party leadership engaged with, the better they got at it. 'The more we did the more I realized that Fianna Fáil local organizations were chronically incapable of selecting the right candidate. Actually what they sometimes did is pick the biggest gobshite,' said one figure closely involved in the process. When this did happen it was because the incumbent TD controlled the local organization and wanted no threat to his or her primacy, or, where there was more than one sitting TD, because an uneasy truce existed between the rival camps, which held that whatever their differences, there certainly wasn't room for another local chief.

Another party figure remembers Cork North West as a pretty typical example of the sort of obstacles that headquarters felt they had to surmount. Farrell had come across Michael Moynihan, a young Fianna Fáil activist with a strong local profile, whom he had considered as a potential candidate. At that time, Fine Gael held two seats to Fianna Fáil's one in the Cork North West, a situation that had its roots not just in the strength of Fine Gael historically in the area but also in the fact that the Fianna Fáil organization was content to protect the one seat held by Donal Moynihan (no relation).

'So what does Moynihan do before the convention? He produces three names, and starts telling us, "Oh, we have a woman in Charleville and she has such-and-such a business, she'd be a very good candidate ..."' remembers one party official. Headquarters was not convinced about the possible candidates suggested by the sitting TD.

Farrell travelled to Millstreet, where he met the twelve members of the local officer board. They were seated around a kitchen table which someone had positioned at the centre of a big hall, like a scene from a mafia movie. The entire officer board consisted of reliable supporters of Donal Moynihan. The meeting went along predictable lines, discussing the potential of various running mates for Donal: they have sniffed the wind from the Dublin direction and they know that it's not favourable; they need to head this nonsense off tonight.

'Michael Moynihan – what about him?' said Farrell. Silence. Despite his status as a rising star locally, nobody seemed to know him. Responses varied between 'Never heard of him' and 'Not candidate material'. Like hell he's not, thought Farrell. 'I think he's from Kishkeem – isn't that beside you?' he enquired of one of the officers present.

'I think I might have heard of him,' he replied. 'Now I don't know him but I think my brother might know him.'

Six weeks later, Mara and Farrell made the long drive to Millstreet again and sat this time amid 1,000 delegates for the selection convention. The convention was instructed that it could select one candidate (which would obviously be the sitting TD); the second name on the ticket would be added by headquarters. Uproar.

Knowing it would be a hostile environment, they asked Michael Smith, the Tipperary North TD and front-bencher, to chair the convention. When they knew a convention was going to be particularly difficult, they asked Smith or Noel Dempsey or

Seamus Brennan – guys they knew they could rely on to railroad through the wishes of headquarters, or 'great men for tricky conventions', in the words of one official. 'They'd swarm around you at the table,' recalled one chairman to me, detailing the colour colourful though usually unoriginal abuse that was heaped on them by angry delegates. Other reliables were Micheál Martin or Dermot Ahern or Rory O'Hanlon ('a soldier' says one HQ source). They asked Michael Woods once; it was not a success.

Millstreet was one such hostile environment. 'There was a lot of roaring and shouting, but Smith stuck to it,' recalls one witness. The second Moynihan was duly added by headquarters, over the most strenuous objections from the incumbent. At the general election – and at the subsequent election in 2002 – Fianna Fáil took two out of the three seats. When boundary changes transferred a Cork South Central TD into Cork North West for the 2007 election, he took a seat at Donal Moynihan's expense. Michael Moynihan remains a member of the thirtieth Dáil.

The visits to the constituencies and the candidate selection were complemented by an unprecedented programme of research and polling which endeavoured to give the leadership clarity about which candidates they should run and where. Farrell had discussed the applicability of market research techniques to Irish politics with a neighbour of his, who used market research extensively in his business. 'Where would you get it done?' he enquired. Rather than referring him to one of the Dublin polling companies, his neighbour suggested that he should talk to the director of a unit in the Smurfit School of Business. 'I think he might be in your party, too,' Farrell's neighbour told him. A few days later, Sean Dorgan received a call from Farrell's office.

Dorgan and Farrell held a number of meetings where the lecturer outlined for the general secretary how a pretty simple but methodologically robust model could be designed which would give party headquarters a reading on how potential candidates would fly with local electorates and, once selected, how they were progressing. Subsequently, there were many people who had an input into the plan, which was largely managed by Sean Donnelly. The beauty of the model for headquarters was that the organization could do it themselves, thus keeping the costs down and the circle of information close. And, notes one architect of the process, 'It gave those testosterone-charged lunatics in Ogra something useful to do.'

'We'd hire a bus and send them down the country every weekend,' remembers one senior figure. 'Once they followed instructions it was a remarkably robust model. And they only cost about five hundred quid a go. We'd throw a load of Heineken and chicken and chips into them at the end of the day and they'd all turn up the next time.'

Another source remembers that there were a few incidents early on where Ogra members took issue during the polling process at the stated intention of some respondents to vote for parties other than Fianna Fáil – but they soon learned. In all, the party conducted somewhere in the region of eighty constituency polls over the pre-election period. It gave the party a considerable advantage preparing for the 1997 contest.

But for all these important changes, Ahern was doing badly in the Dáil and badly in the media. Years later, with the benefit of hindsight, Paddy Duffy would tell friends that a complex political project takes time to build. For much of 1995 and 1996, it just looked as though Ahern was floundering.

Ahern's task was made more difficult by the assured and confident start made by the Rainbow administration. And divisions in the party which transcended the rift between the Haughey camp and the country 'n' western gang were exposed when health minister Michael Noonan published his Regulation of Information (Services outside State for Termination of Pregnancies) Bill in February 1995 seeking to make information on abortion available to the public, in line with the referendum result of 1992. The Fianna Fáil reaction was confused and contradictory. On the first day, the party was in favour of the bill; on the second day when the front bench met, the party was neutral. And on the third day, when the parliamentary party met, Fianna Fáil opposed the bill.

In the *Irish Times*, Dick Walsh saw 'a political hole from which comes the sound of digging: "Fianna Fáil at work" ... Bertie Ahern,' Walsh continued, 'who started the hole, had taken his stand near by in the hope of seeing Michael Noonan fall in. Unfortunately for Fianna Fáil, the party's back-benchers took a hand; they undermined Mr Ahern's position and, ignoring their senior colleagues, all but buried his leadership.'

It wasn't the first or the last time that the end of Ahern's leadership or authority would be proclaimed. For the next decade anyway, they would all be wrong. But Walsh's assertion wasn't without a grain of truth. Ahern's authority was weak and threatened, and he simply did not have the power to impose his will on the party at this time. It was the first test of his authority, and he flunked it. Or rather, he chose not to sit the test at all. It was to become a manoeuvre characteristic of his leadership.

Ahern and his advisers watched as TDs trundled out to voice their opposition. Of the loudest was Noel Ahern. One of Ahern's advisers called his office to tell him the delicate news that his brother was refusing to follow his leadership. 'Your latest problem on this is Noel,' the adviser told Ahern. Ahern's reply was curtly dismissive of his brother.

Younger TDs like Micheál Martin and John O'Donoghue also opposed the bill. Another front-bencher had more personal objections. 'I have two adopted children,' he raged at a member of Ahern's staff who was trying to persuade him to back the bill. 'They might never have been born if abortion was allowed!'

'But you can't let your personal circumstances influence a political decision,' the staffer replied.

'I'll let whatever I want influence my decision,' the front-bencher replied testily.

Day by day, Ahern's office watched his initial position disintegrate. The uneasy compromise that was made was that Fianna Fáil would oppose the bill when it was first presented to the Dáil, offer amendments during debate and then abstain on the final vote. Ahern knew this wouldn't get him off the hook, and the media reaction to the Fianna Fáil back-bench rebellion and Ahern's capitulation to it was savage.

'The windows that Mr Albert Reynolds attempted to throw open on the modern world are being shuttered again,' wrote Denis Coghlan in the *Irish Times*, striking an incongruous note of nostalgia for the Reynolds days, 'as the Fianna Fáil party chases the votes of the 40 per cent of the electorate which opposed the provision of abortion information in the 1992 referendum.' Absent was any suggestion that the Rainbow might have been chasing the 60 per cent who favoured the provision of abortion information.

'Planning and hard work' had won Noonan's victory when the bill was passed, Coghlan later declared; Fianna Fáil had been pandering to 'the rural red-neck vote'.

The criticism stung. Ahern told the following week's parliamentary party meeting that he would not allow 'leader writers or columnists' to dictate Fianna Fáil policy. At which point, according to newspaper reports, someone shouted from the floor, 'Or cartoonists!', a reference to the scathing portrayals of Ahern's dithering by the *Irish Times*'s Martyn Turner. However, Ahern added that the party's stance on the abortion question should not be taken as an indication of its position on other social issues. His support for a removal of the ban on divorce was well known, he said, and it would remain. This was a signal to the back-benchers: don't push it. As for the leader writers and columnists, well, they'd have to get used to the odd U-turn. Rural rednecks have votes too.

Similar pressures were to arise for Ahern later that year when the government moved to bring forward another referendum on removing the constitutional ban on divorce.

There was a strongly conservative element in the parliamentary party, reflective of a support base that was noticeably more traditionally conservative on socio-sexual and 'moral' issues than any of the other mainstream parties. 'It was a huge problem for us,' says one party figure of the time.

In addition, several of the front bench believed that Ahern's own situation as a separated man living openly in a second relationship compromised his authority to give leadership on these issues. At the very least, many of them were queasy about it. And friend and foe alike (inside and outside the party) could see that it was a potential political weakness.

These included the several members of his own party – some of them on the front bench – who believed it could 'blow up in his face', remembers one.

Ahern's personal situation was always going to make the divorce referendum a tricky issue for Fianna Fáil. But it was more than just the leader's personal life. On a purely political level, Ahern and his advisers knew that the country was changing and they knew that the brand of Fianna Fáil was associated with an old Ireland, which would become an increasingly difficult sell. As it was they were weak among the Dublin middle classes; Ahern and his strategists knew they could write off much of that vote if they opposed the divorce referendum.

But the fact was that the Fianna Fáil organization remained a largely conservative one, especially in rural Ireland, and a majority of its members were opposed to the introduction of divorce. However, Ahern knew that if he wished to attract new votes to Fianna Fáil, he needed to send out signals to them that things had changed at the top. He needed to support the referendum. It was a tightrope between supporting the referendum, though not campaigning too vigorously, and keeping his own parliamentary party within tipping distance of the leadership line. It was a shaky position, but it was the most he could manage.

So when the Fianna Fáil policy group on the subject, headed by Michael Woods and including among others Professor Patricia Casey, a supporter of Catholic positions on many social matters, produced a draft report that warned of the consequences of divorce in society, the alarm bells began to ring loudly on the fifth floor of the Leinster House annexe. If the report was published in its original form, Fianna Fáil could not credibly support the referendum – which Ahern had decided that the party must do.

One adviser who saw a draft of the report told his colleagues that if word leaked to the media, it – and the party – would look ridiculous. He worried that it ascribed all sorts of difficulties with children to the divorce of the parents, 'up to and including bed-wetting', he told other staff. It was like something from the divisive first divorce referendum, Ahern's advisers thought. One of them told his colleagues that it would set Fianna Fáil back forty years.

The report was largely rewritten by Ahern's staff, with Paddy Duffy responsible for most it. Woods himself was told in plain terms that he had better get a handle on his group. He should warn its members that Ahern would disavow them if they went public and then come out and support the referendum. Woods did as he was told. Patricia Casey was furious, and her annoyance was made public. This worried Ahern to the extent that he turned up at her office one morning to discuss her concerns. She was taken aback at his presence, but thought he was pleasant and polite. He still buried her report, though.

A few weeks later at the Fianna Fáil ard-fheis, there was controversy when a vote after a debate on divorce was called in favour of the leadership position – despite a clear majority speaking and voting against it. The order from party chiefs was clear: the vote will be in favour of divorce, no matter what the delegates say. The party couldn't wait for the whole thing to be over, but just getting through it was an important milestone for Ahern's leadership.

But if preparations for the 1997 contest progressed well through 1995 and the early part of 1996, much of the progress was invisible to the media and to the rest of the political world. Ahern came under significant pressure for his performance in the Dáil particularly, and the perception of him as a weak and ineffectual opposition leader was beginning to harden in the minds of many. Despite the important strides that had been made organizationally, Ahern's leadership was looking as though it was floundering. Before a late 1995 ard-fheis, several delegates felt free enough to express their reservations about his leadership to the media. Seamus Cooney, a Wexford delegate, told the *Irish Times* that Ahern had been 'somewhat disappointing' as leader; a Longford delegate and self-professed supporter of Albert Reynolds, Ned O'Reilly, told the paper he was disappointed in Ahern's performance. 'He should be a bit more aggressive,' he said.

The start of Ahern's public recovery came in the shape of two by-elections, one in Donegal, the other in Dublin. They were to signal a turnaround in his fortunes, and provide a huge fillip to the parliamentary party and the broader organization at a vital time. With just a year to go before the general election, the two April 1996 by-elections showed that Ahern could be a winner. They couldn't have come at a better time for him.

As ever in politics, though, there was a complication. Following the death of Brian Lenihan, the gaze of the party fell – as it always does – on his family for a possible successor. The obvious candidate was his eldest son, Brian, a clever and politically savvy barrister who had been closely involved in his father's campaigns.

Lenihan junior was willing to stand. But he would not do so, he told Ahern, without a clear public commitment from Fianna Fáil and its leader that the party would oppose – and in government prevent – the building of the proposed casino in the Phoenix Park, then a huge issue in the area. Ahern had enjoyed the hospitality of one of the promoters of the casino, Norman Turner, at Manchester United games, and had assisted Turner's application for an Irish passport. Turner had given $10,000 in cash to Ahern's associate Des Richardson. According to Richardson, Turner told him it was to offset fundraising expenses. PJ Mara was retained by the casino consortium. If they didn't have Ahern's support, they certainly hoped to get it.

Ahern demonstrated his willingness to think only of the forthcoming election. Reviewing his statements, he told one meeting of his staff, 'Well, I never actually said I was for it . . .' A letter was sent to all homes in the constituency pledging Fianna Fáil's committed opposition to the casino plan. Ahern gave the guarantee under duress, but this didn't stop him from subsequently claiming to have always opposed the casino project. He was making a virtue out of necessity.

Lenihan had a trump card, and he knew it. Bertie Ahern needed to win the election, and he needed Lenihan junior to do it. Deal-making is central to all politics, and the aspiring politician had just made his first big political deal. He had also made a political enemy. Ahern never forgot the temerity of the young by-election candidate. Lenihan was overlooked and ignored for promotion long after it seemed inevitable. The animosity between the two men became a part of parliamentary party life. Ahern resisted all entreaties, including several from Charlie McCreevy, to bring Lenihan into cabinet. Even allowing for Ahern's latent dislike of the entitled classes of Fianna Fáil ('He had a thing about the party aristocrats,' says one high-ranking officer, citing as an example of this his sacking of Eoin Ryan, the son of a senator and grandson of a party founder, in 2002), his treatment of Lenihan was capricious, and keenly felt by the Dublin West TD. He was finally elevated to cabinet in 2007 by Ahern, probably about a decade after he deserved it.

'Two defeats would have been catastrophic,' says one insider. 'And Brian Lenihan would not have been elected without the casino guarantee.'

In 1997, with a general election looming and a keen appreciation of the perishability of political promises, Lenihan again pushed for a similar commitment. Ahern's constituency abutted the Phoenix Park and he was well aware of the strength of feeling about the matter. In late April, the script of a speech he had given in the Dáil on a debate about investment in Dublin reaffirmed Fianna Fáil's commitment to block the casino. The script was widely distributed to local and national media, pushed by the press office on the instructions of Ahern's office. However, the speech that was actually delivered in the Dáil was shortened by time constraints and contained no such commitment. A leaflet distributed in the relevant areas at election time quoted from the speech that Ahern had circulated, rather than the one he actually gave in the Dáil, promising that there would be no casino under

Fianna Fáil. Fine Gael's Austin Currie objected that no such speech had been made in the Dáil, but few paid heed. Days before the general election, Ahern categorically ruled out a casino in a phone-in on Pat Kenny's radio show. There was, says one source involved at the time, no going back after that. Two seats in Dublin West were more important. Ultimately, Ahern was as good as his word – or his lack of words, depending on how you view it. There was no change in the law to permit a casino. The developers later sold the land for housing, netting a massive profit.

If there was an obvious candidate for Dublin West, the same couldn't be said in Donegal. Headquarters liked the look of Cecilia Keaveney, though: a young teacher whom Farrell had travelled to meet and who had impressed him. As well as her own qualities as a candidate, she was ideally located in Inishowen. In the sprawling constituency, geography was a more important factor than most. She wasn't, however, quite so obvious to the local organization.

Pat Farrell travelled to the constituency where he spent two days convincing the local barons, the 'Donegal mafia', to accept Keaveney as the candidate. It was tedious; he had to spend an evening in Bernard McGlinchey's house listening to his political war stories and had to spend more time squaring off other bigwigs. But it was worth it. Crucially, Jim McDaid, displaying an awareness of the party's broader interests not often found in incumbent TDs, agreed to co-operate.

On the day the votes were counted, it looked for a long time as though Joe Higgins of the Socialist Party and independent Harry Blaney would take the two seats – with all the possible consequences for Ahern that this might entail. One journalist, having her lunch in the self-service restaurant in Leinster House, was joined by the Galway East TD, Noel Treacy, one of the Dáil's occasional plotters. According to one person who witnessed the conversation between them, Treacy warned of the consequences of the results, suggesting to the journalist that moves would start to be made against Ahern. 'Oh, things will be bad,' he told her. 'It could be game on, game on.' Earlier the same day, a senior Fianna

Fáil figure told the *Irish Times*, 'No courtship with Mary Harney will put us into the next government – we must have Labour.'

Fianna Fáil won both seats with transfers – from Fine Gael in Donegal and, more quixotically, from Tomas MacGiolla of the Workers Party in Dublin, just pipping Joe Higgins by 300 or so votes.

The transfer pattern in Dublin didn't just demonstrate the entertainingly fratricidal politics of the far left; it showed that under Bertie Ahern, Fianna Fáil was playing a different electoral ball game: it was now in the market for transfers. This would become a powerful factor in changing the way Irish elections worked. It showed Ahern, Mara, McCreevy and the others that they could move to an electoral landscape that was not simply Fianna Fáil versus the rest. That would be a profound change to the advantage of the largest party.

A few months later another event was to trigger a profound change in the public debate, and one that also worked to the advantage of Ahern and Fianna Fáil.

On the Wednesday morning of 26 June 1996, Ahern was in the Dáil chamber addressing questions to the Taoiseach, John Bruton, on economic policy. The Dáil term was drawing to a close, TDs were tired and the exchanges were testy, with Dermot Ahern and Mary O'Rourke weighing in with their assistance to their leader. 'The Taoiseach is a joke,' Dermot Ahern blurted out at one stage. The day's business included oral questions, statements on a recent European Council meeting in Florence and expressions of sympathy on the death of the former Greek Prime Minister Andreas Papandreou. It was a normal enough day in Leinster House, and when deputies weren't in their offices or the chamber, some of them enjoyed the sun on the plinth.

Ahern was summoned from his seat on the Ceann Comhairle's right by a note delivered by an usher. Jackie Gallagher waited outside the chamber for him. 'Veronica Guerin has been shot dead,' Gallagher told him. The news was not yet public, but Gallagher had heard early through his network of journalist contacts. The gardaí had privately confirmed it to the security correspondents. There was no doubt. It was a hit.

The two men quickly made their way from the chamber to the Fianna Fáil offices. They talked urgently but sporadically as they went; both knew Guerin, who had been for a time active in Fianna Fáil circles and worked for the party at the New Ireland Forum in the early 1980s. Both men were shocked and upset. 'Veronica was a good friend of mine,' Ahern would tell the Dáil that afternoon in a short contribution suffused with obvious grief. 'I knew her well since we both lived in Artane twenty years ago.' But even as they shared their disbelief and horror, their minds were churning – how do we react, what do we say, what does this mean? They got into the lift and fell silent. Then Ahern said: 'This completely changes the dynamic.'

The country was genuinely and thoroughly shocked at the murder, not just because Guerin was a journalist, but because she was a young wife and mother. It was more than an appalling crime: it was a tragedy. And it was a political bombshell.

The airwaves exploded with the anger and grief of ordinary people. The *Irish Times* was moved to declare, in a front-page editorial, that 'The country is anguished, as not in living memory, over the murder of Veronica Guerin. There is palpable anger in the streets, on the airwaves . . .'

Crime and law and order moved to the very top of the political agenda. For a time, they *were* the political agenda. Only two weeks previously, a garda, Jerry McCabe, had been murdered by the IRA during a botched bank robbery. Ahern had actually met and spoken to Veronica Guerin at the funeral in Limerick. In latter years Irish politics has been given to periodic bouts of hyperventilating about crime, largely on the back of unreasonable fears and sensationalist reporting. But in the summer of 1996, the fear and the anger were very real, very widespread and politically very potent.

Fianna Fáil made hay. Justice spokesman John O'Donoghue had been savaging the government on law and order since his appointment, and now he and the party were able to play a devastatingly effective 'We told you so' card. The government was forced to accept legislation prepared by O'Donoghue's justice group (principally by the barrister Eamon Leahy, husband of the future TD and minister Mary Hanafin). From the start of the crisis, the government was on the back foot, and Fianna Fáil gave the lead. A week after the murder of Guerin, the Dáil held a special debate. When the Labour junior minister Joan Burton lectured Fianna Fáil deputies about the need to tackle poverty and the 'causes of crime', it was music to Fianna Fáil's ears. The public weren't interested in the causes of crime; they wanted to nail those responsible for the murder. And Fianna Fáil were the ones talking as though they had a hammer.

The murder of Guerin and, to a lesser extent, Garda Jerry McCabe played an important part in diminishing the Rainbow government's massive advantage on the economy in the subsequent election, held less than a year later. Fianna Fáil's oft-professed 'zero tolerance' approach to crime would be meaningless in terms of policy – as subsequent events bore out – but it was brilliant opposition politics.

Crime is always good opposition politics. There isn't an election anywhere in the Western world in which voters aren't attracted by a promise of more resources for the police and tougher sanctions for criminals, and Fianna Fáil colonized the issue for themselves in advance of the 1997 election. The only remarkable thing is that a Fine Gael-led government let them get away with it. It was further evidence, in Fianna Fáil's eyes anyway, that the government was really run by the soft-shoes in Labour. They couldn't wait to get stuck into them in an election.

But beating the drum on crime wasn't just smart politics: it was entirely in tune with Ahern's own instincts. On several occasions during periodic debates on crime throughout his period as Taoiseach, Ahern expressed his support for tougher laws and harsher treatment of offenders; he was fond of extolling the pugilistic approach of the famous Lugs Brannigan. Latterly, he frequently used the term 'draconian' in an approving fashion, pointing out how criminal justice laws in Ireland were some of the most draconian in Europe, as evidence of his commitment to a tough line on crime. Indeed, he frequently indicated that they weren't draconian enough for his liking.

In this, as in so much else, his instincts were in tune with those of much of middle Ireland. Research subsequent to the election, reported by academics Michael Marsh and Richard Sinnott in the *How Ireland Voted* series, found that voters concerned with crime and law and order were much more likely to vote for Fianna Fáil, and much less likely to vote for Labour. Concern about crime was particularly strong among those who voted for Labour in 1992 and defected in 1997.

It is a telling finding. Fianna Fáil still faced an uphill battle in the forthcoming election. But now they could make a fight of it.

3. Power Regained

The general election of 1997 was epoch-making, one of the most important in the history of the state, on a par, at least, with those of 1932 and 1948. The hindsight of history has shown us that the stakes were vastly greater than was understood at the time. The prize for success was glittering, immense and unprecedented: control of government for a period in which the realization of almost any modern political vision was possible.

Put it another way – had Fianna Fáil lost the 1997 election, what would have been the consequences? The fracturing of the coalition within the party between the Haughey and Reynolds wings certainly, the deposing of Ahern and consignment to opposition for at least ten years probably. And maybe more – the end of Fianna Fáil's dominance of Irish politics.

Had Labour contained its meltdown in a few constituencies and remained in government with Fine Gael to dominate the policy agenda of the following decade, the years of the Celtic Tiger would have been guided by a social democratic government, rather than the economic liberalism and tax cutting of Charlie McCreevy and the Progressive Democrats. From whatever perspective you look, the 1997 general election changed the course of political history in Ireland.

Writing about Fianna Fáil in 1996, the historian and commentator Joe Lee realized the importance of the forthcoming general election.

Bertie Ahern's leadership will obviously be at risk if Fianna Fáil fails to re-enter office after the next election. Indeed, the party itself will face a trauma. Because office has been the glue that has held it together – it has never been out of office for two successive elections – a failure to recapture office would deal it a particularly severe blow. Other parties have long adjusted to opposition as a way of life. Fianna Fáil is psychologically orphaned in opposition. With party politics now so fluid, the fortunes of Fianna Fáil for a generation may depend disproportionately on whatever the fates have in store for the next 18 months.

Bertie Ahern knew none of this at the time. Not what was to come, nor what it might mean. He just knew he wanted to win. He knew he had to win.

But winning was a tall order. Despite Fianna Fáil's healthy opinion poll showings in the early months of 1997, Ahern and his aides were all too aware that Fianna Fáil usually tended to under-perform the polls when the election came, often quite drastically. Moreover, the outgoing Rainbow government enjoyed an advantage that no Irish government in living memory had had in its favour: the Irish economy was growing rapidly, adding jobs, increasing output and putting more money in people's pockets.

And Ahern himself was still something of an unknown quantity, as a leader and as a campaigner. He had worked assiduously to unify the party and prepare it for the general election. He made smart appointments, and let them do their jobs, even if he often sought to avoid any responsibility for the decisions they made. But he hardly looked like a Taoiseach-in-waiting. In Britain, Tony Blair was obviously poised to become prime minister, having remade his party and reshaped public debate; Bertie Ahern often looked as though he was just hanging on and hoping that the post-election maths might work out. Even his closest aides, in their private thoughts, were not optimistic. 'I thought winning the election was a long shot, to be honest,' says one aide now. 'He just didn't really show any firmness of purpose or sureness of foot.'

Generally, the fortunes of opposition politicians depend less on their own efforts than on the performance and popularity of the incumbent government. Government sets the news agenda, and can manipulate and shape it to its advantage. In government you can do things; in opposition you can just talk. In opposition, Bertie Ahern's Fianna Fáil had to contend with a Rainbow government that was stable, coherent and relatively popular. People had tired of the constant drama of the stormy Reynolds–Spring marriage, and they quickly got used to the civilized domestic arrangements of the Rainbow administration. If a little unorthodox, the harmonious tripartite administration was just fine by them. Well over half of all voters professed themselves satisfied with the government and the Taoiseach.

The Rainbow was also beginning to appreciate perhaps the greatest fear of Ahern and those Fianna Fáil ex-ministers who understood that economic growth was gathering pace. They could not have expected at this point that the boom would last so long and change Ireland so much, but they knew which way the winds were blowing and were acutely conscious of the political dividend that any government could generate from the first result of growth: bulging taxation receipts.

From the time they left office, Fianna Fáil noticed that the public was beginning to notice. The 1995 budget, delivered by Ruairi Quinn, the first Labour minister for finance in the history of the state, on 8 February of that year, was well received by voters; an *Irish Times*/MRBI opinion poll found it better received than either of Ahern's two previous budgets. More people thought that living standards would rise; more people thought that job opportunities would increase. There was one consolation for Fianna Fáil supporters: their new leader was well thought of by the voters – some 70 per cent of whom had a favourable view of him, considerably in excess of either of the two other main party leaders. But after the loss of office and when faced by a popular government, it was scant consolation at the time. In fact, it was to become a more important factor than anything else measured by the poll.

During this entire period, Ahern was getting access to Department of Finance numbers that revealed just how much economic growth was gathering pace. He was plugged into an extraordinary information-gathering network – semi-state boards, civil servants, trade unions, even political opponents formed part of that network. They were all telling him the same thing.

He knew that every week that passed, the policy horizons for the incumbent government were expanding as it became clear that they would have more money to spend than they had dared hope. In the model of politics that Ahern carried imprinted on his DNA, this was a huge electoral advantage, allowing the latitude for vote-generating promises and policies to be rolled out before and during a campaign. It also meant that the prize for victory in the general election was growing in magnitude.

Economic trends are the tectonic plates of politics, and by 1997 the irresistible movement of the landscape was in favour of the Rainbow government. The economy was now growing at a rate that had never before been seen; the public finances were in rude good health – for the first time ever, the 1997 budget, introduced in February by Ruairi Quinn, forecast a surplus by the end of the year. A surplus! Whoever was in office after the general election was going to have resources at their disposal that no government in the history of the state had ever enjoyed, and the Rainbow held all the aces. If Bertie Ahern were to win this election, he would have to steal it out from under their noses.

A few weeks before the general election, Ray Burke and Charlie McCreevy were in conversation in the Fianna Fáil offices on the fifth floor of the Leinster House annexe. Pointing out at the cranes that dotted the Dublin skyline, Burke addressed McCreevy ruefully, 'Look at that. How can we possibly win this fucking election?'

'We will,' promised McCreevy. 'We will.'

McCreevy knew that Fianna Fáil had never prepared more thoroughly for an election. He also knew that because Fianna Fáil had changed the way it selected candidates, it would be possible to win more seats on a much smaller share of the vote than was previously required. It had been a slog, he knew, beating the organization into shape over the previous two years. But Fianna Fáil was about to catch everyone – maybe even the voters themselves – on the hop. PJ Mara used to tell them they were 'sneaking up' on the electorate.

McCreevy also knew that Fianna Fáil had a secret weapon ready for the 1997 campaign that it had never had before. It wasn't just on the high roads and byroads of Ireland that the party was preparing for the election. Fianna Fáil eyes had turned towards Washington, DC, where politics is taken more seriously and treated more professionally than anywhere in the world. American political consultants Bob Shrum, Tad Devine and Mike Donilon had been retained by the party for strategic and communications advice and their input was already giving party managers priceless intelligence on what worked with voters.

The connection with the Americans had come about on two twin tracks. Seamus Brennan had been a student of American politics since he was a young man, and he travelled there regularly, maintaining a network of political contacts across the country. His friend Bob Manson had spoken to him about the idea of using American consultants. Months before the election, Brennan had also approached Ahern with the idea, and he asked Mara what he thought.

Mara was sceptical. 'The campaign is going well,' he told Ahern. 'I don't think we really need them. We're really motoring.'

Ahern agreed. 'But look,' continued Mara, 'Brennan is shrewd. You should maybe meet them anyway.'

At the same time that Brennan was talking about their advantages, Des Richardson had made contact with the Americans. He had attended the Democratic Convention in 1996 where he been introduced to Bob Shrum at an event hosted by the Kennedys.

Jackie Gallagher, Mara, Chris Wall and Richardson attended the first meeting with the Americans in Dublin. Ahern may not have trusted Seamus Brennan, but they all liked what they heard.

American politics is a lucrative business, and there are about five thousand such consultants in the United States. 'There are pollsters, direct mail specialists, GOTV [get-out-the-vote] people, internet people, campaign finance and lawyers,' Professor James Thurber of the American University in Washington told me while

I was preparing a newspaper profile on Shrum in 2004. 'Then the media people are top of the pack – and Shrum is the top of the top of the pack.'

Bob Shrum was a political legend in the US, both as a consultant and as a speechwriter. He had penned the famous lines of Teddy Kennedy's concession speech at the 1980 Democratic convention – 'The work goes on, the cause endures, the hope still lives and the dream will never die' – and had made his reputation (and his fortune) as a consultant to Democratic candidates all over the US in the decade and a half that separated those golden lines and from the ascension of Bertie Ahern to the impatient second man of Irish politics. He was also retained by Tony Blair for the forthcoming British general election. With his partner Tad Devine, a rangy and urbane consultant who developed friendships with several leading Fianna Fáil operatives, Shrum was to have an impact on Irish politics beyond the 1997 election.

What did they actually do that was so valuable? Joseph Napolitan, a hardy Massachusetts political operative who worked for John F. Kennedy in the 1950s and 1960s, was perhaps the first to call himself a political consultant. He explained their work as succinctly as anyone has. He said, 'They would say: "That might work in New York, but it won't work here." The truth is, it was the same stuff and it worked everywhere.'

The same stuff, and it worked everywhere. When Mara met them, he told colleagues that he had been impressed, particularly with the way they used polls and research to craft effective messages which would appeal to voters. They had precise polling questions that would give them specific information. 'They would look at it and say, "Look, this is an issue, this isn't an issue,"' remembers one staffer who dealt closely with them. All parties did political research; the novel skill that the Americans brought to Irish politics was giving their clients productive actions arising from it. They soon learned that many things that put the media into a tizzy went completely over the heads of the public. They also had an influence on the speechwriting.

Communicating to voters is the most important skill that a

politician needs in his armoury. In Ireland, that communication has been traditionally done on a small-scale, localized basis – to a large extent, it still is. The number of voters who are routinely canvassed in the course of an election campaign is staggering – approaching over three quarters, according to a 2002 study – and, crucially, canvassing and personal contact remain the most effective ways of garnering votes, researchers have found. But in a more urbanized, more anonymous society, that's changing. Media communications have increased in importance, and in an election campaign the party leader only really gets to talk to ordinary voters through the media and in a mass communications context. That's why an understanding of how voters digest political communication and how they react to particular political messages is of paramount importance in modern campaigns. That's really the secret of what the American consultants have taught Fianna Fáil.

'Tad and Shrum really tightened up the language. They worked mostly on our message and how we would deliver it,' says one insider at the time.

Another insider explains how they came up with the widely derided but actually very effective 'People before Politics' slogan. 'What does it actually mean to people? It means that we care about real things – and they only care about politics. The Rainbow were promising "Partnership that Works" – in other words, they were all about process, all about politics. Fianna Fáil on the other hand were saying, "We'll cut your taxes and put more guards on the street." Now who's going to win that?'

With the help of the Americans, Fianna Fáil was putting out messages that were heard. They had been tested to death in focus groups, of course, and nowadays nobody would dream of adopting a political slogan without first testing it in focus groups. But you have to know how to do that, too. In 1997, Fianna Fáil was learning fast.

'They also tightened up our polling and how we would read it. They brought it to a new level. We used Des Byrne [of polling company Behaviour and Attitudes] for national polls and of course we had the ongoing constituency polling. But the US guys talked about combining our quantitative research with the qualitative stuff from focus groups. When you combine those, that's when you get the magic darts,' recalls one senior figure.

Despite the misgivings of some of his advisers – notably Paddy Duffy – Ahern was happy to have the input of the Americans. But he insisted it was kept completely top secret. Ahern had an innate fear that the leadership would be seen to be out of touch with the grassroots, more interested in high politics and grand strategy than local issues – and he didn't want to see stories in the press about Fianna Fáil's hotshot American consultants. They were practically spirited in and out of Dublin.

Devine was so anonymous that one night he ended up in a restaurant sitting at a table adjacent to the government press secretary Shane Kenny and a Democratic Left adviser. They talked about their political strategy all night, while Devine just sat there and listened.

When I learned of their involvement in the 2002 election and wrote about it in the aftermath of the event, Fianna Fáil sources barely admitted their involvement; those who did emphasized it was the first time the Americans had been consulted. In fact, the Americans were an important part of the team in 1997 and in the preparations that preceded it.

'They quickly became part of the family. They came and they stayed. They maybe reinforced a lot of the stuff we wanted to do, but I couldn't say a bad word about them,' says another senior figure. But they were, everybody complained, shockingly expensive. The only indication of exactly how expensive was revealed after the 2002 election when I conducted an analysis of Fianna Fáil's statutory declarations of campaign expenditure. There was an entry of €45,000 under the heading of 'research'. Was this the Americans' fees for just three weeks? I asked. I had to ask several times. Eventually after much obfuscation, it was reluctantly confirmed to me. In a political system still character-ized by a large degree of volunteerism, this was big money. But Fianna Fáil clearly thought they were worth it.

The influence of the American consultants was brought to

bear early on one enormously sensitive issue in advance of the election. The spectacular fall from office of Fine Gael minister Michael Lowry in November 1996, following revelations that the supermarket tycoon Ben Dunne had paid for an extension to his house in Tipperary, had given much pleasure to Fianna Fáil. But the glee was short-lived. Rumours abounded that a senior Fianna Fáil figure had also received large sums from Dunne. Inevitably, the name leaked out. *Phoenix* magazine named Charles Haughey in early December, and the following weekend, the *Sunday Tribune* reported that Haughey was identified in court documents as a recipient of the Dunne's largesse. The cat was well and truly out of the bag.

It was a sensational story, one of the biggest ever in Irish politics, and it had the potential to derail Fianna Fáil's election preparations. Since the 1960s, Charles Haughey had occupied a central place in Irish politics, so much so that for much of the 1970s and 1980s it often seemed that the only question that mattered was whether you were for him or against him. And Bertie Ahern had been unequivocally for him.

The Fianna Fáil ard-fheis was scheduled for 18–20 April 1997 – a few days before Ben Dunne was due to give evidence to the McCracken Tribunal, the investigative body set up to inquire into the Dunne donations. But it was well known that Dunne would confirm the donations to Haughey, whose magisterial denials were by now widely disbelieved. Clearly, Ahern would have to address the issue. But what would he say?

In one of the most significant speeches of his career on the Friday night of the ard-fheis, Ahern effectively disavowed his old mentor, condemning the receipt of large gifts from businessmen and insisting that there was no room for such ethically shoddy behaviour in his Fianna Fáil party. That was then, he insisted. This is now. He was unequivocal:

There would be no place in our party today for that kind of past behaviour, no matter how eminent the person involved or the extent of their services to the country ... Even if in the particular instance there were no favours sought or given, we could not condone the practice of senior politicians seeking or receiving from a single donor large sums of money or services in kind ...

The point was driven home by extensive briefing of journalists that weekend, and for the following weeks. On the televised Saturday night address the following evening, Ahern drove home the point: 'No one – no one – is welcome in this party if they betray the public trust. I say this and mean this with every fibre of my being.'

Even by the standards that govern these things, this was pretty brazen. According to several people who have reliable claims to know his mind at the time, Ahern was extremely reluctant to offer any sort of condemnation of Haughey. His preference was to say nothing, and keep his head down. The denunciation of Haughey had to be 'dragged kicking and screaming out of Bertie Ahern', says one of his intimates. He was told by several staff and front-bench colleagues: you simply have to do this. We cannot win the election unless you do it. You must say these things. We're not talking to Fianna Fáil, we're talking to the voters. The staff were adamant: 'You won't get a chance to come this way again,' one told him. 'This is your only chance to do this.' But for days he hesitated.

As drafts of the speech circulated between the advisers, it was clear that Ahern would distance himself from Haughey's actions; but would he repudiate him? There was one particular paragraph and there must have been about twenty drafts of it back and forth, says one of the authors. It was a crucial few days in the direction of his leadership.

Even though Ahern had frequently discussed Haughey with his *chef de cabinet*, Duffy still didn't really know what Ahern's opinion of him was: did he really believe Haughey was corrupt? He never really got to the bottom of it.

While Duffy had primary responsibility for the main ard-fheis speech, Mansergh wrote most of the Friday-night speech, in which he was to address the Haughey issues explicitly. The repudiation of their former boss was difficult for both Mansergh and Ahern; neither of them liked doing it. They told each other it had to be done. They told each other weakly that Haughey would have done the same thing; in fact, he had done the same thing, and worse, to Brian Lenihan Sr. At a personal level, Ahern was particularly reluctant, according to one person involved in some of the various drafts of the speech. But he made no serious argument against the necessity for it. Though with Ahern, as his staff had by now learned, that didn't mean that he would actually do it.

Ahern was 'paranoid' (says one person involved in the preparations) that the old Haughey loyalists such as Burke would hear what was planned and force him to abandon it. Besides, in a parliamentary party that until relatively recently had been divided sharply between the country 'n' western wing of Reynolds and Flynn on one side and the Haugheyites on the other, Ahern's support base was very much in the latter camp. If he lost the election, a heave would surely follow, and he would need the Haughey camp's support. And his natural caution weighed heavily against such a bold move. His staff, even those involved in the scripting of the speech, weren't sure that he was going to actually do it until the very end. Some of them didn't think he would until they actually heard him say the words.

The weight of the opinion of the American consultants was brought into the argument. They were unambiguous. It could be an election-losing mistake not to firmly distance himself from Haughey, they said. They were looking at polling and research data which told them that the electorate was still suspicious about Fianna Fáil, and the Haughey stories were reinforcing all that; but they also believed there was an opportunity for Ahern to show the public that the party had changed under him. The public always has an appetite for reinvention. There were a lot of floating votes up for grabs, but they were held by the sort of people who needed to hear Ahern draw a line under the past. To do that he needed to denounce his old mentor, unequivocally.

Those close to Ahern feared that unless they got an absolute commitment to using specific forms of words about Haughey, Ahern would weasel out of it.

'He didn't want to do it, and he never really did it again,' says one of the backroom team. Later, the repudiation of his old mentor clearly weighed on Ahern's mind. 'I said some very hard things at the ard-fheis in 1997,' he told journalist and author John Downing in 2004. 'But I had to say them.' He did, however, claim many times subsequently that he had said difficult things about Haughey repeatedly. No one has said as much about this as I have, he often said. In fact, years later, after another such pronouncement by the Taoiseach, one journalist asked the government press office for a list of all the times that Ahern had denounced Haughey. A trawl by the office found a small handful of occasions when he had referred to the issue.

Nonetheless, his statement electrified the ard-fheis. One front-bencher who was sitting on the platform when Ahern made his comments about Haughey gasped: 'Jesus!' Afterwards, he approached Ahern. 'Well done!' he said. 'That'll help.' But Ahern appeared dejected, he thought. 'Ah Jaze,' he replied. 'It had to be done.'

Writing in *The Sunday Business Post*, Emily O'Reilly noted: 'What was remarkable was the almost manic willingness shown by the party spin doctors and others to cast Haughey into oblivion – his name, his reputation, his contribution to the party and to the state, would all be sacrificed or conveniently forgotten if revelations about him proved true.'

Ultimately, the repudiation of Haughey, whatever Ahern's true thoughts on it, was an unqualified success. There was much weeping and grinding of teeth from Labour politicians, particularly in the years after the 1997 election, about how the result showed that the Irish people didn't care about ethics; in latter years, many commentators have barely been able to come to terms with the public's attitudes to standards in public office. In fact, as Ahern was himself to discover years later, the public do care about standards in public office. It's just that they often make a different – one is tempted to say more nuanced, but relaxed is probably a better word – judgement on its importance relative to other political issues than many columnists and leader writers.

Jack Jones of the pollsters MRBI, recalling his evaluation in the *Irish Times* about the findings of an opinion poll commissioned by the newspaper in the wake of the revelations at the McCracken Tribunal in April 1997, reflected:

My interpretation of the results was that Bertie Ahern had already succeeded in distancing himself, and his party, from any unfavourable spin-off resulting from the Haughey disclosures. Fianna Fáil support was holding firm, as was Bertie Ahern's satisfaction rating at 59 per cent . . . The final resting place of the floating vote was not yet apparent, but the Fianna Fáil leader had positioned himself and his party on a solid basis in preparation for the election campaign.

As well as the big strategic and communications preparations, Fianna Fáil headquarters had been engaged in a nuts-and-bolts programme of preparation for the election for well over a year. Part of this process was doing post-mortems on the disastrous 1992 campaign and trying to remedy its many failings. One of the things that were discovered was that the election-fighting expertise was essentially kept in the heads of a few party stalwarts. One person might know how and where to get the posters printed; another would know how to get polling done; and so on. 'They kept it like that because knowledge is power,' says one insider. 'We knew we had to change that.' Prior to 1997, the notion of a fearsome Fianna Fáil election-fighting machine was largely a myth.

One of things that Farrell and Mara were determined to change was the arrival of a group of Fianna Fáil-supporting barristers into the Mount Street headquarters as soon as the election was called. They would take up occupancy in a mews building to the rear of the Mount Street building and offer a valuable intellectual and organizational resource, or generally get in the way, depending on one's perspective. The latter point of view was more prevalent among those such as Mara and Farrell who were actually tasked with running the campaign. Farrell liked to recall for people one outburst from the 1992 campaign by a frustrated party official: 'Why the fuck,' the official wondered, 'don't they fuck off out and canvass their own constituency instead of wanting to be in here annoying us?' It was resolved that the barristers would not feature in the 1997 election campaign.

A project manager, Joe O'Rourke, who had previously worked in the clothing industry, was brought in to handle the logistics of the forthcoming campaign. He broke down the election preparations into a book that detailed thousands of single actions to be taken which would contribute to the campaign strategy. For example, he had scoured the country looking for the best sites for large billboards, which could be hired for election posters. A map of where every large election poster was to go was drawn up and the sites verified by photos.

Various advertising agencies and creative consultancies were brought in to make presentations in Mount Street. The one that caught Mara's eye was a group called the Power of 7 – led by Philip Walsh. Various samples had been produced for consideration by the campaign, but Mara was unimpressed. 'This is all shite,' he told one meeting which considered various offerings.

Later, he was driving down to his holiday home in Kinvara, near Galway. At the time, Guinness had begun to sponsor the All-Ireland hurling championships and had produced a striking advertising campaign, with distinctive images of hurlers and heroes on a dark background. Purring down the Dublin–Galway road in the capacious comfort of his Jaguar, he considered the need for a strong look for the campaign, how it needed to feel different from that for previous general elections. The new party with the young leader needed a modern visual appeal. It was before the age of the bypass, and he had plenty of slow driving time through the small towns and villages that stageposted the way: Maynooth, Kilcock, Tyrell's Pass. All along the way, he met the striking Guinness posters, with their powerful dark backgrounds and their fusing of the modern and the traditional.

That's it, he thought. At the next meeting in Mount Street, he was insistent. 'I want the whole campaign to look like this Guinness stuff,' he said. The following morning, Phil Walsh came in with some samples of how it might look. Everyone agreed: that was it. That was what they wanted. The posters became known as the Darth Vader posters.

Perhaps the biggest strategic decision that Ahern made was to enter the general election campaign effectively as part of an alliance with the PDs. There was not, it is true, a formal vote-sharing alliance; but there was everything short of it. In Ahern's ard-fheis speech in April, he made no mention of the PDs; characteristically, he was trying to keep his options open as long as possible. But he had spent the previous two years manoeuvring the PDs and his own party into a position where they looked like natural partners.

Mary Harney – the leader of the PDs since Des O'Malley had retired – had known Ahern since the 1970s when they were both young members of the Fianna Fáil parliamentary party. They were obviously different then – he a patient builder of the constituency machine, she a rapidly promoted leadership favourite – and they were obviously different now. But they were both new leaders of their parties on whom the public and media juries were out, and they were both in opposition. Circumstance as much as anything else pushed them together.

Like McCreevy, Harney had never really considered Ahern as a future leader of Fianna Fáil or Taoiseach during the earlier part of his career. She had always figured there was more to him than the haughty dismissal of George Colley – that all he knew how to do was leaflets and Christmas cards in Dublin Central. But where did he stand, what did he stand for? She spent years answering those questions.

In the early part of 1995 following Fianna Fáil's entry to opposition, Harney consulted both Bobby Molloy and Dessie O'Malley about Ahern. They regarded him as decent and reasonable. She could read the politics as quickly as anyone, so she wasn't amazed when the invitation to lunch in his house arrived. As the Rainbow government powered ahead, and following the out-and-out rejection by Labour of possible PD involvement, she knew that her party didn't have many options. Equally, neither did Fianna Fáil.

The two leaders met and talked for a few hours in the house off Griffith Avenue that the Mahon Tribunal was to make probably the most famous semi-D in the country. Later Harney told friends she had been impressed with the house, but she certainly didn't think that Bertie Ahern had decorated and maintained it.

From the outset, a coalition government was explicitly discussed. Ahern bluntly told her that Fianna Fáil wouldn't win an overall majority – and that he wanted to form a coalition government with her party if the numbers could be made to add up. She was under no illusions that Fianna Fáil would do a deal with the Labour Party if circumstances dictated that it had to; but she believed him when he said that the Progressive Democrats were his first choice. The two agreed to develop further contacts. Apart from the firm intention expressed by Ahern, there were few specifics. But this low-key meeting laid the foundations for a decade and a half of coalition government.

As the Rainbow government gelled closer and closer, it became more likely that Fianna Fáil and the Progressive Democrats would be fighting the next election as an effective non-government bloc. McCreevy's increasing influence with Ahern, combined with his closeness to Harney, served to bring Fianna Fáil and the PDs closer together. Ahern was cautious, but he could read the political landscape, too. In 1995 and 1996, he didn't have the appetite that McCreevy and, from the sidelines, PJ Mara displayed for an alliance with the PDs; but he did not recoil from the idea.

McCreevy continued to force the pace with the PDs, though that made some members of Ahern's gang in Drumcondra nervous. They didn't like McDowell, whom Mara was courting assiduously; McDowell's world, bordered by the Law Library and the Kildare St Club, was alien to them, even if Mara flitted through it effortlessly. Despite the cultural differences, the political truth was banal and powerful: the two parties, and the two leaders, needed one another.

Labour had cast the election as a straight fight between 'centre right and centre left', in the words of Dick Spring. In April 1997, a week before the Fianna Fáil ard-fheis and barely a month before the general election, Spring ruled out any coalition with Fianna Fáil, no matter what. Some media commentators, frustrated for years that the dreary dominance of the civil war parties had denied Ireland a 'proper' left–right political debate, were exultant. Though really, Spring's announcement was less an attempt to remake the Irish political landscape than a desperate attempt to shore up support for Labour among anti-Fianna Fáil voters who had backed the party in 1992, and to prevent their mass defection to Fine Gael. Ahern took suitable umbrage in his ard-fheis speech:

It's not about principles, in this government, it's about power. Power at any price. Power without purpose. Power without principle. Power without respect for the people. That is what gave Dick Spring the idea, that his personal preference was far more important than the votes of the Irish people. This is Labour Party arrogance at its worst. We reject it. And on election day, the people will reject that Labour Party and its arrogance.

Ahern's condemnation for an attachment to power might have been a bit rich, but his anger at Spring was genuine and felt across the organization. It was Fianna Fáil, he felt, that had suffered by Labour's treachery. How dare Spring now have the gall to declare that Fianna Fáil were too mucky to sit at his elevated table? Maire Geoghegan-Quinn, by then a columnist with the *Irish Times*, put it more pointedly and spoke for much of the party when she wrote:

In essence what Dick Spring has said to the nation is this: 'It doesn't matter that the majority of you will vote for Fianna Fáil. I will do my best – and use my party – to ensure that your choice on the ballot paper is rendered meaningless. I will parlay the votes of less than 20 per cent of the Irish people into a weapon to stymie the votes of almost half the Irish people.'

Ahern's anger at Spring was also grounded not just in the existential insult done to his party, but in the fact that it cut off a route to government for him. Much as he detested the Labour leadership, he would have done a deal with them if he had had to – an option he had already discussed with McCreevy, who was even more fervently anti-Labour than Ahern, but equally pragmatic about a possible coalition. When before the election *The Sunday Business Post* asked a senior Fianna Fáil official how long the party would spend wrestling with its conscience before going into government with Labour, the reply was frank: 'About ten minutes.' But the problem wasn't Fianna Fáil's conscience. It rarely was. It wasn't even Labour's conscience, really. It was Spring's political calculation that was ruling out Fianna Fáil, not his conscience. The contest had become simpler, but the stakes for winning every vote had just gone up.

Fianna Fáil brought one remaining advantage into the campaign that was about to commence: Northern Ireland. Wary of being accused of playing politics with the Northern peace process, Ahern had nevertheless been determined to carve out a greener space for Fianna Fáil in public debate than the one occupied by the Rainbow government, and particularly by its leader, John Bruton. Ahern did this because it was true to his own and his party's traditional beliefs, but he also thought it could be electorally advantageous. The end of the IRA's ceasefire, negotiated under Reynolds, had convinced many voters – and not all of them Fianna Fáil supporters – that the peace process would progress only under a Fianna Fáil government. This was a notion that Fianna Fáil was happy to encourage.

From his entry to opposition, Ahern had said that he wanted to maintain in Dublin the bipartisan approach to the North, but he would not support the Fine Gael-led government uncritically.

In truth, there was a chasm between Bruton's views on the North and his own. In rough summary, Bruton wanted to be an honest broker between two warring tribes; Ahern wanted to negotiate as leader of nationalist Ireland. Sinn Féin could see this and responded. But it was delicate; the political advantage couldn't be pushed, but it could be nudged. In truth, Fianna Fáil's biggest ally in this was not Gerry Adams but Bruton himself, not so much for his handling of the peace process: clumsy though that might have been, he was obviously sincere and, by his lights, well meaning. But when he addressed the heir to the British throne in Dublin and told Prince Charles that his presence had made it the greatest day of his life, he unnerved people at an instinctive and emotional level. It was one of the great gaffes of Irish politics. Ahern made a number of speeches in which he outlined a stance of what Mansergh called 'critical bipartisanship'. In addition, Fianna Fáil kept up close contacts with Sinn Féin during this period. Mansergh in particular was a regular visitor to Belfast.

Clearly, Ahern hoped that the Northern Ireland issue would work to his advantage, though there have been repeated suggestions that he went farther than that. The belief endures in some quarters that Fianna Fáil quietly advised against a resumption of the IRA ceasefire before the 1997 general election, a suggestion that found its way into a number of accounts of the process. It's true that some Fianna Fáilers, including one member of the front bench, told journalists that they didn't want a ceasefire, but there's no evidence that Ahern was either of this view or communicated it to Sinn Féin. In fact, one reliable source with an intimate knowledge of the process says that Ahern had urged the IRA to renew the ceasefire in the summer of 1996, expressing the belief that it would lead to direct entry to talks for Sinn Féin. He was rebuffed; the IRA wasn't ready internally, and anyway, they didn't trust Bruton to ensure the British delivered. The IRA may have been content to wait for Fianna Fáil's possible return to power the following year; but more so for the end of the Tory government in Britain. At that stage, while Fianna Fáil's return to office was a very uncertain bet, Tony Blair's New Labour was the unbackable favourite to win the next general election in Britain. Walking down a West Belfast street in the August of 1996 discussing a possible ceasefire, Joe Cahill turned to Mansergh and said, 'I think we'll wait until the elections.'

'The Rainbow had two and a half years to get their lines of communication clear,' one Fianna Fáiler told the *Sunday Tribune* after the election. 'We had just two and a half weeks.'

One of the great electoral advantages that a sitting government has is its ability to name the day the votes will be cast. In the competing interests of projecting reliability and predictability to the public, Bertie Ahern tended to dilute that advantage greatly by going until almost the last minute with his choice of dates. But in 1997, when an election could have waited until November but was widely anticipated before the summer, it was a significant card in John Bruton's hand. It was one he chose to play awkwardly and ineffectively.

Even as the momentum built to an unstoppable level, there were good reasons to wait. The tribunal was inquiring into Dunne's donations, and Haughey was in its sights; the economy continued to gather strength; even on one of the government's weak points, the Northern peace process, the impending inevitable election of a Labour government in Britain promised hope of a breakthrough.

Opinion was divided among the leaders of the Rainbow government as to when to call the election – John Bruton was minded to wait until after the summer, but Labour were insistent that the vote should be held before the summer. 'They had this idea that the party conference was going to turn everything around for them. They were obsessed with it, and we were trying to help them,' a senior Fine Gaeler recalls.

If Labour really wanted something, they generally got it. Bruton conceded a pre-summer election early in the new year. In truth, his own natural caution warned him against waiting until the very last minute. The publication of an opinion poll in the

Irish Times in early April that showed some movement in support for the government parties cemented the exact timing. The paper's chief political correspondent, Denis Coghlan, wrote admiringly, 'The public has recognised that Mr Bruton has grown into the job. Fine Gael, the Labour Party and Democratic Left are now offering themselves for re-election as a Government that works, with a proven track record.'

A few days later, Coghlan pinpointed exactly what the results of the poll would mean: 'With the tide flowing strongly in their favour, the three party leaders have virtually no option but to complete outstanding Dáil business and call an election.' He was in no doubt about what it meant, or who would start the campaign in better shape: 'Publication of the poll findings on Wednesday sent Fine Gael officials into paroxysms of delight. Support for the party had hit a seven-year high; John Bruton had never been more popular and the Government's satisfaction rating was exceptional.'

It wasn't just wishful thinking on Coghlan's part. The Rainbow was in an immensely strong position, and while Fianna Fáil ratings remained high, there were signs that the party's vote, particularly in Dublin, was beginning to totter. Nonetheless, Fianna Fáil also wanted an early election, fearing – and some of them knowing – what was likely to come down the tracks at the McCracken Tribunal. Even though the polls were beginning to turn flaky for Ahern, they weren't likely to get any better.

There was a deliberate strategy formulated by Spring and his advisers to use to the tribunal to damage Ahern and Fianna Fáil. This was hardly unfair – both the party and its current leader had facilitated and colluded with Haughey's behaviour in many respects. But it ignored the fact that in early 1997, the questions about Michael Lowry and Fine Gael's fundraising seemed to many people to be just as murky as any rumoured donations to the respectable, retired and, for some, revered CJH.

In *The Sunday Business Post*, Emily O'Reilly noted that Labour 'thought it was the perfect plan'. It would call the election 'just as Ben Dunne and Charlie Haughey exited the witness stand', and then rule out any possible coalition with Fianna Fáil. The strategy backfired, and Fine Gael leader John Bruton ended up answering questions about contradictions between his evidence before the tribunal and his evidence to the Beef Tribunal regarding his involvement in fundraising for the party. Fianna Fáil spinners played it for all it was worth and in the next opinion poll, Fine Gael and Bruton dived in the numbers. Ahern began to believe he could get through the Haughey storm.

'We tried to push them to go early,' says one of Ahern's advisers. Ahern himself told friends he wanted to go to the polls as late as possible before the summer break, but not afterwards. In practice this meant early June; July was out because of the school holidays, and certificate examinations took up most of June. In the event the date selected by Bruton was 6 June, the anniversary of the D-Day landings in 1944 which began the liberation of Europe from Nazi occupation. It was D-Day for Ahern, too.

Bruton announced the dissolution of the Dáil on a sunny Thursday 15 May. The retiring Ceann Comhairle, Sean Treacy, a man never likely to use one word where several might suffice, issued his benediction to the departing deputies in three languages and with characteristic orotundity – '*Nois tá an Dáil ar athlo sine die* ... I bid you all a fond farewell, *Slán agus beannacht le gach uile.*'

As Treacy made an appropriately episcopal exit from the chamber, deputies scrambled in all directions, three weeks of murderous schedules and stress ahead of them. The three leaders of the Rainbow left the Dáil and proceeded on a choreographed walk from Leinster House to the Shelbourne Hotel for the first press conference of the campaign. Immediately, though, there were obstacles: building works in the National Museum meant there were restrictions on the Kildare Street footpaths. They were hardly out the gates of Leinster House when a party flunky began to shout 'Bollards! Bollards!'

The Fianna Fáil campaign took off like a shot out of a gun. 'Bertie was bursting to get out,' handlers boasted. He would spend most of the next three weeks on the road.

*

The campaign had been ready to go for months, and for several weeks previously the Fianna Fáil campaign staff had been head-quartered not in Mount Street but in a building on St Stephen's Green that had been specially outfitted for the purpose. More importantly, the party immediately swung into action with its policy platform, launching its tax proposals on the day after the election was called, and immediately seizing the initiative from the Rainbow.

Fianna Fáil promised cuts in the top and standard rates of taxation – a more immediately understandable (though arguably less redistributive) alternative to the Fine Gael proposal to cut taxes by changing various bands and allowances, though Fine Gael had also pledged to cut the top rate of tax. Amid the post-election controversy about the Fianna Fáil and PD plans for tax cutting, many tended to forget that tax cuts were a central plank of the Rainbow platform, too. On the morning after the election was called, the lead story in the *Irish Times* was headlined 'FG offers £1.5 bn in tax cuts'.

A significant part of the campaign became a battle between opposing tax policies – though this was a concession to the benefit of Fianna Fáil, unquestionably. 'The 1997 tax package was vintage McCreevy,' says one civil servant, who subsequently came to know McCreevy well as minister for finance. The decision to concentrate on cutting tax rates rather than the more complex reform of tax bands was simple and comprehensible to the majority of voters who take an interest in politics and policy only when they have to. Tax rates coming down was something they could instantly recognize and support.

On the evening of the launch of the FF tax package, *Irish Times* political correspondent Mark Brennock joined a number of friends in Toner's pub on Baggot Street, including Derek McDowell, a Labour TD and subsequently the party's finance spokesman. McDowell was dismissive of McCreevy's tax-cutting plans. 'No, you've got it wrong,' Brennock told him. 'This will work. It's simple, but it's very clever.' Brennock's judgement was acute. Three days after the votes were counted, he would offer this blunt assessment of the campaign: 'It started with tax and ended with tax.'

The three-party coalition began the campaign by publishing a document entitled *21 Goals for the 21st Century*, which was immediately sent over to Fianna Fáil headquarters and deposited in Mansergh's hands. He was amazed at it. He couldn't believe there was so little substance to it. This has the look of something that was knocked up on Fergus Finlay's computer the night before, he told colleagues. They won't win any arguments with this.

Fianna Fáil set out to rubbish the twenty-one points on one page, and immediately published an attack called *21 Holes in the 21 Goals*. In contrast to the 'wishy-washy' Rainbow document, party spinners boasted to the political correspondents, its 39,000-word manifesto was the most detailed in the party's history and ten times longer than that of 1992. Not many of them had read it, but what did that matter?

In truth, Finlay and the rest of the Labour team were exhausted from five years of government. One senior civil servant remembers looking at them – Spring, Finlay, et al. – and thinking, These guys are wrecked. They can't fight a campaign. Expending all your time and energy on governing is a trap for all parties, and it's particularly dangerous for small parties. It's what killed the PDs. Fianna Fáil has always been wary of it. Fianna Fáil campaigns tend to have people around who don't care too much about government – as long as they're in it. In 1997, they had plenty of them.

The barnstorming start to the Fianna Fáil campaign soon stuttered, though not because of anything the party had done, or not done. The PDs, Ahern's prospective partners in government, were self-destructing. At the launch of the party's manifesto, journalists – prompted by party staff – had asked about the party's plans to 'encourage' single mothers to stay at home with their parents rather than move out to secure social welfare benefits. Principally because of the reporting that evening by Una Claffey, the RTÉ political correspondent, the issue exploded. Even more serious from Fianna Fáil's point of view was the promise in the manifesto to shed 25,000 jobs from the public sector. Fianna Fáil was terrified it was going to be damaged by association, and rushed out statements promising that none of this nonsense would be part of any programme for government agreed by Bertie Ahern. Only weeks previously, Ahern had shamelessly pandered to public-sector workers in his ard-fheis speech: 'Fianna Fáil is proud of our public sector workers and of their honourable service to their country . . . I say to the Rainbow government tonight: Go and cut your government's waste, but do not cut our government workers.' Now the PDs were threatening to sack 25,000 of them! At Fianna Fáil headquarters, there was confusion and anger. 'Jaysus, Charlie,' Ahern complained to McCreevy. 'You told me everything would be all right. Ah Jaysus, Charlie . . .'

At a quickly assembled meeting Chris Wall raged: 'These fuckers! They're losing us the election! What the fuck is going on with them?!'

He was beginning to shout: 'I fucking told you about them fuckers. They're only fuckers!'

'Ah now, there's no need for that, Chris,' said Mara emolliently, puffing on a cigarette.

McCreevy contacted Harney, who was initially unconcerned about the public service cuts story, believing that it was deniable. 'What's the problem?' she said to McCreevy. 'Some economist has done a few calculations and come up with a number.'

'Mary, it's in the manifesto. The 25,000 is in the manifesto!'

'It's *what*?'

The PDs' campaign was going up in flames.

Disputes have continued among the PDs since about the 1997 election, though Harney, unlike others, has accepted responsibility for all that happened. But at that time, she didn't know what was in the manifesto. McDowell continues to blame Harney. The only good thing about it, Chris Wall reflected after the election, was that McDowell lost his seat.

Reacting to the PDs' implosion, the two leaders and their

entourages met for a crisis session in the hardly imposing venue of the Green Isle Hotel at the south-westernmost boundary of the capital, where the city ended and the country began.

Although the 'crisis' meeting at the Green Isle Hotel was regarded by the PDs as purely for the optics, Ahern did take the opportunity to tell Harney that she could not expect to achieve all her policy aims on taxation. Typically, he indicated this in an elliptical way, and Harney left the meeting unsure of what if anything had been decided, other than a vague commitment to stay in closer touch during the campaign.

Behind the scenes, however, an argument was raging amongst Ahern's closest advisers about whether the PDs should be thrown overboard altogether. In fact, there were several debates at the highest levels during the campaign about this, though one campaign insider says Ahern never really considered this to be a viable option. 'To be honest, I think he thought he probably had them where he wanted them,' he says. And some members of the inner circle, notably Mara, who had the Haughey-era veteran's appreciation of how the party was loathed and feared by a chunk of the electorate, believed that the PD alliance was essential in making Fianna Fáil look different this time. Anyway, Fianna Fáil wasn't exactly overburdened with prospective coalition partners.

On the ground, though, Fianna Fáil candidates and canvassers laid into the PDs on the doorsteps. The Laois-Offaly candidate, Sean Fleming, called headquarters and told them: this PD stuff is hurting us. We're going to cut loose on them – and you'll have to leave us at it. His example was followed all over the country.

Mary O'Rourke was among those to be incensed. Her Athlone base was home to part of the Department of Education, and she encountered considerable hostility about Fianna Fáil's closeness to the PDs. 'You'll have to put a bridle on her! She'll have to calm down!' O'Rourke demanded of Ahern.

Aside from the difficulties with their prospective partners in government, Fianna Fáil was having a rollicking campaign. The leader's tour was in full swing, and the investment in time that Ahern had made over the previous two years was being repaid: he was returning to places and people, rather than seeing them for the first time.

In previous elections, headquarters would write to or telephone the local cumann secretary and tell him that the party leader would be visiting the area on such and such a date and could he kindly have an enthusiastic reception organized. Some did, some emphatically didn't. Some told nobody because they wanted to be the only one there to greet him. Not this time. In the years prior to the election, Pat Farrell's staff had compiled a database of every Fianna Fáil member in the country – some 58,000 of them. Farrell liked to boast that Fianna Fáil had more members than the Democratic Left had votes. Every member was written to and informed when the leader would be visiting during the campaign. They showed up in their droves.

'You're great to come out,' one party apparatchik told a foot soldier at one meeting. 'Why wouldn't I be here?' came the proud reply. 'Bertie wrote to me!'

The tour was frantic, frenetic, high-octane stuff. The Taoiseach and Fine Gael leader, John Bruton, travelled mainly by train, and in the time it took him to go from Dublin to Cork Ahern would have been in three towns and met hundreds of people, greeting the attendees like long-lost friends, cementing their votes. One Fine Gael adviser remembers an afternoon spent on a train – Fine Gael had hired the CIE 'executive' train – travelling from Ballinasloe to Ennis, 'one of these half-closed lines that you could only go about 30 miles an hour on'. The train ambled for hours through the countryside; Bruton and Clare TD Donal Carey lounged across the couches in the bar suite, having a long, cool beer. It was very pleasant, they all thought, but maybe not the best use of their time, nor the way to win an election. 'Bertie was probably in Cork, Limerick and Galway during the time it took us to get from Ballinasloe to Ennis,' the adviser remembers.

For RTÉ, Charlie Bird was detailed to follow Ahern and report on the leader's tour. Bird is probably the country's best-known – and maybe best-loved – journalist and he has a record of scoops matched by few. He faithfully reported the excitement that Ahern was beginning to generate on the campaign trail; Fianna Fáil's opponents claimed that he was building it up himself. According to one of the architects of the Fianna Fáil campaign, Bird 'projected the frenzy', allowing it to build on itself. One of the Dublin-based team remembers the coverage of the campaign as 'Charlie Bird running after the Bert shouting "This is amazing!" on the *Six One*.'

One day early in the campaign, they arrived in Boyle, Co. Roscommon. Despite a continuous downpour, the crowds were out, and Charlie was bouncing around the mob. He said half-seriously to Farrell, 'I've never seen anything like this ... but you need a slogan, like Lemass had – something like, I dunno, "I'm backing Bertie!"'

The next day, Farrell had thousands of stickers printed with the 'I'm backing Bertie!' slogan. It appeared on T-shirts and posters, banners and campaign literature.

'Fine Gael were right,' one handler told me. 'Charlie amplified it completely. But that's what TV does. If it was going wrong, he would have amplified that too. Television does that. Charlie does it more than most.'

Fine Gael were so incensed at Bird's coverage of Ahern that they lodged a formal complaint about it, and on *Questions and Answers* a few days before polling Ivan Yates accused RTÉ of putting out 'video promotional material on Bertie' and of not asking the Fianna Fáil leader 'a single hard question'.

RTÉ was outraged and the chapel (branch) of the National Union of Journalists passed a motion commending Bird. At Fianna Fáil headquarters, they were beside themselves with amusement. Yates later apologized for the comments. 'RTÉ completely leveraged the Fianna Fáil campaign by putting Charlie on it. I think they put him on because they wanted a tough fucker on us, but he got caught up in the whole thing,' one Fianna Fáiler told me, still chuckling about it more than a decade later. Fianna Fáil certainly didn't think Bird was on their side; but nor did they think he was hostile. And Ahern had a particularly good relationship with him; after the election, he offered him the job of government press secretary.

On and on the tour went, with crowds building as they went. It was neither as spontaneous nor as accidental as it seemed: Farrell's staff would position themselves around the crowds, starting the applause and cheering. The iconic *Irish Times* front-page photograph, carried across five columns, of Ahern kissing an attractive – really kissing, it looked like – young woman in Galway came about because Farrell knew her mother, a nurse with whom he had worked previously. He brought Ahern over to her because he knew she was a big Fianna Fáil and Bertie fan. She wasn't just some random passer-by. 'It wasn't on the mouth,' the young woman told Liveline later. It was. 'It shows that Bertie is attractive to the young people of Ireland.' Perhaps it did.

A week into the campaign, there was a publicity event in Dublin to advertise the forthcoming opening of a Planet Holly-wood restaurant in the city. Despite – or perhaps because of – the gaudy décor and dreadful food, the movie star-backed franchise had expanded all over the world. In its small way, it was an indication that Ireland was joining the modern, international world. Sylvester Stallone, who was to acting what the restaurant menus were to haute cuisine, was due to perform the honours.

PJ Mara had an involvement as an investor, and he prevailed upon the promoters to co-operate with an appearance by Ahern. Mara delightedly told staff he was 'killing two birds with the one Stallone'; the whole event was as unsubtle as the gag. If he got there, they agreed, Stallone would share the podium with him and give him one of the chain's signature jackets. But the movie star wouldn't be waiting around for the would-be taoiseach. Ahern was actually nervous about how it might look, and was hoping he would miss it. 'Is there any way I can get out of this?' he asked one adviser beforehand.

As ever, the tour was running against the clock. They arrived in Dublin in good time, but by the time they got to Harcourt Street, leading to St Stephen's Green, the traffic had glued up. Farrell received a call in the car. 'You've got to be here now,' he was told. 'Let's go,' said Ahern. The two exited the car, pursued from the trailing motorcade by aides and henchmen. They sprinted down Harcourt Street and across the Green towards the restaurant. They arrived in a welter of excitement and pushed their way through the crowds. Rock music boomed out over Stephen's Green. Ahern climbed on the stage and was greeted enthusiastically by Stallone. Jesus, one watching handler said to himself, we can do anything.

Some of the tactics were pretty fast and loose. Before every general election, all political parties are subject to lobbying by every manner of special interest group, from nursing unions to vegetable growers, from local groups protesting against the building of a mast to schools looking for a new building – with many colourful stages in between. Usually, parties give them a sympathetic ear; the trick is to appear to be as supportive as possible – in order to garner a few votes – without ever actually giving a demonstrable commitment to doing whatever it is they want. But some groups are more determined than others. So the election headquarters invented someone who would write to them promising that in government, Fianna Fáil would ensure that the mast would never be built or the road would be built as a matter of urgency, or whatever. The letters were signed by a name someone had simply made up. Another aide says that he didn't make up names as such, but he might have signed a few signatures that were pretty much illegible. And in Irish.

Afterwards, someone had to do an audit of what exactly had been promised to whom in the course of the campaign. A few supplicants came back afterwards, and had to be placated. The practice was by no means widespread, but it was an indication that the party would do anything to win.

There was a take-no-prisoners approach. Headquarters got a tape of John Bruton's infamous 'fucking peace process' comment – an irritated Bruton had replied testily to a local reporter in Cork in those terms the previous year – and 'we hawked it around radio stations shamelessly' until someone was persuaded to play it.

One afternoon some of the Fianna Fáil staff went to the political correspondents' room in Leinster House with a statement. There was nobody there. They quickly invented 'some mad statement' purporting to be from Bruton, printed it out and left it on everyone's desks. 'I don't think any of them fell for it, though.'

At the Stephen's Green headquarters, the atmosphere was excited, determined, aggressive. Opponents were fuckers; so were recalcitrant TDs who wouldn't stick to their boundaries; journalists were pricks, the *Irish Times* worst of all. The customarily obligatory Fianna Fáiler's belief that the *Irish Times* was run by a combination of ageing socialists and Blueshirt snobs united against Fianna Fáil was turned up a few notches during the campaign. They were particularly dismissive of an older generation of political writers in several papers, for whom this would be the last election. Journalists often forget what politicians sometimes really think of them.

In fact, the media relations were more advanced and more effective than had ever been the case. The staff set up a proper media-monitoring operation, for the first time in Irish politics. In government subsequently Ahern would receive no end of grief from the opposition and the media for setting up a media-monitoring unit in the Department of the Taoiseach, staffed by civil servants. The genesis of the idea was two volunteers on the third floor of the campaign HQ on St Stephen's Green, listening to the radio.

It was simple, but it was effective. A political charge would be made, or an unfavourable report broadcast. The unit would report it immediately to one of the media team. A statement would be drafted in the name of a front-bench spokesman and put to him for approval. If he couldn't be reached, someone else was (usually); otherwise they just put it out in the spokesman's name anyway. It would be fed to the media outlet concerned, and invariably reported on the following news bulletin. Jackie Gallagher and Martin Mackin – who covered much of the media beat – had a feel for how journalists constructed stories, and what lines appealed to them. Gallagher also had a reporter's ability to write quickly under pressure. They drew inspiration from the 'instant response' and pre-buttal techniques of Bill Clinton's campaign 'war room'. They were good at it and they were fast.

Headquarters provided a candidate-specific service, sending out a sort of mini-newspaper to each by fax every evening with briefing on issues for the following day and draft press releases for them.

For the first time in Irish politics there was a concentrated targeting of local radio as a key medium of political communication. 'Local radio', wrote the (that time) unsuccessful Fine Gael candidate Charlie Flanagan in the 1997 edition of the *How Ireland Voted* series, 'played a far more important role on this occasion . . .' Fianna Fáil put a studio in its Stephen's Green headquarters and installed an ISDN line so that the audio material from the day's press conference could be provided direct to the local stations in studio quality. Press officers would then hawk around interviews with the party's spokesman on whatever issue was current that day.

They would marshal people to take part in phone-ins. Frequently, though not always, a caller might be located in headquarters, masquerading as a farmer from Kildare, or a housewife from Ballybofey. One volunteer managed to inveigle himself into a radio debate with party leaders not just in 1997 but again in 2002 and 2007. When he managed to get on radio, a muffled cheer would go up: he's done it again!

One of Mara's qualities as a leader and organizer is that he is good at identifying young talent, and he is brave enough – or reckless enough – to give it its head. In 1997, he let Mackin and Gallagher and Johnston and the rest of them at it. They fed off each other's enthusiasm and strove to outdo each other in their partisanship. They arrived in their office before seven; usually, it was after one in the morning when they left. They used to take particular pleasure in knowing that the Labour Party headquarters, around the corner on Ely Place, used to close earlier than they did. They left the lights on in the Fianna Fáil headquarters all night, leading the Labour campaign to dub it the 'Starship Enterprise'. In fact, there was a nightshift, staffed in some cases by former *Irish Press* journalists, including Ken Whelan, later to co-write a highly favourable biography of Ahern. The election headquarters even had a few beds on the top floor; they were like mafia soldiers, going to the mattresses during a gang war.

Pre the widespread use of email and the internet, some of the staff would often drive to D'Olier Street to collect the first edition of the *Irish Times*, before heading to Middle Abbey Street for the following day's *Irish Independent*. Then back to HQ to digest them and plan rebuttal strategies for the following morning.

They would try anything. Early in the campaign, De Rossa, Spring and Bruton held a pretty contrived walk-around planned in Temple Bar. Fianna Fáil headquarters had ordered Michael Lowry masks, and organized for volunteers wearing the masks to wander around the Rainbow party, crossing their path with increasing regularity; eventually there was to be a crowd of Michael Lowrys hanging on their every word. In one of his uncharacteristically less exuberant moods, the stunt was vetoed by PJ Mara.

Ahern was never there – he was constantly on the road. His absence from campaign HQ became a running joke with some of the team. One day, the receptionist – who, as a previous contestant in Miss Ireland (everyone believed), had excited a good deal of attention from the male members of the team – received a call from someone who called himself Bertie, calling from Limerick. Who? Bertie. Bertie who? The leader, came the terse reply. The call was put through to the press room. *The Limerick Leader* was on the line.

Not everything went to plan, of course. The most spectacular failure was probably Kerry South, where a long-time party activist, Jackie Healy-Rae, had been denied the nomination he felt was his due and ran against the party candidates as an independent. With his leprechaunish demeanour, flat cap seemingly surgically attached to his Brylcreemed pate and absurdly pronounced accent, Healy-Rae resembled a cartoon character. The Kerry electorate got in on the joke; it became a thing among young women to kiss him.

One of the local activists called headquarters one morning. He had been out in a nightclub the previous evening and Healy-Rae seemed to be holding a rally there! Young women were queuing up to kiss him! 'This fucker is going to get elected!' the activist told Mackin. He has been twice re-elected.

The Northern issue hummed in the background. On 14 May, the day before the Dáil was dissolved, Ahern had met the Sinn Féin leader, Gerry Adams. Afterwards, Ahern issued a statement saying that the British and Irish governments should meet Sinn Féin before an IRA ceasefire. Adams praised the 'pivotal role' that Fianna Fáil had played in the peace process compared to the record of the Rainbow government, and though he emphasized that he was being 'quite cagey' in what he would say, he acknowledged, 'It was a Fianna Fáil government that helped initiate the peace process and a Fine Gael-led government that squandered it.' The message was clear: Fianna Fáil could fix the peace process.

Now, in the dying days of the campaign, Fine Gael made the decision to target Ahern, and Bruton, previously perhaps the most shielded taoiseach in Irish history, went out to tell reporters that Ahern was 'the most overestimated man' in Irish politics. The Fianna Fáil leader was inconsistent and indecisive, Bruton warned. There was more to politics than 'a handshaking marathon'. It stung, because there was a grain of truth to it. Ahern reached for the national question as his defence.

If Bruton had felt Ahern's weak point, then the challenger responded in kind, focusing on Bruton's handling of the peace process. A taoiseach should adopt the role of leader of nationalist Ireland, Ahern suggested, but Bruton had not done so. The message was hammered home on the doorsteps. Previously, Ahern had been wary of using the peace process as a route of political attack. It was never clear to what extent this was a tactical or a principled objection; but whichever, it had now been overcome. It was not an unprofitable decision. Writing after the election, two of the country's most prominent political scientists, Richard Sinnott of UCD and Michael Marsh of Trinity, concluded that 'Concern with Northern Ireland affected the choice between Fianna Fáil and all the alternatives: if a voter spontaneously mentioned Northern Ireland as a factor influencing his or her vote, he or she was substantially more likely to vote for Fianna Fáil in preference to any other party save Sinn Féin.'

The campaign ran down the days towards 6 June. Ahern was everywhere, except in headquarters, and though he was given daily briefings on progress, he was content to be managed. Mara in particular was determined to use him on the campaign trail as much as possible. 'Bertie was never there. He was on the road practically all the time. We hardly ever saw him,' says one headquarters staffer.

He insisted, though, in getting back to Dublin Central every evening. Often returning in a helicopter, he would be met by his car and driver and immediately call one of his constituency bosses. 'Chris? It's Bertie. Where are you now? OK, I'll be there in ten minutes . . .' The canvassers never knew when he would appear.

As election day approached, the polls were clear: Labour were going down, and Ahern was flying. A late victory for John Bruton in the televised leaders' debate couldn't swing things back. 'We all watched it and cheered at the Bert's contributions. We thought he was doing brilliantly. Then papers came out the next morning and said he had been creamed. They were probably right,' says one Fianna Fáiler.

Fianna Fáil had been aided by the Rainbow's mistakes, it's true, and by the legacy of mistrust among the electorate of the Labour Party because of its coalition with Fianna Fáil in 1992, but more importantly its decision to change horses mid-stream in 1994. But the election was also a stunning success for Fianna Fáil's tactics, its strategy and its new leader, with whom the Irish public were beginning a very long love affair.

Fianna Fáil had made Bertie Ahern the central motif of the campaign. They had marginalized the Rainbow's issues, and pushed their own to centre stage. As the biggest scandal in the history of Irish politics broke, they had let it just wash over them, and continued unaffected, absurdly claiming that sleaze was as big an issue for Fine Gael as for Fianna Fáil. They had got away with it, got away with it all.

On the night of the count, they ordered in supplies of drink and food, and settled in to wait for the results. The mood was giddy and optimistic, and the euphoria set in as results were announced, beers were consumed and Labour seats began to fall. Every time a Labour name went down, there was a huge cheer. The biggest cheer, remembers one participant, was when Liam Lawlor took out Joan Burton in Dublin West. 'Jesus, little did we know . . .'

4. An Uncertain Beginning

The oratorical gods did not make their presence felt when the twenty-eighth Dáil met for the first time on an afternoon in late June 1997. Unlike in the days of Edmund Burke, the modern Irish parliament is not known as a hotbed of political rhetoric, but even by the dreary standards of the place, Ahern's acceptance speech was colourless prose.

'I assure the wider public that I have an honour which has been bestowed on only a handful of people. It carries responsibility and is a job at which a person must work extremely hard. I like working hard, but this job is harder than any other and I look forward to it.'

The words were the opposite of the election campaign that had just concluded. After an energetic, glitzy campaign, fuelled by far-reaching promises, his acceptance speech was workman-like, humble, ordinary, determined. In its substance, there were only two important messages that the new Taoiseach chose to emphasize. Firstly, he would work hard. That was not a surprise to anyone who knew him. Secondly, more importantly perhaps, he would do anything to keep his government together. Again and again he emphasized his determination to make the coalition work and the partnership with the Progressive Democrats last. He knew the scale of the prize he had won. He was not about to let it slip. He would not do an Albert, and throw it all away over some stupid row. He was there for the long haul, come what may. Pretty soon, that commitment would be tested. It was Raphael P., not Edmund, Burke who would arrest the workings of this assembly.

The first meeting of the Dáil had been preceded by three weeks of deal-making to cement the prospect that had looked inevitable since the election results had become known. A resurgent and tactically transformed Fianna Fáil had gained 9 seats, while the Labour vote had collapsed, wiping out the historic gains of 1992 and destroying the chances of a return of the Rainbow government. The Rainbow's failure to be re-elected could be laid entirely at Labour's door; the party's vote just self-combusted. In five constituencies, Labour lost entire quotas; overall, the party suffered the loss of 16 seats, just one short of half its parliamentary representation. Even the strong Fine Gael performance, winning 7 additional seats (though only one from Fianna Fáil), could not save the tripartite coalition that had entered the contest with such high hopes of re-election.

The margin was slim, but decisive. The Fine Gael-led combination returned with 75 seats; the Fianna Fáil-Progressive Democrat camp had 77 plus 4: just two short of the bare majority of 83. With a number of Fianna Fáil-inclined independent TDs available for duty, there was no other way. It would be a minority government, but even at this stage Ahern's record as a conciliator and bridge-builder seemed to fit him particularly for the task. There were those in Fianna Fáil who had feared that for all the shape-throwing before the election, the numbers might force Ahern and Labour to renew acquaintance, but once the numbers were there, they need not have worried. 'He never considered a deal with Labour afterwards,' says one influential backroom figure. 'It was immediately clear to us that we could make up the numbers with the PDs and independents.' That's what they immediately sought to do.

McCreevy was especially jubilant at Labour's demise. He knew that had a Labour–Fianna Fáil administration been formed, he would have been marginalized; now that a coalition with the Progressive Democrats seemed inevitable, he thought he could be at the very centre of policy-making. And he had pretty firm ideas about what he wanted to do with that.

Like several of his cabinet colleagues, McCreevy had enjoyed good relations with the Labour ministers on a personal level. As the 1992–4 coalition came apart at the seams in November 1994, he had made extraordinary efforts to put together a deal first between Reynolds and Spring and later between Ahern and Spring – efforts that, as we have seen, came within a few hours of being successful. When those efforts were scuppered at the last minute, it only added to the sense of betrayal and anger that pervaded Fianna Fáil at all levels for years afterwards. Brendan Howlin had warned McCreevy that his (Howlin's) 'arse was out the window' trying to rescue the Fianna Fáil–Labour coalition; McCreevy couldn't help noticing that after the dust had cleared, it was Howlin's backside that was still sitting in the soft leather seats of the ministerial Mercedes.

Nonetheless, like Ahern, McCreevy knew that the electoral arithmetic meant that a Labour–Fianna Fáil arrangement would work after any election, and if there was no alternative, such a deal could be struck whatever the pre-election rhetoric. He kept in contact with senior Labour figures, particularly Pat Magner, throughout the period before the 1997 general election. Remarkably, the contacts – with precisely the same purpose – also continued throughout the period of the 1997–2002 government. McCreevy and Ahern knew that they might need the Labour Party to stay in power and they ensured that it would be possible to at least open negotiations should the Dáil numbers dictate it. 'Are you keeping the lines open there?' Ahern would ask his finance minister. McCreevy and Magner continued to speak occasionally. Both acknowledged that the other party was not the first choice; both knew it could be the only choice.

And yet privately, Ahern and McCreevy despised much of the leadership of the Labour Party and their metropolitan, middle-class hinterland, replete with media supporters; they bridled at the self-righteous pieties that the two Fianna Fáil men thought they luxuriated in. Individual TDs and people like Magner they tolerated and respected. But they loathed Spring and his backroom cohort and the tone that they felt pervaded all Labour criticisms of Fianna Fáil. Ahern in particular felt they were con-descending, dismissive of him and infused with snobbery towards his overtly working-class background and persona. Hide it though he did, it really riled the Taoiseach. He remembered the awful humiliations that they delighted in piling on Albert Reynolds when he struggled to keep the coalition together, insisting he went into the chamber, and as Fianna Fáilers saw it, abase himself by regretting the appointment of Harry Whelehan, and acknowledging that Labour's opposition had been right. No, they didn't just want to get their way, he felt: they wanted to be seen to assert their moral superiority over Fianna Fáil. They wanted Fianna Fáil to admit it.

McCreevy's antagonism was ideological, too. He believed that they actually didn't want to see the country's growing wealth transferred to the people themselves, because they believed wealth was corrosive and that the working class and lower middle class – whose members were, he liked to observe, significantly more likely to vote for Fianna Fáil than the Labour Party – would make the wrong sort of decisions about what to do with their new-found wealth. Better that the state should spend it.

Above all, McCreevy and Ahern wanted to be in a position to exclude Labour from government again. 'O Jesus, if we could do it without them,' they would say to one another. They both knew that the tyranny of the numbers might force them to cut a deal with them; but their ultimate goal was to give Labour the two fingers after the election, after every election.

'We would have done business with them, no question,' one senior figure who had access to the McCreevy–Ahern conversations told me. 'But we really, really didn't want to. We formed an opinion of them in the 1994–7 period, but we kept quiet about it in case we needed them. The truth is we fuckin' hated them.'

Much of the Labour Party and several left-wing commentators seemed to blame the *Irish Independent* for the election result, focusing on the newspaper's page-one editorial which urged a vote for the Fianna Fáil–PD alliance. Later several senior figures in Fianna Fáil told me that they believed that the *Independent* editorial lost them votes. In the immediate aftermath of the Rainbow defeat and the Labour humiliation, Dick Walsh in the *Irish Times* appeared to blame the Independent group newspapers, RTÉ and the media as a whole, in that order. The *Indo* was doing a 'passable imitation of the *Sun* in the days when loadsamoney was its catch-cry'; corporately, Independent Newspapers (now Independent News & Media) was 'one of the biggest obstacles to press freedom here'; many ordinary reporters kept their coverage 'trivial' to the benefit of Fianna Fáil, while Pat Kenny and Gay Byrne kept up 'an endless whine' about tax and crime. The left was beginning to realize what it had lost, and it was sore.

It was true that Fianna Fáil had cultivated a relationship with the Independent group.

Relations between Fianna Fáil and the Independent group had been smoothed by Mara having a foot in both camps (he was an adviser to the Independent group), but also by the presence of McCreevy in the pivotal finance brief and the emerging alliance with the Progressive Democrats. If the shared political preference of all newspaper moguls above all else is that they wish politicians to make the world safe for rich men to become richer, Ahern's Fianna Fáil was more likely to fit that bill than the Rainbow government. Bruton's reluctance to move against illegal TV deflector systems, which were threatening a cable television business in which Tony O'Reilly had an interest, reinforced that view.

While John Bruton was turning down O'Reilly requests for action on the TV deflectors, Fianna Fáil sent out a number of signals that it could do business.

At the time, Mara used to meet O'Reilly quite frequently. The Independent chairman used to complain from time to time in a general way about specific issues, such as the TV deflector controversy. But Mara never understood him to be telling anyone – either executives or editors – that they had to work to get the government out. Mara told his intimates in Fianna Fáil that O'Reilly was 'pissed off' about the deflector issue, but it wasn't a huge issue for him. He felt that chief executive Liam Healy was more likely to be proactive in that way, if anyone was. The *Irish Times* reported subsequently that Independent executives had warned the Bruton government that it would lose the newspaper group 'as friends' if they did not act against the illegal TV systems.

The relationship with the Independent group was cemented with a number of meetings, usually over lunch between Ahern and his lieutenants and the *Indo* top brass, though one of his advisers remembers the meetings being unpleasant – 'the *Indo* guys just wanted things'. It should be pointed out that in the period following the closure of the *Irish Press*, representatives from across the newspaper industry came to see Ahern to lobby him to support their proposals and positions. The former *Sunday Business Post* editor, Damien Kiberd, was one, seeking support for his consortium, which wanted to buy the *Press* group; the chairman and then chief executive of the *Irish Times*, Major Thomas B. McDowell, was another visitor. McDowell's visit to Leinster House caused amusement when his car was too large to enter via the customary one open side of the Kildare Street gates and the ushers had to open the second gate. But nothing came of any of these meetings, and the titles (over which the Independent group had a charge, giving them a veto on any sale) remain unpublished. Fianna Fáil hadn't replaced the *Irish Press* as a loyal supporter, but it had established a special relationship with the *Indo*.

It was given concrete expression two days before the general election when the *Irish Independent* published a front-page editorial – 'It's payback time' – urging a vote for the Fianna Fáil–Progressive Democrat alliance on the basis of their promises to cut tax. The editorial caused a sensation – and it infuriated the government, their supporters and much of the non-Independent group media, who saw a corporatist, political agenda behind it. Fianna Fáil staffers suspected Mara's representations might have had a hand in it, and certainly Ahern would use Mara as a conduit of communication with the group when Taoiseach.

During all the subsequent controversy about the *Independent* editorial, few remembered that on the day of the election, the *Irish Times* published something very close to an endorsement of the Rainbow government. It was certainly an attack on the Progressive Democrats:

The single strongest argument which has been made to the electorate is the stability and the general – though far from universal – competence of the Rainbow. It has shown that it can work together while sustaining the framework for consensus among the social partners. If there is a wholly convincing argument for a change of Government it has not been presented ... The principal argument against Fianna Fáil is its commitment to alliance with the Progressive Democrats, the desirability of whose influence in Government at this time must be doubtful. Outdated neo-Thatcherism, clothed in the political vocabulary of the 1980s, has little relevance in the Ireland of the millennium. This society must eschew inclinations which, however unintentionally, tend to being divisive and retributive ... Vote for stability and competence. Vote for whoever is most likely to form a Government with a commitment to justice and equality.

Perhaps it wasn't just the *Irish Independent* whose editorial wanted to influence the outcome of the election, though obviously the *Irish Times* did not have the broader corporate interests of the *Independent*.

With Labour licking its wounds and Fine Gael raging impotently, the deal-making was as straightforward as these things can be. The negotiations with the Progressive Democrats were pretty perfunctory. Much of the policy – particularly the plans for tax cuts – had been agreed prior to the election campaign. The PD negotiators were Liz O'Donnell and Bobby Molloy, while Fianna Fáil was represented by Dermot Ahern and Noel Dempsey. 'The PDs had such a terrible result, they couldn't really push for things in the talks on government,' remembers one participant in the negotiations. There were just six short negotiating sessions between the parties.

The document – 'Action Programme for the New Millennium' – was 'a decent mix of specific commitments and political aspirations', wrote Denis Coghlan in the *Irish Times*. His colleague Walsh was less willing to compliment; he decried the promises of tax cuts as pandering to the new cheerleaders in Independent

Newspapers, and observed brutally that 'a pat on the back from Glenda Slagg is no substitute for an administration that's sure of itself and the direction in which it's heading. The new minority Coalition is neither.' Walsh's almost palpable disgust at the result of the election only fed the glee of Fianna Fáil.

But the PDs and Fianna Fáil needed help. The preliminary discussions had established pretty quickly that the votes of the independents were for sale; all that remained was haggling over the price.

The process of acquisition and retention of political power in democracies has always involved trading some of the fruits of that power for the support of particular identified groups; the culture of politics is one of deal-making, frequently at the last minute. In few places is this model practised as assiduously as Ireland – sometimes to the exclusion of all else. Few have been as willing, or as able, to deal as Bertie Ahern.

Discussions with the Donegal TD Tom Gildea didn't come to fruition – Ahern's staff found it difficult to contact him – though he later joined the ranks of the government-supporting independents. There were no such communications difficulties with Wicklow, Donegal North East or Kerry South; they were all very clear about exactly what they wanted in return for their support. Ahern's officials, in their turn, were clear about what they could provide: whatever the independents wanted. The transaction turned out to be quite transparent.

Declaring her intention to vote for Ahern on the day the new Dáil met, Mildred Fox, the Wicklow TD, told deputies that prior to deciding who to vote for as Taoiseach, she had studied the programme for government produced by the Progressive Democrats and Fianna Fáil, which much of the House understandably found hilarious. Before long Fox helpfully gave a list of the projects for her constituency with which she had been purchased – a secondary school in Kilcoole, a district veterinary office in east Wicklow, a sub-office of Wicklow County Council in Blessington ('as a matter of urgency') and so on.

The comical Jackie Healy-Rae followed, with a demand that

a tights factory be replaced and the tourist season in south Kerry be extended. He didn't actually demand that the weather should be better, but that was certainly the direction in which he was headed. It was admirable in its brazen honesty: 'During my campaign many matters were raised which I wish to have dealt with by the incoming government ... Since the closure of the Pretty Polly factory in Killarney very few industrial jobs have been created in south Kerry. Many people travel long distances to find work. We require significant new industry for Killarney and other areas of the constituency. We want to extend the tourist season in south Kerry.'

On and on he went with the shopping list: the resumption of live cattle exports ... a new pier at Cromane ... cheaper car insurance for the under twenty-fives ... various grants ... before finishing his singular contribution with an uncompromising warning: 'Do not write me off, I am warning you!'

For both Ahern and Harney, buying the support of the independents with promises of public money for their constituencies was an acceptable price to pay for power. Harney – it was the same for McCreevy, and the two had privately discussed this – was taking up office with perhaps a greater sense of urgency than Ahern, convinced as she was that she would have, at best, a few years in which to exercise her influence on government policy. During all this time, Ahern constantly reassured Harney that his intention was to go the distance with the coalition; she took his words at face value, but privately she didn't expect the government to last more than a few years. The record of Fianna Fáil coalitions was that they collapsed. If meeting the demands of the independents for favouritism for their constituencies was the price of implementing her policies in government, well, that was just how politics was done. But she didn't escape ridicule for it. Taking aim at the deals done with the independents, Pat Rabbitte sneered in the Dáil that Kilgarvan (homeplace of Jackie Healy-Rae) and Kilcoole (in Mildred Fox's constituency) would have more influence on government policy than the PDs. He could not have been more wrong.

Much of the dealing between Ahern and Harney related to ministerial jobs, and a reorganization of the departments of state. The question of Ray Burke was a source of friction and uncertainty. Before the election, Harney had discussed his possible appointment with both Dessie O'Malley and McDowell; they agreed that, in the event of Ahern proposing Burke for cabinet, they would seek firm assurances from the Fianna Fáil leader. This would not just seek to insulate the PDs from any contamination from Burke-related fallout but put Ahern on notice that if the stories circulating about him proved to be true, the PDs could not simply stand by. Harney was loath to be cast in the role of moral guardian of Fianna Fáil, and she had attempted to make clear to Ahern that she didn't see it as the smaller party's role. But nor could she ignore a calamity affecting a member of the cabinet.

Privately, Harney thought that the PDs had lost a sense of perspective when they forced the exits of Brian Lenihan and James McDaid from the 1989–92 government, explicable perhaps by Dessie O'Malley's personal history with Fianna Fáil and the need to define the PDs as being separate from the larger party. She resolved that unless the tribunal revelations directly impinged on someone at the cabinet table, they would 'grin and bear it', in the words of one of the participants in those conversations. Of course, the improving economic news made it easier to grin in the face of the tribunal troubles. Finally, she resolved that if Ahern wished to appoint Burke, there wasn't the evidence to object to it. Soon enough, though, there would be.

Harney herself wanted an economic ministry and the position of tánaiste, or deputy prime minister. The position of enterprise minister was an obvious fit, and she was to form a very close alliance with the department's top civil servant, Paul Haran, who connected with her on an ideological and political level. The two formed a formidable partnership.

The tánaiste's position was significantly downgraded from the previous government, where an Office of the Tánaiste had been created within the Taoiseach's Department to ensure that the junior coalition partners were sufficiently represented at the centre of government and forewarned about future problems. That office was disbanded, though Harney's quota of staff and advisers was greater than her cabinet colleagues'.

The diminution in the trappings of the position of tánaiste didn't prevent Mary O'Rourke from staking her claim for the post and she approached Ahern to tell him so in plain terms. She made her case forcefully. She was deputy leader. The PDs had only four seats. He was giving them more than he had to, she told him. Ahern listened, and shrugged. 'Ah, Mary, you know the way it is,' he pleaded. O'Rourke did one of her harrumphs. 'Mmmm. Yeah. I do.'

To placate her, Ahern told O'Rourke that he had turned down Harney's requests for the Department of Public Enterprise, the wide-ranging and important department (formerly transport, energy and communications) that he wanted O'Rourke to manage. 'Jaysus, you couldn't let her off with the semi-states,' he told his deputy leader. This was a piece of management by Ahern – Harney told friends she had got the job she wanted, and didn't ask for anything else.

But Harney also had her problems. Deeply depressed by the election results and traumatized by the campaign, she was desperate to keep the now seat-less and angry Michael McDowell in the party and wanted to bring him into government as attorney general. Ahern was not enthusiastic; neither was Liz O'Donnell, whose hope of a junior ministry would have been a casualty to such an arrangement, she surmised. She made her feelings clear to Harney. 'He can fuck off,' O'Donnell said. 'I got elected. He didn't.'

Harney's efforts to make McDowell attorney general came to nothing. After much prevarication, Ahern eventually said to Harney that he had promised the job to David Byrne, a barrister who had become close to him in recent years since being retained by him in November 1994. Before the general election, Byrne had prepared a report outlining the financing and ownership of St Luke's, which concluded that the building was owned in trust for Fianna Fáil (through trustees, all part of Ahern's gang) and that Ahern's own position was that of tenant there. Ahern's people intended to rely on the report in dealing with any awkward questions during the campaign. Afterwards, following the tragic death of Ahern's solicitor, Gerry Brennan, Ahern recommended a friend of his, solicitor David Anderson, to take charge of Brennan's practice, which he did with the approval of the Law Society. Byrne had been approached by Des Richardson about the matter. Brennan was Ahern's friend, benefactor and family law solicitor in his High Court proceedings against his wife, Miriam; he was also involved in setting up and attending to the legal machinery of Ahern's constituency organization. For Ahern, the files in Brennan's office were of the highest possible sensitivity, and he was grateful for Byrne's ability and his tact. At Ahern's request, channelled through Byrne, his files in Brennan's office were released to another solicitor, Hugh O'Donnell. Both O'Donnell and Anderson, well-regarded lawyers, were later made judges by Ahern's government. The political dealer with the complicated past came to trust the urbane senior counsel. Harney's cunning plan would have to wait. Besides, like most of Fianna Fáil at this time, Ahern didn't much like McDowell.

In general, Ahern was faced with the perennial problem of prime ministers forming governments: not having enough jobs to meet all the promises, half-promises, cast-iron commitments and vague undertakings that have been made in the years and weeks before the election. The dilemma is most acute when it comes to the selection of the cabinet, where being passed over for preferment – especially when it is anticipated by the candidate and/or the press – is a very public and very enduring insult. It is also a financially costly snub for the failed supplicant, something more acutely felt after a period in opposition and an election campaign. Ahern hummed and hawed over several of his selections, and decided eventually that there was no room for Seamus Brennan. Rather than break the news to the disappointed Brennan himself, he indicated to one of his advisers that he should casually suggest to Brennan that he was unlikely to make the cabinet team – perhaps while they were discussing something completely different. Great, thought the adviser. Nice job. But he did as he was asked, calling by Brennan's office and dropping the suggestion into the conversation that you know, perhaps he might not make the 'first team' on this occasion. Brennan's razor-sharp political antennae were already twitching. No sooner had the adviser mentioned it than Brennan was out of his seat and practically running out the door, headed for Ahern's office. Brennan knew enough about Bertie Ahern to know that if he got to him early, before the decision had been communicated to too many people and had become a fait accompli, he had a fair chance of changing the new Taoiseach's mind.

As Brennan made his way to Ahern's office as fast as his little legs would carry him, the adviser grabbed the phone in his office and rang Ahern's private office. Brennan is on his way up looking for him, he told them. It was too late for Ahern to escape. An angry confrontation followed between the two men. Ahern only partially backed down, offering Brennan the post of chief whip, which brought a seat at cabinet but not full cabinet status. Brennan took off in a funk, holing up in the Davenport Hotel for much of the day to consult friends and advisers before eventually accepting the post. Last-minute compromise it may have been, but it was one of Ahern's most successful appointments; Brennan's mixture of affability, political skills and sense of strategy was an important factor in the stability that existed between the government and its independent supporters.

Not all his cabinet appointments were so problematic. Some of them were automatic. The night before the Dáil met, Ahern called McCreevy at his office in Naas. 'I'm only ringing a few senior fellas about tomorrow, about being in the cabinet,' he told him. The two men then talked about who else might be in the cabinet, with Ahern as usual non-committal, and McCreevy offering opinions and advice. Ahern kept saying, 'Yeah, yeah . . .' McCreevy understood he was in the cabinet, and he presumed it was the finance job. But he didn't ask, and Ahern never actually told him.

The next day, McCreevy drove to Dublin with his wife, Noeleen, in the assumption, but not the certain knowledge, of his appointment as finance minister. He had bought a new suit for the occasion but he chose to bring it with him in the back of the car – he was confident, but not over-confident.

Throughout the day, TDs, prospective cabinet colleagues and others approached him with the predictable question: did you get finance? McCreevy's responses varied from shrugging it off to telling people he didn't know. To those he trusted, he revealed that he assumed he was, but he didn't know for sure. The Dáil adjourned following Ahern's election, and some time later McCreevy went to his office. I'd better change into the new suit, McCreevy thought. Then a member of Ahern's staff arrived – the Taoiseach would see him now. In fact, when he got to the Sycamore Room in the Department of the Taoiseach, there were several members of the new cabinet (they assumed) waiting there. They compared notes and attempted to figure out who was going where. There was some tension; Dermot Ahern had made an attempt to secure the justice portfolio, infuriating John O'Donoghue, who had been spokesman in opposition. The new ministers trickled in, then Harney. But McCreevy himself was never called into the Taoiseach's office. He deduced that he must be the new minister for finance, if only by process of elimination. He was still in the old suit when Ahern came in and read out the full list. The new cabinet proceeded to make their way for the procession into the Dáil chamber.

Protocol dictates that cabinet seniority runs from the Taoiseach, to the Tánaiste, to the minister for finance and then to the other members in order of the length of service in previous cabinets and the Dáil. However, in 1997, there was a mix-up, and Ahern and his Tánaiste Harney were followed not by McCreevy as minister for finance but by the longest-serving minister – Michael Woods. 'Oh Jesus,' thought Noeleen McCreevy when the new cabinet walked in. 'He's after making Michael Woods minister for finance!' She wasn't the only one thinking it. Later, when the two became much closer, McCreevy and Ahern used to joke about it.

'I don't know if I'm actually minister for finance at all,' McCreevy would say. 'You never actually asked me to do the job.'

'Ah, Charlie, you knew, you knew.'

'Ah, I don't know, I don't know. I don't think I'm properly appointed at all.'

Ahern gave cabinet jobs to all his opposition front-benchers – except Michael Smith, the Tipperary TD and Reynolds loyalist whose comments about the strength of Reynolds family life had so angered Ahern in 1992. Much was made of Smith's exclusion; in fact, Ahern privately promised him that he would be in the cabinet at the first vacancy. He would soon get an opportunity to make good his word.

Ahern had barely appointed his government when the Haughey story exploded. Through a combination of luck, Ahern's dis-avowal of Haughey and John Bruton's clumsiness in dealing with the tribunal, the strategy pursued by Dick Spring to use the tribunal to win the election had backfired. But the Haughey train was still coming down the tracks, and Ahern was in its path.

Ahern wasn't as surprised as he appeared to be by the Haughey revelations. In the autumn of 1996 a senior Fianna Fáiler who was close to Ahern had learned, through a family connection with the Dunnes, of Ben Dunne's generosity to Haughey. He immediately told Ahern, who remained impassive. Ahern continued to affect that he, like everyone else, was waiting for the tribunal to ascertain if there was anything to these wild rumours. But actually, he had had first-hand information from this impeccable source for months. His crucial condemnation of Haughey and the distancing of the party from its former leader got him through the election; in fact, it was vital in the election success. But the problem wasn't going to go away.

When the tribunal resumed on 30 June after the election, it

was only a matter of time. After months of denial and evasion, Haughey was forced to admit he had received £1.3 million from Dunne when his legal team – to whom he had lied as much as he had to everyone else – threatened to walk out on him.

The country was enthralled. Even the sober *Irish Times* gave the reputed Haughey wealth the *Hello!* treatment:

He lives in a 200-year old mansion, Abbeville, in Kinsealy, Co. Dublin. He keeps horses and the extensive wooded grounds contain a lake. His redbricked wine cellar is said to boast some of the wine world's most prestigious labels – a Chateau Margaux 1956, a Mouton Rothschild 1967 and a Chateau Lafite 1920. He is the owner of a £200,000 50-foot ketch, the *Celtic Mist*. Inisvickillane, Mr Haughey's Co. Kerry island, is accessible only by helicopter in the calmest weather ... The dining room is believed to contain beams fashioned from beech trees felled by storms in Abbeville. The table can seat twelve comfortably and the host's bedroom is said to contain a healthy stock of expensive clarets ...

And this was before the shirts and the dinners, the trips to Paris with the gabby mistress, before the full detail of the baroque corruptions of Charles Haughey would retrospectively define a political era.

The opposition were tearing their hair out, while Ahern, for his part, affected to be as agog as everyone else by the extraordinary tales of Dunne's generosity and Haughey's mendacity about it. But crucially, Harney decided she could hardly hold Ahern responsible for his mentor's failings. She knew that if she made an issue of it, the government was doomed. So she sat tight. 'If you're just back in government after being out of it, you knuckle down,' says one of Ahern's cabinet. 'You're determined to stay.'

Nonetheless, the atmosphere in the new government was tense and sometimes uncomfortable in those muggy July days. Because it wasn't just the long-retired Haughey's past that was coming back to haunt his successor. There was something rattling in the closet of a member of the government, too.

*

There had always been a whiff of dodginess about Ray Burke. He had risen to political prominence with a reputation as a bruiser and a bully; he was also able and canny. 'I was very nervous of Ray Burke, you couldn't but be nervous of him,' says one of his cabinet colleagues. 'He had a way about him.'

But he was an important assistant to Bertie Ahern in managing the parliamentary party whilst in opposition and he played, says one participant in the negotiations, bad cop to Bertie's good cop with the republican movement in negotiations both before and after Fianna Fáil entered government. 'He always favoured a tough approach with Sinn Féin,' he recalls. In fact, so hostile was Burke to Sinn Féin that some government backroom staff suspected republican involvement in the drip-drip of stories about him in the media, a suspicion that was elevated to evidence of a conspiracy against him by Burke. The truth that was slowly emerging was more prosaic: Burke had been avaricious, using his political position to amass personal wealth.

He had been questioned by the gardaí more than twenty times about land deals during the 1970s and, while nothing was ever pinned on the auctioneer-turned-politician, there was a general assumption in politics, inside and outside Fianna Fáil, that Burke was, well, vulnerable to revelations about his past. Asked during the election campaign about rumours circulating about a member of his front bench receiving money, Ahern observed, 'We all know who we are talking about.' With the Haughey revelations, the question of senior politicians receiving sums of money became immediately much more believable.

Before Ahern made the final decision to appoint Burke to his cabinet, he made discreet inquiries with a senior garda officer. Was there anything about Burke he should know? Were any investigations likely? The officer answered honestly: no. It didn't hurt Burke that he had been popular with senior gardaí when he was minister for justice. But the senior officer was being truthful. They had nothing actionable on Burke.

But the net had begun to close on Burke even before it ensnared Charlie Haughey. Since the mid-1990s, the *Sunday*

Business Post had been publishing stories about planning corruption in Dublin, but the newspaper's editor, Damien Kiberd, trod carefully in running the stories that his investigative reporter Frank Connolly kept unearthing. When Labour TD Joan Burton alleged planning corruption in Dublin, she was sued by forty-two county councillors; when Trevor Sargent of the Green Party held up a £100 cheque he had been sent by a developer, asking if anyone had received one of these, one of his colleagues grabbed him in a headlock. The *Post* didn't want to be sued or put in a headlock, but by the spring of 1996, the newspaper was sufficiently confident to publish a story about how a senior Fianna Fáil politician had received £80,000 from a developer, citing the word of a former company executive who was present when the cash was handed over. Connolly had made contact with James Gogarty, the retired executive who was himself mired in the planning abuses of Co. Dublin, but who had fallen out with his builder employers over his pension. Now we were getting somewhere.

The stories began to leak out that Burke was the politician involved; they always do. The *Sunday Tribune* named him in July; the *Sunday Business Post* identified the donor, a company called Joseph Murphy Structural Engineers (JMSE). The press was momentarily distracted by the IRA ceasefire. Ahern had moved quickly on his election, telling the new British Prime Minister that he needed a month. He didn't quite need it. On 18 July, following extensive contact between Dublin and the republican leadership, Adams and McGuinness 'called on' the IRA to renew its ceasefire. The following day, the organization announced its second and final ceasefire. All-party talks were scheduled for the autumn. But even as he shared the plaudits, the political chatter about Burke's ethical exposure went up several decibels.

It was once said of Burke that he had the ability to sense danger coming over the horizon and the political kingpin of north Co. Dublin could now. The pressure was building on the minister for foreign affairs, and he could feel it. One minister who worked closely with Burke at the time thought he was 'very nervous – he could see the storm clouds were gathering. He was nervous and erratic at times.' As the media leaks continued, Burke was 'paranoid', says another person who dealt with him continuously at the time. He was afraid that Ahern was getting ready to dump him. He was.

On 7 August, Burke issued a statement decrying 'a vicious campaign of rumour and innuendo ... a campaign of calumny and abuse', and declaring that he had done nothing illegal. He also confirmed a donation of £30,000. It was, needless to say, 'totally unsolicited'. A government spokesman expressed confidence that this would put the matter to rest. Like hell it would. Harney was quoted in the following day's newspapers expressing full confidence in the Taoiseach's judgement about the Fianna Fáil members of the cabinet.

Her language was carefully chosen. In private, Harney was becoming highly uncomfortable about the series of revelations, admissions and fudges. She had of course known about the rumours about Burke before his appointment; she had, after all, repeatedly discussed them with Ahern. What she was becoming agitated about was the gap between how much Ahern had known about Burke's dealings and how much he had chosen to share with her. It wasn't so much that Burke was turning out to be crooked, as she and many others had suspected; it was that she felt Ahern wasn't telling her the whole truth.

She was right. Ahern had known the details of the Burke payment not since his flawed investigations prior to Burke's appointment to cabinet – a process he memorably recalled as being up every tree in North Dublin – but since before the general election, according to a member of his staff with whom he discussed it. According to the same staff member, Ahern had also known before the election that Burke had received a payment from Rennicks, a subsidiary of Fitzwilton, which was not revealed until May of 1998 – at which time Ahern declared he had only recently become aware of it.

Before he left for Kerry in early August, he had discussed the inevitable fallout that would ensue when the Burke story became public. Clearly, the Tánaiste and the PDs would have to be told what was coming. However, Ahern instructed one of his staff, 'Wait a few weeks before you tell her.'

When Harney was eventually told, she exploded, directing an angry tirade at the staffer. She apologized the following day, but pointedly told him, 'I'm fed up of being told the truth in instalments.' She would get used to that, but it was a constant problem in her relationship with Ahern.

The leaks and the media speculation about Burke's future continued throughout July and August. In early September, Burke made an emotional personal statement to the Dáil and answered TDs' questions for an hour afterwards. He had rehearsed his Dáil statement for a group of senior advisers. One of them thought he was like 'a cat on hot bricks; he was hyper'. None of them thought that he looked like an innocent man wrongly accused.

In the Dáil, Burke laid it on with a trowel: 'I have come here today to defend my personal integrity, the integrity of my party, of this government and the honour of this House. I have also come here to reassure the public and in particular my constituents that I have done nothing wrong.'

Burke's explanations and especially the emotional tone of his delivery appeased the opposition. Afterwards, he was triumphant. One official who met him coming from the chamber with his adviser Tony Lambert remembers him being jaunty, 'euphoric even'. Speaking to the media afterwards, he declared: 'Whatever comes out of the woodwork from now on, a line is in the sand. From this day on, D–Day, I am going on to the peace process, the United Nations and to Europe and no further.'

Trouble was, he had lied his head off. Later that evening, some government advisers gathered, having watched Burke's combative performance on the television news and the broadly positive coverage of the day's events in the Dáil. The group included officials who had helped Burke prepare his speech. 'Course, the only problem,' reflected one, 'is that he is a fucking crook.'

Even by the later standards established by those who found

themselves in the full glare of the tribunal's headlights, Burke's bravura performance that day was brazen stuff. It was also a doomed attempt to avert the inevitable. Ahern was in full-scale retreat from his friend now, and Burke could sense it. One evening shortly afterwards, enraged by a less than full-hearted backing for him in some media responses issued by Ahern's office, he went into a fury and made for Government Buildings. He arrived in a highly agitated and – staff thought – menacing state. Worried officials had already called from Leinster House to say a furious Burke was on his way over and was gunning for Ahern. The Taoiseach's staff tumbled out of their offices to distract Burke while Ahern fled out the back door of his office, took the quick elevator down to street level and sped away in the waiting Mercedes. The Taoiseach's office had been equipped for just such an emergency getaway for the leader of the country in times of strife or national emergency; it is doubtful the designers had in mind the avoidance of a minister bent on angry remonstrance at his boss's cavilling. Then again, maybe they did.

Burke veered between paranoia and depression. He called an old political ally from the Haughey administration and asked him to come to the Department of Foreign Affairs, where the two men had tea. He was trying to gauge Ahern's support. 'Am I in trouble?' he asked. The longer they discussed it, the more it became clear he could not survive. 'I want to ask you one question,' Burke finally said. 'Do you think I will go to jail?' Of course not, his friend answered. It'll never get that bad.

To others, he continued to swear his innocence. Before one cabinet meeting at the time, Burke sought to reassure Mary Harney that he was being unfairly targeted, that the stories were false. In the small antechamber off the cabinet room, where ministers would drift in for tea and coffee before meetings, colleagues observed Burke and Harney deep in conversation. 'Burke was telling what he hadn't done, and how he was being vilified. He was gesticulating, laying down the law,' says one cabinet member who witnessed the exchange. Ahern came in and observed the exchange. 'Everything OK?' he asked nervously.

Harney's face hardened. 'I don't know. We'll see,' she replied.

In late September, with the pressure continuing to mount, *Magill* magazine published a letter from the developer Michael Bailey of Bovale Developments to JMSE offering to 'procure' planning permission for 700 acres of land. The trickle of allegations was becoming a flood, and it was flowing towards the minister for foreign affairs. The Taoiseach and the Tánaiste, wrote Geraldine Kennedy in the *Irish Times*, 'arrived at the understanding that a new inquiry ... could be required to stop the drip-feed of allegations engulfing and damaging Mr Burke'. So there would be a new tribunal. But it was too late.

The *coup de grâce* was delivered on Saturday 4 October, when the *Irish Times* published a story that revealed that Burke's granting of eleven Irish passports to a wealthy Arab family had been investigated not just by the Department of Justice but by Bertie Ahern. There were a number of irregularities in the way the passports were authorized, identified in the story.

The story was the breaking point. On Monday, Harney went to Ahern in St Luke's and told him what he already knew. 'This can't go on,' she said.

Burke was furious, and Fianna Fáil purported to be outraged at the leak of a story designed to cause maximum damage to Burke, though the investigations had not found any wrongdoing on his part. Various fingers were pointed about the source of the leak. Nobody noticed that the author of the story, reporter Sean Flynn, lived a few doors away from Bertie Ahern.

Burke's resignation from the cabinet and the Dáil marked a bitter break with Ahern, and Burke appeared to many afterwards to be incapable of accepting what he viewed as Ahern's treachery. There was an angry encounter in a pub in Swords during the subsequent by-election and many of Burke's former colleagues reported that he appeared unable to talk about anything else but what he perceived to be Ahern's perfidy on the increasingly seldom occasions when they sought out his company.

'I kept waiting for Burke to sink Bertie. I thought it would happen during the by-election. There was an altercation one night in a bar, but it never went further than that, in fairness to Burke,' reflected one cabinet minister afterwards.

Ahern soon had another delicate problem to deal with. Months of lobbying – the *Irish Times* described it as the most intensive lobbying ever carried out by the Department of Foreign Affairs – had paid off for the President of Ireland, Mary Robinson, who had been appointed to a job in the United Nations. By accepting it she would be unable to complete her term as president. A presidential election was inevitable.

Despite her abrupt departure from the position before her term of office was completed, Robinson's presidency had been a ground-breaking success. Her election was a cathartic event for many people, particularly women, in Ireland and her presidency had reached and recognized many in corners – both geographic and social – that had long been ignored or excluded by the official state. It had been transformative of the office and had marked the transition to a more modern society. Her election had also changed the face of presidential contests for ever.

Her departure presented Ahern with a threat, and an opportunity. After the Robinson presidency, it seemed inconceivable that the office should revert to the sleepier existence it had had under Paddy Hillery, or that it should go to a Fianna Fáil grandee like Albert Reynolds, to whom Ahern had already all but promised the Fianna Fáil nomination.

This was not, however, Reynolds' view. With characteristic single-mindedness, he hired staff and commissioned research and lobbied hard during the summer, determined to win the contest before it really got going. He spoke to members of the parliamentary party, with some of them reflecting that he hadn't spoken to them in years, telling them about the research that showed he would win handsomely. Many of them just didn't believe it. One back-bencher who had been recently lobbied spoke to a minister's adviser in the Dáil self-service restaurant. Reynolds' research was rubbish, he told her. With Reynolds as a candidate, the party might not even come second. They were joined by another back-bencher from the constituency. 'The only thing I care about,' he said, 'is who will keep my seat.' First things first. Ultimately, Reynolds was to underestimate fatally not just how many of his colleagues disliked him but how much the election of Robinson had changed the way voters thought about the presidency.

As Reynolds' campaigning for the job over the summer became more overt – in part as a counterpoint to the ongoing humming and hawing of SDLP leader John Hume – several members of the cabinet made clear to Ahern that they didn't believe that Reynolds could win the presidency in an election. They were probably right, though it was noticeable that it was those on the anti-Reynolds wing of the party who were making the arguments; the mathematics didn't seem quite so obvious to Cowen and many of those who owed their advancement to Reynolds.

Not untypically, Ahern sent out signals to the various camps that he was with them all the way. Signals had even been sent out to camps that hadn't been pitched – including one that would have housed Maire Geoghegan-Quinn, had she been interested. After a bit of inevitable flirting with it, she wasn't. Ahern had more or less told Reynolds he would back him, and continued this fiction until the very end when, on the morning of the selection vote, he rang Reynolds to ask him who he wanted to run his campaign. But behind the scenes several of his advisers and some members of the cabinet were working to the Anybody But Albert agenda. Mary McAleese was the answer to their prayers, though it took them a little time to realize it.

McAleese had flitted in and out of the margins of the Irish political world in the previous decade and a half. A Belfast Catholic, she endured an unhappy time as a journalist in RTÉ in the early 1980s when a powerful Workers' Party clique led by Eoghan Harris and John Caden viewed any deviation from their strongly anti-nationalist view on Northern Ireland to be evidence of sympathy for terrorism. McAleese further infuriated them by turning up as a legal adviser to the Catholic bishops during the New Ireland Forum in 1984: to be a nationalist was bad enough; to be both Catholic and nationalist was intolerable. Harris and Caden were hardly surprised to see McAleese surface as a candidate for Fianna Fáil in the general election of 1987 in Dublin South East. She flopped.

McAleese returned to academia, and taught law at Trinity College and later Queen's University in Belfast. She watched the transformation of the South with pride but also concern that in the rush to modernization traditional values were being eroded. She also saw how the North was being left behind, how for many people in the Republic, the North was a foreign country. By 1997, she was ready to try to do something about all that.

McAleese was encouraged by Harry Casey, a secondary teacher in Navan who contacted the newly elected Mary Hanafin. Hanafin, the daughter of the old pro-life and anti-divorce warhorse Des Hanafin, afforded her a sympathetic hearing. The Catholic element to her campaign was always understated, but it was there. McAleese tapped that element of Irish life, but she did it skilfully and tactfully; when, in a last-minute throw of the dice it was alleged by the *Sunday Times* that she might be a member of Opus Dei, the dramatic allegation had no effect. For one thing, in a country with the highest weekly mass attendance in Europe, being a practising Catholic was not a bar to high office. In fact, many people thought quite the reverse.

Over the summer, McAleese worked the party and she worked the cabinet. Mary O'Rourke hosted her in Athlone one evening and saw not just a woman who could make an impressive president but someone who could stop the dreaded Reynolds from winning the nomination. But it was still a long shot.

Ahern was cautious, but some of his advisers and ministers were increasingly enthusiastic. Though subsequently some in government would try to claim that the nomination of McAleese was a masterstroke planned for months – in 2008, Ahern's former adviser Paddy Duffy told the makers of the documentary pro-gramme on Ahern knowingly that 'a small group of people knew it from early' – the reality was more prosaic, and certainly more chaotic. With little leadership from Ahern, several members of the cabinet proselytized for her in the final days, claiming that she had Ahern's backing. This was only true at the very end. Panicky attempts were made to persuade Ray MacSharry and even David Andrews (whose putative candidacy Ahern had earlier kiboshed because his success would mean a by-election) to enter the race; Michael O'Kennedy, campaigning busily but fruitlessly among the parliamentary party, was given fresh encouragement. At a cabinet meeting on the day before the parliamentary party was due to select its nominee, Ahern asked for views. Several present, including Micheál Martin and Dermot Ahern, were vocally opposed to a Reynolds candidacy, arguing forcefully that it would be an electoral disaster. Others – the Reynolds loyalists such as McCreevy – said simply that they would vote for Albert; they couldn't do otherwise. Typically, Ahern digested the mood of the majority and then swung with it. He indicated to the cabinet that the party had to face electoral realities. Labour's decision, leaked a few days earlier, to nominate the charity campaigner Adi Roche had suddenly left Reynolds looking very old, and very Fianna Fáil. It probably sealed the former taoiseach's fate. Ahern would have accepted Reynolds if he thought he could win, but he wanted to win more than he cared about Albert. The list of the parliamentary party members whose votes could be won was divvied up between the ministers he trusted to bring the votes in for McAleese. That evening they sat in their offices and worked the phones. 'Now,' began one minister speaking to a back-bencher, working his way through his list, 'first of all, this call never happened . . .'

Reynolds' fate became clear the following day at a parliamentary party meeting which has passed into legend. Ahern famously showed Reynolds his vote as a means of assuring the older man that he had kept his word and voted for him, a gesture that was aptly characterized by the cartoonist Graeme Keyes in the *Phoenix* magazine, when he depicted Ahern's vote for Reynolds pinned on the former taoiseach's back – by a knife. When the story was reported it was understood by many as a depiction of Ahern's ruthlessness. Perhaps. But it was also evidence of his indecisiveness and his tendency to postpone difficult decisions until the very last moment. According to several of those who participated, Reynolds' demise was only partly the calculating takedown of political myth; it was also a chaotic scramble to avoid an electoral disaster.

After the meeting, TDs stumbled out on to the Leinster House plinth, some of them in a daze. 'What the fuck happened there?' one aide asked. Nobody had a ready answer. Brian Lenihan, who had proposed Michael O'Kennedy but subsequently emerged as McAleese's election agent, prompting some suspicions among the Reynolds supporters that the whole O'Kennedy candidacy had been a ruse to deflect them and split the vote (without O'Kennedy's knowledge), told people that he knew the game was up for Albert when Cork TD Danny Wallace turned to him and asked, 'How do you spell McAleese?'

The election itself became a sort of referendum on whether it was OK to be a northern Catholic and have a role in southern life. McAleese was subjected to assaults for her northernness, her nationalism and her Catholicism throughout the campaign. The *Sunday Times* columnist Eoghan Harris later admitted that he supported and advised one of the candidates, Derek Nally, purely as a means to stop McAleese, whom he described with a typical Harrisian mixture of pungency and overstatement as 'a tribal time-bomb'. Years later, he recanted his views on McAleese.

Key members of McAleese's campaign remember an extra-ordinary hostility to McAleese amongst many of the media, especially, as several of them noted to me, among women journalists. 'Mind you,' added one. 'She [McAleese] didn't exactly go out of her way to make friends with them.' One female reporter noted her tendency to throw 'reporters' questions back at them like badly constructed essays from dim undergraduates'; not, in fairness, a completely inaccurate characterization of many of the reporters' questions.

When the candidate did an interview with Emily O'Reilly of *The Sunday Business Post*, the interview started with formal pleasantries on the part of each woman. Soon O'Reilly reached for her Dictaphone. 'Do you mind if I tape you?' she asked, indicating that the pleasantries were over. McAleese assented, and then produced her own Dictaphone. She placed it on the table between them. 'Just so you don't misquote me,' she said deliberately. The atmosphere in the room dropped by several degrees.

The other candidates scarcely got a look-in – the whole campaign seemed to be about McAleese. Adi Roche imploded spectacularly; the more worldly-wise Labour handlers sensed something was up when they noticed she was signing autographs, 'It's about love and peace – Adi.' The Fine Gael candidate, Mary Banotti, was competent but colourless; Derek Nally was irrelevant and Dana never broke out from the Catholic right, which constituted her base. McAleese ran a tightly organized and effective campaign, but her opposition was weak and divided.

The result and the way it was achieved emphasized the importance of the campaign and of the necessity to have a professional, organized campaign in modern elections. Adi Roche had started as the favourite, and ahead in the polls. In the end, the campaign destroyed her, as it made Mary McAleese. The primacy of campaigning was a lesson Ahern would bring to his greatest priority of all – retaining power at the next general election. More significantly, the presidential campaign ended Dick Spring's tenure as leader of the Labour Party. Spring and the group that surrounded him were perhaps the most important and dynamic force in Irish politics in the first half of the 1990s. They changed the national mood with the election of Mary Robinson and then changed the make-up of the Dáil in the general election of 1992, coalescing first with Fianna Fáil and then with Fine Gael to give the country technocratic and policy-driven governments of a type it had never had before. Now, exhausted by office, outfought and out-thought in two successive elections, their day was passing. They would be replaced by Ahern's lean and hungry cadres at this crucial point in the nation's history.

Ahern finished 1997 with his party's poll ratings at 50 per cent and his approval ratings among his own party at over 80 per cent. He had restored Fianna Fáil's electoral supremacy and returned the party to government. He was becoming very comfortable there. A year that started with such uncertainty was ending not just in triumph but with great promise for the future. Because the Celtic Tiger was clearing its throat and was about to roar.

5. Tiger, Tiger, Burning Bright

It was a cold November day, five eventful months after the government of Bertie Ahern had taken office. Finance minister Charlie McCreevy was closeted with his senior officials in the grey, imposing Merrion Street headquarters of the department, working out the details of his forthcoming first budget, due to be delivered on 3 December.

The officials had learned in the first months of McCreevy's tenure in the department that he was operationally unorthodox and possessed of radical instincts – much too radical, some of them thought. But nothing had prepared them for what was to come.

Out of the blue – it seemed to the mandarins – McCreevy announced that he was thinking of reducing capital gains tax. It would free up capital currently constrained by what he saw as the penal 40 per cent rate, and would lead to new investment and business expansion, he said. What sort of cut was he thinking about? the officials asked nervously. 'I'm going to reduce it to 20 per cent,' he announced. 'I'm going to cut it in half.'

The officials were stunned. Some assumed they had misheard. Paddy Mullarkey, the secretary general, began to protest. It would decimate the tax projections, he said. No, it won't, said McCreevy, who had anticipated precisely this reaction, and was warming to his theme. Receipts from the tax will go through the roof, he said. The whole budget would be undermined, Mullarkey protested. No, it won't, the minister insisted.

In their incredulity, the officials had underestimated just how radical McCreevy intended to be. They had assumed that he meant halving the rate of capital gains tax over the lifetime of the government – that is, over five budgets.

If you want to do this, one official began to suggest, then you'll have to have a small cut to start, and not say that more would come. Don't commit yourself to further cuts. Then the position could be reviewed in a year, and if you're right we can proceed to another reduction.

McCreevy cut him off. 'I'm not going to do it over five years,' he replied. 'I'm going to do it all in one go.' On Wednesday week. For good measure, the cut was effective from budget day forward; he didn't even wait for the Finance Bill.

The mandarins had never seen anything like it. It was the most extreme budgetary measure that anyone could remember. The officials would see more of this from McCreevy, but they would never quite get used to it.

McCreevy brought a potent combination to the finance minister's job. An accountant by profession, he was able, hard-working and absolutely committed to taxation reform – by which he meant significant cuts in all areas of taxation. According to one of his senior civil servants, McCreevy believed that high taxation had stifled the country, 'stifled its spirit'. He wanted to change that and he didn't know how long he was going to get to do it. So he went at it at with 'a terrific energy'.

This was another important characteristic: impatience. He didn't expect to be finance minister for five years, much less longer. He thought he would get 'two or three years' at it, he told friends. Whatever he wanted to do, he had to do it fast.

The finance minister had one further qualification for the job. He had an intimate understanding of the complex and often arcane architecture of the government accounting system. He had been given tutorials in the system when he was minister for social welfare by a mid-ranking civil servant famed for her detailed knowledge of the workings of government finances, known to everyone as 'Handbag'. McCreevy spotted her capabilities early during his period in the department, and he learned as much as he could from her. He knew more about the system than the rest of the ministers put together, and more than most officials. 'He was the strongest personality in there, bar none. And there was no question of government policy that he didn't have an informed view on,' says a cabinet member from the time.

In the Department of Finance, they had never seen anything like McCreevy. It became clear from an early stage to his officials that unlike almost every occupant of the minister's office in Merrion Street, McCreevy didn't want to be taoiseach, and didn't want to use the office to become taoiseach. He just wanted to be minister for finance. 'He really ran the place. He'd be at his desk at seven or half seven in the morning and he was on top of every-thing. As far as I could see there was very little political direction coming from the Taoiseach's office. It was all about McCreevy, and what he wanted. All the tax stuff was him,' one official said later.

His ebullient manner and impatient attitude became a trade-mark. He greeted everyone as 'mister' or 'officer', and sought counsel and opinion from throughout the department before ignoring it. He would call officials down to his office and say, 'I was talking to a fella in Kildare at the weekend and he said if we did this, it would result in that. What would you think of that now, officer? Would that work now, would it?'

The Department of Finance officials were constantly asking him, 'Minister, have you discussed this with the Taoiseach?' He would dismiss their concerns with an insouciant 'Oh yeah, I will, I will'. Sometimes he did, sometimes he didn't.

He refused to be distracted by convention or diverted by advice. A few nights before one of his budgets, whilst he and his senior officials put the finishing touches to the document before printing, the fax machine was 'going crazy' in his office, as request followed advice, following special pleading, flowed in. The machine was beeping constantly with these vital – to the senders anyway – communications. 'What can I do to stop that bloody thing?' the minister demanded. One of the officials answered, 'Well, minister, you could plug it out.' 'Plug it out, so,' McCreevy replied. So they did.

His work rate and attention to detail became legendary in the Department of Finance and throughout the public service.

In many departments, officials would say that they often didn't see too much of Fianna Fáil ministers. Tuesday, Wednesday maybe a bit of Thursday, that'd be it. Not McCreevy. 'We were amazed that he spent so little time in the constituency,' said one official. They called him a 'five-day minister'. He once explained to one of his civil servants who enquired about his lack of attention to his constituency: 'I pissed off so many of my constituents in the first half of my career that I decided to keep as far away from them as possible during the second half.' On the day of the 2002 general election, he was in his office in Merrion Street.

McCreevy's first budget, delivered by him on 3 December 1997, was a signpost to where he intended to bring economic policy.

The lower and higher rates of income tax came down by two points each; corporation tax on many businesses was reduced, part of the planned reduction to 12.5 per cent; capital gains tax was halved, allowances were increased and social welfare payments went up. But there was no doubt about the character of it: it was a tax-cutting budget. The tax cutting would cost £500 million, reported the *Irish Times*; the social welfare package just one fifth of this. On the opposition benches, Ruairi Quinn declared that it showed the 'clear ideological gulf across Leinster House'. Damn right, thought McCreevy.

The Progressive Democrats were cock-a-hoop, and briefed the media like crazy about how involved in the budget discussions they had been. This was rubbish. Nobody had been involved in the budget discussions at cabinet because there weren't any; McCreevy had prepared it on his own, without reference to cabinet. He simply briefed them on the morning about what was in it. He did keep Harney advised about his intentions, and the Progressive Democrats had 'a shopping list' every year; but the budget tax package was something that McCreevy always kept *in pectore* until the last minute.

There were discussions between McCreevy and Ahern in 1997 – fractious discussions. It was the first serious test of their relationship since the formation of the government and it centred on the size of the social welfare package, which Ahern wanted to increase and McCreevy wanted to keep down. In the end, Ahern mostly got his way, and the increases in the old age pension and social welfare payments were substantial – and substantially more than McCreevy had intended. According to several sources with knowledge of the exchanges between the two men, Ahern effectively forced his finance minister to allocate more money for social welfare spending. Ultimately, he did so by sending a letter to McCreevy on the Friday before the budget stipulating what he wanted the social welfare increases to be. McCreevy, realizing that he had pushed the envelope rather too far, acquiesced, but only on condition that any copies of the letter were collected and sent to him. The few people who had been circulated with copies complied, except the social welfare minister, Dermot Ahern, who kept his copy.

Arguably, this relative generosity was also one of the reasons for the largely benign reception that the budget received in much of the media. But if the welfare package was a defeat for McCreevy, it was one in which he conducted a strategic retreat. Because he had learned a very valuable lesson, one that he would apply in future budgets. It was this: as long as he kept his Taoiseach happy with social welfare increases, he was free to remake the tax system. 'That was really how Charlie bought Bertie off,' concludes one formerly high-ranking official. McCreevy's realization that he could do this was to change Irish society.

The constitutional relationship between the Taoiseach and the minister for finance is somewhat ambiguous on budgetary independence, though McCreevy was subsequently fond of pointing out that he was a constitutional officer like the Taoiseach, the only member of cabinet to enjoy such status. McCreevy wasn't shy about exercising his influence and his walk-in privileges to the Taoiseach's office. He would occasionally tell advisers and staff that he needed time with the Taoiseach alone; sometimes he could be brusque. 'I was often told get the fuck out by Charlie,' remembers one staff member, though not unfondly. Politically, finance ministers have enjoyed significant though varying degrees of independence in the formulation of their budgets; nobody pushed the boat out as much as McCreevy did.

He excluded Ahern almost completely from the formulation of many of the details of economic policy and completely from taxation policy. There is unanimity among people involved intimately with the process at a high level that McCreevy did not disclose the content of his budget tax packages to Ahern until almost the last minute – a few days, or sometimes the day before their delivery. He did enough to reassure Ahern about the content of the social welfare package, but the tax reforms that were McCreevy's lasting legacy – and which changed Irish society profoundly – he did not discuss or agree with Ahern in advance. He would call to St Luke's on the Sunday or Monday before a Wednesday budget and show Ahern what he intended to do, the full extent of the tax package, at which stage, it was too late to change it. In the first year, he did this because he wanted, after Ahern's letter, to emphasize his independence; subsequently, he did it because he got away with it then.

On one occasion before one of his early budgets, McCreevy called at St Luke's with the first printed copy of his speech. He gave it to the Taoiseach, and said, 'I'm going out for a walk. I'll be back in twenty minutes. See if you're happy with that.' When he returned, the two men discussed it for a while, and then McCreevy took it back from Ahern. It was an astonishing way to treat the Taoiseach.

One finance official recalled, 'We'd be working through the last few weekends. You'd be in at half six or seven in the morning. Then it would be finished – but the Taoiseach's office didn't seem to know what was coming.' The same finance official, bringing the finished copy of the budget over to the Taoiseach's office, gave the document to Ahern's special adviser Martin Mansergh on the morning the speech was to be delivered. Mansergh read through the text and suddenly looked alarmed. 'We're cutting taxes by *this* much?' he asked the official. 'Well, yeah,' was the reply.

One of Ahern's senior advisers at the time said cautiously, 'I'm not sure the extent to which McCreevy let Bertie Ahern into his confidence about what he was doing.' Others are more forthright about the nature of the relationship between the Taoiseach and the finance minister. According to a senior cabinet member, Ahern seemed to have little input into not just the budgets – apart from social welfare spending – but broader economic policy during the 1997–2002 government. 'I wouldn't think Bertie was involved at all in economic policy,' the minister told me.

It gradually became clear to Ahern's staff – and the rest of his cabinet – that he had effectively allowed McCreevy and Harney to assume control of the most important parts of government policy-making. 'Yes, Charlie ran economic policy with Harney all right,' admits one of his most senior advisers, 'though Bertie was very strong on the social partnership stuff.'

Ahern's senior political officials in that first government – Jackie Gallagher, Joe Lennon, Paddy Duffy, Gerry Hickey – would come to St Luke's on Monday mornings for a meeting with Ahern about the coming week. Usually, on budget week, Ahern would be in a position to tell them what was coming in the budget and they would discuss how to prepare for it. The political staff, wary of landmines in the text, were always desperate to know. On one occasion, Gerry Hickey was in St Luke's when McCreevy called to brief Ahern and leave the speech with him for half an hour. Hickey rang Government Buildings and hissed urgently at another staffer, 'I'm going to read this very quickly – take down as much of it as you can!'

On the morning of budget day, the cabinet met in Government Buildings for a breakfast, where McCreevy would brief them on the general thrust of his plans, omitting the exact detail of the speech he would deliver to the Dáil that afternoon. Nothing could be changed at this stage; the document was being printed. Ministers knew this and were under no illusions – they weren't being consulted, they were being given a heads-up. Later in the day, around lunchtime, officials from the Department of Finance would conduct a more detailed briefing for ministers. McCreevy never bothered to attend.

But if McCreevy was keeping Ahern in the dark about what exactly his intentions were to reform the tax system, he and Harney kept in close contact. They were personally as well as politically close, and had been for years. McCreevy almost joined the PDs at their foundation and despite his last-minute decision to stay with Fianna Fáil, their friendship and shared political outlook grew. They holidayed together, and socialized frequently, part of a group that included the *Irish Times* journalist Renagh Holohan and Labour MEP Bernie Malone. They were a tight-knit group, and no one was closer than Harney and McCreevy.

McCreevy knew what Harney would think about things without having to ring her. She was the same. He would often say to Ahern, 'Oh, Harney will never stand for that,' even without talking to her.

Harney shared McCreevy's assumption that they would get a few years at best to implement their policy agenda. Though it seems pessimistic in hindsight, the shared expectation that the coalition would last at best two or three years was not an unreasonable supposition given the history of Fianna Fáil coalition governments. Therefore, they reasoned, the reforms of the tax system had to be front-loaded; if they waited until the fourth of fifth year of the government's term, they might never see it.

Harney and McCreevy were the axis on which the government's economic policy turned. They set out to remake the tax system, incentivize business and transform the economy, and were prepared to get around Ahern if they had to. In fact, they found it pretty easy.

The two never sat down and discussed overtly how to pull the wool over Ahern's eyes as a long-term strategy; in any event, they found it unnecessary. But they did frequently discuss how best to approach him on an issue, and which of them should do it. 'Will you raise it with him or will I?' Harney would say to McCreevy. They learned rapidly that when the two of them were united on an issue – as they almost always were – they nearly always got their way.

★

The virtual control of economic policy that Harney and McCreevy exercised was strangely unremarked upon, though the fact is that much of government, and the manner in which policy decisions are arrived at, remains shrouded in secrecy. Partly that's because people aren't asking questions about it, and because of the inability of a daily news schedule to deal with longer-term policy stories; partly it's because that's the way the system likes it. Initially, Harney and McCreevy didn't even think of it in those terms themselves. About a year and a half into the first administration, the former Progressive Democrat general secretary, Stephen O'Byrnes, still an influential figure in the party, told Harney that a businessman asked him about it at dinner one night: how did Mary Harney and Charlie McCreevy get to be running the economy? At the time, Harney hadn't really thought about it like that, but she was flattered. But the more she thought about it, the more she knew it was true.

Why did Ahern allow it? Without any strong ideological objections to their approach or any other, Ahern appeared happy with whatever worked, and wasn't overly concerned about the way the enormous tax cuts were reshaping government economic policy. The economy was booming, and there were enough short-term problems that required his attention. Some ministers quietly worried that it was a shift to the right that was out of step with Fianna Fáil's traditions, but because Ahern was ensuring that the social spending was keeping pace with the expansion in the government's revenues, they felt they had little to complain about. And they felt that Ahern was happy with whatever worked politically. More than one came to the same conclusion as the minister who told me: 'I don't think he gave a shit that he didn't control economic policy.' Another says: 'Bertie was happy. The economy was going very well. And if there was ever a man with an instinct for not fixing things that were not broken, it was Bertie Ahern.'

'What Charlie used to do before budgets,' explains another cabinet minister, 'is he'd ask Bertie, "Now do you have 'ere a little project that you want?", and Bertie would have a few things in his own constituency that he wanted funding for and he'd get it. Bertie would be delighted, and McCreevy would then write the rest of the budget according to what he wanted.'

It's an overly simplistic view of the relationship and of the way the two men interacted, but there is a grain of truth in it. As Denis Coghlan of the *Irish Times* observed after the first coalition budget, 'Mr Bertie Ahern's fingerprints were absent from the document until Mr McCreevy got around to announcing a £20 million development grant for Croke Park, located in the heart of the Taoiseach's own constituency.'

As he prepared his first budget, McCreevy was tuning an engine that was about to roar. For the *Economist* magazine, Ireland was 'Europe's Shining Light', a booming economy committed to lowering taxation and controlling public spending. Two days after the 1998 budget, the government reported that the Live Register numbers had fallen again, now coming in at under 10 per cent for the first time in twenty years. Within a few years, unemployment would fall to 4 per cent – virtually full employment, despite a rapid growth in population and, later, massive immigration. By the end of 1998, just a year and a half after the government had taken office, unemployment had fallen to just 6 per cent. Economic growth that year was nearly 9 per cent. This was astonishing progress for any country, and it was not just because of the Good Friday Agreement that the government's satisfaction rating in opinion polls that year ranged from 68 per cent to 73 per cent.

In the years between 1996 and 2000, economic growth in Ireland averaged 8.5 per cent per annum; the average for the EU was less than 2.5 per cent; for the Organisation for Economic Co-operation and Development (OECD) it was less than 3 per cent. Ireland had become an international star performer.

Tax revenues exploded. In the Department of Finance, where they received daily updates on the tax take, they were flummoxed as their forecasts were smashed and then revised forecasts were smashed again. 'We couldn't believe it,' says one official, 'because it was unbelievable.' McCreevy was clear what he wanted to do with it: he wanted to return it to taxpayers. He assumed that they would be suitably grateful.

But tax policy wasn't the only thing that would turbo-charge the Irish economy. McCreevy was about to make a decision that would have arguably an even greater effect on the economy than any of his budget renovations. Europe was getting ready for the euro, and Ireland was on board the train.

McCreevy had warned in opposition that joining the euro should the British decide to stay out could create 'immense problems', especially for exporters. But as minister for finance, he knew that not joining had become a political impossibility.

The Irish government had committed as far back as the Maastricht Treaty of 1992 to join the single currency, and all parties had committed to joining the European Monetary Union (EMU) in their manifestos for the 1997 general election. The question that faced McCreevy in the first months of 1998 was at what exchange rate Ireland should join. In other words: how many euros should Irish consumers receive for their punts? Too high a rate would pour money into the economy and risked sparking inflation; too low would act as a brake on the economy and make imports more expensive – also risking inflationary pressures.

Ireland's central rate within the exchange rate mechanism was 2.41 Deutschmarks, though at the start of the year it had been trading considerably above that rate, at about 2.50 DM and slightly higher. The assumption, however, among most commentators was that the 2.41 European Exchange Rate Mechanism (ERM) rate – and the D-mark was the anchor of the whole euro project – would be observed. A higher rate would, after all, effectively involve a revaluation of the currency, for which there was little justification in a rapidly growing economy. The debates raged throughout the early months of 1998: as is often the case in Ireland, they were conducted in terms of which groups would win or lose – a higher rate put more euros in people's pockets, while a lower rate would give a boost to competitiveness, and was favoured by farmers and other exporters. Either way, it was a decision that would have huge consequences for ordinary people. It wasn't entirely up to McCreevy to decide Ireland's rate – it would be agreed with the finance ministers and the emerging European Central Bank apparatus – but his attitude would be crucial. Ireland was good at getting what it wanted in Europe.

Characteristically, McCreevy kept his deliberations to himself. He figured that he would get 'one bite at this cherry', he told friends later, and resolved to keep his thoughts to himself. To those who enquired about his thinking, he cited what he called the 'Mickey Doherty experience'. Doherty was a loyal Fianna Fáil retainer of Albert Reynolds in Longford, who had offhandedly responded to reporters' questions about the whereabouts of the then Taoiseach in the hours after the election disaster in 1992. Reynolds had gone home for a cup of tea, but Doherty, loath to reveal the prime ministerial prandials, told reporters that he had gone back to Dublin to sort out something about the currency, which was then undergoing a period of great volatility within the European ERM. When the reports hit the newswires, the Irish pound dropped 4 pfennigs against the Deutschmark. So McCreevy kept in mind the Mickey Doherty experience, and said nothing to anybody about the currency. In fact, he said little about any policy matters either. With some delight that conveyed a measure of his disdain for most of the media, he described it as his 'button lip' policy.

'If I signal what my preferred rate would be, I would simply be giving licence to the financial community to make a lot of money,' the finance minister told an Oireachtas committee in February. He would continue, he said, his policy of 'the less said the better'. Senior officials, most of whom had experience of the devaluation trauma of 1992–3, told his press secretary, Mandy Johnston, secrecy was paramount. Under no circumstances could the minister's thinking or intentions be revealed, as they would open up huge speculative possibilities. Currency policy, they told her, was the one area where she absolutely had to lie. If only they knew, she thought: Charlie would have her lying to the press on anything that suited him.

The joke in government circles was that McCreevy's press officers had to have several ways of telling the press to fuck off. There was much truth to it. His advice to Mary Harney when the press enquired about her controversial holiday arrangements (she and McCreevy were staying in airline tycoon Ulick McEvaddy's villa in Provence at a time when McEvaddy was seeking to build a second terminal at Dublin Airport) was, 'Tell them to fuck off. F–U–C–K O–F–F.' Another of his press officers thought that *Morning Ireland* used to ring seeking an interview simply as a charade to amuse themselves. He stopped telling his boss in advance when the programme was looking for him. He would mention it later. '*Morning Ireland* rang looking for you to go on, minister.' 'What did you say?' 'I told them to fuck off, minister.' 'Good man.'

Opposition politicians complained bitterly that McCreevy's secrecy on the currency was a denial of their democratic rights, and many resented the fact that senior officials were kept in the loop about the EMU intentions, while democratically elected politicians were not. They needn't have worried. McCreevy didn't tell his officials about his thoughts either. Nor did he discuss it with the cabinet.

McCreevy wasn't too worried about losing control of Irish monetary policy, seeing it as more theoretical rather than practical independence – in effect, Ireland largely had to follow British interest-rate movements. What was clear was that Irish rates would have to come down substantially to enter: at the beginning of the year, German rates stood at 3.3 per cent; the Irish Central Bank's rate was 6.25 per cent. Clearly, the movement was going to be on the Irish side, prompting what one commentator predicted would be a 'wall of money' hitting the Irish economy.

The decisions weren't just economic calculations: they were also political. Within the general band that a currency might operate in against the euro – or the D-mark before it – fixing a rate at the higher end of the scale would offer a country an advantage – exchanging its currency for more euros than might strictly be warranted. McCreevy knew that the German Bundesbank president, Hans Titmeyer, believed that Ireland had a competitive advantage even at the 'resolved' 2.41 rate after devaluation in 1993.

In fact, McCreevy had decided that a rate of around the €2.50 mark (to the D-mark) represented the best option, and would act as a further stimulus towards his primary goal of economic growth. Quietly, on a weekend in March, he sent his officials, led by assistant secretary Tom Considine, to Brussels to negotiate a revaluation of the Irish pound within the ERM. That would be the base for the eventual euro rate of 1.27.

It wasn't true that McCreevy had spoken to nobody about it. He had, after a fashion, spoken to Bertie Ahern about it. The decisive conversation took place the previous Sunday. McCreevy rang Ahern and told him: 'I need to see you.'

It was during the campaign for the Dublin North by-election, caused by the resignation from the Dáil of Ray Burke the previous October. The government would lose it (and the Limerick East contest held the same day following the death of Jim Kemmy), but Ahern, as usual, was campaigning hard.

'I'll be at an after-mass meeting in Garristown,' Ahern replied. Grand, replied McCreevy. I'll come over to you. He hadn't a clue where Garristown was, but his driver located the church and he met Ahern as he came out of mass.

'I'm going to do the currency this week,' McCreevy told him simply.

'OK, great,' Ahern replied. 'Have you told the Tánaiste?' 'No, but I will.' The rate wasn't mentioned. Cabinet wasn't told when it met later that week. Nobody was. The revaluation was announced after the officials' meeting in Brussels the following Saturday, and it was made clear that there would be no further changes to the ERM rates. Ireland would join the euro at a rate just shy of 2.49 DM, translating to the 1.27 rate. The agreement on the rate was a success for McCreevy, but more significant than the rate was the near-halving of Irish interest rates that would take place over the coming months.

On the Monday following the meeting, the newspapers reported the accidental death of the Cork TD Hugh Coveney, who drowned after a fall from a cliff near his home in Cork. But the main headline on page one of the *Irish Times* focused on the weekend's momentous decision: 'Push for fall in interest rates following revaluation'. McCreevy's tiger economy had just received another shot in the arm. He would later reflect to friends that this decision probably contributed as much to the Celtic Tiger as any single policy.

Few ministers were upset at being kept in the dark about the currency decisions; they had got used to McCreevy's secretive approach, and anyway, few of them understand the complex architecture constructed to underpin monetary union. Though they might have cavilled if they had heard McCreevy's insistences to Ahern – 'It's too complex to bring to government,' he told him.

However, one of the Taoiseach's advisers, Gerry Hickey, was greatly put out when the decision was announced. He had briefed a journalist who had asked on Friday that nothing involving the Irish rate would be decided that weekend. So upset was he at having – albeit inadvertently – misled the journalist that he threatened to resign to Ahern – a fact which McCreevy, when he heard about it, found hysterically funny. The finance minister had little time for what he felt was Hickey's overreaction. Ahern mollified Hickey as only he could – displaying the complete lack of ego, allied to a willingness to bend the truth beyond its normal breaking point, that could defuse almost any situation. 'Ah, Gerry,' Ahern told him when the revaluation was reported in the newspapers, 'sure I didn't know about it until this morning!'

Ahern might have been bluffing to Hickey, but he would soon be complaining bitterly about being really kept in the dark.

McCreevy's second budget followed the same pattern as the first, restructuring the tax system profoundly with the introduction of a system of tax credits and reducing taxes (though not cutting rates) for all. 'The Minister,' wrote Jane Suiter in the *Irish Times*, 'managed to deliver on significant tax cuts, spending increases and more investment, as well as paying a large chunk of the national debt.' Even the unions were happy.

One of the effects of the change to the system of tax credits was that it made it easier to use budgets to achieve specific policy goals. Exactly what McCreevy had in mind was revealed in the following year's budget when he introduced one of the most controversial measures of his entire tenure: the 'individualization' of the tax code. Essentially, this meant changing the tax code to favour two-income families – incentivizing married women, who otherwise might have stayed at home to look after children in many cases, to join the workforce. Conversely, it meant that if women chose not enter employment, they could feel they were being discriminated against for staying at home.

That was exactly how it appeared to George Lee, RTÉ's economics correspondent, who, in a remarkable appearance on the station's six o'clock television news, denounced the proposal as 'Thatcherite' and one of the most regressive budget measures he had ever seen. Later on another news programme, Lee raged that McCreevy was trying to 'twist the tax system against one-income families'. 'It's about society and what this budget is likely to do to the way we live in this country ... Family operations are likely to be changed by this.' And not in a good way. Government ministers and their advisers, watching Lee apparently quivering with anger, were taken aback. It couldn't be that a billion-euro giveaway, which slashed tax rates again and put more money in everyone's pockets, was going to blow up in their faces. Could it?

Lee's intervention was cathartic. Although the following day's newspapers were full of glee – 'Everyone's a winner: tax perks for all but two-salary families hit the jackpot' trumpeted the *Irish Independent* – the airwaves soon filled with outrage about the disadvantage to single-income families. McCreevy pleaded that no one was being disadvantaged by the move, but it was intended to compensate working mothers for the costs – such as childcare –

of going out to work. He was fighting a losing battle. Portrayed as an attack on stay-at-home mothers, the landmine at the heart of the budget exploded under the government's feet. Fianna Fáil back-benchers scuttled to the microphones, demanding that the minister revise his plans.

As usual, McCreevy had previously received plenty of advice from his officials warning him about what he was about to do. As usual he ignored it and went ahead anyway. On individualization, he was especially bullish. He told his officials about families he knew in Kildare, with both parents working to pay the mortgage, and consequently being crucified by childcare costs, and compared them to well-heeled women in Dalkey, heading out to play tennis in the morning. Why should there be the same tax treatment for playing tennis and then getting your hair done as there was for working full-time? Like the high rates of personal taxation that he was bringing down, it appeared to him that it was as much about justice and equality as economic philosophy.

But his officials continued to warn about the possible political consequences when people didn't see it like that. One frank official with whom he had developed a healthy understanding, and who was both good at reading McCreevy and canny enough not to show it too obviously, discussed the possible political fall-out with him a few days before the budget. In response to the minister's brash pre-budget predictions that the individualization measure would be popular among women and the plain people of Ireland, the official told him frankly: 'Minister, you have no idea how this is going to go. It could go any way.'

A few days after the budget, McCreevy complained to him: 'Jaysus, whatever happened, I didn't think I was going to be accused of ruining marriages and wrecking homes!'

His colleagues were accusing him of wrecking the government. On the night after the budget, with the public and political outcry gathering volume, Ahern told the annual Cairde Fáil dinner that the budget was 'a real contribution to equal status'. But he knew it was also a real contribution to blowing the political gains not just of a giveaway budget but also of the historic developments in the North, where the executive was finally up and running. After his staunch defence of the budget, Ahern mingled among his TDs, many of whom were deeply uncomfortable about anything that could be construed as diminishing the status of women in the home, and more uncomfortable still about anything that might diminish their own status.

Despite his public defence, Ahern was already orchestrating the climbdown. Standing in the middle of the floor of the ball-room, he told Mary Hanafin, then a back-bench TD, to make herself available to the media the following day and ask for some compensation for stay-at-home mothers to be introduced to soften the effects of the budget changes.

The measure itself had been largely welcomed by the unions and by McCreevy's old foes in the Combat Poverty Agency, who described the controversy as affecting only 'the well-off taxpaying households'. But as the government was to discover, well-off taxpaying households are a vocal and determined group. They flooded the airwaves and the letters pages of newspapers. The lobbying of Fianna Fáil TDs over the post-budget weekend was intense, and even before TDs returned to Dublin, Ahern's political antennae had told him that a quick climbdown was the easiest way out of the hole.

McCreevy remained insistent about his policy, but he could see the political inevitability. He told back-benchers: 'I wouldn't like to be going into war with you guys. I'd have to keep looking behind me.' A week after the budget, he announced a partial climbdown, conceding a special allowance for stay-at-home spouses, though it contradicted the logic of the move. In the *Irish Times*, Mark Brennock observed, 'The result is a highly in-coherent policy, with the tax system now giving an incentive to spouses of taxpayers on the standard rate band to stay out of the paid workforce, while encouraging spouses of top-rate taxpayers to join it. This is because spouses of standard-rate tax-payers will lose £660 if they take up paid employment, while spouses of top-rate taxpayers will gain £1,200 by taking the same step.'

Ahern was furious that the political opportunity of a giveaway budget had been blown, and he was angry with his finance minister. He complained to Mary O'Rourke that McCreevy had never told him about it. 'He never confided in me. The minister for finance is supposed to work with the Taoiseach. I knew nothing about it until the day.'

Despite the embarrassing public climbdown, the individualization project was to have a secret sequel the following year. McCreevy further extended the same tax changes in the 2001 budget – delivered in December of 2000 – which allowed families where both parents worked to be assessed individually and advantageously. Though on this occasion he simply didn't say he was doing it. One oblique reference to the measure was included in the budget speech, and nowhere was the word individualization mentioned.

Prior to the budget, one amazed and nervous official asked the minister, 'Minister, are you really going to do this again?'

'Didn't I do it last year?'

'Are you going to tell them in the speech?'

'No, I'm not going to use the actual words. But I am going to do it.'

None of the opposition and only one commentator understood that the individualization project was continuing. Garret Fitzgerald, writing in the *Irish Times* a few days later, professed himself incredulous that nobody had noticed it. Fitzgerald was almost breathless at McCreevy's gumption. 'He actually had the nerve,' the former Taoiseach spluttered, 'to hide an increase from £34,000 to £40,000 in the standard-rate income tax band for double-earning married couples by suggesting that it was a relief for taxpayers with incomes just above the average industrial wage . . .' Fitzgerald went on to explain in some typical – and even less pithy – terms how the budget change would leave double-income-earner families £1,100 better off than a single-income family on the same salary.

McCreevy had guessed that if he simply avoided using the term individualization, nobody would notice what he was doing.

With the exception of Garret, he was entirely right. Fitzgerald observed: 'No one else but Charlie McCreevy would have attempted such a con trick.' Needless to say, McCreevy was delighted at this.

But Ahern wasn't the only member of the cabinet who was angry with McCreevy over the individualization fiasco. Dissatisfaction at his high-handed approach to restraining government spending whilst giving priority to his own tax-cutting agenda had been growing among ministers for some time.

McCreevy had promised not just to run a current budget surplus but to limit the spending growth to 4 per cent. This sounded fine in 1997, but as the money flowed into the coffers, it began to look pretty parsimonious to many ministers. McCreevy bowed to pressure and began to loosen spending policy, but he never satisfied his colleagues. The muttering about him began early, and never really went away. This is the lot of all finance ministers; but in the case of McCreevy there was an extra edge to it. Many ministers felt he was dismissive of them, arrogant, aloof. Some also felt there was an inside track with him. Some ministers were more equal than others.

'Charlie had a very clear view of what he wanted to do with tax from the word go. But not with spending,' one insider told me. 'He had no strategic sense of what he wanted to do with spending.' With a growing economy and population, spending growth was inevitable, said another. 'But Charlie had no real engagement with it.'

'Many of us felt that there was more money available for Charlie's pet tax projects than there was for party policy,' reflected one minister later. At the time, their grumbles were sharper. 'He's treating us like mushrooms,' hissed one to his colleagues. He meant they were being kept in the dark and having manure poured over them. 'The minister for finance has to control things, but he doesn't have to act as if he owns the government. We stood for Fianna Fáil, not for Charlie McCreevy,' complained another.

McCreevy's tight control over their budgets made ministers

chafe at how McCreevy was deciding the priorities for government spending. They felt that there was a certain amount of money available to the government, but that one man was personally deciding where a large chunk of it would be spent. 'Nobody had an ideological problem with tax cuts, but we had a big problem with them in terms of where they came in our list of priorities,' said one political adviser. 'Charlie's tax cuts in 1999 and 2000 were over the top and irresponsible. The last thing the country needed was tax cuts,' he recalls.

When they learned of the 1999 tax cuts, several of the cabinet were enraged by them. 'Inflation once again,' one muttered, in a refrain that echoed around government whenever dissatisfaction with McCreevy was aired. That annoyance increased with every 'Champagne Charlie' headline.

'There were times when the only one around the cabinet table who disagreed with a proposal to spend money was Charlie,' says one minister, close to McCreevy but in sympathy with some of the criticism of him. 'The only one around the table! And he wouldn't release money. After a while, there was a lot of resentment about it.'

Every so often, a minister would try to bounce McCreevy into agreeing something at cabinet by leaking a story about its impending approval to the Sunday papers, or to the daily papers on the morning of cabinet. Almost on a point of principle, McCreevy would then seek to block it at the cabinet.

He adopted various devices to restrain public spending, varying from insisting that contrary to appearances, the exchequer was actually very tight for money, to blank refusal. Even some of his policy monuments like the National Pension Reserve Fund and the SSIA saving scheme seemed contrived as ways to get around giving ministers what they wanted. One official describes it as 'simply a way of keeping money away from ministers'. The SSIAs were a different response to a similar problem. 'I want to give people more of their own money,' McCreevy told officials. 'But I want them to save some of it.'

★

But despite his bluster about restraining spending, McCreevy was quite content to acquiesce with Ahern's preferences for large social welfare increases for pensioners, child benefit, widows and other groups. Irish welfare provision quickly rose to one of the most generous in Europe. He committed the government to tripling child benefit over three budgets; old age pensions increased similarly sharply. The volume of spending increased hugely. Despite the popularly repeated mantra that the economic boom had massively widened the gap between rich and poor, a study by the ESRI, the economic think-tank, concluded that inequality did not 'uniformly or substantially increase during the boom'.

The analysis, by Brian Nolan, showed that while government budgetary policy contributed to a small widening of the gap between rich and poor in 1998–2000, the budgets in 2001–2 had the opposite effect. In another study, the ESRI found that the numbers in consistent poverty fell from 11 per cent of the population in 1997 to 6 per cent in 2000.

But it suited McCreevy politically to keep the perception of him as favouring the rich, the business sector. 'You have to have an enemy,' he told friends. He was happy to number the 'poverty industry', the left and the *Irish Times* among his.

One minister complained that the government was spending more on social services than any of them had ever thought possible. 'But we were constantly being told that we were right wing. Of course, Charlie loved that.'

But if McCreevy was happy to increase old age pensions and children's allowances – though electoral considerations were on his mind at the same time as his social conscience – he was explicitly determined to keep down the rate of unemployment benefits. He wanted to keep a substantial gap between the dole and the sort of living one could expect in even the lowest rank of employment; he believed that if that financial incentive weren't there, there was a feckless class of people who would be happy to live on benefits. He intended to look after both sides of that gap – not just taking the low-paid out of the tax net, but also minimizing increases to unemployment benefit. He didn't just believe in carrot: he believed in stick.

He was also happy to play politics with the economic cycle. As the coalition government moved into the second half of its life, he began to bow to spending pressures. He received a memo from one government adviser – copied to the Taoiseach – which began: 'It's time for the minister for finance to rejoin Fianna Fáil . . .' McCreevy was savvy enough to know that an impending election – and he was by no means sure that he could persuade Bertie Ahern to wait until 2002 – would change the political calculus of the government's spending plans. He had always been preparing for this shift. As far back as 1997, he had criticized Ruairi Quinn's election year budget, telling an interviewer, 'No matter what the minister says at the cabinet table, they [ministers] will not listen in a year of an election. I understand the politics, but throwing money into a rapidly growing economy and adding fuel to the fire is extraordinary.'

McCreevy wasn't just prepared to add fuel to the fire; he was prepared to throw petrol on it.

6. Showtime!

'OK, folks, it's showtime!'

PJ Mara swept to the front of the ballroom in the Shelbourne Hotel, raised his arms and addressed the rows of journalists, cameras, ministers, aides and hangers-on. Outside, the sun shone brilliantly on St Stephen's Green. Inside, the speakers boomed as the big screen flashed into life showing the forthcoming Fianna Fáil party political broadcast. 'All together now! All together now!' sang The Farm, as images of the bright new Ireland created by Fianna Fáil and Bertie Ahern appeared before an occasionally startled audience. 'All together now!' Then somewhat incongruously: 'In no-man's-land!' The general election campaign was on.

The tone and the look of the party political broadcast was unsurprising to anyone who knew that Fianna Fáil had spent years studying the methods and tactics of Tony Blair's New Labour. The broadcast was emblematic of the entire campaign to come: concentrating on the feel-good factor; emphasizing the achievements of the government. The none-too-subtle message: why in the name of God would you want to change the government now?

Like much else in that campaign, the party's broadcast was hailed as a huge success; but it wasn't quite as smooth as it looked. A previous version of the broadcast had been made by the party, centring on Ahern and featuring – among other things – footage of him tending to his hanging baskets. Known to the staff as 'Bertie: the Movie', it was dispatched to RTÉ before it had been tested in front of a focus group. When the results of the focus group came back, they were disastrous. Nobody swallowed the guff about Ahern and the hanging baskets. The Taoiseach was certainly a huge asset to the Fianna Fáil campaign – but there was a limit to what voters would put up with. They knew he was an ordinary fella, but that wasn't enough any more. The broadcast was recalled and a new one put together hastily. Fianna Fáil campaign managers expected the old broadcast – with the hanging baskets – to surface during the campaign, but incredibly, to their minds, RTÉ appeared to have handed back their only copy. But then, in 2002, Fianna Fáil got all the breaks. It was Fine Gael, by contrast, that would soon find itself in no-man's-land.

The choice of the Shelbourne for the launch was apposite. The venue for the drafting of the constitution of the Irish Free State, it was a haven of old gentility and respectability lately colonized by the brash new Ireland. The hotel's famous Horseshoe Bar heaved with new money that spilled across the lobby into the newish side bar, its high walls adorned with Martyn Turner caricatures of politicians from the 1980s and early 1990s. If the cartoons poked ridicule at the stewards of political failure, the inhabitants of the bar (and the inflated prices it charged) bore testimony to the political and economic success of Ireland in the millennium. It was congested, sweaty, exorbitantly priced. It was the place to see and be seen.

The Showtime election was the one that most accurately summed up the approach of Fianna Fáil to politics during the Ahern era, meticulously researched and tested in focus groups, limited in its policy proposals: a giveaway government grown fat on spectacular economic growth wooed a contented public with massive spending increases and goodies in the pot for any interest group that sought them loudly enough, all set against a weak opposition and reported by an ineffective, often frustrated media. There was practically no policy debate; it soon became clear that the only question was whether the country trusted Fianna Fáil enough to see the party in government on its own. Fianna Fáil ran a slick and professional campaign in which it was clear that it would say and do almost anything to win. End hospital waiting lists? No problem. Medical cards for the elderly? Say no more. They didn't need any of the gimmicks, but they did them anyway. In a three-week period, the 2002 campaign told the story of the politics of Bertie Ahern's boomtime Ireland. And it left behind it, in the immediate post-election period, a political and economic hangover of enormous proportions.

The Fianna Fáil hierarchy, people like Mara and McCreevy, knew they had picked the 1997 general election from the pocket of the Rainbow government. Proud though they were of that feat, they were determined that no such thievery would be required again. The work of building on the hugely successful new candidate selection strategy began afresh, and party general secretary Martin Mackin and Mara began a series of visits to local organizations. Latterly this was complemented by a renewed programme of local polling orchestrated by Sean Donnelly. The purpose of the polls was twofold: on the one hand they gave the party managers a picture of the relative political strengths of various candidates, and the viability of the various possible strategies and local divisions; on the other hand, the very existence of the polls strengthened the hand of the party headquarters in their efforts to manage the election tickets. The contest between what the local polls said and the wishes of the local organization was an ongoing and controversial one – sometimes the data (and the way they chose to interpret it) gave headquarters the excuse it needed to push through unpopular or difficult selections.

Constituency preparation was one part of an overall package. Another, more innovative and certainly more clandestine, was launched in 1999 by Peter MacDonagh, an adviser to education minister Micheál Martin, who would later join Ahern's staff in Government Buildings. It was a large project of qualitative and quantitative research, which MacDonagh believed could generate a considerable political advantage when it came to designing and preparing the general election campaign. A close observer of American politics where such techniques had been used extensively, MacDonagh also visited the New Labour election headquarters in London in 2001 with Mackin to study their methods. Mara immediately bought into the idea. Ahern was on for any strategy that could offer an electoral advantage.

The research project didn't just look at political issues and attitudes: it tried to paint a broader picture of the Irish public. 'Rather than just get a snapshot of who's up and who's down and where's the thermometer, we tried to tap into the mood of the public on a number of levels,' one insider told me for a post-campaign piece in *The Sunday Business Post*. The surveys and focus groups asked questions not just about political affiliation and support across a range of issues, but also about people's sense of themselves and the country, and how they had changed over the past few years. They surveyed attitudes to things like poverty and sense of community. 'The most striking thing to come out of it was that, politically, no one was talking to modern Ireland,' the source continued. 'Political discourse was stuck in a ya-boo-sucks mentality. Mr Angry from Sandymount [Ruairi Quinn] and [John] Bruton would stand up and attack Bertie [Ahern] in the Dáil or the media would attack him over something, but none of these attacks were having any effect. Why?'

The answer that the team came up with, I wrote then, was to have far-reaching consequences for how the campaign was eventually run, how its message was delivered and the level at which that message was pitched. 'We found the public had moved on from the discourse of the élite. They were being talked to in a language they didn't understand. The focus groups told us lots of important things – one of them was that we didn't have to respond to every charge and another is that there isn't a crisis every time the *Irish Times* says there's one.'

Liberating though this finding was, it didn't mean that there was no such thing as a crisis for the government. In fact, even as the economy thrived in the late 1990s, Bertie Ahern's government appeared to be determined to draw attention away from its successes with a series of self-inflicted wounds. One of them would almost derail the coalition.

In February 1999, Dublin legal circles began to hum with a rumour that was, even by the frequently unreliable standards of that forum, sensational. There had been untoward judicial interference in the premature release of a prisoner which could be explained only by political interference, it was claimed. Even more amazingly, when journalists began to investigate the story, they discovered that there was at least some truth to it. Philip Sheedy, a young Dublin architect, had been jailed in 1997 for dangerous driving causing death, having been drunk at the wheel of his car. He was sentenced to four years in prison in the Circuit Court, though the judge gave leave to apply for a review after two years. A year later, he was free. In a bizarre twist, he was seen on the street by a relative of the dead woman, who made inquiries with the gardaí. It emerged that the gardaí and the DPP had not been notified that the case had been – in a highly unusual move – relisted for hearing a year after the initial sentencing. At that hearing, the judge, Cyril Kelly, had suspended the remaining three years of the sentence.

The circumstances that led to Sheedy's release (he subsequently returned to prison) were to transfix the legal and political worlds for the following two months, and lead to the resignation of two judges and a court official. It would also cause the most serious wobble that the 1997–2002 coalition would endure.

Dáil inquiries revealed that a judge of the Supreme Court, Hugh O'Flaherty, had been approached by a sister of Philip Sheedy. He explained to her that her brother could seek to have the sentence reviewed, citing a recent precedent. Oddly, O'Flaherty didn't leave it at that. He summoned a court officer, the county registrar, and explained about the case to him. The registrar then sought out Sheedy's solicitor, who duly applied to have the case relisted. It was heard by the then Circuit Court judge, Cyril Kelly, without the state side being properly notified. In a hearing lasting no more than a few minutes, Judge Kelly ordered Sheedy's release. 'I have grave concerns in relation to his mental condition,' he said. And that was it. Except it wasn't.

The controversy was to cost Judges Kelly and O'Flaherty and the county registrar their jobs. If some had expected a white-wash by Law Library good ole boys, they were greatly mistaken. A highly critical report by the Chief Justice, Liam Hamilton, exposed conflicts of evidence between the two junior judges in the case – one of whom must perforce have not been telling the truth – and laid out very clear and damning criticisms of O'Flaherty. The government decided that if the judges did not resign, it would take the unprecedented step of removing the two men from their posts. The evidence assembled by the Chief Justice and by other inquiries, including one in the Department of Justice, was clear that both had acted improperly; but everywhere the suspicion mounted that the two men had actually discussed the case between themselves. If that was so, justice minister John O'Donoghue told one of his colleagues at lunch one day, 'Neither of them can ever admit it because it's a criminal offence.'

O'Donoghue was under immense pressure – not alone was he from the same Co. Kerry town of Cahersiveen as O'Flaherty, but the two men were personal friends. But to his credit, he played the affair with a straight bat; he told the cabinet the same thing: we don't know if they spoke about the case, but there is no doubt that they will not and cannot admit it if they did, because it is a criminal offence. 'But we cannot stand by and do nothing.'

If the legal side of the affair was causing turmoil, the politics was only a few weeks behind. For a while it seemed that there was a real danger the government would fall. Ahern had been approached by Sheedy's father, who wanted to enquire about early release for his son, and Ahern had passed the representation on to the Department of Justice. Allied to the fact that Ahern's friend Joe Burke had visited Sheedy in prison, this revelation, Ahern knew, could light a political tinderbox. He also knew he would have to tell Harney. Walking into the Dáil, Ahern, in a typical manoeuvre, casually mentioned to the Tánaiste that he, too, had made representations on Sheedy's behalf. 'You had better put that on the Dáil record,' she said. But Ahern said nothing about it.

A few days later, the *Sunday Tribune* reported Ahern's representations on its front page. After Ahern didn't put it on the record of the Dáil, Harney was annoyed. When the *Sunday Tribune* got wind of the story and splashed it all over their front page, she 'went bananas', according to one of his aides. She was in Donegal on official business and offered herself for a doorstep interview to RTÉ. Asked if the government could survive, she said, 'I don't know,' and walked away across a windswept car park. It was a pretty hammy dramatic gesture, but on television it was dynamite. In Dublin, the phones lit up across Government Buildings. The following day, a regular meeting of all the special advisers across government waited for the Progressive Democrat representatives. The political machine of the Ahern administration chatted worriedly among themselves, wondering how serious the rift between the two leaders really was. Then Gerry Hickey's phone rang, and he spoke briefly into it. It was Harney's adviser, Katherine Bulbulia: there would be no PD representatives attending. Nor would there be any PDs at the cabinet the following day. The feeling in the room was universal and instant: this means real trouble. One adviser asked Hickey what the prognosis was. He replied dejectedly: 'I don't know. We'll just have to see.'

Facing questions, Ahern twisted and weaved. He hadn't been asked to put it on the Dáil record, he had been asked to put it in the public domain. He had tried to do it in the Dáil, but couldn't find an opening. Then he had told a few journalists, he said. Anyway, if he had told the Dáil, it would have 'gone into its usual ballistic self and looked for a suspension of standing orders'. There would have been 'ructions'. 'It's a lot of nonsense,' he told reporters. One of the political staff was looking out the window on to the forecourt of Government Buildings when they saw Ahern come out for the 'doorstep' interview. The adviser knew no line had been agreed, and whatever Ahern was saying, it was likely to make things worse.

He was babbling now, and it looked increasingly as though the government was on the brink of collapse. Harney was livid. Seeing the danger, McCreevy tried to mediate between the two. His first task was to ensure things didn't get any worse. Don't say or do anything, he told Harney on the phone. He went around to the Department of Enterprise and Employment on

Kildare Street and the two disappeared into her office. 'I can't work with someone who says that I'm telling lies,' she told him. The officials waited outside, unsure if the government was falling apart inside.

McCreevy went to Ahern. Just apologize and get on with it, he advised him. It's worth it. Ahern went into the Dáil and apologized. 'His approach was "If that's what I have to do, that's what I have to do. It'll be forgotten in a week's time,"' reflected one of his aides. Privately, Ahern seethed with anger about the affair. But he duly issued the statement 'I accept that I was at fault ... I have expressed my regrets to the Tánaiste.' He would do anything to keep the government together, just as he had promised. Ministers were bemused by the whole turn of events, and few believed that they had been told the whole truth about it. One muttered to colleagues about Celia Larkin's high-profile visit to the O'Flaherty home, apparently having tipped off photographers – 'Celia going out to kiss the judge in the high boots, it was outlandish.'

Reflecting on the crisis in *The Sunday Business Post*, Emily O'Reilly was unimpressed with the PDs' panic at the media exposure of something they already knew. 'It is now taken as gospel that this latest spat marks the beginning of the end of the coalition. Perhaps it does.' However, if the government was going to survive, O'Reilly noted, the Progressive Democrats would 'have to find some way of coping with the odd screw-up by Fianna Fáil without having to resort to the kind of death-defying political stunts we witnessed last week. Because they won't go away, you know ...'

It was advice that would be useful when the second leg of this strange controversy reared its head a year later. The O'Flaherty affair would prove to be more damaging with the public than the Sheedy affair. It was also an entirely self-inflicted wound.

One of the first rules of all politics is patronage. From the humblest municipal governorship to the presidency of the United States, electoral systems function in part on the expectation that some bounty from the office might make its way to supporters of the successful candidate. Some want to just bask in the reflected glory; others want tangible rewards. The Irish government has thousands of appointments in its gift. Among the most coveted – and often, most lucrative – are the European offices. In the spring of 2000, one of these, a directorship of the European Investment Bank (EIB) – salary £147,000 a year – was becoming available. The minister for finance had somebody in mind.

McCreevy had mentioned to Ahern at the end of a parliamentary party meeting that he intended to appoint O'Flaherty to the EIB, indicating that he would consult the rest of the members of the cabinet. 'He's been badly treated,' McCreevy told him. Ahern shrugged his assent. It was Charlie's call, and Fianna Fáil looked after its own. Probably nobody would notice anyway. McCreevy rang the other ministers to let them know what he proposed. 'McCreevy rang me to say he was going to put this judge on the European Bank or whatever it was,' said one minister. 'I didn't know what it was.' None of the members of the cabinet raised an objection.

After cabinet meetings, the secretary general to the government briefs the government press secretary about the decisions made and any other matters that arose for discussion at the meeting that the Taoiseach has decided are to be communicated to the press. The press briefings are not a complete record of the cabinet meeting, but rather what the government wants to release from it. Sometimes the government press secretary will hold back nuggets he or she wishes to pass on to particular journalists; sometimes ministers will want to brief people themselves about it, or wait until a formal launch of a policy or programme. Sometimes the government just doesn't want people to know what it has decided. It's an incomplete, ad hoc system in which all the power rests with the government, and it drives the political correspondents crazy. Often cabinet briefings, usually held on a Tuesday evening when the Dáil is sitting, contain little more than notice of some diplomatic appointments, the agreement on heads of an already announced bill and a few annual reports.

But even when the gruel is thin, effective press secretaries know where in the dull officialese of the decisions and actions of the government the journalists will hunt for an edge, an angle, anything to sell to their editors for a few minutes of airtime or a few hundred words. A press secretary is often a journalist's opponent; but sometimes he's his friend. As the numbers of journalists covering politics have increased and their demands multiplied, more often the press secretary just does damage limitation on good days, and fire-fighting most of the time. On a quiet Friday afternoon in May 2000, when Joe Lennon learned that the government intended to appoint O'Flaherty to the European Investment Bank, he knew he was going to need his hose.

Lennon's well-attuned political alarm went haywire. A career civil servant who had worked for Ahern in the Department of Finance before joining him in the Taoiseach's Department as government press secretary, Lennon was relied upon by politicians and respected by journalists. He was one of that breed of bright civil servants who had developed a sharp political sense after years of working with ministers. And he was one of the few people in the habit of being completely frank with the Taoiseach. He immediately rang Ahern and told him he had shot himself 'in both feet'. He told him that the O'Flaherty appointment would be a huge political problem. Alarmed, Ahern wondered if the appointment could be stalled in time for a rethink. He told Lennon to ring Mandy Johnston, McCreevy's press officer.

Johnston herself knew that the appointment would ignite a political conflagration. 'This is going to cause a lot of shit, and you're going to be blamed,' she told McCreevy. 'Ah, I don't care, it'll blow over,' he replied.

Johnston rang Gerry Hickey, the Taoiseach's programme manager. 'You're not going to believe who they've just appointed to the EIB,' she said. 'Who?' 'Hugh O'Flaherty.' 'No!' 'Yes.' 'No! No!' 'I'm writing the press release.'

Lennon rang soon after. Can we stop it? Too late, Johnston told him. The press release was already issued. McCreevy had moved fast to notify the press on this occasion – not something he was accustomed to doing.

Shaking his head in bemusement, Lennon wandered down the corridor in Government Buildings, where most of Ahern's advisers were housed. Lennon brought with him a copy of the press release. They were incredulous. 'You're not serious,' one of them said. The media would go ballistic, they knew. It did. And if the media was going crazy, they predicted, it wouldn't be long before the PDs discovered they had problems with the appointment, too. It wasn't.

Never mind that Harney had agreed to the appointment, or that she had consulted Bobby Molloy and Dessie O'Malley: the PDs decided to have a near mental breakdown about the O'Flaherty appointment.

Liz O'Donnell declared her outrage, and alternated between trying to get the government to abandon the appointment and trying to distance herself and her party from it, describing the decision as a 'Fianna Fáil appointment by a Fianna Fáil minister of a Fianna Fáil person'. One of the party's senators, Helen Keogh, left the party and joined Fine Gael, though her decision was hardly unrelated to the fact that Fiona O'Malley had been parachuted into her constituency and the two sitting Fine Gael TDs, Monica Barnes and Sean Barrett, were going to retire. She would later run unsuccessfully for Fine Gael. Ahern and McCreevy thought the PDs should just grow up.

But it soon became clear that matters were becoming serious for the government. As the controversy blew up in his face, McCreevy took panicked steps to retrieve the situation. He rang Mary O'Rourke and said, 'Get over to Bertie, will you, and just keep him happy?' O'Rourke hurried over. She found Ahern depressed and angry at the PD acrobatics. 'Mary, you know, that judge has done nothing wrong.' A year previously, he had presided over a cabinet meeting that resolved to remove Hugh O'Flaherty from the Supreme Court if he refused to resign, a monumental step unprecedented in the history of the state. Now the judge hadn't done anything wrong.

Just as Joe Lennon and the advisers had predicted, the controversy wouldn't go away. It got worse, not better. When the affair was the subject of special notice questions in the Dáil, a bad-tempered exchange turned nasty when McCreevy, after a half-hour of questions and abuse from the opposition, suddenly flared up. Replying to Fine Gael deputy Michael Noonan, McCreevy spat, 'Deputy, there are members in your party around and about you and sitting in the front row to your right who were given a second chance and some of them should recall that very well.' This was understood to be a reference to the civil way that the Labour deputy, Emmet Stagg, had been treated several years previously after he was stopped by gardaí in a part of the Phoenix Park frequented by male prostitutes. The opposition exploded in fury, and even the Fianna Fáil deputies sitting behind the finance minister were horrified. McCreevy hightailed it out of the chamber and made for Baldonnel, where the government jet was awaiting to take him on an official visit to the Lebanon. Johnston's phone almost combusted with calls. Chief whip Seamus Brennan, who had been in the Dáil chamber at the time, was insisting that he come back and apologize in the Dáil. 'I'm telling you he simply has to come back,' Brennan insisted. Johnston employed the stalling device of last resort. 'I can't hear you Seamus, you're breaking up, I'll have to ring you back.' She got to the plane and turned off her phone. McCreevy was in the Lebanon for five days. It was, his staff reflected, going from one war zone to another.

The affair festered all summer. A succession of polls, some of them published, others private to Fianna Fáil, tracked the extent to which the affair was damaging the government with the public. Nearly 70 per cent of the public thought the decision to nominate O'Flaherty was wrong, one poll found. 'It was pretty plain to everyone that if we didn't deal with this we were toast,' says one insider. Ahern and some of his ministers couldn't understand why the public was so exercised by it. The advisers nearly screamed at them: because he has already been convicted by the government! Other ministers wondered why on earth McCreevy had brought it on the government. They stuck with it until it became obvious that the bank itself was leery at a scandal-tainted appointment.

Even then the finance minister refused to budge. 'I'm not asking him to withdraw his name. I won't do it,' he told aides. And what if he asks that his name be withdrawn? 'Well, then that would change things . . .' McCreevy conceded. Johnston told Hickey. Soon O'Flaherty bowed to the inevitable and asked that his nomination be withdrawn. The government, which should have been riding the crest of a wave as the economy boomed, was severely damaged in the public mind, having spent months reminding voters about its propensity for cronyism. The ability of Ahern's government to distract the public's attention from its own economic achievements never ceased to amaze.

It had been a long few months in the Taoiseach's office and for the Taoiseach's staff. They had been disrupted by departures: Jackie Gallagher had left for a career in public relations and, more dramatically, Paddy Duffy had resigned following the revelation that he had joined the board of a firm of public relations consultants and lobbyists while still working as Ahern's adviser. More seriously, the public relations and lobbying firm Dillon Consultants had acted for the cable television company NTL in a successful bid to buy Dublin cable provider Cablelink from two state-owned companies, Telecom Éireann and RTÉ. Confronted by the story, Duffy panicked, telling reporters that he had been appointed to the board of the company without his knowledge. 'Paul Dillon did this as a gesture to me before Christmas. He intended it as a surprise.' However, the Christmas present wasn't that much of a surprise – Duffy's signature was on Companies Office documents recording his appointment. He claimed to have had no role in the company, but admitted to attending meetings. In a later Dáil debate on the controversy Ahern reflected, 'I have to say that I have come to the conclusion that it is so stupid it is probably believable.' Duffy clearly had no choice but to resign, an ignominious end to a productive and loyal career on Ahern's staff.

The ejection of Duffy was painful for Ahern, whom he had served since the 1970s. It was even more painful for Duffy. Faced with the inevitable, he retired to his office in Government

Buildings and closed the door. He wasn't taking calls and staff ended up pushing notes under the door. Tense phone calls buzzed around advisers' offices, veering between amusement and concern. Joe Lennon rang one adviser: 'What the hell is going on?' Duffy came out in his own good time and went on to have a highly successful career in his own communications consultancy and he maintained his closeness to Ahern. A subsequent cabinet meeting was held at Farmleigh when Ahern, clearly still furious about the incident, according to one witness stared straight down at the table, saying, 'Paddy Duffy is a long-time friend of mine and somebody went out to do him and I know who it is and I won't forget it.' The fingers were pointing at Mary O'Rourke, who had been told of Duffy's role by the former Fine Gael leader Alan Dukes, and under whose department Telecom operated. O'Rourke was able stand up for herself. 'Well, I don't know who he's talking about,' she said in a stage whisper to those sitting around her, 'because it certainly wasn't me.' Duffy was among those who didn't weep when O'Rourke lost her seat in 2002.

Ahern also ran into a sticky public reaction when the government granted permission for the Independent group's chief executive and controlling shareholder, Tony O'Reilly, to accept a British knighthood in the New Year's Honours List of 2001.

O'Reilly had been one of Ireland most successful exports. His remarkable business success, following a dashing rugby career, had been breathlessly chronicled in the newspaper group he had controlled since the 1970s and which he had built into a global brand. Elsewhere, his success was regarded with a mixture of admiration, envy and old-fashioned begrudgery. While the *Irish Independent* had historically been a Fine Gael paper, where the *Irish Press* was solidly pro-Fianna Fáil, O'Reilly had displayed little interest in politics beyond a suspicion of Charles Haughey. But after Haughey's departure, he had accommodated himself to Fianna Fáil, and the *Irish Independent*'s famous 'payback time' editorial before the 1997 general election had advertised that relationship in political Technicolor. He retained PJ Mara as a corporate adviser.

O'Reilly had contacted Ahern in November and told him that he had been offered a knighthood by the British government to be announced in the New Year's Honours List. This was routine plámásing for a British press proprietor – in fact, a knighthood might be the least of what one could expect, being pretty far down the pecking order of these things. But it would be unusual for such a prominent Irishman to accept and use the title. Other Irish (and indeed American) recipients of British titles, such as Bob Geldof, had contented themselves with 'honorary' knighthoods, which did not involve their customary use outside the tabloid press, but this wasn't for O'Reilly. It might be considered an odd move for someone who had traded on his Irishness internationally as O'Reilly had, but all men have their little vanities, and this was exactly what he intended. He wanted the real thing – Sir Anthony and Lady O'Reilly – and an edict would soon go out to the staff of his newspapers in this regard.

There was only one problem: the Taoiseach didn't appear inclined to play ball. As an Irish citizen, O'Reilly could not accept the title without the express permission of the government – there is an explicit prohibition in the constitution – and Ahern was queasy about giving it. O'Reilly was the owner of the dominant newspaper group in the country and Ahern didn't want to make an enemy of him. But the notion of a knighthood went against Ahern's own republican instincts and he knew it would annoy a lot of people. So he did what he always did when faced with an unpalatable choice where he didn't like either option. He did nothing.

November ticked into December without any word from the government. O'Reilly continued to press for approval. Because his father was born before independence, O'Reilly was entitled to British citizenship, and so he was technically able to accept the gong without the government's approval, though this could have seemed like a revocation of his Irish citizenship, and O'Reilly knew how that would look. Besides, he *was* – and is – Irish. He just wanted a British title, and he wanted the government to give him the OK for it. But Downing Street needed to know one way or another, and time was running out. The secretary to the government, Dermot McCarthy, was being pestered by O'Reilly's people. He needed a decision.

On the last day that the Department of the Taoiseach was open before Christmas of that year, Ahern repaired around the corner to Doheny & Nesbitt's with about twenty members of his office staff for a Christmas drink. He wasn't long there when he was interrupted by Dermot McCarthy. Ahern was surprised to see him there, and he knew he wasn't coming over for pints. McCarthy needed a private word. O'Reilly has been on again, he told him. He needs word today, one way or the other. If you want to approve it, we can organize an incorporeal cabinet meeting now. This was a rarely used device whereby ministers were contacted by telephone to give their approval for an urgently needed decision. The procedure was hardly designed with the current circumstances in mind. Still, Ahern knew that he had run out of road. OK, he said. Go ahead. McCarthy thanked him and left the pub, bringing some of the staff with him. He went back to the department and made the telephone calls. Ministers were nonplussed. 'What does Bertie say?' one of them asked. McCarthy replied: 'He says OK.' 'Well, OK so.'

When they weren't dealing with such episodes, Ahern's advisers were trying to find a way in which the government's increasing vulnerability on the health issue could be neutralized. Despite vastly increased budgets, public dissatisfaction with the state of the health services was growing steadily. The inherent imbalance of the media reporting of the issue – in news terms, one bad case trumps a hundred good outcomes – meant that there was no obvious solution to the growing political damage. Ahern had also been mulling over the issue, and he had concluded that a change in the Department of Health would be the first step.

Public concern about health had the potential, Ahern thought, to derail the re-election plans. Brian Cowen was clearly unhappy in the department and, Ahern feared, losing interest. A broad political strategy would be needed, and that included a change in the minister's office. There was an obvious candidate: the bright and youngish minister for education, who had turned into one of the successes of the government – so much so, in fact, that he was being openly talked of as a future leader.

'You've done fantastic, a brilliant job,' Ahern told his education minister, Micheál Martin in 1999. 'Everyone's talking about you.'

And you'll have to do something about that, Martin thought to himself.

David Andrews was thinking of retiring, Ahern told him, and he was keen to move Brian Cowen. There would be vacancy in the Department of Health. He should look on this as an opportunity. 'It would be good for you. You'll get more experience, and it will be good for the party. You know I have to think of the party.'

Martin left the meeting thinking, Sure, it might even be a good idea for me. *Like an eejit*, he subsequently reflected. McCreevy repeatedly told him that he would be mad to take the job; John O'Donoghue joked that if nothing else, he would 'have a good bedside manner'. Martin and Ahern discussed the move on a few more occasions over a period of about two months. Then, finding himself at a funeral in Cork which Ahern and Celia Larkin were also attending, Martin fell into conversation with the pair as they walked out of the church. 'Andrews is going,' Ahern said, almost as an aside. 'Will I pack my bags, so?' Martin replied. 'Yeah, yeah ... Oh, and we'll do an abortion referendum as well,' the Taoiseach muttered over his shoulder as he walked away. For fuck's sake, Martin thought.

Martin moved to health at the beginning of 2000 while Cowen replaced Andrews at foreign affairs. Martin's move was also intended to address the growing public concern about the state of the public health system, and to present a more emollient face on the issue than Cowen had heretofore managed. This imperative grew into an effort to define a new departure on health policy. Twelve months later, with an election on the middle horizon and public concern growing, the government was preparing to give concrete form to this desire. To emphasize the seriousness of the initiative, Ahern decided that the cabinet would have a special all-day meeting at an out-of-Dublin venue.

Gerry Hickey called the health minister to discuss how they might set the media agenda for the cabinet meeting at Bally-mascanlon, Co. Louth. The political correspondents, Hickey told Martin, were 'sniffing around' for something on Ballymascanlon. The two men discussed the health strategy and agreed that Hickey would pass on a few 'nuggets' to shape the coverage. Martin followed it up himself by speaking to journalists, and the government's spin doctors told the political correspondents that something big was coming and it would be in their interests to make the trip to Louth. It was teed up as a major departure in government policy.

The only problem was that nobody appeared to have told Charlie McCreevy. The *Irish Times* headline on the day of the meeting ('Cabinet to hear extra billions are needed for health') was followed by a report which the finance minister felt was an attempt to bounce him into a new policy. 'The Government will be told the health budget needs to be at least quadrupled and extra billions spent if the crisis in the State's health service is to be tackled,' the report predicted. 'At a special Cabinet meeting in Co Louth today the Minister for Health, Mr Martin, is expected to tell his Cabinet colleagues that the doubling of the health budget to £5 billion annually has not been nearly enough . . .'

Martin knew that the interview with the *Irish Times* – and the treatment the paper had chosen to give it – would get up McCreevy's nose. 'I didn't say that, I didn't say that,' he protested when he saw the story. He wanted his staff to ring the reporter, Alison O'Connor, and – what, they asked. Get the story changed? 'Are you mad?' one of them replied. 'She has the whole thing on tape.'

McCreevy's reaction was just as Martin had expected. 'He went ballistic,' recalled one person who was in the room. 'Bertie and Dermot McCarthy had to smooth things out between them afterwards.'

McCreevy arrived into the meeting with a face like fury,

banged his papers down on the table and launched into an angry rant. 'Now, I'll tell you . . .'

The substance of the first half of the meeting was a presentation from Michael Kelly, the secretary general of the Department of Health, accompanied by several officials. Kelly was forthright with ministers, more forthright than some ministers thought suitable for an official, no matter how senior. McCreevy bridled at his suggestions that a set percentage of GNP had to be set aside for health spending. It's not his job to be dictating to ministers about spending decisions, McCreevy later told his colleagues when the officials withdrew. Of course the finance minister had a very clear view of how spending decisions should be reached, and of his own position in that process – right at the centre of it. If McCreevy wasn't going to listen to his own officials about policy and spending decisions, he certainly wasn't going to offer too much deference to an official who headed what he regarded as the worst department in the government.

For someone who disdained the media, McCreevy now showed that he was willing to use it when it suited him. He emerged from the meeting and told reporters that there was no new money for health, that health budgets – like all other budgets – would be decided in the annual estimates process and that anyway, health appeared to be wasting much of it. 'Our whole communications message after that was "Fuck health",' one finance official told me. Instead of being bounced into more spending, McCreevy was now doing the leaking, announcing health developments before Martin did. Ahern's aides were reduced to briefing that the Taoiseach believed the health service was 'excellent'.

The whole operation had been an unmitigated disaster, an example of the cack-handed political management from which Ahern's administration seemed unable to escape. It was only when it came to elections that they were able to truly find their gear. It was the old failing of Ahern's Fianna Fáil: winning power, not using it, was what they were really good at.

★

There was one great exception. Ahern had moved early to assert his own centrality in the Irish government's approach to the North, and the growing relationship between the Taoiseach and the British Prime Minister became first a facilitator and latterly an engine of the process. Both were young and recently elected, both lacked the history of some of their predecessors, though especially in the early part of the process, they clearly came at it from different perspectives and with different agendas. They both displayed a quite astonishing degree of political skill and commitment throughout the long process. Ahern's government played a firm uncle to the republicans – generally on their side, but demanding they behave themselves – while Downing Street played a similar role for the unionists.

Ahern was superbly suited to the political and diplomatic landscape. He was young enough not to have any baggage from the days of the Arms Trial, he was inclusive rather than ideological and he had spent the middle, reputation-making part of his career as a consensus-building, deal-making minister for Labour. Though sprung from the Haughey wing of the party, from the North he looked a lot more like a deal-making Reynolds than an irredentist Haughey. When he had met the Ulster Unionist leader, David Trimble, at the annual conference of the British-Irish Association ('Toffs against Terrorism') at St John's College, Oxford, in September 1996, the two men had spoken for half an hour. They were both cautious, but they were both encouraged.

While Ahern's claim that he would spend forty hours a week on Northern affairs before turning around to spend a normal working week running the government of the Republic was hardly true of every week, the claim is a measure of the importance he attached to it and the dedication he brought with him. 'The North was all about patience,' says a long-time close aide. 'He took all the insults and he just outlasted them.'

But the process that evolved was also entirely suited to Ahern's skills and his personality. The very traits in his character and his modus operandi that were to strangle policy-making and, eventually, lead to runaway public spending in the South – the

determination to keep everyone within the process, the willingness to compromise with all sides, the reluctance to make hard
decisions – these were the very things that enabled him to keep
the peace process on track. He would be criticized in the South
for his elevation of the social partnership process as a policy end in
itself, rather than a means to an end; in the North, it was precisely
this devotion to the process that allowed the ceasefires to bed
down and made a return to large-scale violence unlikely, and in
the end impossible. In the words of one senior government
figure, 'It was the deal that mattered, not what was in it.'

Ahern was also facilitated by Harney's attitude to the North:
it just wasn't a priority for her. She always saw the PDs' role
as being primarily an economic one and with McCreevy at the
helm, she knew they had an historic chance of fulfilling that role.
She didn't feel she needed to watch what Ahern was doing on
the North; she knew his attitudes to Sinn Féin, and she knew he
wasn't Charlie Haughey. Nonetheless, Ahern made sure to keep
Harney updated on progress, though sometimes the updates were
less welcome than he might have understood. Sometimes the calls
would come at 6.00 or 7.00 a.m. on Sunday mornings, outlining
meetings or contacts the Taoiseach intended to have during the
day, or had conducted the previous day. 'For God's sake, they're
impossible,' she used to say to him. She was impressed with his
tenacity, and she wondered at his forbearance and his work rate.

From early into their respective careers as prime ministers,
Ahern and Blair established a level of contact and co-operation
that was unimaginable by previous incumbents of their offices,
and probably unparalleled between the leaders of two modern
states. They became that rare thing in politics: genuine friends
(a closeness underlined when Blair made an appearance in the
Fianna Fáil election broadcast before the 2007 election).

As their relationship developed they talked informally all
the time. According to one source familiar with Blair's office
in Downing Street, if Blair found himself with a spare twenty
minutes in his schedule he would often ring Dublin directly for a
chat about progress in the North. As the former secretary to the

government Paddy Teahon told the makers of the 2008 television documentary, in the 1980s setting up a phone call between the British Prime Minister and the Irish Taoiseach used to take about a week. In fact, much of the tortuous negotiations took place over the phone in advance of formal sit-downs. Teahon told David Trimble's biographer Dean Godson that on one weekend in January 1998, whilst the two leaders – one in Spain (Ahern) the other in Japan (Blair) – struggled to reach agreement in advance of talks, some three hundred phone calls were made between their two offices.

Occasionally, this was a source of some concern to Ahern; he had told staff previously that he was worried about being bugged, and some staff even claimed that a device had been found in St Luke's. Many other participants in the talks simply assumed that they were being bugged by British Intelligence.

By the time the all-party talks convened at Stormont in April 1999, in advance of the deadline imposed by the independent chairman, Senator George Mitchell, there had already been several hiccups, suspensions, walk-outs and collapses. As has been chronicled in great detail in many places, the talks themselves were a roller-coaster ride through high politics, historic compromise and constitutional horse-trading; or 'ludicrous' (Blair) and 'awful' (Mitchell). Blair's press secretary, Alastair Campbell, records that Ahern told him at the start of one day that if he was exposed to too much of Adams or Trimble that day, he would end up thumping them.

The achievement of the Good Friday Agreement had been a shared political triumph for all the participants; for Ahern, having buried his mother in the midst of the proceedings, it was an immense personal achievement. As the country exhaled its wonder – 'Historic agreement marks a new beginning for us all' declared the *Irish Times* headline – Ahern and Blair knew that they were beginning a process rather than drawing a line under anything. They could not possibly have imagined how long and difficult the road would be; had they done so, it would surely have muted the celebrations.

The process that followed was about slowly reeling in these two constituencies to the institutions and the peculiar politics envisaged by the agreement. To say this process took longer than expected doesn't quite cover it. It was not until the end of 1999 that power was devolved to the new Stormont executive, when Trimble finally sat at the head of a cabinet that included nominees of the Ulster Unionist Party, the SDLP and Sinn Féin – but not Ian Paisley's DUP. The devolution of power was followed by a meeting of the British–Irish Council in London and a meeting of the North–South Ministerial Council in Armagh. The IRA appointed an interlocutor to lead with the international body set up to supervise decommissioning of its arms. 'On this day,' wrote the editor of the *Irish Times* in his front-page editorial, 'we witness nothing less than the birth of a new Ireland.' There would be a few more such editorials and declarations before the process was through.

Twelve days after devolution, Ahern's government put on a show for Sinn Féin. The first meeting of the North–South Ministerial Council in Armagh was a big day for nationalist Ireland; and a big day for Bertie Ahern. It was, he told reporters, 'the biggest thing that has happened in my political life'. For unionists it was something to be endured. David Trimble busied himself ostentatiously reading his papers while Ahern spoke, but nationalist and diplomatic fears of an outbreak of Trimble irascibility went unfounded when he conducted himself with relative good humour throughout, especially in the four-handed press conference afterwards.

On what Ahern's spin doctors insisted was a day of high symbolism for Ireland and the United Kingdom, the most telling symbols were made in Germany. As the appointed hour of the council approached, a stream of ministerial cars appeared in convoy over the brow of the hill leading to the Palace Demesne. Twelve black 98 and 99 D Mercedes, each carrying a Fianna Fáil minister, drew up in front of the building and disgorged their smiling cargoes. 'You should have seen it,' a participant told me. 'It was magnificent.' Some unionist commentators sneered that it was like a mafia funeral, but for the Irish government, in all the years since the ambitious Pee Flynn had first revealed his ambition to fold his gangly frame into the 'Car with the Star', there had never been a greater expression of ministerial puissance and presence. A few minutes before the appointed time, the Air Corps helicopter whirred into view and landed on the lawn, scattering winter leaves. The Taoiseach, the Tánaiste and the minister for foreign affairs stepped out. The message to the unionists was clear: you are dealing with a new Ireland now.

Actually, like the British-Irish Council, the North–South body was a sideshow. The political focus remained on the twin holes in the entire edifice: the willingness of the republicans to commit to (and demonstrate) exclusively peaceful means, and the acceptability to unionists of sharing power with Sinn Féin. In practice this meant decommissioning and working devolution; neither was within a country mile of being achieved in 2002.

Nonetheless, by the time Fianna Fáil faced the general election it was trumpeting the slogan 'Peace, Prosperity, Progress'. In his foreword to the party's manifesto, Ahern was cautious – 'We finally have in place the foundations for building a just and lasting peace on this island' – though the document went on to claim credit for the IRA ceasefire and the Good Friday Agreement for Fianna Fáil. Throughout the campaign, Fianna Fáil didn't try to over-egg the peace process pudding; in a sense, the achievement of the Good Friday Agreement and the ceasefires was so obvious that it didn't need to.

Its achievements in the North notwithstanding, Fianna Fáil faced a political threat of a potent nature from the continuing revelations at the two tribunals of inquiry into possible political corruption, Flood and Moriarty, which continued their tardy and often tedious work at Dublin Castle. Requests for the discovery of thousands of documents had arrived in party headquarters from the legal teams of both tribunals as they continued to pick away at the seams where business and politics met. The party's general secretary, Mackin, having consulted senior counsel Rory

Brady, simply ordered that everything be given over. Ahern appeared happy with this openness, though others seemed less enthusiastic.

Property developer Tom Gilmartin alleged that he had been tapped for donations by a coterie of Fianna Fáil ministers who included Ahern, recalling that he had uttered the memorable line 'You guys make the mafia look like monks' while he was being, as he saw it, subjected to a shakedown. By his own admission, he was willing to be shaken down, at least up to a point. Gilmartin's later allegations were to have the most serious consequences for Ahern, but at the time, they were more serious for Padraig Flynn. 'The Commissioner' – as Flynn sometimes referred to himself – saw his political career destroyed by Gilmartin's revelation that he had given the politician £50,000 in 1989 – money which it later emerged had been lodged in a bogus non-resident account.

The continuing revelations of the Moriarty Tribunal effectively destroyed whatever reputation Charles Haughey still enjoyed. They also threatened to engulf Bertie Ahern, especially when lurid tales of Charvet shirts bought from the leader's account with blank cheques signed by Ahern were aired. The corruptions exposed by the Flood Tribunal investigations into planning practices on Dublin County Council, where builders bought councillors almost by the dozen, were of altogether less grand and grubbier measure. When the lobbyist-turned-briber-in-chief Frank Dunlop was finally backed into a corner and began to sing in April 2000, his testimony just confirmed what had been assumed for years: many planning decisions were politically corrupt. Despite Ahern's initial reaction to one of his officials on the day that Dunlop broke – 'Ah, this is all so long ago,' he told officials – Fianna Fáil referred the matters to its grandly titled Standards in Public Life Committee, a body which gave much scope for amusement to amateur political satirists up and down the country.

Its report identified payments to a number of its public representatives, but chose as its scapegoat the likely figure of Liam Lawlor, who had made several spirited attempts to mislead the committee. He resigned from the party before he was expelled,

and went on to be sentenced to three terms in prison for contempt towards the tribunal before the 2002 election. To the fury
of the opposition and the media, the tribunal failed to have an
appreciable effect on Fianna Fáil's poll ratings, or subsequently on
electoral performance.

Why did the revelations at the tribunals not damage Fianna
Fáil politically in 2002? Or at least, why did they not damage the
party enough to deny it electoral success? Because voters did not
care enough about them. It wasn't that they didn't think it was
important; it was that they thought other things were more
important. That same calculus would again come to Ahern's aid –
to the renewed fury of the opposition and much of the media – in
a later election. Ahern's high standing with the public also
allowed him to get away with an amazing conceit: that despite
the mountain of sleaze that the tribunals were uncovering, the
past really was a different country. The Fianna Fáil of the present
was a different beast from the Fianna Fáil of the past.

For the 2002 election, it's useful and instructive to refer to
the work of a team of political scientists from the country's
universities. They analysed the results of the election, utilizing
an in-depth election study conducted among over 2,500 people,
the largest of its kind ever undertaken in Ireland. With the sense of
urgency that often characterizes such endeavours, it was published
after the 2007 election as *The Irish Voter: the Nature of Electoral
Competition in the Republic of Ireland*. Many of the conclusions are as
equivocal as academics often are when commenting on current
events; in any case, they point out that they have no way of knowing if what they have discovered is generally true of Irish elections,
or just true of the 2002 election. But it remains a treasure trove of
data. Much of the research is extremely detailed, but one of their
central conclusions is disarmingly simple. Fianna Fáil went into
the 2002 general election with an enormous advantage because
it had presided over five years of rapid economic growth. Ireland
had become a wealthy country; unemployment was at historically
low levels; forced emigration was ended; corporate and personal
taxes had been slashed, while the yield to the exchequer from

them had soared. The wealth was both public – evident in budget surpluses and falling government debt – and private, in rising incomes and house prices that had doubled in the intervening five years. 'Over the five years the Fianna Fáil–Progressive Democrat coalition was in power, the performance of the economy reached levels never experienced before in the history of the state . . .' the study observes. It was, the authors conclude, not at all surprising that Fianna Fáil won the 2002 election; it may well be surprising that they did not win it by more.

An earlier account of the campaign from another political scientist came to a similar conclusion. In the 2002 edition of *How Ireland Voted*, Dublin City University academic Gary Murphy noted: 'The single most important fact for the government was that it had presided over the greatest boom in the country's history and electorally this is what would be stressed during the election campaign. It was to be Fianna Fáil's trump card, and one that the opposition found almost impossible to counter.'

Aside from the booming economy and the meticulous preparation of the political operation, Fianna Fáil brought another great advantage into the 2002 general election: its opponents.

In the early months of 2001, Fine Gael had deposed John Bruton and replaced him with Michael Noonan, supported by the deputy leadership of Jim Mitchell, a combination proposed implausibly by some Fine Gaelers as 'the Dream Team'. It turned out to be a dream team, all right – for Fianna Fáil. In an age where general election campaigns were becoming increasingly presidential, Fine Gael had replaced an ageing balding man who had been a popular and respected taoiseach with a slightly older, balding man who had never been taoiseach. Voters found it difficult to imagine him in the role. When he was clobbered by a custard pie – which engagement was of course caught perfectly on camera – it seemed to sum up the entire Fine Gael campaign. Fianna Fáil was overjoyed when Noonan won the leadership. Shortly afterwards, Mara met Sean O'Rourke of RTÉ. 'Happy days,' Mara told him. 'There's no way this guy can touch us.'

Another of Ahern's advisers told me: 'This is the best thing that could have happened for us.'

Noonan struggled to establish himself as a credible leader and shake off the shadow of the Bridget McCole controversy. McCole, one of hundreds of women infected with hepatitis C by blood transfusions, sued the state when the scandal came to light at the time Noonan was minister for health; the state mounted an aggressive legal defence. She died, and the episode was dramatized by RTÉ in early 2002, compounding the damage. Meanwhile, Fianna Fáil was putting the finishing touches to the most detailed campaign plan in Irish political history. The research and the planning were done, the slogans crafted and tested. 'A lot done, more to do' was the party's chief catch-cry, a copy of a Blairite line and chosen in preference to Mara's suggestion of 'Let Ahern lead', a nod to an old Lemass slogan. One of the campaign team wondered: 'Why does PJ want to revive a forty-year-old slogan when all we need to do is steal New Labour's one?' The supporting line was 'Peace, Prosperity, Progress', or the three Ps, as it became known.

The prosperity was to be evidenced by a massive programme of public spending increases in the year and a half before the election. Previously, McCreevy had been unwilling to bow to the incessant demands of ministers to fund programmes and expansions in their own departments. But in his 2001 and 2002 spending plans he allocated huge increases in current and capital spending programmes, with, in many cases, limited justification. Few examples were more egregious than the decision to allocate medical cards to the over-seventies in the 2002 budget. Officials in the Department of Health were called a few days before the budget: how much would this cost? The calculation was a 'back of the envelope one', says one source very familiar with the process. McCreevy didn't care, and went ahead anyway. Six months before an election, he knew that politics would trump economics every time. Many of the spending plans were on a much smaller scale, though no less politically effective: local improvements, grants for schools, sports facilities, hospitals –

whatever. Announcements of National Lottery grants to sports clubs were brought forward to before the election in April, months ahead of the usual schedule. TDs were given lists of good-news announcements for their constituencies. For all the sophistication of the market research and the message delivery techniques of the party's election campaign, this was the retail politics for the ground war – votes for fixing footpaths, writ large. Fianna Fáil ran the most modern political campaign in Irish history; but it didn't trust it. In the first half of 2002, public spending grew by an astonishing 22 per cent. There would be a reckoning for that, but not until after the election.

By December 2001, it was all ready. In January, a full five months before the election would take place, Mackin met Ahern and presented him with the final plan. 'Are you happy with everything?' the general secretary asked the Taoiseach. Ahern was typically non-committal. 'Are you happy with it yourself?' 'I am, Taoiseach.' Ahern paused. 'Well, if you're happy with it, then I'm happy with it.'

As long as it works, thought Mackin, as long as it works. Nonetheless, they *were* ready, he knew. All that remained now was for Ahern to name the day.

Having scrapped for his seat for two decades around Tallaght and Clondalkin in the constituency of Dublin South West, Pat Rabbitte knew that the hard yards are gained by the unglamorous grind of tireless lobbying, parliamentary questions and raising the issues that your constituents are concerned about in adjournment debates when you might prefer to be in the pub with a pint. So at nine o'clock on the evening of Wednesday 24 April 2002, Rabbitte sat in an almost empty chamber facing Mary Hanafin, the junior health minister, asking her to reconsider a cut in funding for care and services for people with an intellectual disability. One of the Dáil's most skilled debaters, Rabbitte linked the slashing of services to vulnerable people in his constituency to the government's grandiose plans for a national stadium.

'The cost reduction measures have very serious repercussions,'

Rabbitte explained. 'The closure of six respite beds at Old Bawn, Tallaght, will in turn mean a 50 per cent reduction in the respite services available to support the students in the St John of God School, Islandbridge, the discontinuance of the summer camp, reduced extended day and holiday break programmes and the deferral of the move of sixty clients to a new day centre in Tallaght, planned for August and September 2002 … Wherever cutbacks have to be made, they should not be visited on people who are so vulnerable and in need of the very limited services that are in place. I hope the minister of state will be able to tell us that the government that thinks it can afford to spend €1 billion to build a football stadium can at least provide respite care for people who are badly in need of it.'

Hanafin gave the standard reply scripted by her officials. The government had increased funding for such services, budgets were under review, the minister had asked to be kept informed and so on. Nobody was listening. They were looking at the normally somnolent Ceann Comhairle, Seamus Pattison, who had read a note passed to him and suddenly perked up. The Taoiseach had entered the Dáil chamber. Pattison told the slowly comprehending participants in the adjournment debate that the Taoiseach had indicated he had an announcement to make.

'I wish to inform the House as a matter of courtesy,' said Ahern, 'that I intend to proceed to Áras an Uachtarán at 9 a.m. tomorrow to advise the President, pursuant to Article 13 of the Constitution, to dissolve Dáil Éireann …' Polling day would be Friday 17 May. It was game on.

Less than five minutes earlier, in the rooms adjacent to the Taoiseach's offices, a few of the Taoiseach's staff were finishing for the evening. The door to Ahern's office was closed; he was alone. Olive Melvin, the Taoiseach's personal assistant, sat at her desk. Suddenly, the door to the Taoiseach's office burst open and Ahern emerged almost in a jog. He hurried down the corridor past his startled officials, calling after him over his shoulder. 'Watch the monitor! Watch the monitor!' One of them thought that someone had said something about him in the Dáil and he was rushing to have the record corrected. The officials waited at television screens showing the live feed from the Dáil chamber. Like everyone else, his announcement caught them completely by surprise.

Several of the Government Buildings staff had gone to the nearby Doheny & Nesbitt's pub. Like everyone else, they expected that the announcement of the election would be made in the normal way in the Dáil the following morning. Brian Murphy, a special adviser, had remained behind and now rang them frantically. 'He's after calling the election!' Murphy told Gerry Hickey, who was with Mandy Johnston.

'Don't be stupid, he's calling it tomorrow.'

'I know, I know, but he's after calling it in the Dáil!'

They left their drinks and hurried back to Government Buildings. They got there before Ahern had returned from the chamber. When he did arrive back, he had a grin on his face.

'Heh, heh,' he greeted them. 'I got ye all by surprise!'

Later Ahern chatted about the campaign with a few of his staff. They thought he was amazingly cool, very relaxed. One of them thought, He knows he's going to win. The polls were certainly telling him he was going to win. The question was: by how much?

Incredibly, it wasn't until just before the general election that the realization began to seep into the body politic that Fianna Fáil could be on course for an overall majority. I wrote a piece in *The Sunday Business Post* pointing out the mathematical reality, and drawing up a hit list of the important constituencies. Fianna Fáil strategists and spin doctors went crazy. 'It's just not on. Nobody can win an overall majority. Those days are over. You'll look stupid.' A few weeks later, one commentator observed that the Fianna Fáil spin was that no matter how many votes it won, it still couldn't achieve an overall majority. But the numbers were obvious. If PJ Mara had tried to coach Fianna Fáil into 'sneaking up' on the electorate in 1997 (as he had told people), 2002 was like sneaking up on them in a tank.

'The overall majority was like the love that dare not speak its name,' remembers one member of the campaign team. 'Nobody wanted to say it. It was only in the final week we started to allow ourselves to think, Jesus, it *is* on.'

From the outset, the focus of the Fianna Fáil campaign was on the economy. The backroom staff – with considerable assistance from the economist Colin Hunt, a strong party supporter who would later become an adviser to Brian Cowen in the Department of Finance – had prepared an attack on the Fine Gael economic plan, alleging a €6.5-billion hole in their costings. 'Remember the huge deficits and taxes of the 1980s? Well, Fine Gael in government would return Ireland to those days,' wrote Charlie McCreevy in the *Daily Mirror*, of all places. 'Fine Gael have been caught telling fibs on how they will fund the economy with their spending plans set to return the country to €5 billion debt within four years.'

'Actually, we had decided in advance that there would be a black hole in their plans – whatever they were,' says one participant. Fianna Fáil knew from its research that the public instinctively distrusted politicians who promised them too much. In response to this, they had dialled down their own promises and costings, and devised a strategy to attack from the outset the costings that underpinned the opposition proposals. This led to days of repetitive argument about the costings and economic projections – the Fine Gael senator Maurice Manning characterized the exchanges as the 'it's a biscuit, it's a bar' debate – culminating in a proposal to let a team of independent economists assess each party's spending plans. It was tedious stuff, but it achieved precisely what the Treasury Building guys wanted: it kept the focus on the economy. Having presided over an economy that had experienced five years of rapid growth, rising living standards and rocketing employment levels, Fianna Fáil couldn't lose as long as this was where the debate was. 'The economic skirmishing early on was intended to undermine them on their costings and establish a credibility fault in the minds of the electorate. Once we had them on that particular ground – economics and spending – we let them flail about for a while and then we killed them,' one insider told me at the time.

The campaign ran like clockwork. The day started with a morning meeting in Mount Street at 7.00 a.m. The core team was relatively tight: Gerry Hickey, Gerry Howlin, Brian Murphy and Peter MacDonagh from Government Buildings; Joe O'Rourke and Martin Mackin from Mount Street; Chris Wall from Drumcondra; Mandy Johnston; Tad Devine, over from Washington for the duration of the campaign. Retiring politicians Chris Flood and David Andrews sometimes attended. Mara chaired the meetings. They reviewed the agenda for the day and decided on tweaks to the strategy and the 'grid' – the all-important day-by-day plan of the campaign – as events demanded. Sometimes they were presented with polling or focus group research, either nationally or from individual constituencies, which was then refined into actions or statements. Murphy would write local concerns or flavours into the Taoiseach's stump speech.

During the day the staff divided into those 'making snowballs' and those throwing them. The snowball makers did the research on the issues and the opposition; the snowball throwers did their best to get it reported in the media.

Mara had imposed a no-drinking rule on the Treasury team for the duration of the campaign. Most of them adhered to it; some, to my certain knowledge, did not. This (temporary) asceticism, combined with their enthusiasm, led Mara to dub the staff at the Treasury Building headquarters 'the Taliban'. Before they went to face the media at the morning press conferences, he would often send them out with the exhortation 'Kill! Kill! Kill!'

Mara's typically catchy characterization aside, there's no doubt that Fianna Fáil enjoyed a significant advantage in the campaign because the standard of the election staff was very high. A younger coterie including Dan Pender, Caitriona Meehan, Grace Cappock, Ciaran Ó Cuinn and Deirdre Gillane all went on to serve various ministers in government – some have since departed for the private sector – but in 2002 they were a highly effective second tier of staff who minded candidates, briefed journalists and bad-mouthed their opponents.

The efficacy of the Fianna Fáil campaign and especially of its media management became a theme in the reportage. After barely a week, the *Irish Times*'s Mark Hennessy was noting that journalists were complaining that 'too many strings' were being pulled; the campaign was too slick. But if the media were played, whose fault was that? In the Treasury, with each successful diverting of a journalist, the contempt for the media as a whole – and for individual journalists, often colourfully expressed – only rose higher.

The opposition struggled to move the focus to public services, but even here they floundered. There was widespread concern over the state of some public services, notably health, and the government had made extensive efforts to neutralize it as an issue before the election. In this, Ahern and his strategists were remarkably successful; though many voters still cited their dissatisfaction with the health service as a major issue when deciding how they would vote in the election, the coalition was successful in convincing voters that they were taking the problem in hand, and that the opposition did not offer anything better. This remarkable achievement is borne out by the 2002 election study, which concluded that while health was a concern for many people, the issue was actually a marginal positive for the government! A quarter of voters credited the government with effecting improvements in the health service, while just 20 per cent believed that the opposition would do better. This is almost completely at odds with the conventional wisdom of the time. It also suggests that the widely derided commitment to ending waiting lists in two years worked as an electoral device, though it would obviously entail a political price to be paid later.

As the campaign moved into its final stages, Fine Gael was facing meltdown, Labour irrelevancy. The only slim hope for Noonan was to crush Ahern at the televised leaders' debate. But Fianna Fáil was stalling on agreeing a date. Fine Gael obviously wanted a debate; in fact, if they could have had a debate every night, they would. It might have given some hope of reviving the campaign. With such a strong lead in the polls, Fianna Fáil knew that if nothing changed in the campaign, they would win handsomely. So the debate was a risk to be minimized. The campaign discussed in meetings how to put Fine Gael and RTÉ off as long as possible, circulating drafts of letters between one another in an effort to find the right tone of willingness to debate without agreeing to any specifics. 'We had a deliberate tactic of pushing it out as long as possible,' says one participant. Endless correspondence dragged on between Fianna Fáil, Fine Gael and RTÉ. Meanwhile, the clock ticked on.

Ahern's meticulously planned schedule had included a number of rehearsal sessions for the debate, but it was thrown into confusion when Ahern read a story in the *Irish Independent* a few days before the debate was due. It revealed how Ahern had been doing intensive preparation for the debate and how Brian Cowen had been playing the part of Michael Noonan in the rehearsals. It was, says one insider, 'from beginning to end an invention'. Ahern was furious, and immediately cancelled all preparation sessions. He angrily upbraided Mackin, whom he wrongly suspected of leaking the story to the reporter. Eventually, with his staff despairing, he consented to one rehearsal, with his friend and sometime voice coach Patrick Sutton playing the part of Noonan.

The debate was a widely watched anti-climax. According to RTÉ's viewing figures, 1.2 million people tuned in; few of them found it memorable. Conforming to the boxing analogy uniformly employed for such events, the *Irish Times*'s verdict was that it was a points victory for Noonan, but there was no sign of the knockout blow that he needed at this stage of the campaign. 'The killer punch was never landed,' wrote the paper's political correspondent, Mark Hennessy. In fact, despite the massive audiences, the whole thing was a damp squib. Which suited Fianna Fáil just fine. The reports of the debate were mixed; more importantly the following morning's editions of the *Irish Times* also carried details of the last poll of the campaign: on 45 per cent of the first preference vote, Fianna Fáil were comfortably ahead. Asked about their choice of taoiseach, voters preferred Ahern by a margin of almost five to one. Over 60 per cent of voters were happy with the way the government was doing its job. There was no stopping him now.

The most-managed campaign in Irish electoral history had one final twist, however. With his unlikely shimmy up a lamppost in Ranelagh to hang his 'One-Party Government? No thanks!' poster, Michael McDowell elbowed the PDs into the heart of the election debate. Astutely concluding that attacking the opposition would get them no more than incidental media coverage, McDowell instead conceived a remarkable strategy to attack Fianna Fáil and paint its leader, with whom he had sat in government for three years (and with whom he nowadays enjoyed extremely cordial personal relations), as a communist-era megalomaniac dictator, bent on self-aggrandizement through his plans to build a national sports stadium at Abbotstown – a proposal that was actually one of Ahern's most cherished projects. McDowell's charges were all the more wounding to Ahern because he knew how attached the Taoiseach was personally to the plans. 'If I lose this election,' the Taoiseach had told one of his aides, 'the last thing I'll do before leaving is sign the orders for that stadium.' (Six years later, after leaving office, he told the *Sunday Independent* editor that his 'one big regret was not building the stadium'.)

Fianna Fáilers had bristled when Labour portrayed them as needing to be supervised by adults in government; now here was the attorney general in their own cabinet doing it! Many were furious. Ahern, demonstrating his at times unbelievable tolerance and ability to soak up personal attack, shrugged it off in public. He was pretty annoyed about the Ceaucescu stuff, but it was just business.

McDowell's intervention – which had excited the anger of some of his colleagues, such as Liz O'Donnell, who feared for the Fianna Fáil transfers they needed – fed into a public mood in the final days of the campaign. That mood accepted the inevitability of a Fianna Fáil-led government and was preparing to select from a variety of accompaniments. At least as damaging for Fianna Fáil was an *Irish Independent* headline which boomed 'It's all over bar the voting' in the days running up to polling day. That front page was probably more significant than the *Indo*'s 'payback time' editorial of five years earlier. When the paper arrived in Treasury Building, the Fianna Fáil reaction was clear: that's not going to help.

It didn't. The day of the count brought triumph, and eighty-one seats, but no majority for Fianna Fáil. Ahern quickly announced that he would seek to form a government with the Progressive Democrats – who, despite their own expectations of a wipe-out, had doubled their numbers from four to eight.

For Dick Walsh, writing in the *Irish Times* after the election, 'It was the tabloid press wot won it.' It was the second election in a row in which Walsh blamed the media for the left's failure. The Fine Gael meltdown, he asserted, and the Labour atrophy were the result of PJ Mara's dual role as Fianna Fáil handler and consultant to the Independent group, and the decision of the *Irish Sun* and the *News of the World* to support the Ahern-led government. If only the Irish people could be left alone and allowed to form their own opinions free from the influences of foreign tabloid media and the depredations of the Independent group, it seemed to the writer, they would revert to their European social democratic natural state and vote for a left-of-centre government. Within two years, it would appear that the leader of the supposedly centre-right government thought much the same.

7. After the Party, the Hangover

'SCREWED BY LIARS' screamed the front page of the *Irish Daily Star* on the day after the government published its spending estimates for the following year in November 2002. It was less than six months after the general election triumph and Bertie Ahern's government had spent almost the entire intervening period on the defensive, trying desperately to justify the curtailment of election promises and explaining the need for cutbacks in public spending. Given that the same ministers had spent the general election campaign publicizing their wizardly management of the economy over the previous five years, the public was understandably having some difficulty swallowing the new reality. The growth in government spending was indeed being slashed, and the adjusted figures would later show that spending increases fell from a whopping 14 per cent growth in 2002 to 7 per cent growth in 2003. A more explicit illustration of the effect of the election on the national finances was that spending growth in the first six months of 2002 was an eye-watering 22 per cent, before McCreevy slammed on the brakes in July.

The *Star*'s pithy bile was an accurate representation of the media climate, but the national mood had also turned quickly against the new government. Ministers argued and briefers briefed that these were not cutbacks but reductions in planned increases, but neither press nor public were minded to accept that. Few in government were that worried; they thought it would pass. In fact, something important and profound was happening in the way that the public thought about the Fianna Fáil–Progressive Democrat coalition.

It wasn't just that the government had become unpopular, though it had, as poll numbers made clear. It wasn't just that ministers were establishing in the public mind traits – arrogance

was one of the most frequently cited – that would prove ultimately to be terribly damaging, though they were. It was that
the government was losing the trust of the electorate. Simply
put, many people came to believe they had been lied to during
the preceding general election campaign. That lack of trust
among voters for the second government was to be among the
salient political dynamics of the following five years. It drove
the unpopularity of Ahern's second government, unpopularity
that the government would spend tens of billions of euros trying
to buy its way out of. Low poll ratings would dissuade ministers
from taking corrective action to deflate a dangerous property
bubble and address a dangerously imbalanced economy. The
government's fall from public acclaim after the 2002 general
election was to have profound political and therefore economic
consequences.

The roots of the trouble went back to the general election
campaign and the immediate aftermath. As ministers and advisers
toasted their success and watched Ireland's roller-coaster World
Cup in Japan for the month of June, officials in the Department
of Finance were putting the finishing touches to a budget strategy
memorandum that would have far-reaching political consequences.

At this time every year, the minister for finance presents a
budgetary strategy memo to government, signalling the start of
the process of deciding budgetary allocations for the following
year. Colloquially, it became known as the 'end of the world
memo', such was its gloomy tone and pessimistic outlook for the
government finances. The Department of Finance was engaged in
a perennial battle to control the spending of the line departments;
hence its tendency to emphasize the negative. In tandem with this
process, McCreevy was in the habit of tweaking his spending
plans mid-year. Given the front-loading of spending in the first
(pre-election) months of the year, allied to the deteriorating
financial position of the government, the 2002 tweaks were
always going to be pretty severe. Though Fianna Fáil had romped
home in the election on the back of the economic boom, the

government's finances were actually declining quite precariously in the first months of 2002. The fact that most journalists and commentators – Garret Fitzgerald was a notable exception – hadn't noticed this before the general election was only sharpening their attitudes now. The fact that the opposition's spending plans were more lavish than Fianna Fáil's was neither here nor there.

The trigger for the change in the public mood and the damage to the government was the revelation that McCreevy was demanding post-election cuts in spending in each department. Later a cabinet memorandum was released to Stephen Collins and published in the *Sunday Tribune*, though under the terms of the Freedom of Information Act, it should never have been allowed through. Its release was a mistake, something which McCreevy accepted after an initial suspicion in some government circles that it was a malicious leak.

The cuts memorandum seemingly stood in direct contradiction to McCreevy's assertion during the election campaign that 'no cutbacks whatsoever are being planned secretly or otherwise'.

This was where the damage came from. Most people accept that a government has to manage its finances according to its resources, and the international climate at the time was highly unfavourable. But it hadn't changed since Charlie had told them everything was hunky-dory. It was the lying, rather than the screwing, that the public took exception to.

McCreevy had some justification in pleading both that spending adjustments were a normal part of the government's financial year, and that some action was needed in the light of declining government revenues. However, he could hardly object to the accusation that he had inflated spending hugely in advance of the general election, and slammed on the brakes in the immediate aftermath. All summer and into the autumn the news trickled out of more spending cutbacks, driven by organizations and interest groups which knew that their best chance of avoiding the cuts was to make them sound as severe as possible. Certainly, growth in the world economy had plummeted as a result of the

9/11 attacks and the bursting of the technology bubble on the stock markets. But to the charge of playing the economic cycle for electoral purposes, McCreevy had no real defence. Nor did he see any particular reason to give one.

'Look, it was my job to win the election for Fianna Fáil – not to do it for Fine Gael, Labour or anyone else,' he told reporters with commendable though politically unwise candour. His public comments and his private explanations to ministers at least had the virtue of consistency. 'Look,' he told a cabinet meeting that cavilled at instructions to cut back spending, 'do you want to win the next local elections *or* the next general election?'

The finance minister was right about one thing, though: the popular notion that overall government spending was being massively reduced was rubbish. By end of the year, the total reduction in planned expenditure was something of the order of €100 million – or about a quarter of 1 per cent of total government spending.

Ahern was furious that such a relatively trifling amount should be the cause of such political pain. He assured McCreevy that he was absolutely convinced of the need to rein in spending and supported him publicly, but he complained to other ministers that the political damage was completely out of proportion to actual cutbacks. 'One hundred million – that's all we cut, for fuck's sake,' the Taoiseach said to one minister. 'We've destroyed ourselves for the sake of 100 million.' Another minister reflected later: 'We said things in 2002 that we didn't have to. Then we had to have the cutbacks, and we made a balls of them.' Another told me: 'We took huge flak for small money.'

What Ahern immediately understood was that it was the political management of the cutbacks that was to cause more damage than their actual effect. What is remarkable is that he seemed so reluctant to do anything about it. It was a failing that would dog his second government again and again.

But if McCreevy was determined to follow a business-as-usual approach, Ahern was already signalling that some things would be changing. This much was evident as soon as the second programme for government was published. The negotiations between Fianna Fáil and the Progressive Democrats after the election were largely perfunctory. They were entrusted to a team comprising Brian Cowen, Noel Dempsey and Seamus Brennan; Ahern still disliked Brennan, but he grudgingly admitted that he had been a highly effective chief whip. He was also, on economic policy, halfway towards the PDs; more importantly, he was a born conciliator and deal-maker. Just in case the negotiators should get ahead of themselves, they were aware that the back-up team of officials to support them were all Ahern's men – Gerry Hickey, Peter MacDonagh and Brian Murphy. The Fianna Fáil ministerial team was faced across the table by Michael McDowell, Tom Parlon and Fiona O'Malley. To say that the Fianna Fáilers regarded it as a mismatch doesn't even approach their feelings about it. McDowell they knew, of course, and they respected his intellect, even if they were still smarting from the frontal assaults he had made on their party and their leader in the course of the campaign. But that was politics, and they would get over it. Parlon and O'Malley they regarded as political lightweights. Conducting their own sessions during breaks in the negotiating, the Fianna Fáilers laughed about the political inexperience of the PD's negotiating team. They didn't rate Parlon or O'Malley.

When the two sides met, Fianna Fáil produced a draft programme for government and handed it across the table. 'They said, "Yeah, er, OK ..."' says one participant. They had no answering document. The amount of actual negotiating was negligible, and confined to a few small points. They dragged on for far longer than was necessary. 'Their principal concern was that negotiations should go on long enough for people to think there were negotiations,' says one participant on the Fianna Fáil side. 'We spent most of the time telling stories and then coming out and saying we were working away,' says another.

Nonetheless, the document that emerged from them was significant in some respects. In stark contrast to the tax-cutting pledges of 1997, there were no promises of further tax cuts in the

2002 programme for government. 'Fianna Fáil and the Progressive Democrats have delivered dramatic reductions on taxation over the last five years,' the final document stated. 'We will keep down taxes on work in order to ensure the competitiveness of the Irish economy and to maintain full employment.' The old commitment to cutting taxes had become one to keep them down. The programme stated that the parties were 'committed to the achievement of the taxation objectives set out in the "Action Programme for the Millennium"', the previous programme for government. Actually this included the commitment to reduce the top rate to 40 per cent 'if economic circumstances permit'. However, the 2002 document didn't include this explicitly. Tax cutting was no longer a core part of the government's agenda.

Partly that was because the discussions and their conclusion were informed by knowledge of the rapidly worsening economic situation, but it was also because Ahern believed that the tax-cutting agenda had gone far enough. McCreevy concurred, for the present at least – he knew that the finances were declining rapidly. In fact, he had told people that the election manifesto should be a 'blank page': that is, there should be no promises in it, an argument that ran up against opposition from some of the Taoiseach's advisers. But it was also a signal that McCreevy's power could not last for ever. A new government would not be as easily dominated as the previous one had been. The Taoiseach would not be as easily circumvented as he had been. 'This is a Fianna Fáil document and I'm very happy with it,' he told people. When he went before the parliamentary party, he was even more effusive. 'This is a Fianna Fáil government and it will be more in tune with our social policies,' he told TDs.

These overt signals sent out by Ahern were testament to the fact that he had become uncomfortable not so much with tax-cutting policies of the 1997–2002 administration but with the way the government was being portrayed as right wing. He had kept the 1997–2002 government together through conciliation and compromise. Ahern would never abandon that side of his political nature, but he would be more assertive in future. Especially with

his finance minister. Soon, ministers began to notice tension
between the two men that hadn't previously existed.

Nonetheless, McCreevy remained a powerful force at cabinet,
and still Ahern's most important collaborator and adviser. He
intervened to save his friends and cabinet allies Joe Walsh and
Michael Smith when Ahern was selecting his ministers, though
his entreaties to promote Brian Lenihan went unheeded. The
new cabinet contained some new faces – Michael McDowell,
Seamus Brennan, Martin Cullen and Eamon Ó Cuiv – replacing
Michael Woods, James McDaid, Frank Fahey and the defeated
Mary O'Rourke. It may have been a Fianna Fáil programme for
government, but it was a more economically PD cabinet than its
predecessor – a typical Ahern contradiction.

Despite his supposed willingness to share government with the
PDs even with an overall majority, Ahern was hopping mad about
the results in a few constituencies – the few hundred stray votes in
a few constituencies that cost Fianna Fáil its first overall majority
in twenty years. When one cabinet minister met Ahern in
St Luke's, the minister thought he was going to have a discussion
about his own place in cabinet. But this was preceded by a long
tutorial from Ahern about the failings in a few constituencies
that had cost him an historic majority, about how this fucker and
that fucker had cost him the overall majority. The Taoiseach
ranted particularly about Galway West, where he blamed 'fucking
Frank' (Fahey) for the failure of the third candidate, Margaret
Cox, to gain a seat for the party. This was a little hard on Fahey,
but Ahern's interlocutor noticed that when the new cabinet
was announced, Fahey was not a member of it. His constituency
colleague and rival Eamon Ó Cuiv was.

Ó Cuiv was a curiosity in the party. The grandson of Éamon
de Valera, he bore a passing physical resemblance to his exalted
grandfather (exalted by nobody more than Ó Cuiv himself),
though where the Chief's stern morality and the Catholic
asceticism of his times seemed to be embodied in his thin, upright
figure, the current generation concealed a growing paunch under
his plain suits. He had grown up, he surprised people by telling

them, in Dublin 4; a less typical representative of that much-derided (and much misunderstood) postcode it would be difficult to find. He left Dublin to become a creamery and co-op manager in Connemara; he speaks Irish fluently; he thinks, speaks and acts like a countryman – often an eccentric one. When he ascended to stewardship of the Department of Community, Rural and Gaeltacht Affairs, it soon became known as 'Craggy Island', the home parish of the television character Fr Ted. Many of the Dublin political establishment thought he was half mad. Ahern thought he was mostly reliable. He was responsible for the administration of thousands of small grants under various schemes; politically, it was his job to keep rural Ireland content with thousands of small grants. A lot of the time, he did.

Micheál Martin spent an hour or so with Ahern, discussing Martin's future in health. Martin had said during the campaign that he looked forward to returning to the department after the election, though like any sane politician – and especially one who might have ambitions to lead the party in the future – he was lying about this. He also knew he would have to return. They had a long talk about health policy and the implementation of the new health strategy. At the end of their discussion, Ahern summarized: 'So what you're telling me is that you'll take it if I'm stuck?' That was about the size of it, all right.

Martin had also indicated that if he was going back to health, he would want some assurances about budgets and about having able and reliable junior ministers to assist him, which Ahern was happy to give. Some weeks later, when Ahern appointed Ivor Callely and Tim O'Malley – neither of whom Martin subsequently placed in both the able and reliable categories – he began to wonder about how safe his budgets were.

Ahern and McCreevy quelled most of the public rumblings in the party in the autumn of 2002, telling the party at its Killarney gathering that they were five years from an election as long as they kept their heads. McCreevy in particular delivered a bravura performance to one of the parliamentary party sessions, described by one TD as 'mixing wit and economics', an unlikely cocktail. But he continued by turns to surprise and infuriate his cabinet colleagues. Nothing was more surprising – and for some, infuriating – than his choice for the new ombudsman and information commissioner a few months later.

The introduction of the Freedom of Information Act in 1998 had greatly discommoded both civil servants and politicians, providing a window to the exercise of power and the policy-making process that served occasionally to embarrass the government, but more routinely just to inconvenience officials. But bad and all as the FOI Act was for government, in early 2003 it was about to get an awful lot worse. The 1997 act, which came into operation in the spring of 1998, contained a provision that would effectively open cabinet records to be released under the act after five years – a dramatic reduction in the previous thirty-year rule – which meant that the innermost workings of the first years of the Fianna Fáil–PD coalition would be due for release in April 2003. To the government, that was intolerable.

Amending legislation, which it fell to the minister for finance to introduce, was needed. Everyone could see the storm of media protest that would ensue, though as ever, ministers thought that the public wouldn't mind all that much, and they figured that they had a greater claim to know the public's mind than the media did. Still, McCreevy came up with what he thought was a masterstroke to confound the inevitable criticism of the restrictions and the vastly increased charges that were to be introduced simultaneously. He proposed to appoint the journalist Emily O'Reilly to the joint positions of ombudsman and information commissioner. O'Reilly was one of the country's best-known and most able journalists, and while in recent years her work had occasionally exhibited signs of a weary and worldly cynicism, she was unquestionably among the most able critics of the government. Though friendly with McCreevy, O'Reilly was capable of being witheringly dismissive about individual politicians – as she had been about Bertie Ahern in an article written during the 2002 general election campaign. She had referred to Bertie Ahern's 'monstrous ego' that needed constant stroking, describing the Taoiseach as an insecure man with a manic desire to be liked. In fact, McCreevy's calculations that the appointment of one of their own would mollify the media critics of the Freedom of Information restrictions was the direct opposite of the truth, and another example of political incomprehension of how the media actually works. O'Reilly had led a charmed life in journalism and the reaction of most of her colleagues was not a warm glow of satisfaction at her achievement but bitterness and envy. 'The response of Emily O'Reilly's fellow journalists this week to her appointment . . . "was shock and awe,"' noted one newspaper profile. 'Very few of them instantly exclaimed with pleasure and approval about the news. More typically, they paused and then struggled to compose a measured response that didn't sound grudging. Many failed in this regard.'

'Ah, Jaysus, Charlie . . . ' was Ahern's reaction when the finance minister proposed O'Reilly's appointment. Harney's was a good deal more direct, and less polite. Nonetheless, McCreevy made the case with some vigour and was ultimately successful, though Harney later told friends that she thought Ahern would block it and Ahern thought she would block it. Officials were even more surprised than the politicians. Dermot McCarthy was contacted the night before the cabinet decision and told by McCreevy. There was a long pause. 'And what,' he finally said, 'does the Taoiseach think of this?'

The first half of 2003 was a tough time for Fianna Fáil but it was also a tough time for Ahern personally. His relationship with Celia Larkin had come to an end and he was dealing with the necessary and unpleasant social and personal consequences from that decision. Some intimates found him subdued and even morose on occasion; but typically, there was no let-up in the work rate. The Drumcondra boys, many of whom loathed Larkin, were exultant. 'I think he was in a pretty difficult space at the time,' says one official who dealt with him on a regular basis at that time. 'The Drumcondra lads were ecstatic, of course. But it was a black few months for him.' Larkin had left Ahern's staff a few years earlier; in truth, her departure was also welcomed by many staff in Government Buildings. Working with the boss's partner is never easy. She was in the habit of dropping in to the staff's offices and offering advice and instructions – a practice which did not endear her to many of them. 'She was a pest,' remembers one staffer. Some felt that she was trying to tell them how to do their jobs.

Sometimes her behaviour seemed almost designed to court controversy and notice. On one occasion, travelling to Cork by helicopter, she was reading a copy of a book on John F. Kennedy's relationships, entitled *Kennedy's Women*. On another occasion, she was carrying a copy of 'something like *How to Keep Your Man Happy*, or something like that,' recalls one staffer. Ahern eventually turned to her and said, 'Jaysus, would you ever take off the dust jacket.' There were numerous diplomatic headaches because of her unofficial status as Ahern's partner, at home and abroad. Some were easier than others to overcome. Ahern threatened abandonment of at least one official visit when controversy arose over Larkin's programme. Other parties were more understanding. Chinese officials assured Ahern's staff that there would be no problems with Larkin's status. 'It's OK, it's OK, in China also. He has secretary. Wife stay in China. Secretary travel.' The officials had to explain that it wasn't quite like that.

Her departure was obviously a blow to Ahern. They had been partners for more than a decade, and – like a good political wife – she had devoted her life to his political career. But there was to be no wedding, despite her hopes, which she had the temerity to make public. Another wedding would underline her departure: there was no place for her at the wedding of Ahern's daughter Georgina to pop star Nicky Byrne of Westlife in France in the summer of 2003. The antipathy of Ahern's daughters to Larkin was the subject of some lurid tales among Ahern's staff.

All relationships and marriages are in part unknowable to observers, but Larkin's desire to marry Ahern was well advertised, including by herself. Nobody else thought it would happen. 'Why he never married that woman I just don't understand,' reflected one of his female ministers. But of all the dozens of Ahern's colleagues and staff whom I asked about this question, not one ever thought the pair would marry. Larkin was to make a life apart from Ahern for herself, though she would remain semi-detached from public life, speaking occasionally to journalists and maintaining a public profile. When the National Consumer Agency was set up, staff in Micheál Martin's office received a call from Gerry Hickey, to request that Larkin be appointed to the board of the new body. Over the protests he said simply: 'The Taoiseach wants this. It has to happen.'

Despite a successful second referendum on the Nice Treaty in October, the Taoiseach had much else to occupy him during those jumpy months: fires were breaking out all over government. None would generate more heat than the tortuous saga of electronic voting.

For an issue that was to become one of the running sores of the second Ahern administration, and a byword among both media and public for waste and expensive incompetence, the plan to introduce an electronic system for voting in elections and referenda had a remarkably uncontroversial birth. All the main opposition parties were generally supportive of the measure, and the passing of the relevant legislation was marked by an unusual degree of political consensus. Partly, this was because Noel Dempsey, the minister responsible for its introduction, was acknowledged even by his opponents as someone who was serious about the reform of the political process and the electoral system. This was occasionally derided among his colleagues; he won no friends in Fianna Fáil, for example, for his suggestion that the system of proportional representation by the single transferable vote – played so successfully by the party – should be abandoned. By the end of Ahern's second term, Dempsey had developed quite a reputation for landing himself and the government in the soup for making radical policy proposals without reference to his cabinet colleagues. 'The usual Dempsey fucking foot-in-the-mouth manoeuvre' was how one senior government source characterized one of his mishaps to me in the autumn of 2007.

But the acceptance of e-voting (as it was to become known) by all parties was also motivated by a simple though seldom acknowledged fact: politicians hate elections. No matter what they may say in public, the experience of sitting through a proportional representation count, especially if their seat is uncertain (as most congenitally believe it to be), is excruciating for politicians, whatever their rank. They would have been, and most still would be, happy to see the end of it.

Just like Dempsey, Martin Cullen was delighted to find an easy issue to hang his hat on. He had been elevated to the cabinet after the election, and though he was hardly the clownish figure of subsequent newspaper characterization, his promotion probably owed much to geography – he was the only minister in the south-east, a region that had keenly felt its absence from the cabinet table – as it did to his abilities.

Cullen had joined Fianna Fáil from the PDs in 1994 at the invitation of Albert Reynolds, following the departure of Pat Cox from the PDs over Harney's election as leader. His recruitment was a quiet coup for Reynolds, who had cultivated him for months, though the actual announcement had to be postponed at the last minute as it would have clashed with the IRA ceasefire declaration of 1994. 'Look, we have the ceasefire and it's going to be announced on the same day as your thing,' Reynolds told him in a hasty phone call a day or two before his press conference was due. 'It would be a feckin' disaster for you. Can you leave the country for a day or two?' Cullen complied, travelling to see a relative in London.

Cullen's move to Fianna Fáil was for a mixture of motivations, not least among them his own self-interest. Waterford yearned for a cabinet minister, and Cullen could see that he had a better chance than any of the existing TDs or prospective TDs. He certainly knew there was little chance of becoming a minister in an FF–PD coalition as long as he remained in the smaller party; the axis of power in the PDs had moved definitively to Dublin after O'Malley quit the leadership and Cox left the party. Cullen could see little future for himself in the PDs; he would be serving the people of Waterford better, he told himself, in the larger party, and serving them even better if he could wangle a promise of a ministerial job in the future. There was even a vacancy for a junior minister at the time he joined, which he had pushed Reynolds for, though without much hope of securing it. Not this time, he was told. 'You're not getting it. But we'll start the process in 97.'

However, if Cullen could see this, so could everyone else, and many of his new colleagues in Fianna Fáil never welcomed him to the fold with quite the warmth he might have hoped for. Many back-benchers remained cool towards him, and when he ran into trouble later, he lacked a constituency of supporters or friends to speak up for him. A non-drinker, he didn't spend hours in the members' bar trying to win them over, either. When he did make it into government, he was entirely dependent on the goodwill of the leader. He had a constituency of one to please.

Not that progression to government was exactly a smooth path. He was only weeks in his new party as a government back-bencher when that government began to disintegrate. First came the report of the Beef Tribunal and then the controversy over the extradition of Fr Brendan Smyth and the appointment of Harry Whelehan to the High Court. 'Fuck me,' Cullen asked himself at one point, having moved from opposition to government and back to opposition within three months or so; 'What am I after getting myself into?'

But the new leader moved quickly to assuage the worries of everyone in the party and he took time to ease Cullen's concerns about his ministerial future, too. 'You've got a few years to really establish yourself,' Ahern told him. He was as good as his word, appointing Cullen to a junior minister's job in 1997, and promoting him to the cabinet after the 2002 election. John O'Donoghue had wanted – and was expected by many to get –

the environment job. He wasn't pleased when it was given to Cullen, especially as his own appointment to the Department of Arts and Culture was widely perceived as a demotion. Having finally made it to cabinet, Cullen was overjoyed. He was fêted in Waterford, where the absence of a cabinet minister had been the source of much anguish, and the existence of many ills was explained by the lack of a Waterford presence at the cabinet table. One local commentator, speaking through the pseudonymous Phoenix column in the *Waterford News and Star*, had kept up an almost Catonic chorus about Waterford's lack of a cabinet minister for years; the news of Cullen's appointment was greeted with some satisfaction.

Cullen's elation was not dented by the warnings by some of his colleagues, who told him the department was 'completely dysfunctional'.

Cullen wasn't discouraged. He had got along well with his officials in the Office of Public Works; he was going into the new job eager to learn and willing to work hard. He would have hundreds of civil servants working for him – including several to look after his constituency affairs. He wasn't a stubborn fucker; he had always been ready to compromise. Too ready, some said, but wasn't compromise the currency of politics? Now, at last, he had a ministerial car under him to drive him home every week to Waterford. He had a big budget and would have plenty of good-news stories to tell the local papers. Sure, what could go wrong?

In the summer of 2002, early in his tenure amid a sprawling brief, Cullen wanted something that would afford lots of announcements and photo ops, easy publicity and no political risk. What politician doesn't? He fancied himself as making his reputation in his new brief, perhaps catapulting himself into the front line of the cabinet. And the department seemed enormously keen on the idea. So when David Davin-Power of RTÉ asked for an interview with him on the subject of e-voting Cullen was delighted, even though some of his political staff, observing the reactions of the media to the piloted introduction of e-voting in three constituencies at the just-concluded election, were beginning to have some reservations about nailing his colours to the mast on this issue so early.

While Davin-Power and his cameraman waited in the board-room of the ministerial suite of offices in the Customs House, Cullen's press adviser, Dan Pender, went through the talking points with him. 'Are you sure about this?' Pender asked again. 'Do we really want to go strong on it? Maybe if you were a little softer?'

But Cullen was bullish. He could feel the presence of the TV cameras. 'It'll be grand,' he assured Pender. 'It'll be grand.'

In fact, many in the media were beginning to have second thoughts about the prospect of e-voting, and this was feeding into the political world. Later, Cullen himself became utterly convinced that a media campaign against e-voting was building after a meeting with RTÉ executives who Cullen believed did not want to lose the spectacle – and the chance for RTÉ to hog the limelight – presented by two days of vote counting.

But it wasn't just the media. There was genuine and wide-spread sympathy for the way the former Fine Gael justice minister Nora Owen had been treated by the new system at the May election. She had been told, live on television and without warning, that her seat was gone.

While there were no serious questions being asked about the system's reliability at this stage, many inside politics and outside were thinking simply, What's wrong with the old system? It was a question to which Cullen never really found a worthwhile answer.

Meanwhile, an independent technology consultant called Joe McCarthy had embarked on what was initially a one-man crusade against the proposals. A self-declared election junkie, he was a politician's nightmare – independent, intelligent and au fait with the technology, armed with formidable communications skills and in-depth knowledge of the programme culled from hundreds of Freedom of Information requests for which he had paid himself.

At first, McCarthy was dismissed by Cullen and his staff as a crank, and jokes about his conspiracy theories became currency in the department and among Cullen's staff. (One of his concerns was about the effect of cosmic rays on the counting machines, which really set the staff off.) But McCarthy soon found allies in the university at Maynooth, where a Ph.D. student called Margaret McGaley, who had completed a thesis on the subject, founded a group called Irish Citizens for Trustworthy E-Voting (ICTE).

The dissenters were beginning to find their feet and their voice. They were encouraged by Cullen, who took to making idiotic statements – such as describing the proposed Nedap system as 'the most secure electronic system that exists in the world'. In fact, as was becoming clear, Cullen knew little about the technicalities of the system; he was simply taking the supplier's word for it.

As would become painfully clear to the minister, some of his officials didn't know much more about it. In meeting after meeting, Pender remonstrated with the officials. 'Do you realize,' he asked them at one stage, 'the significance of the political problem we are having with this?' He thought they were stone deaf to the politics. They thought he and his boss should just get on with it and implement the government's decision.

One day, Cullen was having a regular meeting with his senior staff, reviewing the disaster that the issue was turning into. Cullen's advisers were wondering was it possible to abandon the thing completely. Without warning, the civil servants dropped a bombshell: the department had gone ahead and placed an order for the machines in accordance with government policy and policy the minister had adopted as his own. The cost was €42 million. Jesus Christ, thought one of Cullen's advisers. They're supposed to be on our side; this is going to bury us.

The Oireachtas Environment Committee scheduled hearings in early December 2003, at which the opposition put a hapless minister and his officials on the rack. The Department of the Environment – still intending to introduce the system in the local elections six months later – was frantic to get the issue settled and out of the committee. As the Dáil prepared to break for Christmas, the opposition proposed more hearings and a delay in the introduction. One evening, Cork North Central TD Billy Kelleher, the Fianna Fáil whip on the committee, met a worried Pender in the corridors of Leinster House. 'We're going to have to call a fucking vote on this,' the normally laconic Kelleher told him. 'And we'll have to whip them to vote on party lines.'

Whipped votes on committees are unusual. Cullen's staff knew what this meant: e-voting was going to become a point of political attack for the opposition. At the final meeting, Labour's Eamon Gilmore spelled out the political trap into which Cullen was enthusiastically hurling himself: 'If the Government parties insist on putting a proposal to the committee asking it to fully endorse a system that some of us are unhappy with, we will not support it. Subsequent to this, the introduction of electronic voting in this country will become a party political issue. It will be the introduction of electronic voting by Government parties in the face of opposition from the two largest Opposition parties.'

Opposition to e-voting had become more than just technical: it had become political. The fact that a public relations company – run by the party's former general secretary, Martin Mackin, and Ahern's former adviser Jackie Gallagher – had won the public tender to promote the project added a whiff of political sulphur that the opposition couldn't resist. Labour leader Pat Rabbitte raised it repeatedly at Leaders' Questions in the Dáil.

Cullen's advisers tried to scramble out of it. 'We need to get a commission or something. We need to get out of this. It's going to be a big problem,' one of them told the minister. He felt they were at a tipping point. The whole thing was moving from being a problem to a crisis.

Cullen shrugged it off. They were too far in, he told

Pender. The civil servants were all for it. It would be OK. Most importantly, the Taoiseach and the cabinet were onside. They would just have to handle it. He would have to handle the press, Pender took this to mean. The press had already whipped itself into one of the frenzies that were to become customary for the rest of the lifetime of the government.

'It'll be grand, it'll be grand,' Cullen kept saying. He had been through political and personal crises before. He was, above all, a survivor. 'We have to keep the head down and just keep driving forward. This thing will work itself out.'

In fact, the disaster was only beginning to get really going. It would rumble on for several months until finally being abandoned before the 2004 local and European elections, months after it became apparent that a U-turn was inevitable. The e-voting fiasco became a sort of totem for government waste, political myopia and politicians' vaingloriousness about pet projects. Cullen's increasingly strained defences of the project only served to highlight the fact that, actually, nobody thought there was anything wrong with the existing system of counting votes. In fact several public and painfully slow and – for the politicians involved – excruciating recounts in recent elections had only gone to show it was transparently honest and fair. This was the most glaring fact of all about the e-voting project: nobody, apart from a handful of politicians and civil servants, wanted it.

It would destroy Cullen as a serious political figure among the public, though he continued to prosper under Ahern and had a number of policy achievements to his name when he became minister for transport later. Though they had been acting in accordance with government policy, and his own department's policy, when Cullen looked for someone to blame for the mess he was in he looked at his officials. While the political controversy was raging, they had gone ahead and ordered the machines – acting on something that had been agreed by their political bosses, but oblivious to the emerging politics of the situation. He felt that he had been made to look 'a complete eejit' and blamed the civil service. 'If you get hung out to dry,' he told his ministerial colleagues, 'they don't give a fuck.'

The e-voting saga wasn't the end of the trials of Martin Cullen. In December 2004 *Ireland on Sunday* reported that his communications adviser, Waterfordwoman Monica Leech was employed on very generous terms, and had initially been the only person invited to apply for the job. Much of the press went after the story with excess – an excess that was to cost several of them hundreds of thousands of euros in libel settlements.

Ultimately, it was the excesses of the press pursuit of him that saved Cullen's ministerial career. Although Cullen commanded little loyalty and no real close political friendships around the cabinet table, several ministers including Brian Cowen were disgusted at his treatment by the press, and they had no appetite for delivering up a head for the press's satisfaction. Most politicians by their nature mistrust the media; many of them actively dislike it. They saw in the pursuit of Cullen a vision of the future in which their own foibles were illuminated for the edification of the more bovine elements of the press, and they recoiled from it. There was no great love for Cullen, whom ministers saw as accident prone and, by now, a political liability; but there was sympathy for him, and there was a fear of setting a precedent of letting the press destroy a minister. By most objective standards of political accountability, he would have resigned or perhaps been fired for the e-voting fiasco; but Bertie Ahern wasn't prepared to play by those rules.

'We can't be seen to give in to this kind of stuff,' Ahern told a cabinet discussion about setting up the inquiry into the Leech contracts. They all knew what he meant.

'The one thing you'll get out of all this,' Ahern told Cullen, 'is fairness.' Having made the judgement that Cullen shouldn't be fired, Ahern asked Dermot Quigley, a former chairman of the Revenue Commissioners, to examine the circumstances of Leech's employment. The inquiry would be fair and honest,

Ahern promised, and he would withhold judgement on his embattled minister. Cullen's own staff were ecstatic when they learned of the inquiry, judging correctly that it meant he was safe. The minister himself was more cautious – 'They could say I know it's unfair but you have to go anyway,' he reasoned – but ultimately his advisers were proved right. Following a mild slap on the knuckles, and a public declaration that future consultancy contracts would have to be approved by Ahern (which many doubted would be the case), Cullen gained a reprieve. He gained in the process a reputation as a political survivor, one which would be augmented in the months and years to come.

Cullen was probably no more ill-equipped to be head of a department than many ministers, though he displayed spectacularly poor political judgement throughout the lengthy e-voting saga, allied to a seemingly congenital ability to get on people's nerves. But his long and somewhat self-inflicted torture on e-voting was also a good example of how unwary ministers can be over-reliant on their civil service officials. Typically, the centre of government didn't involve itself in the fiasco until it was too late. Also typically, Ahern managed to support his minister whilst ensuring that what one of Cullen's staff called 'the avalanche of shit' that descended on his boss's head didn't come anywhere near the Taoiseach's office. By the time that e-voting was shelved, Cullen was at war with his own civil servants. His experience also demonstrated that in conflicts with their officials, ministers usually end up carrying the can.

Everything in politics comes at a price; Cullen's survival came at a price for Ahern. Leaving the transport minister in the cabinet would cost Ahern and his government dearly in political capital. Cullen, his consultants and his e-voting became bywords for the government's perceived arrogance and incompetence. This perception was driving the continuing unpopularity of Ahern's administration.

Other ministers were playing their part too. Noel Dempsey had been appointed after the election to the Department of Education in succession to Michael Woods, whose disastrous legacy would be a murky deal with the religious orders to compensate the victims of child abuse in orphanages and other institutions run for the state by the orders. That agreement, championed and nego- tiated by Woods, supported by Ahern and Dermot McCarthy, was signed hours before the first government left office and would cost the state more than €1 billion.

Dempsey was happy to leave the Department of the Environ- ment, and as a former teacher, he looked forward to taking the reins in education. But he worried his officials with his talk of reforms. He was barely two months in the job when he mentioned as an aside in a radio interview that he might consider looking at the possibility of reintroducing third-level fees. *The Sunday Business Post* followed up his comments and the following week's headline, 'Dempsey looks to bring back university fees', kicked off a political controversy.

There were a number of scraps at cabinet, culminating in what one witness described to me as 'a heated row' between Michael McDowell and Dempsey. Dempsey later told colleagues that he felt like punching the justice minister. McDowell accused Dempsey of being an 'ideologue'; Dempsey replied sharply, 'Well, coming from an ideologue like you, that's a compliment.' The Progressive Democrats were opposed from the outset.

Dempsey had a stubborn side to his nature which comple- mented his reformist instincts. Combined, they had the tendency to land the government in political trouble, on which occasions government ministers and functionaries tended to elide the Dempsey's county loyalty and his character; he was frequently described as 'that thick fucking Meathman'. 'Noel Dempsey,' noted one colleague, 'could start a fight in an empty room.'

The cabinet row over fees subsided, but the media seized on the issue and it simmered for months. The more Dempsey pleaded that the abolition of fees by the Labour minister Niamh Bhreathnach in 1995 had effectively ended up as a gift to the middle classes, the more the middle classes (in the media and else- where) found reasons to justify it. Government TDs wondered aloud why the minister had contrived to create another problem for the government where there were so many existing ones to choose from.

Ahern didn't have strong feelings about the third-level-fees issue one way or another, but Harney had made clear to Ahern that it was a red-line issue for the PDs – the party always had an acute sensitivity to issues affecting the middle class. Anxious to defuse the row, Ahern sought to discuss the issue quietly with Dempsey in a side office off the main cabinet room. It was one of those elliptical Ahern conversations that frequently left the other participant none the wiser about what the leader of the country actually wanted. Ahern explained how when you made a decision, there invariably were going to be people who were upset by the decision, which was why you had to carefully weigh not just which way to decide any issue but whether the decision had to be made at all. 'You can't take too many decisions together,' he told an increasingly puzzled Dempsey. 'Now, take this decision about the fees . . . It'll annoy the students, the farmers, the PDs . . . so we'd need to think about it.'

Fuck it, Dempsey thought. If he wants to tell me to do something, then let him bloody well tell me. The minister for education stuck to his guns, but there was no real political support for him. Eventually, McCreevy came to him. 'Look we have to stop this fees thing from dragging on,' the finance minister told Dempsey. The two men had a good relationship and a high regard for one another. 'I can't,' said Dempsey. 'I'm too far out on it now.' Well, what would get you off the hook? McCreevy enquired. This is how political deals are struck and, often, policy is made. Dempsey agreed to drop the fees proposal in return for extra funding for promoting greater access to higher education for students from underprivileged backgrounds and the fig leaf of a funding review of the sector. Perhaps because McDowell had been so precipitate in his opposition, Harney chipped in money from her department's budget. Nobody worried too much about the underlying principles.

But if McCreevy was trying to solve some political problems, he seemed to relish creating others. His willingness – some of

Ahern's aides saw it as eagerness – to court unpopularity where he saw it as necessary was becoming almost a fetish in the eyes of some. Nowhere was this more apparent than in his approach to disability funding during the Special Olympics.

The stadium was thronged to its 80,000-plus capacity and the playing surface was packed with 7,000 athletes from 160 countries and their coaches. The opening ceremony of the 2003 Special Olympics about to begin would be a glittering extravaganza of music and dramatic performance, including U2, The Corrs and the largest Riverdance group ever assembled. Among the audience were Nelson Mandela and Arnold Schwarzenegger. Waves of goodwill washed around Croke Park on a warm June evening, as a worldwide television audience looked on. The public address system boomed into life, asking participants to welcome the arrival of the Taoiseach, Bertie Ahern, on to the stage. The foreign athletes and spectators clapped politely. Some sections of the crowd cheered. Others began to boo. The booing reverberated around the ground. It wasn't universal, but it was loud, sustained and unmistakable.

Later, Ahern brushed it off. If there was booing, he said, he didn't hear it. Or maybe he did a little, 'on the left'. 'But I didn't even notice ... If there was some, it was very little because normally I'd pick it up.' Privately, though, he was furious.

Worse was to follow: other crowds began to pick up on the new trend. He was booed by a section of the Dublin football supporters at a game in Clones a fortnight later. It was like being rejected by his family. 'Booing Bertie,' noted Frank McNally in the *Irish Times*, 'has become a new sport.'

'I was galled to see Bertie Ahern standing up on stage and giving a speech. Has the man no shame?' demanded one irate letter writer to the *Irish Times*.

Disability groups had been warning for months that they would try to embarrass the government at the Special Olympics. In April, the chairman of one group, Frank Flannery – who would also become Enda Kenny's most important backroom strategist – warned that unless the government released promised funding, his group would give serious consideration to picketing the Olympic events. Several other groups also warned of pickets or boycotts. In the days before the opening ceremony, Ahern had engaged in a round of meetings with groups to avert official protests. But that didn't stop activists and parents from giving him the pip in Croke Park.

Ahern was not only angry at this treatment: he believed it to be unfair. 'I spent six years directly involved with the games committee,' he told Pat Rabbitte in the Dáil a few days later. 'I am glad that through this period I took the political flak and invested money in Croke Park, Abbotstown and other centres so that we would have the Special Olympics . . . Like all good things in this country, when the occasion arrives everybody agrees it was a good idea.'

In public, he alternated between unconcerned and wounded. In truth, it would have been impossible to satisfy the demands and requests of all the different disability groups – they wanted different things, for a start. But in private, he was furious with his finance minister. McCreevy was refusing to release funding for disability services.

The minister for finance refused entreaty after entreaty from a variety of government supplicants. Gerry Hickey repeatedly made the case for releasing funding, pointing out that the minister was doing the government unnecessary damage to no avail. He was repeatedly rebuffed. Both Micheál Martin and Ahern made repeated attempts to get him to relent – the Department of Health could say they were using money from a contingency fund so as not to upset their agreed budgets. McCreevy thought the government had to be tough; everyone else thought he had to open his eyes to the political reality. When Martin again complained to the Taoiseach, Ahern told him the money was there. Harney told him it was there, but they couldn't get McCreevy to release it. For fuck's sake, Martin raged. These guys are supposed to be the leaders. Eventually, McCreevy relented. He would release the funding, he said. But there was to be no announcement until after the Special Olympics. He would not be seen to bow down before any lobby, no matter how strong, no matter how deserving. Martin thought it was just perverse. It was the opposite of politics. Later, Martin told friends that he thought this was some sort of a breaking point for Ahern.

Ahern's annoyance at the whole episode must have been subdued when a mysterious plane carrying a massive trailing banner appeared over the Croke Park sky at the closing ceremony. The banner read: 'Thank you, Bertie'. Ahern himself denied any knowledge of the curious flyby.

A few weeks after the Special Olympics concluded, the Department of Health announced that it was making an extra €50 million available for disability services. The Taoiseach, said Micheál Martin, pointedly omitting the minister for finance, had 'prioritized disability'. The press all reported that the funding had been released because of the reaction to the Taoiseach at the Special Olympics. 'Isn't it amazing,' asked the *Irish Times* editorial writer, 'what a public boo can do?' Martin insisted that the money would be from existing resources, and was included in a contingency fund in the department's budget from the start of the year. So why weren't people told before now; why weren't they told before the Special Olympics? he was asked. 'The cynics would have been in full flight,' he responded meekly. That wasn't what kept the funding under wraps; it was the obduracy of Charlie McCreevy. Nobody was booing him, though. At least, not in public.

There was one great effort to revive the party fortunes, one great dramatic gesture, which the leadership hoped would give the flagging poll figures a lift. It would fall flat on its face. Actually it would do worse: it would backfire badly and become another symbol of the government's policy and political failures. Again, McCreevy was the central figure in the drama.

Charlie McCreevy was only getting into his stride in his seventh budget speech when he dropped the bombshell. 'It is important that the growth we expect should be regionally balanced. In this regard, I am announcing details of decentralization of government departments and agencies . . .'

It was an astonishing plan, involving the transfer of entire departments, including their ministers, out of Dublin. There had been no consultation, much less debate, in advance of the announcement. McCreevy just pulled it out of the spacious hat in which he stored many of his budgetary announcements. 'No longer,' he declared, 'will policy be made entirely in Dublin on the basis of a Dublin mindset.' Whatever that was.

However, despite much subsequent commentary and political charge, decentralization in fact wasn't something that had suddenly parachuted into the political agenda. The policy had been announced as a government policy as far back as the 1999 budget, when it was widely reported that 10,000 civil servants would be transferred out of Dublin under the programme. The announcement triggered a widespread lobbying campaign from towns all over the country seeking to have state bodies and government departments decentralized in their direction. Leinster House became a place of pilgrimage for local action groups, town councils and chambers of commerce seeking to promote their respective homes as especially suitable, carefully prepared and deserving of a political decision in their favour. It was good old patronage politics at work, and TDs and ministers were pestered on a weekly basis.

The cabinet discussed the possibility of announcing a pro-gramme of decentralization in one 'big bang' in early October of 2003, as part of the budget. 'I'll do it,' McCreevy told ministers. 'I'll do it in the budget, but if there's the slightest leak outside this room it's cancelled. One leak, and that's it.'

McCreevy told the cabinet that they could talk to only two officials about the plans – his press officer, Dermot Ryan, and Michael Scanlan, an assistant secretary. The two civil servants met the ministers and asked them to identify the units of their depart-ments that could be decentralized. The ministers also had requests for towns in their constituencies to be allocated decentralized offices. The officials then tried to match up the lists – and see if they could comply with the government's previously published blueprint for regional development, the National Spatial Strategy. They couldn't.

The secrecy was thorough: even when the budget speech was written, a blank space was left for the decentralization announcement.

It was a measure of how McCreevy had come to dominate the cabinet that he could treat ministers in this way. But they didn't risk leaking it. A few, he later discovered, had told their secretary generals. But there were no leaks to the press. In the few days before the early December budget, McCreevy called ministers in to his office, and the final programme was put together. The night before the budget, McCreevy called in the leaders of the largest unions and briefed them on what was coming. You can condemn it if you want, he told them. Do what you have to do. You can deny that you knew anything about it. It's up to you.

For some ministers, it was done over the phone. One minister was travelling abroad on official business a few days before the budget when he received a phone call from McCreevy. 'It's the big D,' the finance minister told him. The line was bad and McCreevy seemed to be whispering. 'What?'

'The big D!' McCreevy repeated.

'The big what?'

'D! D! De-fucking-centralization! What do you want and where do you want it?'

And so it went. The back-benchers loved it. 'Whatddya think of that, Pat? Whaddya think of that?' an excited Donie Cassidy, the Westmeath TD, asked Labour leader Pat Rabbitte outside the members' bar in Leinster House that evening. 'Sure you couldn't oppose that!'

The media reaction to the budget was less giddy, with much of it focusing on the lack of major initiatives and the essentially neutral taxation package. 'Mr McCreevy,' sniffed one editorial writer, 'has lost his radical touch.' Back-benchers couldn't have cared less. With government bodies heading for fifty-three locations around the country, most of them had something to bring home at last. Surely, as Donie Cassidy said, nobody could oppose it?

But instead of being a magic bullet for the government, decentralization would be another nail in McCreevy's coffin. Ahern was already measuring him for it. The decentralization budget would be McCreevy's last.

8. The Inchydoney Conversion and the Exile of Champagne Charlie

Bertie Ahern is an unlikely but occasionally prolific journalist and his work has appeared in all the major newspapers. In early January 2004, he was on the job again, adorning the front page of one of those typically worthy special supplements with the *Irish Times*. This one was to mark Ireland's six-month presidency of the EU, which had begun on New Year's Day. 'More than ever,' the Taoiseach's bylined article asserted, 'the European Union's member states need to work together if we are to overcome the many challenges facing us.' Now that, thought one adviser, will be considerably easier than getting Fianna Fáil to work together.

Party managers were becoming increasingly worried about the forthcoming local and European elections. Published opinion polls in the autumn of 2003 had confirmed that the drastic slide in the government's popularity since the 2002 election was continuing, with support for Fianna Fáil registering at twenty-year lows – around 30 per cent. Ahern's personal popularity had plummeted by an astonishing thirty-three points since before the general election. Local and European elections were scheduled for June, and ministers would spend much of the time between January and then on EU business. In urban constituencies like Ahern's, Sinn Féin was organizing steadily and opinion polls showed Labour resurgent. The polls even showed that Fine Gael, left for dead after the 2002 election, was making some modest gains. As Ireland stepped on to the world stage, the party's private research was confirming that its leaders were heading for a fall at home.

Mara had tried to get a handle on the elections early on, instituting campaign meetings between headquarters' staff and the political advisers in each minister's office, but over time he gave up. They fizzled out, says one participant, because nobody trusted anyone else. A fissure had opened between Ahern's advisers based in Government Buildings and the Mount Street party headquarters, one that would endure until Ahern left office.

The local and European elections would be the first battlefield test for the party's new general secretary, Sean Dorgan, after the departure of Martin Mackin in late 2002. Mackin had been a highly effective general secretary and a close collaborator with PJ Mara in the management of the organization in advance of the 2002 election. He was also a skilful briefer of the media, something of which Ahern grew increasingly suspicious. Some of Ahern's Drumcondra acolytes were also less than impressed with Mackin's insistence on complying to the letter – as advised by Rory Brady – with every request for information and documentation from the Flood Tribunal.

Dorgan had never met Bertie Ahern before he sat down with him for the second interview for the general secretary's job. He had given some advice and assistance in setting up the party's extensive constituency polling operation in 1995 and 1996, while working as a lecturer in market research in the postgraduate School of Business at UCD. But in Fianna Fáil terms, he was an outsider.

Ahern learned to trust his new general secretary and to pay attention to his meticulously prepared briefs. At first, he tested Dorgan, throwing out little nuggets of confidential information to see if he heard them back from different sources. 'Between ourselves . . . ' he'd begin, before imparting some piece of gossip or some signpost to a future leadership decision by him. Dorgan sensed what he was at, but he wasn't one to tout around confidences of the leader anyway – besides, he was still finding his feet in the organization. There are some advantages to being an outsider. And he knew Ahern viewed media leaks – or at least, those not authorized by him – as a form of grievous disloyalty. One Monday morning after the *Sunday Tribune* had published the details of an internal Fianna Fáil poll, he met for their regular 9.30 a.m. meeting in St Luke's. Only he and Ahern had access to the numbers; he certainly hadn't told anyone. But he was terrified that he would be blamed for the leak – he was always conscious that Mackin's perceived closeness to the press had undermined his relationship with the Taoiseach, so he just never spoke to reporters beyond the most basic exchanges. It weighed on his mind throughout the meeting. At the end, he said, 'Look, I just want you to know, I had nothing to do with the poll in the *Tribune* . . .' Ahern stopped him. 'Don't worry,' he said, 'I know you didn't.' He paused. 'But I know who did.'

The two met every week, and Ahern was assiduous in tending to the party organization. He had an amazing ability to compartmentalize his life. No matter what else was going on, he absorbed the brief quickly and though he didn't always come to a decision quickly, Dorgan felt that Ahern knew as much about what was going on in the organization as the general secretary did. Dorgan's approach was that Ahern didn't have to be told everything, but he had to be told what he needed to know. And he tried never to surprise Ahern. Even during the EU presidency, when Ahern often hosted meetings with other EU leaders, ministers and delegations from the European Commission in Dublin Castle, Dorgan sometimes found himself summoned to an anteroom in the State Apartments; Ahern would excuse himself and meet the general secretary for an hour to discuss party matters. Even then, Dorgan felt, Ahern often knew the answers to the questions he asked. As the two men considered the approach of the local and European elections in 2004, neither the questions nor the answers were terribly encouraging.

Faced with consistent weakness in the polls and the likelihood of a caning in the forthcoming elections, Ahern sought to inject a bit of the old Showtime into the pre-election debate, looking for eye-catching initiatives and promises. But in truth, with McCreevy still keeping a tight hold on spending, it was pretty thin gruel. At the pre-election ard-fheis at Citywest in March, Ahern told delegates that old age pensions would go up to €200 a week and that decentralization would bring state bodies to their towns and villages. 'The challenge is not just to build a better economy; it is to bring government closer to the needs of all our people,' he told cheering delegates. With decentralization, he meant this literally.

But the biggest cheer was reserved for the previously embattled Martin Cullen, who announced a huge loosening of planning restrictions on one-off rural housing – an issue so hot in rural Ireland that the opposition was reduced to welcoming the move.

There was outrage from environmentalists, advocates of sustainable development as well as those (often urban-based) critics whose principal concern appeared to be as much about the aesthetics of yellow bungalows as it was about sensible planning. But Cullen's new policy was a victory for more than just dubious taste; as Frank McDonald noted, 'One factor that has not been noted is the huge vested interest in the sale of sites. It has been estimated that half-acre sites are selling for €45,000 on average and that farmers and other landowners could be making more than €800 million a year from such disposals.' No wonder they cheered Cullen to the rafters at Citywest. Intoxicated with the approval of the crowd, Cullen proceeded to jibe at the English rugby team, that day defeated by Ireland at Twickenham (more cheers), and Sinn Féin. Pointing to the national flag, he declared: 'It doesn't belong to one party. It doesn't belong to Sinn Féin. It belongs to Fianna Fáil!' More cheers.

But it wasn't enough. Fianna Fáil's own core supporters were delighted, but among the crucial and growing number of floating voters, they remained unpopular. The polls barely moved before election day. Voters hadn't forgotten 2002.

One week before polling day, some senior Fianna Fáilers were among the Celtic Tiger cubs drinking at the bar in the Schoolhouse Hotel, near the party's Mount Street offices and the gleaming corporate headquarters of the Grand Canal dock. They were pessimistic about the election but didn't believe that the outcome could be as bad as the *Sunday Business Post* polls, which had consistently been showing Fianna Fáil at around 30 per cent during the campaign, were suggesting. It was ten points worse than the party had secured at any previous election, they reasoned. 'I just don't believe it could be that bad,' one of the Fianna Fáilers told me. 'It couldn't,' echoed another. 'Could it?'

It could. When the votes were cast they showed that Fianna Fáil had secured just 32 per cent of the vote in the local elections; the party lost 80 of its 382 seats. Worse, Fine Gael had a red-letter day, securing 28 per cent of the vote, a complete recovery from the disastrous 2002 election, and more seats in the European Parliament than Fianna Fáil. Sinn Féin was unstoppable, especially across the Taoiseach's native northside of Dublin, winning nine seats on Dublin City Council. The local government landscape had been dramatically redrawn.

In fact, the story of the election was Sinn Féin – increasing its number of local councillors by over 150 per cent to 54, with several of them situated across the northside of the city of Dublin. Ahern's own brother, Maurice, almost lost his council seat in the surge to Sinn Féin, which saw them win a massive 18 per cent of the vote in Dublin. Mary Lou McDonald was elected an MEP for Dublin with over 60,000 votes. It was a stunning result. Ahern reflected: 'We lost this election. There is no doubt about that. Sinn Féin won it.'

It had been building since 2002. While most of the electorate did not base their voting intentions on the North, there were small numbers of voters for whom Northern Ireland was likely to influence their vote – and they were now more likely to vote for Sinn Féin. A *Sunday Independent*/IMS poll just before that election had rated the North as joint fourteenth in voters' order of priority. The more reliable RTÉ/Lansdowne exit polls on the day of the vote found that while 14 per cent of voters rated Northern Ireland as an issue influencing their vote in 1997, by 2002 that had dropped to just 4 per cent. In fact, Fianna Fáil lost nearly 4 per cent of its 1997 voters to Sinn Féin in 2002 – a proportion which, though small, would almost certainly have secured an overall majority for Fianna Fáil. Sinn Féin went from just one seat in the 1997–2002 Dáil to five, winning seats in Kerry North (Martin Ferris), Dublin South Central (Aengus Ó Snodaigh),

Dublin South West (Sean Crowe) and Louth (Arthur Morgan) to accompany Caoimhghin Ó Caoláin from Cavan-Monaghan.

The election of Ferris, a former IRA man who had served a prison sentence for importing arms, at the expense of the former Labour leader and Tánaiste Dick Spring, sent shockwaves through the Southern political establishment. Joining with independent deputies, Sinn Féin formed a technical group in the Dáil to ensure speaking rights and committee representation. Ó Caoláin, the party's leader in the Oireachtas, now had near-weekly slots to interrogate the Taoiseach at Leaders' Questions in the Dáil (though he was lamentably bad at it). While the fate of the Northern Assembly was unclear, Sinn Féin had gained a real foothold in the parliament of the Republic.

Ahern had always been keenly aware of the potential for Sinn Féin to grow. However, he was always prepared to risk this, seeing it as an acceptable risk to promote the peace faction in Sinn Féin and bind the party to politics at the expense of its attachment to violent means. He discussed it with his aides, many of whom had much greater misgivings about the consequences of effectively giving Sinn Féin room to promote themselves at Fianna Fáil's expense than he did. On one occasion he instructed the then general secretary, Martin Mackin, to meet Sinn Féin representatives and advise them on political organization in the South.

Ahern's willingness to encourage Sinn Féin was all the more questionable to many in his own party because of the unshakeable belief they shared that not alone were Sinn Féin's electoral efforts funded by the proceeds of illegal activities on both sides of the border, but the party was spending more money promoting itself and building a political organization than Fianna Fáil was. This was one subject about which ministers, TDs, party officials and spin doctors constantly complained to journalists, especially when Sinn Féin began to open offices around the country. Ahern himself privately told people that Sinn Féin was spending ill-gotten fortunes on its Southern electoral efforts. 'For God's sake,' Fianna Fáil would whine repeatedly, 'they spent thirty years killing people. Do you think they're worried if they violate electoral spending laws?' But by far the largest sources of declared funding for Sinn Féin were the British and Irish governments.

The other reservation that many in Fianna Fáil had about the political consequences of the peace process was that there didn't appear to be very many votes in it for them. The 2002 general election and now the bloody nose it had received in the 2004 local elections appeared to confirm that belief.

The government's unpopularity was the principal reason for the huge defeat, but it doesn't explain the loss of all the seats. It was a measure introduced by itself which exacerbated the scale of the defeat. The abolition of the 'dual mandate', where many TDs also sat on local authorities, meant that many deputies had resigned but crucially kept to themselves the right to nominate a replacement. In many cases, these tended to be either ultra-loyalists who would never challenge the TD – family members, often – or else, if such could not be found, someone who would make a poor candidate. Headquarters did not hold many of them in high esteem, to put it mildly. Voters evidently shared this assessment.

The party's customary approach to an election of promising local patronage and spending fell flat on this occasion. Perhaps it had momentarily worn out this approach; more likely, the party lacked the credibility to carry it off. Privately some ministers despaired. One cabinet member told me: 'It became impossible to keep people happy. If you said you would build a bridge to the Aran Islands, they'd want two bridges. I've sat at meetings up and down the country and some of the requests [for funding] were ridiculous, unbelievable. We'd be telling them that, No we don't have the money. But they knew we did.'

If the lack of enthusiasm of TDs and the proliferation of weak candidates were evidence that the grassroots effort for the local election was going to be below par, the leadership was frequently otherwise occupied too.

Ahern's own movements bear testimony to those distractions. On election day, he was on his way back from Savannah, Georgia, where he had been attending the G8 summit as President of the European Council. Watching at home, many people guffawed when Ahern appeared for the 'casual', walk-on-the-beach photo-call in a bizarre ensemble of a canary-yellow sports jacket and not-quite-matching trousers.

Nobody was laughing in Fianna Fáil headquarters. Press director Olivia Buckley had complained to the Broadcasting Complaints Commission about a story the independent radio stations were running on the day before polling – when a moratorium on political coverage exists – about a campaign by the trade union SIPTU against the government's decentralization proposals, an issue which was causing hell on the doorsteps. Gerry Howlin had blown a fuse when he heard the news item, and had demanded that headquarters take action. 'We can't take this,' he fumed to Dorgan. 'These people are shitting all over us and we have to do something about it.'

Buckley made the complaint and the offending item was taken off the airwaves, but – needless to say – the row leaked and adorned the front pages of the newspapers the following day. Polling day opened with stories about Fianna Fáil trying to censor the media leading the news. The complaint had backfired badly, and there was the usual fallout. Headquarters felt the heat from Government Buildings in sentiments that were relayed back pretty quickly; 'For fuck's sake!' complained one Government Buildings figure. 'Those guys in headquarters don't know what they're doing.' When Dorgan called Ahern to update him, the Taoiseach greeted the news in silence.

The European elections were no more successful. The party lost two seats, including those of the old war-horse Gerry Collins, and the high-profile second Dublin candidate, Royston Brady, self-appointed heir to Ahern's mantle, who imploded in spectacularly entertaining style. Brady was soundly defeated after a pantomime campaign, which started brightly before spiralling into disaster. He thought Yugoslavia was about to join the European Union; he appeared incapable of uttering a coherent political thought. He finished by fleeing a delighted media, literally – broadcaster

Matt Cooper, who seemed to be enjoying the pursuit more than most, took to sending a representative of his programme dressed as a chicken after him. One of Ahern's staff, briefing him on the phone about the day's events, told him about it. 'And er, Taoiseach, Royston is being followed around by a chicken.' Ahern was in the US, meeting the leaders of the G8. 'What? What?' 'There's a chicken running after Royston. It's from the Matt Cooper show.' 'Ah Jaysus ...' Most governments tend to suffer in mid-term, but not like this. Ahern had led the party to its worst ever election result. His pristine electoral record was gone. Ahern was stung by the defeats, and stung badly. He finally resolved to act.

On the Saturday evening as the full horror of the results sank in, Ahern's aides noticed one telling signpost to their boss's reaction to the fiasco. The Carlow-Kilkenny TD, Liam Aylward, had been elected as an MEP for Leinster, and was interviewed at the count. He expressed full confidence in Ahern's leadership, but it was the bit that came next that caused one of Ahern's closest advisers to look up. My advice would be to reshuffle his cabinet, Aylward said. Well now, thought Ahern's adviser. Somebody has just told him to say that.

Though he had discussed the possibility of the European Commissioner's job with Ahern the previous autumn, McCreevy had changed his mind and resolved to stay in Merrion Street. The economy was recovering; he was sure the politics would, too. He thought that Fianna Fáil should absorb a caning at the local elections and move on in the hope that the public, having vented its anger, would give the government a fairer hearing. In his discussions with Ahern, McCreevy came to believe that Ahern shared this attitude. In fact, Ahern had come to believe that there would be no change in the public's attitude to his government without a change in the government. And that spelled trouble for Charlie McCreevy.

The first indication McCreevy had that his days were numbered was when newspaper articles appeared after the local elections talking about a change of direction for the government and the possible appointment of the finance minister to the Brussels job. Politicians routinely dismiss much press speculation but many of them have a sixth sense about a planted story. McCreevy had been a front-line combatant in the Haughey wars of the 1980s and though he had occupied a minister's chair for seven years now, he still had a functioning political threat monitor. Suddenly nervous, he spoke to one friend that day, who told him ominously: 'That's the first sign.'

Things moved quickly following the June elections. At the start of the month the *Irish Times* columnist Drapier was assuring his readers that 'Charlie McCreevy is on target to have a decade as finance minister . . . He is not going to Brussels and he is not leaving finance.' By the end of the month, the paper's political correspondent, Mark Hennessy, was opining that 'the Taoiseach's reshuffle must fundamentally change the political mood, but this cannot happen unless McCreevy quits or is forced to leave Merrion St. Such an outcome would not have been predicted months ago and it may not have even been in the Taoiseach's mind, but it is in the mind of every FF TD spoken to by the *Irish Times* for days.' The idea wasn't miraculously appearing simultaneously in every TD's mind; Government Buildings was briefing heavily against him.

McCreevy was well aware that he was being briefed against, and he suspected Gerry Hickey and Gerry Howlin of being the main culprits. But he wasn't naïve enough to think they were doing it without Ahern's approval. There had been an animus between Howlin and McCreevy for some time; McCreevy had fingered him for leaking details of his holiday at airline tycoon Ulick McEvaddy's French villa in 1999. He had directly confronted Howlin about it subsequently, marching into his office, closing the door – which Howlin habitually kept open – and accusing him directly. Put on the spot, Howlin admitted that he had confirmed the story when it was put to him, but denied proactively leaking it. Relations between himself and McCreevy were even cooler afterwards, and McCreevy refused to sanction a subsequent pay increase for Howlin until PJ Mara intervened.

McCreevy's closest ally could also see a move was afoot. He had discussed the European job with Harney, the previous year, indicating to her that he intended to 'throw his hat in the ring', and checking with her that she didn't want the job. She also knew that McCreevy had firmly decided that he wouldn't go to Brussels. Now she was alarmed for her friend, and for the government – where would the PDs' agenda be without McCreevy in finance? Harney hadn't a huge regard for much media speculation, but nor did she think that stories about McCreevy's possible departure were invented. She could see the pattern and she knew what was happening. Ahern was deliberately giving signals that he was preparing to move McCreevy, whether he would move him against his will or not.

Even before the local election disaster, a *Sunday Business Post* poll had found that only a quarter of voters favoured McCreevy's retention in the Department of Finance; half opposed it. Just 37 per cent of Fianna Fáil voters were confident that he was the right man for the job, compared with 38 per cent who said he was not.

Ahern had already spoken of the need to 'shake things up' in government following the European presidency, and Harney could sense the direction he wanted to move in. She knew what it might mean for McCreevy. She assumed the stories in the media about McCreevy moving were planted by Ahern's staff. He had spoken to her about the need to do a bit of 'scene-setting' in the past – he meant preparing the ground by leaking speculative stories. He thought that some of McCreevy's budget explosions could have been avoided with a bit of scene-setting, but McCreevy always refused to play ball. Now the finance minister himself was the subject of the scene-setting. He knew he was under pressure. He called the health minister, Micheál Martin, who had been trying to get finance's approval for 300 new hospital beds for months. 'Look, neither of us may be around in these jobs for much longer,' McCreevy told him. 'I'm going to give you the green light for the new units.'

McCreevy went to government press secretary Mandy Johnston

to find out the lie of the land. Johnston had previously worked for McCreevy, and the two remained close. She was loyal to him; he trusted her. The whole business put her in an awkward position. She told McCreevy: 'He doesn't have the balls to sack you.' Fortified, he told reporters he had no intention of moving. But the speculation didn't go away; it moved up a gear. When a story appeared in the *Irish Independent* predicting his departure, McCreevy was furious and savaged his officials. He contacted TDs to tell them he was staying, and stories appeared in the media that he was resisting attempts to move him. But privately, he continued to agonize, consulting Johnston constantly.

Johnston may have been right about the Taoiseach's lack of testicular fortitude, but the gambler McCreevy decided not to push his luck. Making his peace with the inevitability, he told Ahern that he wanted to go to Brussels now, if the job was still there. He wasn't surprised to be told it was. Again, a newspaper story foretold his demise; the final nail in the coffin came on a Sunday night, when McCreevy's press officer received a call from Gene McKenna, political editor of the *Independent*. It was as much a courtesy to let him know what was coming in the following day's paper as it was a request for a comment. McKenna spelled it out: the paper was predicting an imminent announcement about McCreevy's departure to Brussels. They were utterly happy with the accuracy of the information. Two days later, the news was announced. Ireland would have a new European Commissioner, and a new finance minister.

Having got the outcome he wanted, Ahern now affected reluctant resignation. 'I felt really sad last night that my best friend and closest colleague was going to leave,' Ahern told reporters. 'You have to have a heavyweight man or woman in that position from now on if you want to be at the centre . . . and that's why I'm glad Charlie has taken up the post . . . but I'm really sorry for the home scene because that makes my life more difficult, and believe me it does.'

'You know,' Johnston told McCreevy ruefully as the two reflected on the briefing against him, 'the fuckers will say they got rid of you.' Blaming Hickey, Johnston hardly spoke to him for months afterwards. McCreevy knew better; the only one who mattered was Ahern. It was one of Ahern's most momentous decisions in government. Harney warned McDowell: 'Things aren't going to be the same.' McDowell had reached the same conclusion. 'It's all over,' he told one of his officials.

'There's no doubt about it – Bertie was more powerful around the cabinet table after Charlie left,' says one minister who served throughout the period. 'The strongest other perspective was gone, and Bertie was in total control. He was calling the shots.'

Having spent his customary few weeks in Kerry in August, Ahern was anxious to show that he was still committed to responding to the changed mood of the electorate. A high-level meeting to assess the political situation took place in the Merrion Hotel on the day after he returned from Kerry – the 'first day back', as one participant remembers it.

Though the supposedly secret meeting was pretty well advertised to the media as a sign that Ahern was listening to the voters, it was more than just a public relations stunt. Ahern himself was badly shaken by the results. They had been particularly brutal on his northside of Dublin, where voters had deserted Fianna Fáil in droves. Digesting the results and discussing their implications he understood intuitively that they meant one important thing for him, says one confidant who was close to him at the time: his aura of invincibility was gone. He would have to go out and really win the next election. That meant changes were necessary. Though all the important decisions would be taken at meetings of which the media very definitely would not be notified – and one key participant says that actually, much of the process was in fact internal to Ahern – the all-day meeting at the Merrion was suggestive of a process that was now irreversible. It was moving inexorably towards Inchydoney.

The parliamentary party's gathering every September had originated as part of Ahern's determination not to lose touch with his back-benchers, but had evolved beyond a hooley for the lads into something of more substance, as well as a formal indication that the new political season had begun. The choice of Inchydoney in West Cork was not just a sop to the departing agriculture minister, Joe Walsh, in whose Clonakilty bailiwick the hotel rested: part of the function of the gig was to get far away from Dublin.

Even if Charlie McCreevy was departing to Brussels with imprecations of gratitude, he must have been tempted to arrive at Inchydoney and stage a protest when he heard who one of the keynote speakers would be: Fr Sean Healy, of the Conference of Religious of Ireland (CORI). This was Gerry Hickey's brainchild. He believed that it would make Fianna Fáil look 'more left-wing' and would attract considerable media attention. He was right about that. It was, reflected one of the participants, the equivalent of buying a national advertising campaign.

No one had been a more persistent critic of the government than Healy; no one made Fianna Fáil, for all its economic triumphalism, feel more uncomfortable, dedicated as he was to focusing on the failures of the government to end consistent poverty and on the enduring and obvious inequalities in society. Healy's budget critiques analysing how the measures affected the worse-off had become a media staple, though his claims that poverty was increasing in Celtic Tiger Ireland were contrary to the evidence that most people perceived around them. His solutions tended towards such electorally unpopular measures as tax increases and wealth redistribution.

If Fianna Fáil back-benchers regarded him as a troublesome priest or a begrudger in a collar (actually he rarely wore one), many of those in government who had to deal with him through the partnership process had come to regard him as a person who greatly enjoyed media attention. One senior adviser to the Taoiseach, reflecting on one of Healy's economic critiques which began with an acknowledgement that Ireland was now a rich nation, told me: 'That's right. We are a rich nation. And one of the reasons for that is we have ignored everything that Sean Healy told us to do.'

Lionized by most of the media, Healy looked as if he had died and gone to heaven when he arrived in Inchydoney. Back-benchers were divided. One told me he wasn't telling them anything they didn't know already; another said he found the session useful and informative. Actually, what Healy said wasn't the important part – his presence there was enough to help Ahern in his ambitious rebranding exercise: 'caring Fianna Fáil' was born. Healy was just being used as a tool in political marketing.

Ahern and his office directed everything, from the photoshoots to the speaking order.

Mary Hanafin was in the shower in her hotel room when the telephone rang; Olive Melvin, from the Taoiseach's private office, was on the line. 'He wants you to meet him and walk on the beach in ten minutes,' was the urgent request.

The subsequent picture of Ahern, Cowen and Hanafin, the two men with jackets thrown over their shoulders, she slinging her sandals nonchalantly in her hand, became the iconic picture of the Inchydoney boondoggle. It ran on page one of the *Irish Times*, beside a headline which – ironically, in hindsight – read: 'Taoiseach rules out "spending spree" to win votes.' The symbolism of the new image was pretty unsubtle. Out went the Ahern, McCreevy and Harney triumvirate of tax cuts, individualization and, latterly, cutbacks; in came New Bertie the pal of Fr Sean, Cowen the traditional Fianna Fáiler and caring, sharing Mary Hanafin.

Throughout the autumn of 2004, there was only one message from Fianna Fáil: we care. Ahern himself put the tin hat on it in an *Irish Times* interview when he declared he was 'one of the few socialists left in Irish politics'. Poor Joe Higgins, the Socialist Party TD who delighted in berating Ahern in the Dáil, was almost distraught:

You can imagine, as Cheann Comhairle, how perplexed I was when I returned to find my wardrobe almost empty. The Taoiseach had been busy robbing my clothes. Up to recently the Progressive Democrats did not have a stitch left due to the same Taoiseach but we never expected him to take a walk on the left side of the street. He said: 'I am one of the few socialists left in Irish politics' ... I thought: Good, Taoiseach. There are two of us in it and we will go down together!

The saga of Bertie the socialist was a constant in political debate for months. Ahern's own staff thought the socialist stuff was ludicrous. Years later some of them were unable to answer serious questions about it without laughing. But it wasn't aimed at the political classes. Ahern was trying to communicate with a wider public who didn't pay daily attention to politics, and that was his way of doing it. 'He knew the political classes were laughing at it, but he didn't care. They weren't the audience.' Judged solely in terms of getting a message out, it was a master-class in political communication. Only problem was, it wasn't working. The party continued to languish in the polls.

The cabinet reshuffle three weeks after the Inchydoney departure confirmed the political sea change. Few things cause more excite-ment or more irrationality around Leinster House than ministerial reshuffles. The prospect of promotion to ministerial or even junior ministerial office can make TDs rigid with excitement, sick with nerves. The difference between life as a back-bench government TD and as a minister is vast; their lives can be transformed overnight. One minister who has been among the appointed and disappointed described it: 'You've been waiting for days and you don't get the call, you're not on the list. You know nothing and no one has spoken to you. So you spend a day or two going, "Fuck this, fuck him, fuck it all, I'm wasting my fucking time, blah, blah, blah"; then you think, Jaysus, what about the juniors, am I in, can I do anything or speak to anyone? And you go through the same process.'

The most dramatic move was Harney's. Privately, Harney had been critical of Michael Martin's performance as minister for health and she shared many of McCreevy's views about the lack of an appropriate return for vastly increased investment in health. She had sat on the cabinet sub-committee on health, and thought better management could deliver results, from the top down. She thought she could do a better job. As well as that, she had been enterprise minister for seven years, and she wanted a change.

Ahern thought she should move to the Department of Foreign Affairs, one of the top positions in cabinet and also one which would conveniently entail her being out of the country for much of the time, and so unable to devote the sort of time to the domestic policy agenda that she had previously. This would also suit Ahern's plans to change the focus of the government to a more 'caring' stance.

Harney discussed her own position with Ahern on a number of occasions. Actually, she spent a few weeks pestering him about promoting her to the finance job after McCreevy left, though she never really believed it was a possibility. Nonetheless, Ahern was reluctant to refuse her straight away and he stalled and avoided her until he finally had to plead that he couldn't give her the job. 'I can't, I just can't,' he told her eventually. 'My fellas would never wear it.'

However, Ahern was surprised when Harney indicated that she wanted to go to the Department of Health. 'I thought you'd go to foreign affairs or education,' he said. 'Are you sure? Have you thought about it?'

'I've thought about nothing else all summer,' Harney replied. 'I want to do it.'

'OK,' Ahern acquiesced. McCreevy told her she was out of her mind.

Seamus Brennan was amputated from the Department of Transport, a move he doggedly resisted. Ahern's staff knew that Brennan was fighting a rearguard action; they saw him go up and down the corridor to Ahern's office 'like a yo-yo'. Ditto Noel Dempsey, who tried to hang on in education, with a similar lack of success. The unions were unhappy with both men, particularly Brennan, whom the highly unionized transport sector found uncomfortably fond of competition and deregulation, and they had made their feelings clear to Ahern. A change would be appreciated. Ahern was listening to them.

After five bruising years, Micheál Martin had also earned his move, Ahern knew. He had implemented much of the reforming health strategy and secured billions more in funding, often from a truculent McCreevy; there were thousands more nurses and doctors, and patients were treated more numerously and successfully. But still public dissatisfaction with the health service was enormous, and conspicuous failures abounded. They were also, as in the nature of these things, widely reported; the health unions still controlled the news agenda, and used it to benefit their members. Martin had also failed to achieve a new contract for the powerful hospital consultants, though Ahern didn't judge him for that. 'Everyone who has taken on the consultants has failed,' Ahern told him. Martin had the scars on his back to prove it. But he had survived, and left the legacy of the smoking ban behind him, a controversial measure (especially with Fianna Fáil back-benchers) that would be copied around the world. 'You want to get out,' Ahern told Martin when the two men discussed it. 'Ah, no, no,' Martin replied. He meant: 'Ah, yes, yes.'

'No,' said Ahern. 'I owe you one.' He swapped places with Harney, moving to enterprise.

After the e-voting nightmare, Martin Cullen was desperate to get out of environment. Characteristically, Ahern was still trying to make up his own mind. When he saw Cullen, he told him, 'I have a great gig for you – something close to my own heart. What would you think of social welfare?'

Cullen could hardly think of anything to which he was less suited. He knew by any reckoning that he was lucky to be still in cabinet, and luckier still to be contemplating a job after the reshuffle. But social welfare? 'Ah, Jesus Christ, Bertie ...' he began. Ahern was smiling to himself, he noticed.

'On the other side,' Ahern continued, looking at the papers on his desk, 'I could give you transport – what would you think of that?'

'Now that's a job I'd like!' Cullen responded eagerly. Ahern told him no final decision had been made at that stage but that he would let him know the following day. When Cullen was summoned to the Taoiseach's office twenty-four hours later, he met an agitated, angry Ahern, who was pacing the room. Cullen thought he had just had a row with someone. Turning to him sharply, Ahern barked: 'You're getting fucking transport and don't fuck me up with the unions. Good luck!' The interview was over.

Cullen wasn't the only minister who was mandated to keep the trade unions happy. Mary Hanafin received similar orders. Politics was something of a family business for the Hanafins. Mary's father, Des, had been a Fianna Fáil senator, sometime head of fundraising (he was sacked by Charles Haughey for properly and bravely refusing to divulge the identity of donors) and party elder for many years, combining this role with his activities as an anti-divorce, anti-abortion campaigner which brought him to public prominence. A third member of the family, Mary's brother John, would later have a short spell as a party fundraiser and a more successful one as a full-time politician, winning election to the Senate.

Hanafin was able, and she was pushy. She was also impatient; she had been knocking on the door of politics for a long time. She had met Ahern when she was first elected to Dublin Corporation in 1985, but she lost her seat in the local elections of 1991. She had also been unsuccessful in the 1989 general election in Dublin South East. Handed another opportunity in 1997 by being added to the party ticket in Dun Laoghaire by the authority of party headquarters – a selection decision that necessitated the unusual move of persuading the selected candidate, Larry Butler, to remove himself from the ticket – she won a seat thanks to an energetic campaign and the co-operation of David Andrews. She enjoyed a good relationship with Ahern, who appreciated her media abilities, and also the fact that she was relatively young and a woman, not characteristics in abundance in the parliamentary party. He had made her chief whip in 2002, and now she was itching for a cabinet job.

Waiting around Government Buildings on the day before the reshuffle, Hanafin could no longer contain herself. She found some spurious excuse to go upstairs to Ahern's private office. He welcomed her in. 'Do you think you're ready?' he asked her.

'I've been brave and I've been strong. I'm ready, Taoiseach,' she answered evenly. Her husband, Eamon Leahy, had died suddenly the previous year. Ahern had been concerned and considerate throughout the grieving process, contacting her regularly.

'Well, if you feel you're ready, come up and see me tomorrow.' The following day, she waited and waited. The staff in her private office watched to see who was going in and who was going out, and she tried to put jobs on names, but it was hopeless. Eventually, she got the call and went up. 'I'm giving you the one you want,' Ahern said. 'It's education.' Hanafin burst into tears.

Ahern's instructions to Hanafin on taking up her new post were the same as they were to Martin Cullen in the Transport Department: get the unions back onside. Relations between the powerful teaching unions and the previous minister, Noel Dempsey, were dreadful, with Dempsey going so far as to refuse to attend their Easter conferences – a very direct and deliberate snub which horrified Ahern. 'We have to rebuild relations,' Ahern told Hanafin. 'Make sure you go and speak at the conferences.' There were no specific instructions – just a general injunction to 'keep the unions happy'.

Removing ministers was a lengthier process than appointing them, and it took Ahern all summer to get rid of Michael Smith.

Smith had a previous reputation as an Albert Reynolds aficionado and a tough guy, and he certainly wasn't afraid to use his elbows; nor was he afraid of strife within his own party. In fact, he had known nothing else; he had spent his entire political life scrapping with his local Fianna Fáil rival, Michael O'Kennedy, for the Fianna Fáil vote in the traditional bell-wether constituency of North Tipperary. Their rivalry – and the conduct of all such constituency rivalries in Fianna Fáil – was summed up when Smith coined the telling and bitter observation in response to reports that O'Kennedy was faltering: 'When Michael

O'Kennedy is in trouble, Michael Smith loses his seat.' For much of the time since Smith had first entered politics, O'Kennedy had been the one in the ascendant: agriculture minister, finance minister, European Commissioner. He had also been a supporter of Haughey. With the rise and rise of Reynolds, Smith saw the opportunity to reverse their positions. So it was. Reynolds sacked O'Kennedy, and as expected, promoted Smith to the cabinet. Worse was to come for O'Kennedy: in the following general election, he lost his seat. Smith, the farmer and quintessential countryman, had long laboured in the shadow of O'Kennedy, a senior counsel and metropolitan, and he now relished the job of a cabinet minister. His civil servants used to joke that because his two predecessors, David Andrews and Sean Barrett, didn't tax them overmuch, Smith looked like a 'supersub' when he arrived and easily got to grips with his brief. He was tough, and he played tough politics. Minister for defence in Ahern's cabinets, he closed barracks and cut army numbers during a time of prosperity, using the proceeds to upgrade the army's equipment and training. He decided to fight the army deafness cases, and under his direction, the bill for the deafness scandal came in at about €300 million; some initial estimates had suggested it could eventually be as high as €1 billion. Mostly his colleagues thought he was a pretty wise old owl around the table. They also knew he had a very close relationship with Charlie McCreevy. And they knew that with McCreevy gone, Smith's days were numbered.

Even had his friend and sometime protector McCreevy stayed in cabinet, Smith would have been in danger of losing his place at the cabinet table. He had broken with the party line on the Hanly Report on the health service the previous November. The report proposed a major reorganization of some health services, centralizing some activities in smaller local hospitals to major regional centres. This immediately aroused the opposition of some groups who feared that their local hospital would be 'down-graded'. One such vocal lobby was in Nenagh, in the heart of Smith's Tipperary North constituency, and he took to repeatedly making critical statements about the report's plans for some services in Nenagh hospital to be transferred to Limerick. Worse, from Ahern's point of view, he had repeated his comments after the Taoiseach had told the Dáil that there was no division in the cabinet about the Hanly Report.

Smith knew the risk he was running when he attacked the Hanly Report. Ahern had already signalled the possibility of a reshuffle after the local and European elections of the following summer, and it was clear that Smith would be one of those in the firing line. McCreevy had pleaded with him not to attack Hanly. 'We can't lose you this way,' McCreevy told him. 'You've had an impeccable political career. Don't let it end like this.' McCreevy believed that Ahern would have to sack him, and told Smith that he couldn't save him. 'He'll have to let you go, you know.'

'Ah, let it off,' Smith replied. 'It's probably going to happen in a few months anyway.'

Smith was eventually forced to issue a statement expressing his regret at having embarrassed Ahern after some colourful ex-changes between Merrion Street and Phoenix Park. Some of Ahern's aides urged him to sack Smith, and the minister himself for a period thought he was finished. But that wasn't Ahern's style: he would wait, and not forget. He would have a reshuffle when it suited him, and not when it suited Mick Smith.

And so in that febrile summer of 2004, when the local elections disaster spelled the end of the McCreevy era, the news vacuum was filled by endless speculation that Smith and agriculture minister Joe Walsh – two of the former finance minister's closest allies at cabinet – would be the losers in a reshuffle.

Smith knew that he was being briefed against. And he knew that there must be at least tacit approval from Ahern for it. He didn't think that Ahern was telling his aides, 'Ring the paper and tell them Smith is for the chop,' but he was sufficiently worldly wise to know that Ahern knew it was going on and wasn't doing anything to stop it. Politics often works like this: a minister's staff will do things that they know he wants them to do, even if he can never actually instruct them to do it. That's one of the reasons why there are often such catastrophic misunderstandings in political communications.

Walsh accepted the inevitable and indicated that he would retire voluntarily, believing that in doing so he might stand a chance of being appointed to the European Commissioner's job, which he made strenuous efforts to capture. Smith declined to go quietly. 'I don't give a fuck,' Smith told Joe Walsh in one of their conversations that summer. 'I'm not going to lie down.'

Smith maintained a spirited, if faintly ridiculous, defence throughout the summer, telling reporters that he wouldn't resign, and hinting heavily that he might become a critic of the government outside the cabinet. The phrase 'sources close to Michael Smith' appeared frequently in the newspapers, and was taken by everyone to mean Smith himself. Sources close to Michael Smith told anyone who was asking that the Taoiseach would be better with him inside the tent pissing out. For one such transgression, back-bencher John Moloney was dispatched to criticize Smith. The writing was on the wall, and he agreed to go, believing he would be fired if he refused.

The Smith affair was an entertaining sideshow, but it was part of a very profound move in the make-up of Ahern's cabinet, the most significant since he had picked his first team in 1997. McCreevy was gone, and his allies Smith and Walsh were gone, too. Ideological comrade Seamus Brennan was gone from transport. Harney moved to health. The influence of McCreevyism was removed completely from economic policy.

The process was entirely internal to Ahern. Ministers had never discussed the abrupt change of direction for the government. 'But we understood it,' says one cabinet member. 'I think he was reasserting control of things,' says another.

A key element of reasserting control was the move of Cowen to the Department of Finance, where – it was made clear – he would be working closely with the Taoiseach in the formation of economic and budgetary policy. Ahern had named Cowen as his deputy leader in 2002 after Mary O'Rourke lost her seat, and though some ministers heard Ahern say unflattering things about him, the elevation to the finance portfolio confirmed his emerging status as Ahern's most likely successor. Cowen was respected by his colleagues and adored by the back-benchers, and as foreign minister he had been instrumental in the successful European presidency. But crucially, the fiercely guarded independence of McCreevy was gone.

Bertie Ahern was now in complete control of his government, and things would never be the same again. The way was open to shower public services with money before the next election, inflating spending in all areas with the aim of buying back the popularity that the government had lost.

Ahern had also resolved to make sweeping changes among his staff and advisers, and he had already discussed a change of role for his programme manager, Gerry Hickey. So much was it a fait accompli that Hickey had told several people that his role in the set-up would be changing, and that he expected the special adviser and former government press secretary Joe Lennon to replace him. Ahern also toyed with a move for Mandy Johnston from the post of government press secretary, where she had become unpopular among the political journalists. 'If that's the way she wants it,' one journalist told me at the time following a snub by Johnston, 'then herself and her fucking boss are going to get it every day with both fucking barrels.'

Rumours of the imminence of Hickey's and Johnston's removal began to circulate in government circles, and soon a report appeared in *Phoenix* magazine. Ahern was infuriated, and did what he often did when angered like that: he did nothing. Hickey stayed. Lennon left to join the Health Service Executive.

'Bertie didn't like the way things were going. He felt he was losing control,' says one of his closest aides of the 2004 changes. He was determined to get it back.

'After McCreevy left the whole thing changed, the whole dynamic changed. The private enterprise Fianna Fáil was no more – it was now social partnership Fianna Fáil,' is how one senior cabinet minister describes it. In fact, this was just what Bertie Ahern wanted.

9. The Gathering Storm

The bars and lobbies of the Citywest Hotel were thronged with over five thousand Fianna Fáil delegates as the pre-election ard-fheis of 2007 prepared for its Saturday evening climax. Red-faced men and middle-aged women mixed with T-shirted Ogra members and self-consciously busy political professionals. Ministers and TDs, all surrounded by knots of admirers basking in their proximity to power, mingled freely with the crowds.

A Fianna Fáil ard-fheis is like a cross between a Munster hurling final and a revivalist meeting of Christian evangelicals. Old friends and comrades meet once a year and talk of epic battles and famous strokes of long ago; the generations mingle and renew their faith, pledging devotion. The Citywest Hotel in west Dublin replaced the RDS as the venue of choice for ard-fheiseanna under Bertie Ahern, and if it is somewhat soulless, it's more convenient for the travelling throng, and it gathers them all under the one roof for the weekend. God knows how many pints they sell there.

This time, some ministers were unhappy, and some were very unhappy. Bertie Ahern's keynote address, in which he would spell out the party's approach to the forthcoming general election, was only hours away. There were rumours among ministers of major policy departures and extensive election promises. And none of them had any idea what he was going to say, or what he was going to promise they could deliver in their departments. Ahern's speech remained a closely guarded secret.

Noel Dempsey grabbed one adviser in the corridor of the hotel a few hours before the speech was delivered. 'What the fuck is going on?' he hissed. Eventually copies of the speech, along with a briefing document on the tax changes it proposed, the pension promises and the associated costings, were hastily put into envelopes and handed to the cabinet, some of them only receiving their copies as they took their places on the stage in advance of the speech. They opened it, many of them wide-eyed. Some couldn't believe what they were reading.

Three days after the party had warned about reckless promises from the opposition, and vowed that it would not compete in a political auction for votes, Ahern's speech was a litany of election promises, including massive tax cuts. Two points off the standard rate of income tax, one point off the higher rate, the halving of the rate of PRSI, increasing the old age pension to €300 a week, new metro lines, Luas lines, commuter rail services, 2,000 extra gardaí, 4,000 teachers – on and on he went. It was a giveaway surpassing anything Charlie McCreevy had ever dared, and it was a complete reversal of the previously agreed strategy of avoiding an auction with Fine Gael and Labour and instead pointing to Fianna Fáil's prudent management of the economy.

Afterwards, many ministers were furious. 'What the fuck just happened?' one minister demanded of a senior adviser. Brian Lenihan grabbed another by the arm in the bar and led him a few steps away from his drinking companions. 'He's lost his bottle, hasn't he? He's lost it. I can see it. That's what that was about.' He meant that Ahern was afraid to fight the election and was now trying to buy it. Completely deflated, the adviser agreed. 'Yeah.'

There had been a behind-the-scenes battle all week over the content of the speech, and by extension, the platform on which the party would fight the general election. Ahern's Government Buildings advisers Hickey and Howlin wanted tax cuts – a big splash, a big story – to be announced in the speech, which they believed would catapult them into the election campaign. Cowen, supported by his special adviser Colin Hunt, and Peter MacDonagh, who had returned from abroad to help with the campaign, favoured a more cautious approach encompassing smaller, targeted, less grandiose proposals. It wasn't just a difference of degree about the size of election promises: it signalled a profound difference in approach to the forthcoming campaign. The plan favoured by Cowen was to emphasize caution and restraint, avoiding big tax-cutting promises; leave Fine Gael and Labour to make the big-ticket promises and attack them for being reckless. This was the strategy they had agreed months in advance; but the others believed it wasn't working. Look at the polls, they said; just look at the polls. Government Buildings believed that the race – which looked to be in the balance – could be transformed by standing on a tax-cutting platform, shifting the focus to the economy and reminding voters of the improvements in their own personal circumstances since Fianna Fáil had taken office. Both sides of the argument believed the other's plan would be disastrous.

All week the argument went to and fro. Ahern rang the advisers repeatedly. 'Go through it again why you want me to do it,' he asked them. This was his way of teasing it out. It was finally settled when Ahern ran through his speech in rehearsal in the presence of the various advisers. What do you think of it? he asked Howlin. I think it needs a bigger message, more oomph, replied Howlin. Johnston concurred. Brian Murphy thought it was OK. Buckley, usually a bitter opponent of Johnston, was consulted. The journalists are going to want a big story, she said. I think we should give them one. Ahern was convinced.

Hunt and the others were furious, realizing they had been outmanoeuvred by the Government Buildings camp; the battle over the speech was a proxy for a power struggle that was going on between the Ahern's advisers Johnston, Hickey and Howlin and another group in which Dorgan, the general secretary, Hunt, MacDonagh and Mara were most vocal. At times some of them barely spoke to one another. But Hunt's side were also convinced it was the wrong strategy, and that the mistake could cost them the election. It was, after all, a reversal of the strategy that had been agreed months ago. They went to Cowen, and put the case. He was completely convinced and went to argue the case with Ahern: don't do it – stick with the plan. 'Cowen pleaded with him,' says one person in the inside of the discussions. But Ahern was not for moving. His mind was made up.

A furious memo was circulated among the advisers. Given that we had agreed a strategy and agreed a means of communicating it, it said, and given that you have now argued that this strategy should be thrown out, could you please give us some indication of what the new strategy is, and how we should communicate it? One of the Government Buildings people, enjoying the triumph, wrote back: 'I'm sure you'll think of something.'

There was one small matter: the cabinet hadn't been told, much less consulted. Nobody thought to do it until the Saturday, by which time the media – in particular those newspapers with early deadlines, such as *The Sunday Business Post* – were screaming for the script. Buckley was plagued with demands. Eventually copies began to trickle out. But still the cabinet hadn't been told. The political correspondents knew the detail of the extraordinary giveaways in the Taoiseach's speech before his own cabinet did. Ahern took the podium at 8.30 p.m. for the television address and proceeded to revert to his ard-fheis style of shouting and rasping his way through the litany of giveaways.

The Government Buildings caucus was jubilant. Privately, Cowen believed the election might well be over, but publicly his attitude was, 'Well, he's done it now. We just have to live with it.' Seamus Brennan was furious. On the say-so of Government Buildings, he had briefed the media extensively at a press conference a few days earlier about the prudent and cautious package that Fianna Fáil would unveil at its ard-fheis. Brennan had warned about the 'alarming' promises of Fine Gael and Labour and rehearsed a line that had been carefully tested in focus groups: 'We will promise less and deliver more.' 'FF says it will not match opposition promises,' read the headline in the next day's papers. It was true. FF wouldn't match them. It would beat them.

The 2007 ard-fheis speech, and Ahern's overruling of Cowen's preferences for taxation policy, underlined how Ahern had asserted control of economic policy since the departure of McCreevy. The former finance minister had maintained complete control of taxation policy, to the extent that he informed the Taoiseach only a day or two before the budget what the taxation changes – which were the most significant and far-reaching parts of his budgets – were. With Cowen in Merrion Street, it was a very different regime. The first paragraph of the new minister's first budget speech, in December 2004, was a tribute to McCreevy; the second was a repudiation of the McCreevy way of doing things. 'The budget,' Cowen told the Dáil, 'is an initiative of government as a whole and not simply the work of the minister for finance.'

'We reverted from a system where Charlie would tell nobody what he was doing to the system of all the lads sitting down and deciding what they wanted,' reflected one senior Government Buildings figure afterwards. 'Bad idea.'

Cowen's first budget, like the four that followed it, marked a change in the government's priorities that was given concrete form in budgetary and taxation policy. Gone were the pyrotechnics of the McCreevy years; gone too the production of rabbits from hats. 'The constant stream of innovation from the Department of Finance ended,' says one minister.

Ahern's spin doctors briefed incessantly about how the budgets were now a joint production between the Taoiseach and his minister for finance. This was actually largely accurate. Ahern's officials immediately noticed they were becoming much more involved in the budgetary process. Ahern wanted an integration of budgetary and economic strategy and political strategy, and the new processes reflected this. Officials from the Department of the Taoiseach now sat in on many budget meetings. This would have been unthinkable in the McCreevy era. Staff noticed Cowen's adviser Colin Hunt constantly coming back and forth to the Taoiseach's Department. 'It was a lot more joined up,' says one official. 'Cowen and Bertie were meeting all the time before the budgets.'

The swerve in government practice was pretty plain to see. 'Gone is Charlie McCreevy's free market agenda,' wrote the then *Irish Times* economics editor, Cliff Taylor, in response to the 2005 budget, 'and in comes Brian Cowen's social concern.' That social concern was incarnated in substantially increased public spending

– rising a projected 9.1 per cent (the eventual outturn would be a lot higher) – and a tax package that was directed at low- and middle-income workers. Taylor's economic analysis was fine, but what the government really wanted was the thumbs-up from the *Star*'s budget supplement, which summarized the new finance minister's first budget for its readers in terms to make Bertie Ahern glow: 'CARING AND SHARING'. The assessment wasn't just a tabloid phenomenon. In the *Irish Times*, the paper's vox-pop reporters solicited the views of Matt Reville, a primary school teacher. He praised the budget's 'socialist leanings'. 'It does seem that this minister is looking after the have-nots, as opposed to his predecessor, who looked after the have-lots,' he told the newspaper. In Government Buildings the spin doctors were tickled pink: the spin was working.

But Cowen's budgets were hardly Robin Hood take-from-the-rich-give-to-the-poor efforts. He depended on economic growth and increased taxation revenues – not increased rates of taxation or better value in public spending – to pay for the extra teachers, care workers, hospital facilities, social welfare payments and so on. The socialist stuff was about expenditure – not revenue. McCreevy might have been gone and his legacy been repudiated, but even the new economic policy engine of the government wasn't forgetting all his lessons. Taxes would remain low, and many tax incentives would remain in place. The change was all on the spending side of the ledger, not the tax side. That might have seemed like good politics, but it would store up economic problems for the future.

But was it good politics? Ahern had digested the results of the local elections and their confirmation of the government's unpopularity, which stemmed, he believed, from a perception that his administration was 'uncaring' and 'right wing'. He was completely allergic to the right-wing accusation. 'People think you're right wing,' he told Harney, 'but you're not.' She thought he meant: people think we're right wing; we have to change that. Before they start thinking *I'm* right wing. He had a terror of being labelled 'right wing' – stemming principally from his close relationship with the trade unions, for whom right wing was just another term for anything bad or nasty. It escaped them that the tax cutting which they negotiated in successive national agreements is normally considered a goal of right-wingers.

Any examination of the first seven years of Ahern's administration undermines the right-wing label. Right-wing governments are supposed to restrict public spending and let the market rip. The Fianna Fáil–PD coalitions vastly increased public spending, interfered in the market via initiatives such as the minimum wage and various (ineffective) attempts to curb and then stimulate property investment, put a special levy on banks, made property developers hand over 20 per cent of their projects for social housing (though it later modified the initiative) and introduced a range of social spending on old age pensions and child benefit that didn't look very right wing at all to anyone looking in from abroad. 'For all its talk, this Government's fiscal record fits perfectly the stereotype of socialist profligacy,' commented *The Economist*'s Dan O'Brien.

Of course, when you look at the record of tax cutting that McCreevy left behind, the right-wing label seems to make a little more sense. But when you consider that the tax cuts were demanded, lobbied for and lauded by the trades unions, they seem a little less Thatcherite. The fact is that the unions did very well out of the McCreevy years; social partnership gave them an unprecedented say in the running of the country – an influence they used to the benefit of their members. From general giveaways such as the benchmarking payments, to sweetheart localized deals such as the favourable tax treatment for the Eircom unions, the 'beards' – as the union leadership came to be known around Government Buildings and the Department of Finance – had reasons to be content with the supposedly right-wing government, whatever their public sabre-rattling said. Their closeness to the Taoiseach and to his secretary general, Dermot McCarthy, yielded benefits far beyond the obviously symptomatic tax relief on members' union subscription, and it increased in later years. 'There was a lot more social partnership after McCreevy left,' one cabinet minister told me. 'In practice this meant Dermot McCarthy ringing you up and asking you to do side deals with the unions.'

Moreover, despite the widely held perception that inequality had exploded during the boom years, even the ESRI – hardly a repository of right-wing crazies – found that inequality had not increased substantially. The think tank found that government budgetary policy contributed to a small increase in inequality in its early years, but later budgets had the opposite effect. By anyone's measure, consistent poverty (the only measure that really matters) fell dramatically. An OECD report on the Irish economy in 2005 found that the Irish welfare system was the most generous in the world. Ahern's governments certainly believed in low taxation – though repeated surveys indicated that the public did too – but they were not right wing by the standards recognizable in any comparable country.

Of course, Charlie McCreevy certainly talked as though they were right wing. But that was largely due to his own desire to stand for something, to have an edge, to have opponents. He had a view of politics that was, in some ways, the opposite of Ahern's. Ahern believed in consensus above all; McCreevy believed in defining yourself by your opponents.

The government's problem was being retrofitted to suit the solution of the exile of McCreevy. In fact, the problem wasn't that the government was 'right wing', no matter what McCreevy sounded like. The problem was that the public had lost trust in the government. People – with some justification – believed that they had been lied to at the 2002 general election about the state of the country's finances. It wasn't about left wing or right wing. A lot of voters didn't care about those labels anyway. It was about trust. By exiling McCreevy, Ahern was trying to fix the wrong problem. And fixing the real problem would be more difficult than any political rebranding, no matter how skilful.

This lack of trust and disbelief in the government's pronouncements made it impossible to convince people that the public services they affected to be so concerned about were improving.

Both the public and an increasingly hostile media had long since discounted the rambling recitations of increased expenditure on schools and health services and so on that so often constituted Ahern's replies to questions in the Dáil. There were objective improvements in the numbers of patients treated and successful medical outcomes, there were more teachers and special needs assistants and doctors and nurses than ever before; such facts neither alleviated the grumpiness of the public nor changed the basic narrative of the media. The neat trick of the public-sector unions in conflating the interests of the public sector with the interests of the public meant that their members had become vastly more numerous and significantly better paid – but the government was yet to see a political payback. In fact, at a time when more money than ever was being spent by the government to provide a level of public services that was objectively higher than ever, the public remained convinced that services had actually deteriorated. It was a paradox that would bedevil the government for the duration of the entire second term.

The Progressive Democrats' fears about their influence in government were already acute by the time Ahern started to declare his socialist credentials. 'We didn't take it too seriously,' says one senior PD figure from the time. 'The Bert may as well have gone into the Dáil and said he was a nudist for all we cared. The real thing was the removal of McCreevy and the shift to left in actual policy.'

It was a shift that the PDs were alarmed by. While Fianna Fáil prepared to reposition itself in the summer of 2004, Michael McDowell delivered a speech that was simultaneously a defence of the Progressive Democrat record in government and a plea that the lessons learned from national recovery shouldn't be shunned in a populist, leftward retreat. Recalling the party's determination to attack the economic consensus of the 1980s, McDowell asserted:

Anyone who challenged state domination of the Irish economy was derided and attacked as 'Thatcherite', 'yuppie', 'selfish' and 'right-wing'

by the elite which brought this country to its knees and kept it there
between 1973 and 1987. It took some degree of courage ... to insist
that there was a better way – a way which involved radical tax
reform, the breaking up of monopolies, which viewed profit as healthy,
which argued that entrepreneurs and risk-takers had to be rewarded,
which argued that workers could and should be incentivised, which
embraced competition, which was open to at least consider the option
of privatisation.

Then the PD president added: 'It still takes some degree of
courage to stand up for those policies.' McDowell was preaching to the converted: his audience was the annual dinner of
IBEC, the business organization, generally men who didn't have
to hire their dinner jacket for the evening. But he also had
another audience: it was in St Luke's, and it wasn't wearing a
tuxedo.

There was a 'definite change in the atmospherics around the
cabinet table', says one senior Progressive Democrat figure.
'McDowell and Harney felt very much alone.'

But the relationship between the two PD ministers was
deteriorating too. It was under pressure from McDowell's impatient expectation that Harney would step down and allow him
to become leader and from Harney's conviction that such a course
of action could tear the parliamentary party asunder. Between
the PD tensions, the loss of McCreevy and Harney's move to
health (which McDowell thought was crazy) the PD influence on
economic policy was enormously undermined.

McCreevy's departure only heightened McDowell's desire to
replace Harney. McDowell is a more intense version of the usual
combination of a politician's make-up – ego, ambition, commitment to public service and an unshakeable belief that what is
good for the individual politician is good for the country. This
cocktail simmered in McDowell, barely below the surface.

The PD parliamentary party had become largely dysfunctional,
even more of a collection of individuals than heretofore.
McDowell disdained several of them; they deeply disliked him.

The relationship, says one insider, was 'just not functioning'. Their staffs briefed against one another ferociously.

Tensions almost boiled over in advance of the citizenship referendum of 2004. Many in the PDs were instinctively opposed to McDowell's proposals for a referendum on removing the automatic right to citizenship for children born in Ireland. They were also puzzled about the origin of the citizenship referendum: it wasn't in the programme for government. They knew that Ahern had previously expressed concern about the numbers of foreigners coming into his constituency, where foreigners tended to be especially visible because many of them were Nigerians. The numbers of Nigerians and the readiness with which they set up businesses and established a visible presence in the community were deeply unsettling to many, especially older people, in Ahern's constituency and he was acutely aware of their concerns. Ahern knew that many of the urban myths of the lavishly-provided-for asylum seeker living a life of ease and plenty on state benefits were just that, but he also knew that Dublin Central was housing a disproportionate number of foreigners and he knew many people were uneasy about it, and some of them were hostile to it. He didn't think that a situation that ignored the numbers coming in was sustainable; it wasn't sustainable in Dublin Central, anyway. His staff had heard him express such concerns before; they knew that some of his constituency workers had concerns about 'the blackies'. They thought he would be happy with any initiative that sought to control the numbers.

Having inherited a system that was completely unsuited to dealing with large numbers of immigrants and asylum seekers, McDowell was committed to tightening the process, something he largely achieved through a combination of better enforcement and greater efficiency in processing applications. He saw the citizenship referendum as part of this process, though the fact that it drove the left crazy didn't diminish its attraction for him, to say the least. He had always entertained an almost childish delight in annoying left-wingers, and anything that got up the noses of their woolly pieties, as he saw it, was worthwhile.

Nonetheless the discomfort felt by many PDs about the measure manifested itself in – among other things – a deep pessimism about the prospects of success for the referendum. A few weeks before the vote was due, the PD parliamentary party and its staff met in Farmleigh, where the cabinet had taken to meeting during the EU presidency. McDowell was last to arrive and was taken aback to find the meeting in a state of agitation about the possibility that the referendum would be defeated. McDowell said little. He and his staff were happy with the opinion polls and they didn't rate the political judgement of the others anyway. If she (Harney) wanted to have a row in front of the children, they joked, then let her. Such were the opinions of McDowell and his aides about many of the rest of the PD parliamentary party that they didn't expect to hear much they considered useful anyway. McDowell's confidence was justified – the measure passed by an overwhelming majority. Its success didn't undermine McDowell's belief in his own judgement; nor did it lessen his impatience to succeed Harney.

The most significant thing in the eventful political year of 2004 was not the socialist rebranding; nor was it any of the associated political ballyhoo. It was that the Irish economy, after a period of relatively slow growth (by the standards of the previous years), was revving up once more. In 2002 GNP grew by just 1.5 per cent; in 2003 by 2.8 per cent. But in 2004, the Celtic Tiger II emerged, and growth surged to 4.9 per cent. It was expected to grow further in the coming years. This would provide huge growth in taxation revenue for Bertie Ahern and Brian Cowen. They knew what they wanted to do with it: they wanted to win the next election.

When newspapers report the findings of their opinion polls, it's common that both the head of the polling organization and the paper's chief political writer pen pieces explaining the significance of the data. It's often the case that both step outside their respective fields of expertise; the pollster writes about the politics and the political reporter writes about the numbers. Often this works; sometimes it doesn't. In the autumn of 2004, after Inchydoney, after a reshuffle and in the midst of the government's attempts to effect its rebranding, the chief executive of the polling company MRBI, Ian McShane, got the politics absolutely right. Commenting on a poll in the *Irish Times* which showed a modest gain from a low base (rising two points to 35 per cent) for Fianna Fáil, he remarked that the party had 'embarked upon the long process of atonement, with attempts to position itself as a more socially-aware organisation, in tune with the needs and concerns of the ordinary voter'. More importantly, he observed, 'With Monday's publication of the third-quarter exchequer figures, which suggested there may be €1 billion to give away at the next Budget, an improvement in Fianna Fáil's fortunes might reasonably have been expected.'

The budget that followed that poll and those of subsequent years continued the general policy of returning the fruits of economic growth to the voters with effective cuts in the tax burden and a number of pro-business initiatives. Tax incentive schemes for certain types of construction projects were continued, even as the annual inflation in new house prices was recorded at over 12 per cent when the budget was published.

At the same time, however, government spending on social welfare, on health and on education expanded massively once McCreevy left – funded from the tax revenues provided by the inflating property bubble. Ministers observed to one another that projects for which they had to wait years to get over the line with McCreevy – even core policy objectives and election promises – they could now propose with a reasonable expectation of success. McDowell's staff told people that they only finally got the OK for the much-heralded 2,000 extra gardaí after McCreevy left.

Ministers' impressions are attested to by the numbers: while under McCreevy public spending grew massively, it remained under 30 per cent of GNP – in fact, in some years, he shrank public spending as a share of the economy. After 2004, there was a steady increase in the proportion of the economy made up by public spending. McCreevy certainly pumped public spending with some eye-watering increases; but it was fuelled by rapid economic growth. When growth eased off, as it did in 2001–2, McCreevy slammed on the brakes once the election was out of the way. After 2004, Ahern decreed that the purse strings were to be loosened, and they duly were. That was fine as long as the economy was growing strongly each year. But if economic growth slowed, it would very quickly run out of road.

It was also clear that a housing bubble was inflating. The economist and columnist David McWilliams had been among a small group warning about the housing bubble and the associated credit binge from the late 1990s, leading to accusations that even if he was eventually right about the bubble bursting, he had been wrong about it for so long it didn't matter. McWilliams's growing celebrity and his sometimes glib social analysis – a world of 'decklanders' and 'breakfast-roll man' – didn't help his credibility but, in the light of hindsight, many of his assertions were entirely accurate. Of course, policy-makers could hardly be expected to heed mere predictions, but the data on which the predictions were based were there for everyone to see. In 2005, just a year before house prices peaked, McWilliams warned:

The only fundamental reason for house prices to rise is if the income from rent is rising. This is not the case in Ireland.

Rents have been falling, according to the Central Statistics Office, for over eighteen months now. If the income from the asset is falling relative to the value of the asset, then we have a problem. But because of the enormous amount of credit in the system and the way in which the system reinforces the original loan with another one, real world economics is suspended and Moonie economics takes over.

Moonie economics is the financial equivalent of a confidence trick. When things are going up, Moonie economics accelerates the upswing. When that confidence is punctured, banks pull in their loans, shut up shop and the opposite of Irish pricing occurs – a credit binge is replaced by a credit crunch.

A few months later, the economist Alan Ahearne, also writing in *The Sunday Business Post*, made much the same point, though without the McWilliamsisms:

Consider the ratio of house prices to rents, which has been shown to provide a useful benchmark for valuing housing in other countries. The price-rent ratio in Ireland has soared over recent years and at 29 now stands roughly 2.5 times above its level in 1996. Irish house prices have surged 300 per cent over the past decade, while increases in rents have been relatively muted. Price-rent ratios at these levels raise legitimate concerns about the sustainability of Irish house prices ... Typically, house prices peak not long after central banks begin raising interest rates in response to emerging inflation pressures.

An *Economist* magazine survey of Ireland in 2004 warned that Ireland was particularly exposed to a burst of its house-price bubble. Ministers had trumpeted the magazine's celebration of Irish successes in the past; they seemed less inclined to heed its advice now. Perhaps because the writer, discerning a change in the political climate in the autumn of 2004, had warned: 'Suddenly Irish politics has become very important for the country's economy.'

But Irish politics was full square behind the surge in house prices. Rather than take steps to alleviate the rapid growth in house prices, the government seemed to actively encourage it, not just in their public statements but in policy changes too. Ahern practically exhorted people to get moving on to the property ladder.

In April 2006, he said that had listened for seven years to warnings and arguments about difficulties in the construction sector.

I mean quite frankly, if you had taken the advice a year ago you would have lost a lot of money. Everybody said we're going to see a huge downturn in 2005 linking into 2006 – they were entirely wrong.

Really we should have an examination into why so many people got it so wrong. My view is there's not a great problem. Really, the bad advice of last year given by so many has maybe made some people make mistakes, that they should have bought last year.

The 2005 budget, which cut stamp duty for first-time buyers, was welcomed effusively by estate agents. 'The announcement is very good news for first-time buyers and the property market alike,' Sherry FitzGerald chief economist Marian Finnegan said. CB Richard Ellis Gunne commended the government for its 'sensible' approach. When estate agents are praising a budget, you can be pretty sure it's not trying to cool the property market.

By the time he came to frame his last budget, Cowen knew that house prices had to come down. Privately, he told people that modest decreases were a good thing. But his policy-making record belied that desire, and the 'soft landing' that he spoke about remained an inchoate aspiration rather than a policy goal.

According to one very senior insider, the budget strategy shifted after 2004 'because we didn't have a strategy after it. The strategy was not to have a strategy. It was year-to-year stuff.'

One of the weaknesses of democratic systems of government is that elected decision-makers are by their nature ill-disposed to taking decisions that may be desirable but will be unpopular among voters. There was certainly no popular outcry for policies that would dampen demand in the property market; nor were such calls a constant – with one or two exceptions – in public debate. Generally, people liked the fact that their houses were becoming more valuable; Ireland, after all, was a country with over 80 per cent home ownership. For all the vocal concern at the plight of first-time buyers, there was little discernible political support for policies, such as property taxes, which could have brought down, or even stabilized, prices. Where bodies like the ESRI called for measures like property taxes to dampen demand, they were dismissed as politically naïve, or simply ignored.

In fact, when the growth in house prices began to level off in the first half of 2006, there were soon loud and growing calls for the government to cut the rates of stamp duty to restore growth to the sector. Columnists in the *Sunday Independent*, including the influential Eoghan Harris, tried to run a 'campaign' on the issue for the greater part of the year before the general election in 2007. It eventually became the stated policy of the junior partner in government to achieve exactly this, when McDowell declared that the state didn't need the income from stamp duty anyway. As he wrote in the *Sunday Independent* (where else?) in September 2006, 'the Irish people respect parties who listen to them and responsibly address their concerns.' A policy of drastic cuts in stamp duty were quickly adopted by Fine Gael, too. As it faced towards the election of 2007 most of the pressure coming at the government wasn't directed at gently deflating the property bubble – it was demanding that the inflation be restarted.

The other salient fact about the Irish public finances which was storing up trouble for the future was that public spending was expanding at a breakneck rate. That was fine as long as taxation revenues kept growing, but what if they stopped growing owing to some economic shock? The teachers and the nurses would still have to be paid. Compounding this threat was the rapid growth in public-sector wages. By February, 2005, the Central Statistics Office was reporting that average wages in the public sector had grown by 9.3 per cent in the year to the previous September – when Ahern began to implement his strategy for increasing public spending. This was almost four times the rate of inflation during the same period. It was also more than twice as fast as wages in industry, which rose by just 4.5 per cent during that time.

But with an election looming over the horizon, the political debate was not interested in talk about housing bubbles or warnings about the unsustainability of the public finances. There isn't, not surprisingly, a huge market for pessimism in the midst of an economic boom. The government was expanding public spending at a massive rate, and still running huge surpluses, while the opposition, rather than pointing out the follies of economic policy, was racking its brains as to how it could get its hands on the levers of power and the pot of riches that came with them. The first promises of tax cuts of the 2007 election campaign came not from Fianna Fáil or the Progressive Democrats but from the Labour Party.

In broad terms, Ahern was attempting the same strategy as proved successful in 2001–2: inflating public spending in advance of a general election. But he was starting earlier and the increases were bigger. Though the National Development Plan had at least attempted to put some strategic shape on the capital spending, increases in current spending were still running at twice the level of growth in the economy. The remarkable thing is that it was plain to all observers what was happening. Despite this, the opposition and most of the media concentrated their critique not on the unsustainable increases in public spending on the back of windfall revenues from the property market but on perceived failures in the provision of public services. The government was criticized certainly for waste and profligacy; but simultaneously for not spending enough on public services. If the government was repeating its old form, except on a greater scale, the opposition was repeating its mistake of describing a dysfunctional and impoverished country that few voters recognized. It didn't make for a very enlightening political debate. It would shortly get even less enlightening.

Rather than the national finances, politics would be consumed by the altogether more prosaic question of Bertie Ahern's finances. As the seeds of economic trauma continued to germinate unobserved, the question of Ahern's finances was to dominate Irish politics until his departure. But not in the way people expected.

On the night of Wednesday 20 September 2006, Bertie Ahern knew that his political and personal life was about to enter a new era of scrutiny and criticism. For the previous two years, the Taoiseach had been dealing with the Mahon Tribunal's inquiries into his personal finances, prompted by allegations that he had received substantial sums of money from the property developer and tycoon Owen O'Callaghan. Ahern had always strenuously denied the charges, and indeed he had won a libel case against a man called Denis 'Starry' O'Brien, the source of an ill-advised

Sunday Business Post story which related a claim that Ahern had received money from O'Callaghan. But the tribunal's inquiries had gone far beyond the curious – and as yet unexplained – inventions of the Cork chancer, 'Starry' O'Brien. It had sought and received discovery of Ahern's financial records, and it had found a series of lodgements which he was having some difficulty explaining. The fact of the tribunal's investigations remained, for obvious reasons, a closely guarded secret. It was about to be blown wide open. Ahern didn't know what the consequences would be, but he knew they would not be pleasant.

When the *Irish Times* public affairs correspondent Colm Keena opened a plain envelope addressed to him in the paper's newsroom, he was opening a new chapter in Bertie Ahern's political life. There was no indication of the sender, though that in itself was hardly unusual. After reading the contents, Keena got up from his desk and went straight to the editor's office. The contents of the anonymous envelope, which revealed the tribunal's inquiries into Ahern's finances, would cause an earthquake in Irish politics.

Ahern had always feared disclosure of the tribunal's inquiries, but the process had been watertight until then. In recent months, however, it had stepped up a gear, with the tribunal seeking discovery of documents relating to Ahern's legal separation from his wife, Miriam. Such documents were normally entirely confidential, and Ahern would go to the High Court – and win – to prevent Mahon gaining access to them. That case was in preparation.

Now he authorized Brian Murphy, his special adviser, to contact a small number of staffers and alert them to what was coming. It was simply a matter of news management. Murphy did his ringaround of a small circle of key people – Ahern's advisers, some press officers and other officials. 'You might get a call from the *Irish Times* on a story about the Taoiseach and the tribunal,' he told them. 'The line is: it's a matter for the tribunal.'

'Is it serious?' one asked.

'It's big. You'll see tomorrow,' he replied.

Later that evening, a few ministers attended a gala ball for the Ryder Cup (the golf tournament was being held in Ireland for the first time that September). Brian Cowen was among the guests, though he was in a grumpy mood. The same Mahon Tribunal had been hearing evidence about a decision which he made as minister for transport back in 1994 which worked to the advantage of clients of Frank Dunlop, and that day counsel for the tribunal had been pushing the line that the decision was made against the advice of his officials. One of the officials declined to characterize it in such a fashion, but Cowen knew what the media reports would look like. He wasn't a huge fan of the tribunal or the media. 'Look,' one adviser told him above the din of the music. 'You won't be the biggest tribunal story in the papers tomorrow.' That was an understatement.

'Tribunal examines payments to Taoiseach', read the *Irish Times* headline the following day. Beneath it, the killer line: 'The tribunal is investigating a number of payments to Mr Ahern in or around December 1993, including cash payments, the *Irish Times* has learned.' Bombshell is a much over-used term in political reporting, but this was a ten-pounder.

Ahern, who was in the middle of an eighteen-day national tour, was in a rage. More particularly, he believed that an organized conspiracy to bring him down was now under way. The following morning, striking the note of angry victimization that was never to leave him throughout the affair, he told reporters in Clare that the leaking of the tribunal's business was 'dirty, dishonest'; the only real question was who was doing it. That was the question the reporters should be pursuing, not whatever money he may have received, which 'wasn't much'. And which anyway, was 'none of your business'.

Mandy Johnston, the press secretary, was on holiday. Her phone rang non-stop when the news broke. Gerry Howlin called from Dublin. 'Do you think it's serious?' he asked. Johnston checked the *Irish Times*'s website. 'Yeeepppp. It's serious.' Government Buildings was in a complete state of panic. 'Will we last?' they asked one another. Nobody had any answers.

Nonetheless, Ahern continued on his tour of the country,

keeping in touch with Dublin through regular phone calls. 'What's happening?' he would ask. 'Well, it's all about this tribunal stuff, Taoiseach,' one staffer responded. 'People don't care about it,' Ahern reported. Sensing the disbelief, he continued. 'No, I'm telling you. Come down here and have a look for yourself. They don't care about it.' One of the senior staff eventually went to join him. Jeepers, it's true, the staffer thought. They don't care about it. Ahern was getting an enormous reaction, especially from the Fianna Fáil organization. It was keeping his spirits up, anyway, and that was a good thing. But whatever about the reaction of the Fianna Fáil organization, the media climate was building to a frenzy. Ahern's reaction became more strained; an atmosphere of gloom was enveloping government. One senior adviser told a younger colleague: 'Be careful what you say when you're defending him. We'll all have to work in this town after he's gone. Don't destroy your credibility.' Harney met Ahern that weekend at the Ryder Cup in the K-Club. She thought he was very depressed, and feared for the immediate future of the coalition.

Over the weekend, the pressure built. Press officers, advisers and ministers were receiving hundreds of media calls about the controversy; every time Ahern commented, it spawned more questions. It became clear that Ahern would have to make a statement.

Olivia Buckley counselled that a straight television interview would give Ahern the opportunity to talk directly to the people, above the heads of the sceptical media. She was convinced that if he explained his situation to people, they would see it differently from the media. Johnston and Gerry Hickey thought he should make the statement in the Dáil, and the usual bitter disagreement between the advisers ensued. Johnston believed that a television interview could be the end of him. The stakes involved the survival of the Taoiseach's political career. It was an extraordinary moment. On the Monday after the story had broken, Ahern decided to do a television interview. Buckley rang Bryan Dobson, the anchor of RTÉ's *Six One News*. 'The Taoiseach wants to talk to someone,' she told him. 'He has a lot of things he wants to clear up. Would you be interested?' Naturally, Dobson was.

The venue would be St Luke's. As the hour approached, the tension in St Luke's was extraordinary, recalls one who was present. The Taoiseach's loyal personal assistant, Olive Melvin, was in tears. Buckley and Brian Murphy waited as Dobson and the RTÉ cameraman, Denis Devane, set up. Most thoughts in the room were simply this: what in the name of God is he going to say?

The story that Ahern haltingly and at times emotionally confessed to Dobson that evening was a compelling one. A man who, at a difficult time in his life, had seen his savings disappear, and had no home of his own, was helped by a few old friends – Joe Burke, Paddy 'the Plasterer' Reilly and others – some of them pals from childhood. They helped him out when he needed it, and though he had always insisted to them that he would pay them back, none would ever hear of it. His marriage break-up had left him all but wiped out financially, as he sought to provide for his children and his estranged wife. He looked forlorn, uncomfortable. 'I don't like giving details of the children, but for completeness, I did that.' He seemed on the verge of tears.

At a function in Manchester, someone organized an unsolicited whip-around. He never asked for it. He never did any favours for anyone. All he did was accept a few bob from a few friends in a time of need. And finally, the brilliant peroration: 'You know, from the position of the Irish public, they've always been kind to me about being separated. They've always been understanding and, em, if I've caused offence to anyone, I think I have to a few people, em, I'm sorry.'

The following day, Miriam Lord reflected in the *Irish Times*: 'You'd want to have been made of stone not to have been moved by his performance on the six o'clock news last night.'

Since his accession to the leadership of Fianna Fáil, and especially since he had become Taoiseach, Ahern had made himself more available to the media than any of his predecessors. Where

John Bruton was carefully and often aggressively shielded by his press secretary and insofar as possible only interacted with the media in controlled circumstances, Ahern appeared happy to stick his face in front of a microphone in any circumstances.

This frequently drove his press handlers to distraction. On one occasion in the summer of 2003 Ahern was under particular pressure from the tabloids for his daughter's decision to marry in France and sell the photographic rights to the event to a magazine. The Taoiseach, attending the Galway Races, had agreed not to speak to any journalists at all. Staff knew anything he said just gave the story further legs. Olivia Buckley, the press director, allowed herself to relax a little. Then she entered the marquee to find Ahern addressing a group of journalists on the subject of his daughter's wedding cake: 'Well, they might make it in France, but the flour and the eggs and everything are from Ireland . . .'

He was addicted to 'doorsteps' – giving a few words and soundbites to groups of, usually radio, reporters. Print journalists grumbled that real access to him, and getting the opportunity to ask substantive questions with answers that might run to more than a few sentences, was another matter, but there's little doubt that Ahern was the most media-friendly Taoiseach ever. This certainly wasn't because he was enamoured of the fourth estate; like most politicians his attitude to most journalists and media outlets varied between hostility and acceptance of them as a necessary evil. But he understood that he needed to communicate constantly with the Irish people. All those doorsteps, all those interviews, all those soft-soap chat-show appearances – they added up to a conversation that he had been having with the Irish people for over a decade. And the upshot of it all would be that when he chose to go before them on the *Six One News* and bare his soul (or at least, some of it), very many of them accepted his words. They had been listening to him for so long, it seemed quite natural.

Ahern's advisers, colleagues and friends looked on agog at the interview and its aftermath. Good God. It might just work. 'Unbelievable, unbelievable,' one figure who spent several years in government summarized to me that evening. He meant that he was wondering at the political skills of Bertie Ahern and his remarkable ability to communicate with the Irish people. Many of the details that Ahern gave during the interview would later be picked apart by the tribunal, but in the autumn of 2006, the Dobson interview bought him crucial time. People laughed about Paddy the Plasterer, rather than question whip-around donations from roomfuls of businessmen. They *wanted* to believe him.

But inside the political bubble of Leinster House, the media and government, it was different. Very many people were saying exactly the same thing: this is unbelievable.

This extended even to some of those who stock was defending him. 'He's lying, of course, he's lying. They all lie in the end, I suppose,' one senior party figure told me shortly after Ahern's RTÉ interview. But whatever they said in private, when they were asked straight out, they had no choice but to affirm their trust in the Taoiseach. Though many feared it would be thrown back in their faces before long, they mostly backed him to the hilt. 'In fairness to them, the ministers never refused to go out and defend him. Well, most of them didn't,' one of his aides told me.

Ahern's Drumcondra praetorians were in overdrive, and they saw conspiracies everywhere. They couldn't see that the roots of all the trouble were in Drumcondra. 'What were you talking to him about?' one of them demanded of PJ Mara, after Mara had spent an hour chatting to Cowen in the Leinster House members' bar. Mara told him to cop on. He knew Cowen's opinion of Ahern. 'Bertie Ahern,' Cowen had told him, 'is a political genius.'

It took a few days for Brian Cowen to find the opportunity. But when he did, he was unequivocal. 'Look, the Taoiseach is our Taoiseach, he's the president of our party. He enjoys the full support of our party and everyone in this organization because we know him and we believe him and we believe in his credibility.' Cowen was a big beast of the party: finance minister, favourite to be next leader, beloved of the grassroots and respected by the parliamentary party. He steadied a lot of nerves.

The PDs, though, were in turmoil. They didn't believe Ahern, but they had no evidence to back up their disbelief. Fianna Fáil had some practice in the art of defending fantastical stories and brazening out media disbelief. But the Progressive Democrats were having a nervous breakdown about it. It was just two weeks into the ill-fated leadership of Michael McDowell.

Harney had actually intended to hand over the leadership at the time of the 2004 reshuffle, and had discussed the move with friends. She had also given McDowell to understand – at least as far as he was concerned she had – that she would move aside to allow him to fulfil his leadership ambitions. However, she faced a revolt in the parliamentary party, particularly from Liz O'Donnell and John Minihan, both of whom nursed occasional loathing for McDowell.

In the autumn of 2006, Harney returned from her summer holidays and called a parliamentary party meeting. McDowell thought it was some sort of ambush, so he arrived at the meeting ten minutes late, to be told she was resigning. The same day, Fianna Fáil's most influential advisers and strategists were meeting in PJ Mara's holiday home in Kinvara to discuss and plan the strategy for the next general election campaign. Watching the television news coverage of Harney's resignation in the Merrion Hotel, the Fianna Fáilers thought, Well, this could change things. McDowell would seek to define the PDs more independently, to give them a sharper political edge. He would pick a few fights with them to emphasize the PDs' independence; *in extremis*, he could look for a convenient issue to break with them before the election. Inevitably, he became leader of the party, though he hardly had time to enjoy his elevation. They had barely changed the party's notepaper when the landmine that was Bertie Ahern's financial past exploded under the Fianna Fáil–PD coalition.

McDowell thought that Harney and O'Donnell were flakey under pressure; now it was he and his guys who wobbled. As the crisis worsened, they closeted themselves in their offices one Saturday, refusing to give a statement to the Sunday papers. They told themselves that by not making a statement to the newspapers, they were sending a message to Fianna Fáil. Of course, Fianna Fáil would have to work out what the message was. 'What do they think they're doing?' one Fianna Fáil adviser asked. 'They're sending a message,' another replied. 'For fuck's sake!'

In fact, the PDs were just paralysed by the magnitude of the decision that confronted them: either accept Ahern's explanations and stay in, or say what you actually believe and cause an election. 'Can Michael engineer a return without looking like he has his tail between his legs?' asked Miriam Lord in her Dáil sketch. 'Or is an unleashed McDowell in Opposition, knowing where the juiciest Government bones are buried, his best option now?' McDowell couldn't make up his mind.

The PDs' distrust was heightened by private information received by the PD leader. A PD nominee to a state board knew the family of the late Tim Kilroe, the friend of Ahern and proprietor of the Four Seasons Hotel in Manchester where the infamous dig-out dinner had taken place. Having spoken to the family, the source reported to McDowell that the Kilroes were outraged at the way Ahern had used their father as a sort of shield. They had got in touch with their father's friends, the source reported to McDowell, who would have attended such a dinner. None of them could recall it. They also checked the hotel's records, he said, but found no evidence that such a dinner had taken place. (Later, Ahern would specify that the dinner had taken place in the restaurant of the hotel, meaning there would be no record of a room booking.)

McDowell had decided that there was no possible benign construction on events, and from that point on, deep distrust characterized the relationship between the Taoiseach and the Tánaiste. Like many of his colleagues, McDowell didn't believe Ahern's story. He was definite about that. What he was much less sure of was what he should do next.

'We wanted the tribunal to catch him or we wanted his own guys to push him. But we couldn't do it. The government wouldn't fall, and when the election came we would be completely irrelevant. We would be political orphans,' said one of his staff.

Eventually, the PDs decided to stay in government, demanding some concessions on what they were now calling 'the corruption stuff' but staying for what they could get on economic and taxation policy. 'We have to grin and bear it,' one of McDowell's advisers told him. 'We have to stay in.'

They hoped that when the election came, people thought economics would be more important than Ahern's house. And, as it happened, it was. What they couldn't know then is that voters wouldn't give the PDs any credit for the economics.

Three weeks after it flared up, the fever broke. The *Irish Times* published an opinion poll which showed that the Ahern revelations had transformed the political landscape all right − but in Fianna Fáil's favour. The party rose by an astonishing eight points (to 39 per cent) since the previous poll in May, while Ahern's personal rating remained high, rising slightly to 53 per cent. Support for Labour and Fine Gael fell away.

Despite what they say, nearly all politicians obsess over opinion polls. Typically, news of a poll circulates a few hours before its official publication, usually on the RTÉ television news. When the news of the Fianna Fáil surge began to beep on the mobile phones of the political community, many assumed it must be a mistake. Fianna Fáil couldn't be up. It was against all the rules of politics.

On the night news of the poll broke, Ahern was in Carrickmacross. A massive crowd turned out to greet him − assembling before the news of the poll. It was tribal. Ahern grinned at his aides. See? I told you. They don't care. Jesus, thought one of the aides. This must be what it was like during the Haughey days.

He wasn't the only one who thought so. The editor of the *Irish Times* was not happy. In an editorial which became a subject of much amusement in government and which several press officers clipped and pinned on walls and noticeboards in their offices, she thundered: 'What sort of people are we? We know now.' She concluded: 'If the rest of us "look the other way" it won't be long before the culture of corruption engendered by Mr Haughey will resurface. But regrettably this poll would indicate that this does not seem to matter.'

The poll demonstrated that the perspective of those inside the political bubble isn't always the same as that of the electorate, many of whom pay little or no attention to the charge and counter-charge of political debate. The poll didn't say, as some assumed, that voters didn't care what Ahern did in his personal finances, or that they didn't think he was wrong. It said they didn't think it was more important than everything else. That judgement was subject to revision, but for the moment, that's where the public was. This is so obvious as to seem simple. But it was an insight into Irish politics that evaded many people – participants and commentators – during the long-drawn-out final phase of Bertie Ahern's career.

Amazingly, Fianna Fáil's political fortunes had been transformed by the affair. The party had shaken off its unpopularity among a key section of swing voters which had dated from the aftermath of the 2002 election. Would they be able to keep the monkey off their backs as they approached another election?

If Ahern's dealings with the Mahon Tribunal were terrifying Fianna Fáil ministers and strategists as they prepared for an election year, they had another very substantial advantage. Record exchequer receipts had transformed a planned €3 billion deficit into a €2.2 billion surplus. Here were the taxation fruits of the property bubble, and by God did ministers know what they wanted to do with them. When he presented his budget, Brian Cowen planned for an increase in spending of a whopping 13 per cent.

One senior figure explained the approach to retail politics as they approached the election. 'There was a list as long as your arm given to every TD, especially in marginal constituencies. PJ used to talk about finding little nuggets. We'd say to them, "If you have to go down and paint the fucking school yourself, that's what we'll do."'

10. A Last-minute Winner

'What if he decides to go tomorrow?'

The question hung in the air in the cluttered room in the Treasury Building, once again to serve as Fianna Fáil's general election headquarters and media centre.

It was Saturday 28 April 2007, warm and sunny without a trace of the rain that had lashed the country intermittently during the month. Soft-top cars, that summer's must-have conveyance for the twenty- and thirty-somethings with twenty and thirty thousand euros to spend (or borrow, more likely), whizzed busily around the city streets below. Three floors above the Saturday traffic, PJ Mara was chairing a meeting of the election headquarters staff. Drawn from ministers' political staff and from the advisers in Government Buildings, the room contained a wealth of professional political ability and experience – as well as some intense personal rivalries. Mandy Johnston, the government press secretary, and Olivia Buckley, the party's press director, had been conducting a personal battle for the past two years, each trying to outdo the other as the principal conduit to the media. Each spent varying proportions of their time briefing against the other.

The rivalry between the two women reflected deeper divisions between most of the Government Buildings personnel, a group centred on the Taoiseach's programme manager, Gerry Hickey, on one side, and a group drawn from the various departments and from party headquarters on the other. Many of the latter didn't esteem Hickey as highly as the Taoiseach did and the fact that he was by some distance the best-paid adviser to government didn't increase their respect for him. They took to reporting to one another how they sometimes saw him play solitaire on his computer during the campaign. 'In fairness,' one of them later told me, 'I think he's pretty good at it.'

Though Ahern had waited until almost the last minute before formally nominating him as director of elections (a slight which did not go unregistered), Mara was the undoubted figurehead and the chief, as ever the flamboyant face of the campaign. His two most important lieutenants were Peter MacDonagh, the former adviser to Ahern and one of the principal architects of the 2002 victory, who had returned from his Prague home for the campaign, and Johnston, who commanded the press operations. Among the rest, the most important figures were Gerry Howlin and Brian Murphy – both advisers to the Taoiseach, but who often found themselves on the opposite sides of arguments – and Colin Hunt, Cowen's adviser, who was responsible for economic policy. Sean Dorgan, the party's general secretary, ran the party's infrastructure and played the most important organizational role in the room. Other staff, seconded from their roles as political advisers and press officers or transferred for the duration from party headquarters a few hundred yards away, hovered on the edges of the meeting.

The Treasury Building offices were once again the nerve centre of a campaign that had been devised, planned and prepared for many months. Posters were printed and ready; the media grid – the detailed schedule outlining how themes and messages were to be pushed during the campaign – was eventually agreed; TDs and their canvassing teams had already been knocking on doors for months. There was only one problem: nobody had a clue when the Taoiseach was going to call the election.

Mara looked around at his senior staff. For the past three days, they had expected the starting pistol to be fired, and there had been several false alarms, which excited flurries of text messages between the staff. The press were half demented from weeks of waiting. A dozen rumours flew about every day. One senior figure told me with a high degree of confidence on both Wednesday and Thursday that the 'election will be called tomorrow'. Ministers and TDs, press and staff all probed one another, often trying to ferret out information by pretending they knew more than they did. But nobody knew. Because Ahern told nobody.

So, what if he did call it? Gerry Howlin volunteered to prepare a draft statement in case the Taoiseach went to Áras an Uachtaráin that evening, though few of them believed it would happen. The President was departing in the morning for an official trip to the United States, which meant that if she were to dissolve the Dáil, it had to happen that evening or, more improbably, early on Sunday morning before she caught her 9.10 a.m. flight to Atlanta. If Ahern was going to call it, the staff reasoned, they would know by now. Ministers would know in advance, for God's sake. They had all expected it by now, and none of them could understand why he was waiting. They all knew well Ahern's reluctance to take a decision that could possibly be postponed, but even by his standards, this was ridiculous.

The meeting finished and some of the staff idled around head-quarters for a few hours. Unlike the previous weekend, there were to be no opinion polls in tomorrow's newspapers. Dorgan went home, wondering if the campaign would ever start. RTÉ's main evening news bulletin led with coverage of the funerals of Ciara Dunne and her two children, found dead in Monageer in Wexford after an apparent murder/suicide. There had been a small earthquake in Kent.

The news finished, and Dorgan's phone flashed into life. The Taoiseach ringing. 'Sean, I told you I'd give you a bit of notice,' Ahern began. 'I'm going up to the Park in the morning. So we'll have to get the posters up tomorrow.'

Dorgan answered respectfully, deferring as he always did to Ahern's rank in the party and his political office. He promised the Taoiseach that the organization was ready and raring to go, and while it would be a battle against a resurgent Fine Gael, he assured Ahern that the organization was up for it. 'You will win a third term,' Dorgan told Ahern.

His mind was already racing. When would they announce? Tonight? Surely it was too late for that now. He was thinking about the posters, and securing the best sites. He could hardly get teams out at this hour. Could he? Incredibly, to his mind, Ahern told him they would not announce until noon on Sunday, hours after the President had formally dissolved the Dáil at his request. No posters up until then, Ahern said. In the event, Dorgan ignored the Taoiseach's orders, and got his teams out as early as he could.

As soon as the Taoiseach hung up, Dorgan called MacDonagh. 'You're not going to fucking believe this,' he told him.

But there was no time to waste on expressions of exasperation. Dorgan rang Johnston, told her the news, and the pair then began to call the staff. It's on, the staff were told. Get in as early as you can in the morning.

Meanwhile, Johnston rang the Taoiseach to formulate a plan to deal with his early-morning dash to Áras an Uachtaráin in the media. Ahern wanted simply to issue a press release in the morning. No word was to go to the press in advance, he said.

In the five years that Johnston had served as his press secretary, she had learned that sometimes the Taoiseach had to be faced down. This was one of those times. If some previous controversies had rocked her confidence – and that of others – in herself, she had always worked best in the white heat of a campaign. And she was ballsy.

'Taoiseach, you just can't do that,' Johnston told him.

They needed to involve the media, she explained, needed to let reporters tell the story of the start of the campaign. She didn't say that it was going to be difficult enough to explain a highly unorthodox start without excluding the media altogether. 'The press has to be told,' Johnston told him bluntly. Reluctantly, Ahern agreed. Johnston called MacDonagh for back-up. Was she doing the right thing? 'Absolutely,' was the reply. Dorgan said the same. The following morning from six o'clock on, journalists' phones began to beep with text messages.

Noel Dempsey awoke on a gloriously sunny April morning to find that RTÉ news was telling him that the general election campaign was now under way. Initially, he wondered if it could be a mistake, until he heard the reports from Áras an Uachtaráin. He called Dorgan.

'What the fuck is going on?' he demanded loudly. Dorgan

tried to mollify him. It wasn't the first such call he had received from a member of the cabinet. Most of them had found out from the radio. One of the most senior ministers in the cabinet found out at midnight when his press officer called from a pub, shouting across the din in the background. 'Mandy just rang me and told me to get in as early as I can in the morning,' the press officer roared at his boss. 'I think that means there's an election on.' Another minister asked Dorgan: 'Does he actually think *we're* the enemy?'

Once an election campaign starts, the advantages of being in government largely fall away. But knowing when it all starts gives a government both a tactical and a strategic advantage. For whatever reason, Ahern had denied that advantage to his party. 'Has the man taken leave of his senses?' one minister asked his colleagues.

It would get a lot worse before it got better. At the press conference at the Treasury to announce formally the start of the campaign, journalists noticed to their delight that there were two spelling mistakes in the press statement circulated. Embarrassingly, the supposedly expert government 'spin machine', as some newspapers had taken to calling it (the reality was considerably at odds with the characterization), had managed to spell 'Taoiseach' incorrectly. It appeared as 'Taoisech'. Waiting for Ahern to come to the podium, the journalist Olivia O'Leary pointed the error out to the director of elections. Mara smiled, slapping his wrist in mock chastisement, but when he went behind the screen later it was a different story – he exploded into profanity. But that's what happens when a campaign starts in a disorganized rush, others pleaded in mitigation; this was the draft statement that Gerry Howlin had composed the previous day. Someone had simply printed the unrevised and unedited text and passed it out to the press.

Amid all the confusion, aides also had to come up with some sort of an explanation for the sudden dash to the Park. Ahern was to claim that he had intended to ask the Presidential Commission to dissolve the Dáil but having checked, discovered that this hadn't been done before and therefore he felt compelled to run to the Park before McAleese departed to the US. In fact, this explanation was concocted by the team in the Treasury that afternoon. The authors had no more idea than anyone else why Ahern did it in the way he did.

When Ahern did appear at the podium, he read the statement, turned his back on the media and left. It took a moment for the journalists to realize what had happened. No questions, no engagement; it was the very antithesis of the legendary campaigning Bertie.

But Ahern had a very good reason for the absence of his customarily sunny disposition, and also a very good one for calling the election when he did, if not in the manner that he employed. The following day at Dublin Castle, the Mahon Tribunal was due to begin its public hearings into Ahern's possible links to the property developer Owen O'Callaghan.

Though the news that the tribunal were investigating payments to Ahern in the early to mid-1990s had paralysed normal politics when it was revealed the previous autumn, the issue had largely died down in daily political debate in the period before the general election. Partly this was because both Fine Gael and Labour were terrified of a repeat of the amazing surge in opinion poll support for both the Taoiseach and Fianna Fáil before Christmas.

However, a small group of Ahern's top aides knew that the story had not gone away or anything like it. Ahern's lawyers had been in constant correspondence with the tribunal, much of it extraordinarily antagonistic. In addition, the tribunal's legal team had conducted a private interview with Ahern and his lawyers on 5 April. It was at this interview that the Taoiseach was first confronted with the tribunal's suggestion that he had received cash sums of $45,000 and stg£30,000.

At the time Ahern was furious, telling his lawyers that he had been ambushed. However, worse was to come. Despite strong protestations and predictions of leaks by the Taoiseach's lawyers, the text of his interview was circulated among the twenty or so witnesses who were concerned with his module. It was duly leaked to Frank Connolly of the *Irish Daily Mail*, who published the dollar and sterling claims in typically forthright fashion. There was some nervousness among other media in picking up on this claim, as they hadn't seen the document themselves and some trusted neither Connolly nor the *Mail*. But Ahern's staff knew that the dollar claim was coming in the tribunal's opening statement, which was due to be read the following morning, and they knew that once it was aired at the tribunal, it would be explosive. Significant damage had been done to Ahern already, certainly. But unless Judge Mahon decided to postpone the tribunal hearings until after the general election, they feared the campaign could be over before it had begun. Mahon had already indicated that he would continue with hearings until two weeks before polling day, which meant that the opening statement was due to go ahead on Monday, irrespective of the calling of the election. On Sunday, Ahern's lawyers wrote to the tribunal one last time to assert forcefully that failure to postpone the hearings would be not alone gross interference in the democratic process but a direct intervention to the clear benefit to one side, in a letter that was received by Judge Mahon and his fellow judges of the tribunal early on Monday morning. The letter was a powerful device: it was effectively an accusation that if the tribunal went ahead as planned, it would be trying to fix the general election for Fine Gael.

Meanwhile, in the Treasury Building, there was 'an air of unreality' at the 8.00 a.m. staff meeting on Monday morning, says one member of the campaign team. The day's press conference was planned and media events co-ordinated. But nobody's mind was on the 'issue of the day' planned on the campaign grid – everyone was waiting for news from Dublin Castle.

'All rise.' Judge Alan Mahon's clerk opened the door from the judge's quarters adjacent to the hall which housed the planning tribunal, and the three judges who comprised the tribunal swept in. Pausing for their chairs to be pulled out for them, the judges took their seats in front of the assembled legal teams, a throng of reporters and a small crowd in the public gallery.

'Good morning,' Mahon began. 'This session was convened for

today to resume the public hearings in the Quarryvale module. In the light of yesterday's announcement, calling a general election for 24 May, that course will not now be followed.'

Rescheduling the hearings for 28 May and observing that the tribunal was following precedent, Mahon swiftly concluded. 'All right?' he asked.

He didn't have to ask Ahern's team twice. Seconds later the phones in the Treasury rang. For now, anyway, they were off that particular hook. There was, recalls one person in HQ, 'the most enormous sigh of relief'.

But the campaign had still started with a car crash. The media treatment on Monday of the rushed start of the campaign was overwhelmingly negative – something the Taoiseach upbraided his advisers about, adopting his familiar 'You made me do it and now look what happened' approach. His failure to accept responsibility wasn't unusual; he frequently looked for someone else to blame, adopting an outlook of patient exasperation with the others who were at fault. But having had to deal with irate ministers, and conscious of how bad a start it had been, most of the staff were furious with him for the previous day's shambles.

Others were beginning to realize there might be something serious amiss, and their concern grew in the opening days of the campaign. Everywhere Ahern went in the early days he was asked about his finances, and he soon began to withdraw from active campaigning. In fact, as the more senior members of the team knew, he had never really committed to it in the first place. It became a constant theme of the early part of the campaign: when would the leader of the party join the campaign? Though it wasn't picked up by the press, who were happy to cover one outing by Ahern most days, there wasn't a leader's tour in the way there had been in his previous two high-energy general election campaigns. Johnston and Dorgan were put to the pin of their collar trying to cover it up.

'Mandy and Dorgan was constantly trying to cover for him,' recalled one insider. 'He'd go to Blanchardstown or wherever for an hour or two. The press would be given a schedule and they'd turn up and harangue him about the money stuff. But they never noticed that there wasn't a proper tour.'

Eileen Gleeson, a corporate public relations expert who had made a reputation as telecoms tycoon Denis O'Brien's media adviser, and who had also been instrumental in Mary McAleese's campaign, had been drafted in to run the leader's tour at the behest of PJ Mara. She found things were not as she expected, to put it mildly. In the 1997 campaign, Ahern had been on the road almost all the time; television footage often featured him literally running around streets, frequently accompanied by an appropriately breathless Charlie Bird. Again, in 2002, according to one of the staffers on that campaign, Ahern had been 'on the go' for all but two or three days of the campaign. In 2007, one senior figure estimates that Ahern spent at most nine or ten days on the road – in a four-week campaign. Ahern, previously the great lover of meeting the people and the natural-born campaigner, couldn't be persuaded to get out on the campaign trail.

Much later, in early 2008, when Dempsey opined in an RTÉ interview that the famous 'Bertie factor' was less of a force in elections than it once was, his colleagues understood exactly to what he was referring. For much of the 2007 campaign, it wasn't just that the Bertie factor was missing: Bertie himself was nowhere to be found.

It was obvious to everyone in campaign headquarters and to the ministers that something pretty serious was wrong. Mara, MacDonagh, Dorgan, Johnston and others discussed it between themselves and with various cabinet members. Some of them concluded that Ahern, riven by worry about the tribunal and believing he was going to lose the election, was suffering from depression.

When Ahern did show up in the Treasury headquarters, several of the campaign team were shocked at his appearance. One of them remarked that he looked 'inches lower' than usual; another thought he was 'withdrawn, beaten down'. He wouldn't make eye contact when he spoke, and he was practically monosyllabic.

Mara realized he needed to intervene, and took to constantly contacting the Taoiseach to gee him up, trying to engender a more positive attitude in him. Others followed suit. 'We were trying to talk him up to himself and get him into a better mood,' says one senior figure. 'You know: "We have them on this, Taoiseach, you'll be the man" – that kind of thing. PJ ended up doing most of it.'

'We were trying to get him to join the campaign and lighten up, and not look as if he was going through a nightmare,' recalls another senior source. Of the rest of those who knew what was actually happening, most of them couldn't believe that this was happening in the middle of an election campaign that had been years in the planning.

It also became clear that in this frame of mind, Ahern needed a lot more preparation for media encounters. Brian Murphy, MacDonagh, Howlin and Johnston began to conduct intensive briefings with him, all the time trying to keep his mood light and positive. He offered them some hope with a forceful performance at the launch of the Fianna Fáil manifesto under fierce and lengthy questioning by the journalist Vincent Browne.

In a dramatic encounter – and the drama was not lost on Browne – the veteran journalist dissected the account of the purchase of the house and the dig-outs as presented by the Taoiseach and concluded: 'It just ain't credible!' In fact, Ahern was well able for Browne. After the encounter the journalist confided to friends that he thought he might just have won the election for Fianna Fáil, by lancing the boil of Ahern's finances.

But despite the Mansion House encounter, Ahern continued to bleed on the money story. The following day during a walk-about in central Dublin, he was again questioned on his finances, on camera. He simply ignored the question, but everybody paused, waiting for him to answer. Six seconds of excruciating silence ensued before a handler intervened: 'Next question!' The exchange was caught on camera and received the full treatment – including the six seconds of silence – that evening. Watching the

six o'clock news on television, there was despair on the third
floor of the Treasury.

The expectations were overwhelmingly gloomy. Ministers
told one another, 'There's no way he can get away with this.'
One minister's adviser, seconded like most to the campaign team,
enquired nervously of Sean Dorgan after one bout of revelations.
'What's going on? Is there more coming?' Dorgan replied: 'I just
don't fucking know.'

That weekend, Brian Cowen, Dermot Ahern and Michael
Martin, the three acknowledged heavyweights of the cabinet,
resolved that they had to do something. Staff expected more
damaging revelations in the Sunday papers (though not because
Ahern had warned them) and so had scheduled their three
big beasts for a press conference on taxation and the economy.
'Hang on a fucking minute,' Mara observed. 'There's nobody
interested in the fucking economy today.' The papers lived up to
expectations; the *Mail on Sunday* led with further excerpts from
Ahern's witness statement. Other papers, with the benefit of a
steer from Progressive Democrats sources, suggested that the
PDs were on the verge of pulling out of government. Michael
McDowell gave a strange press conference in which he indicated
that Ahern had misled him when the controversy first broke the
previous autumn. He wanted a statement from the Taoiseach
clarifying the questions about his finances. He had also contacted
Cowen, wondering what the Fianna Fáil ministers intended to
do about Ahern. The three Fianna Fáil ministers decided they
had to see the Taoiseach. Mara shrugged his agreement, and
rang him.

'Listen,' he began. 'We're over here getting ready to do our
launch. The lads want you to come over and have a chat with
you.' He put things as delicately as he could.

'I'm doing a few churches here. Can I ring them a bit later on?'
Ahern replied cautiously.

Mara's tone hardened a little. 'No, no, that won't work. They
need to have a handle on this.'

'OK, yeah. I'll tell you what. I'm coming over to do a thing for Chris Andrews. I'll come in to them.'

Ahern travelled from Drumcondra and slipped in a back door of the Treasury Building, avoiding the notice of the press. The three men went into a side room and talked for about forty-five minutes. The ministers didn't interrogate Ahern, but he talked them through the sequence of events that was to become his subsequent statement on the finances. He detailed a series of complicated transactions with the Manchester businessman Michael Wall, from whom Ahern had first rented and then purchased his home, and how Wall had given him cash to refurbish the house. He told them about the evidence he retained to back up his story – in the shape of, among other things, receipts from Brown Thomas. Ahern suggested to one of the ministers that he take notes, and he duly copied down the details of the curtains and furnishings and the receipts. The meeting didn't feature demands and ultimatums. Despite the various constructions put on it when news leaked out, they were trying to figure out how to defend him, not whether he was innocent or guilty. Well? asked one staffer when they emerged. 'If he had only told us that a few weeks ago!' was the reply.

The press conference was due to take place at noon, but had to be postponed – a measure that was not entirely incorrectly interpreted by the waiting press as a sign of panic. When the ministers emerged from their meeting with the Taoiseach (he slipped away unnoticed to Drumcondra again) they reported that he had agreed there would be a full statement on his finances in the coming days. They also agreed with suggestions that they would have to come out swinging. 'Someone is trying to manipulate the Irish electorate,' was agreed as the line. Well, of course they are: it's an election campaign, said someone. 'By illegal means,' was added to the statement. Five minutes before the conference started, Mandy Johnston suddenly had a panic: 'Where's the statement on tax?' she asked. The ministers had to deliver that as well, she said. 'Mandy,' Cowen replied, 'do you want us to be laughed out of the room?' The only subject would be the Taoiseach's finances. The press conference was a strong performance, and the handlers hoped that Ahern's promise of a statement on his finances would give the campaign some room to talk about other things. But it didn't stop the questions, inside or outside the campaign team.

The problem now was how could such a statement not cause further damage? Ahern wavered and played for time. Many of the headquarters staff and his own cabinet were completely furious with him by now. Johnston had worked hard to persuade him that he would have to make a statement, at one stage disagreeing vigorously with him. By the time Ahern gave his grudging assent to making a statement on his finances, Brian Murphy was already working on a text. The drafting of the statement was done in greater secrecy than anything else in the campaign, and only a few staff – Murphy, who drafted most of it, attorney general Rory Brady, Peter MacDonagh and Johnston – were given access to it. Everyone else was kept outside the loop. Even Mara was excluded – Ahern explicitly ordered that he shouldn't be given early access to the drafts. Sometimes Ahern was wary of Mara's abilities with the media. Eventually the head of the campaign was given it a few hours before general release.

Late in the week, the small group assembled in party head-quarters in Mount Street to review the finished statement. Rory Brady was concerned about the legal and tribunal implications of parts of the statement. The others didn't care: they just wanted to plug the political leak for the duration of the election campaign. At this stage, none of them thought Ahern could last very long afterwards anyway.

They had one overarching question: does it pass the smell test? Does it still smell bad? Or can we get through it? Eventually, they concluded without any great confidence that they could. Once finished, they left the building separately – they wanted to avoid questions not just from the media, but from their colleagues.

However, despite the media saturation on the issue, Ahern's financial past wasn't the only thing going on in the cam-paign. Cowen's forceful performances at press conferences and interviews were beginning to turn attention to the economic issues that the campaign team, and particularly the finance minister's special adviser Colin Hunt, believed were key to any Fianna Fáil victory. And anyway, voters – and journalists – were simply getting fed up with the constant querying of Ahern's finances. In fact, as they had demonstrated when the news first broke the previous autumn, voters took a more relaxed view of Ahern's finances than either the media or many of his own colleagues. Another factor also focused voters' thoughts on economic matters: confused and messy though the beginning of the campaign might have been, it also coincided exactly with the maturing of nearly half of all SSIAs, the government-subsidized savings scheme introduced by Charlie McCreevy five years earlier, under which the exchequer paid a 25 per cent top-up when the accounts matured. Because many SSIA holders had left it until the last minute to open an account, their schemes matured in April 2007. Overnight, nearly half a million people were an average of €14,000 richer.

Considerable preparation had gone into positioning Fianna Fáil on the economy. One of the most potent charges Fianna Fáil could level at the Fine Gael–Labour camp was that they couldn't really be trusted to run the economy. For this to be effective, Fianna Fáil needed to demonstrate that the opposition had promised lavishly, while their own pledges were prudent, costed and deliverable. Convinced of this strategy (which was endorsed by the American consultants), Cowen had already argued with Ahern weeks earlier that he shouldn't include tax-cutting pledges in his ard-fheis speech, but to no avail. Nonetheless, the economy remained Fianna Fáil's strongest card throughout the campaign, and one which the architects of the strategy believed could still bring them victory, despite Ahern's troubles.

Spirits were lifted, too, by positive reports coming from TDs all over the country who reported to Dorgan and Mara frequently. The interest in the Taoiseach's finances was simply not shared by an awful lot of voters, TDs were telling headquarters. The overwhelmingly negative coverage of the Fianna

Fáil campaign in the national media did not reflect the experience of local campaigns. Predictably, some TDs blamed headquarters. 'What are ye up to up there?' became a familiar question to campaign staff.

Sometimes the atmosphere in the Treasury Building was almost surreal. One day, the advisers started to nudge one another and point over at adjacent desks where Mara and Gerry Hickey were both nodding off in their chairs for a brief afternoon nap. Pointing to the slumbering seniors, Mandy Johnston whispered to her colleagues that it was like an old folks' home.

Two further events, long planned for precisely this purpose, gave Ahern and Fianna Fáil their first real positive news cycles of the campaign. The focus groups had shown that the Taoiseach's appeal for many voters had changed in the ten years he had served as Taoiseach. While he still had, for many voters, an ordinariness they found attractive, they had also come to appreciate him as a statesman and national leader. While Enda Kenny was attempting to match Bertie's retail appeal as a regular fella, Fianna Fáil knew that he couldn't match Bertie as a statesman and national leader. This was the principal reason why Fianna Fáil ministers kept referring to the issue of who would be Taoiseach during the campaign – even though privately most were seething with Ahern for much of the time. The visit of Ian Paisley to the site of the Battle of the Boyne and the Taoiseach's address to the Houses of Parliament at Westminster had been specifically designed and arranged to emphasize this side of Ahern's appeal to voters. The unusual commitment of the British Prime Minister to re-electing a Fianna Fáil Taoiseach was further emphasized when Tony Blair appeared in the party's political broadcast, along with former US president Bill Clinton and the former senator George Mitchell.

So by the time the leaders' debate arrived, there were some positive signs for Fianna Fáil. The rise and rise of Fine Gael in the polls seemed to have abated the previous weekend, and the beginnings of a Fianna Fáil recovery were in evidence. But Ahern himself was still a huge problem, and there was a sense emerging

among the staff that he needed to win the debate – a position he
had not experienced in either of the two previous elections.
Though debates in the past had not affected the races substantially, Fianna Fáil believed the stakes were higher this time
than ever. It could make the difference between government and
opposition for the next five years.

Ahern was not, by any standards, a good debater. While
occasionally capable of delivering fluent and warm speeches on
subjects he knew well to friendly audiences – a side of him
that the public and press seldom saw – his Dáil performances were
usually halting and evasive, while his ard-fheis set pieces tended
to be shouted lists of achievements and promises. His frequent
incoherence and celebrated malapropisms had become almost a
signature; going into any debate, Ahern was the underdog. Going
into one after three weeks of disastrous campaigning was a
daunting prospect.

Practice sessions were arranged for both the day before and the
morning of the *Prime Time* debate, though contracting schedules
meant that Ahern managed only about four hours' preparation
in the end. Patrick Sutton, the director of the Gaiety School of
Acting and a long-time friend who had also acted as an occasional
speech coach to the Taoiseach, had agreed to play the part of
Enda Kenny, while Howlin, Johnston and MacDonagh looked
on. The early run-throughs were not encouraging. Ahern was
halting in his delivery, and not sure of his material. MacDonagh
attempted to get him to concentrate on the material, repeating
over and over the key points of Fianna Fáil policy and the
weaknesses they had identified in the Fine Gael manifesto. Ahern
was happy to get stuck into the detail and asked question after
question: 'Tell me again why their Garda numbers don't add up?
How do we pay for the extra teachers? Why does their plan
for medical cards not work?' On Wednesday evening, Howlin
and MacDonagh disagreed sharply, not for the first time:
Howlin wanted to concentrate on rehearsal with Sutton and
on crafting phrases and soundbites that would stay with voters,
while MacDonagh insisted on staying with a more policy-based

preparation, in essence giving the Taoiseach intensive grinds in his own and Fine Gael's manifesto commitments. 'We've got to stop the fucking policy seminar,' Howlin barked at MacDonagh.

But Ahern seemed to be getting the message. As the time to travel to RTÉ neared, Ahern told MacDonagh to accompany him in the car. As the Mercedes picked its way through the southside traffic, the adviser reiterated his key points: Kenny's numbers didn't add up, his 'contract' with voters was a sham, his pledge on Garda numbers started from an incorrect base and the promise of free GP care for all under-fives was undermined by the fact it would only be introduced gradually. (This was a sucker punch, one senior Fianna Fáiler told me long after the election: of course a policy like that could *only* be introduced piecemeal. He couldn't believe Kenny fell for it.) Fianna Fáil, on the other hand, would promise less and deliver more. Like a coach with a prize-fighter before a big bout, Johnston tried to psyche Ahern up as he waited to go into studio: you've been Taoiseach for ten years; this guy's a lightweight; you're going to wipe the floor with him. Kill the contract, they exhorted him. Kill the contract.

The tension in the RTÉ studios in Montrose was intense. Miriam O'Callaghan, the moderator of the debate, was sick with nerves beforehand. It was obvious to everyone that with the race so finely balanced, the debate could be crucial to the winning and losing of the election. Coming out of the room where he had been preparing, Ahern walked straight into Kenny on the narrow corridor. Everybody paused. 'After you, Enda,' Ahern said, stepping back. 'No, no, no, Taoiseach, after you,' Kenny replied. To Ahern's people, he looked wound up, jaw rigid, fists tightly clenched. The two men stood facing one another, until Ahern strode ahead, not looking back.

Armed with masses of information, Ahern was in his element. He had always demonstrated an almost savant-like ability to master the facts and figures of his government's policies, trotting them out as answers in the Dáil to such an extent that it became a point of parody for the sketchwriters. They often missed how much it demonstrated that Ahern was a master of detail on the workings of his own administration. One of the great failures of his communications strategy was that he had never managed to build a narrative that effectively communicated the successes of his government – he thought the figures simply spoke for themselves. Usually, the press just found them tedious. But in the debate against Kenny, speaking directly to the people over the heads of the media, Ahern's command of the numbers and of the detail of his own and his opponent's policy was a crucial advantage. Ahern was reassuring; Kenny was unsure. For a large section of the public that was still making up its mind, it was a decisive difference.

The debate was an obvious and immediate success for Ahern. Some analysts and commentators scored the contest as a draw – further evidence for Fianna Fáil, if any more were needed, of the determination in some parts of the media to replace Ahern. The following day's *Irish Times* summarized: 'Kenny scores on confidence and Ahern on detail'; Saturday's editorial stuck with this analysis: 'Mr Ahern failed to play Mr Kenny off the pitch. Fianna Fáil's best opportunity to reverse the slide towards a change in government was missed.' In fact, subsequent polling by *The Sunday Business Post* and others was to show that the million-plus voters who watched the debate – especially and crucially the all-important undecided voters – scored it decisively for the Taoiseach. But the reaction of the two teams in the immediate aftermath of the debate in RTÉ was the most eloquent. According to one witness who saw both camps, Ciaran Conlon and Mark Mortell, the two Fine Gael handlers who had accompanied Kenny and who felt they were in touching distance of the Taoiseach's office before the debate, were glum and downcast as they approached the studio, only pausing to brighten up before they went on to the set to greet Kenny. Johnston and MacDonagh, frequent opponents on the campaign team, embraced after the finish; running into the set, Johnston hugged the leader, while MacDonagh clapped him vigorously on the back. Mara hung around, spinning furiously that Ahern had wiped the floor with Kenny, 'by a country mile'.

Later that evening a senior party figure was asked by RTÉ's director-general, Cathal Goan, how he thought the debate had gone. 'I think our man won it hands down and I think we'll get a lot of votes out of it,' he answered. 'I think you're right,' Goan replied. That night at the Treasury Building, for the first time since the election had been called, the team that was running the campaign actually thought they might win it.

Harney was in Courtney's pub in Lucan, watching on television after an evening canvassing. She felt the atmosphere shift even as the debate progressed. Canvassing the following day, she thought the reaction was completely different, she told her team. There might be hope for the government yet.

The following evening, in a *Late Late Show* debate marking the last weekend of the campaign, the *Sunday Independent* columnist Eoghan Harris staunchly defended Ahern, pushing voters to focus on Ahern's achievements as well as the negative stories about his finances. His urgings pushed the same buttons for many undecided voters that the debate did. Things were beginning to turn. The leaders' debate seemed to effect a dramatic change in Ahern. The following day, on the campaign trail, he was mobbed by enthusiastic crowds. Handlers reported back to Mara in headquarters that he was more like his old self. One of Dorgan's sources reported to him that the reaction to him was 'phenomenal'. He seemed to be drawing energy from the crowd's reaction to him, as in previous campaigns. He was enthusiastic about doing events, keen to get going. The leader had finally joined the campaign.

That Saturday, Mara returned to the Treasury Building after a long lunch at the Unicorn restaurant with friends to find spirits were giddy among the troops, despite a coruscating article about the management of the campaign in the *Irish Times* which christened the Treasury headquarters 'Meltdown Manor'. Martin Larkin, an advertising executive who occasionally attended on the fringes of the campaign, had commissioned his staff to produce a few examples of attack ads aimed at Kenny. Though everybody knew that the Taoiseach would veto them – he had an aversion to negative campaigning – some senior figures had earlier in the week concluded that they might be getting to the stage where they had to try anything to rescue the campaign, with or without the Taoiseach's permission. In any event, if they decided not to use the ads officially, they could always leak them to the press as something that Fianna Fáil had considered and turned down. The press would be sure to cover it, reproducing the pictures.

The ad in question was a picture of Enda Kenny with an L plate around his neck. Mara, knowing Ahern's likely reaction, ranted at the staff: 'Why wasn't I asked about this?'

There was silence until someone piped up: 'Because you had an appointment with a bottle of Pinot Grigio, PJ?' In fact, Mara's taste in wines was considerably more expensive than that. But the staff were also busy because Colin Hunt had found a bet that they figured they could make a lot of money on. The reports from around the country had further improved since the debate, and they had got early word of the following day's *Sunday Business Post* poll that showed the FF share of the vote rising to 37 per cent. Worldspreads, a spread betting company, was estimating that Fianna Fáil would win seat numbers in the mid-sixties, and punters could bet that the number would be higher. The staff didn't know if they would win the election, but reckoned they couldn't lose the bet, and guaranteeing the bet with Mara's credit card – Hunt actually spelled out Mara's name for Worldspreads, who registered no recognition – they all piled in according to their means. They would win over €50,000.

The following Monday, an *Irish Times* poll counted Fianna Fáil support at 41 per cent; on Tuesday the *Sunday Business Post* released its final poll of the campaign online, showing a similar rise in support, though putting the level of support at a more conservative 38 per cent. But the movement was clear. After a frantic final few days of campaigning, Ahern retired to Drumcondra to await his fate. As in 2002, the first news of it was from *Morning Ireland* at 7.00 a.m. on Friday. On a clear, sunny morning, as bleary-eyed politicians, campaigners and journalists all over the country shook groggy heads and strained to hear,

RTÉ's political correspondent, David McCullagh, reported what few could immediately believe: the station's own exit poll had reported a share of the vote for Fianna Fáil of over 41 per cent, in excess of the 2002 vote. Despite the most aggressive campaign against him that any modern Irish politician has had to bear, despite the incomprehension of his own party and the disbelief of the media, Ahern was victorious again. Despite himself, it was perhaps his greatest triumph.

If Bertie Ahern's electoral success in 2007 was a damn close-run thing, Fianna Fáil's resurgence at the expense of Sinn Féin was one of the sweetest aspects of that victory for him. For Ahern and for Fianna Fáil, the great conundrum of the peace process had always been how to prevent Sinn Féin from turning the political capital it gained them into seats in the Dáil and political power in the South. The peace process and the ending of violence had transformed the politics of the North and Sinn Féin's advances in two elections in the South made it seem as though the political landscape in the Republic was being transformed too.

The republican peace strategy had been sold to the movement's hawks on the basis that it would ensure political power; the general election result of 2002, when the party won five seats, and local elections of 2004 were signposts along the way. The definitive IRA statement of July 2005, declaring an end to its armed struggle to end British rule in Northern Ireland, instructing its units to dump arms and encouraging its volunteers to 'assist the development of purely political and democratic programmes through exclusively peaceful means', was a landmark in Irish history. That it came after months of pressure on Sinn Féin, following the killing of a man (Robert McCartney) by IRA members in a bar brawl in a Belfast bar and the robbery of £26 million from a Northern Bank branch, didn't diminish its political or historic significance. The southern parties expected it to give further impetus to the growth of Sinn Féin. Forecasts of fifteen to twenty Sinn Féin seats at the next general election abounded. By the autumn of 2006, Sinn Féin was polling at 10 per cent, and

Michael McDowell was warning that Fianna Fáil would welcome them into government (at his expense) after the next election.

Earlier in 2007, at an historic special ard-fheis held in the same RDS venue, Sinn Féin had voted overwhelmingly to support the police service of Northern Ireland, clearing the last barrier to a full engagement with the state they had vowed to overthrow. The war was finally and definitely over, and Sinn Féin looked forward to reaping the peace dividends.

Fianna Fáil had fought the rise of Sinn Féin in Dublin and elsewhere with two weapons. Firstly, it stepped up its level of political activity on the ground significantly, led by Ahern's example. The battering it had taken at the 2004 local elections concealed an underlying strength that did not apply at that contest: it had a lot of sitting TDs. Sitting TDs are significantly more likely to be elected than challengers; in fact, academic research has pointed to incumbency as the single biggest predictor of a candidate's election. Under new electoral rules, sitting TDs were no longer permitted to serve as members of a local authority – a change many of them resented greatly. Consequently, in those places where a TD was neither able nor inclined to place a family member or some other ultra-loyalist on the election ticket, the biggest Fianna Fáil presence in the area was – in many cases – hardly bothered about the result of the election. This depressed the Fianna Fáil performance significantly. Privately, party managers told Ahern that it could have been responsible for as much as 50 per cent of their losses. TDs were told to get their constituency organizations in order and on to the doorsteps. More importantly, they had an obvious direct personal interest in the outcome at the following general election, which most did not in 2004.

Secondly, Fianna Fáil made the strategic decision that they would seek to reclaim the mantle of nationalism from Sinn Féin. While commentators such as Eoghan Harris were advising Ahern that the only way to defeat Sinn Féin was to confront nationalist rhetoric, symbols and history, Ahern thought that the exact opposite was more likely to appeal to the majority of voters.

'Bertie Ahern is about to make a big mistake by competing with Sinn Féin for "control" of the Sinn Féin centenary commemorations next year,' Harris wrote. 'As a result, the RTÉ airwaves will be filled for a whole year with republican rhetoric – ably assisted by hush puppies at all levels. This rise in the republican temperature will benefit Sinn Féin more than Fianna Fáil at the next general election.' In fact, it would do the exact opposite, though Harris was to become a vocal admirer of Ahern and would eventually be appointed to the Senate by him.

The 1916 commemoration parade in 2006 was actually not a Fianna Fáil idea at all – it was Michael McDowell's brainwave. McDowell detested Sinn Féin and he also boasted a distinguished nationalist pedigree: his grandfather, Eoin MacNeill, was a founder of the Gaelic League and the Irish Volunteers, though as Fianna Fáilers sometimes liked to point out, MacNeill was the man who tried to call off the 1916 Rising. Whatever about his family's prior attitudes, McDowell now believed that the Irish state and its mainstream parties had to reclaim ownership of the event. After a cabinet dinner in Farmleigh, a number of ministers stayed on afterwards for drinks. McDowell fell into a discussion on the rise of Sinn Féin – the political topic that was most exercising the southern political establishment – with Mary Harney and Rory Brady and some others. McDowell was animated in his insistence that Sinn Féin should not be allowed to appropriate the symbols of the country and the history of the Irish revolution. He floated the idea of a state military commemoration of the 1916 Rising. Rory Brady agreed enthusiastically. Ahern was quickly persuaded of the merits of the idea. The following Easter, of 2006, over 100,000 people lined the route to see a military parade through the streets of central Dublin after a wreath-laying ceremony in Kilmainham Jail, where the 1916 leaders were executed. The Sinn Féin leader, Gerry Adams, stayed away.

In the Northern Assembly elections in March 2007, the party increased its share of the seats from 24 to 28, firmly closing the door in the face of the SDLP, who managed only 16 seats. The astonishing pictures from Stormont on 8 May, when devolution to a government led by Ian Paisley and Martin McGuinness took place, were broadcast around the world; just as importantly from Sinn Féin's point of view, they were broadcast into the middle of the general election campaign. Polls suggested the party was running at about 10 per cent of the vote; Martin McGuinness confidently predicted that whatever they said in the campaign, the main parties would be knocking on Sinn Féin's door to support or join a coalition government after the election. Expectations of ten or twelve seats were on the conservative side. Giddy with the prospect of government on both sides of the border nine years before the party's own target of 2016, hundreds of Sinn Féin election workers poured south to join their colleagues on the canvass. A shock awaited them on results day.

The party's share of the vote increased slightly, though this was a function of running many more candidates than it did in 2002 – 42 as opposed to just 27 five years previously. It lost one of its five TDs, Sean Crowe in Dublin South West, and another, Aengus Ó Snodaigh, survived by fewer than 100 votes. None of its anticipated breakthroughs materialized and McDonald, the great white hope south of the border who had made the stunning breakthrough to the European Parliament in 2004, flopped in Dublin Central, home constituency of the Taoiseach.

According to one senior figure in Fianna Fáil, the success of the Northern peace process worked to the significant advantage of the party in the 2007 elections. Certainly, the Fianna Fáil campaign was set up to maximize its benefit. Three events emphasized the Fianna Fáil role in the peace process – the establishment of the power-sharing executive, the ceremonial welcoming of Paisley to the Boyne Valley and the Taoiseach's address to the British Houses of Parliament at Westminster. If some of Ahern's political operatives had previously wondered whether there were any votes in the North, the group that ran the 2007 election campaign were determined to prove that there were. And that they would be Fianna Fáil votes. 'There was a bounce out of the peace process bounce,' complained Gerry Adams, 'but Bertie got it.'

In the scheme of things, that was hardly unfair. When Bertie

Ahern ascended to the leadership of his party, the IRA was still at war. In very great part because of his labours, by the time he left office, Ian Paisley, the great angry volcano of not-an-inch unionism, whose sectarian politics gushed forth from the spigot of medieval theology, sat grinning broadly in a local executive beside his constitutional right-hand man, Martin McGuinness, a former IRA commander from Derry, the famous boy-general who vowed and fought to overthrow the statelet he now co-led. The familiarity of that achievement should not dull its enormity.

In another sense, despite many claims over the years that the exact opposite was happening, the Irish electorate pulled a fast one on Sinn Féin. For the long period when the peace process was being nurtured and bedded down, voters indicated that they were likely to support Sinn Féin in great numbers. They were opposed to violence and wanted Sinn Féin to decommission, and play a part in the northern state. If the party did that, the polls and the 2002 and 2004 elections suggested, its vote would grow very significantly. When Sinn Féin did all those things, its support declined – many of the Sinn Féin votes went back to Fianna Fáil. Far from Sinn Féin conning the voters, it appears the voters may have been doing the conning.

The great achievement of Ahern and his governments in achieving concord with the British government on Northern Ireland and persuading the representatives of that bitterly divided society to engage with it was followed by the political trick of pulling the rug from under Sinn Féin support in the South, reversing a trend which had seemed unstoppable. Either would have been a mighty achievement for a leader of Fianna Fáil; to follow one with another was a virtuoso display of political skill.

11. The Long Goodbye

Some of the most acute observers of Irish politics and of the behaviour of Irish politicians are the staff in Leinster House. The wisdom of the bar staff is particularly prized, witnesses as they are when tongues are loosened and innermost thoughts are revealed, though their discretion is trusted by everyone. After half a lifetime in Irish politics, PJ Mara has always been careful to listen when they offer their opinions. One afternoon in the summer of 2007, Mara found himself in conversation with one of the staff. They talked about the election, about the eventual succession in Fianna Fáil and about how the party would cope after Ahern retired. 'You get this into your head,' the barman told Mara. 'Bertie Ahern is irreplaceable.'

Irreplaceable he might have been, but Ahern had entered the final phase of his political career. The victory in the general election was stunning. The turnaround in public opinion towards Ahern and Fianna Fáil in the final days has been ascribed to many things, but it certainly wouldn't have happened without Ahern's performance in the televised leaders' debate. The well of public affection and respect for the Taoiseach had not been entirely drained by the revelations about his personal finances, or by the growing public scepticism about his account of them.

Looked at one way, Ahern was at the height of his power – a third general election victory delivered, the historic accord in the North finally bedded down, a thriving economy, his place in history assured. But as so often in politics, the public triumph marked a private decline.

The public did not see it, but Ahern had used up a lot of his political capital in that general election campaign. By making them cover for his behaviour for most of the campaign, he had cashed in a lot of chips with his own cabinet colleagues and within the Fianna Fáil organization. His ministers marvelled at his ability to pull the campaign out of the fire; but they knew that it was largely his fault that it was in the fire in the first place. After the chaos of the campaign, the reaction among many to his announcement that he wouldn't fight another election was: you're damn right you won't. 'They were pretty pissed off with him,' says one person with regular contact with the cabinet. 'They certainly would have blamed him if they had lost the election.' His ministers had already begun to look beyond him.

Some of his staff thought he understood that decline was imminent. Returning to the Treasury Building headquarters on the night of the general election results, he spoke to a raucous gathering. It was a tough fight, he told the cheering crowd. They were all against us. But we stuck together and we did it in the end. The election workers roared their approval. Triumphant staff had hung a sign over the door: 'Welcome to Meltdown Manor', a reference to the nickname bestowed on the venue when the campaign seemed to be doomed. A few of the Ogra–Fianna Fáil volunteers had purloined a life-size cardboard cut-out of Fine Gael leader Enda Kenny which was the subject of much predictable hilarity, generally centring on favourable comparisons between the cardboard and the real thing. Somebody hung L-plates around his shoulders. The drink flowed. Amid the celebrations, one of Ahern's most trusted aides offered his congratulations. 'We'll just have to keep going as much as we can,' was the less than triumphant reply.

As with all political leaders, Ahern now began to look towards his legacy. He made two typically solitary, but far-reaching, decisions. He named Brian Cowen as his preferred successor, and he instructed his ministers to open negotiations with the Green Party on a possible coalition deal.

Ahern had done a tired and tetchy results-night interview with Mark Little on RTÉ television, complaining about his treatment by the press and the Mahon Tribunal. By the time he sat with Sean O'Rourke a few weeks later, he was back in form. 'Brian Cowen and I have been friends since the mid-1980s,' Ahern said.

This was stretching things. The two had never been particularly close personally. 'My point of view, he is the obvious successor to me in five years or whenever.'

Or whenever. His anointing of Cowen greatly annoyed several ministers. It wasn't just that they thought it would damage their own chances of succeeding him – though several thought of themselves as potential leaders – but rather that the succession wasn't a matter for him. The convention that departing leaders don't involve themselves in succession contests relates more to the fact that departing leaders usually have little power: a leadership contest relates to the future, the departing leader is part of the past. Nominating Cowen as his preferred successor, Ahern was trying to exercise power while he still had it. Several ministers commented publicly on the appropriateness, or otherwise, of the Taoiseach's remarks – a signal that his power had already waned. When Dermot Ahern observed that it wasn't a matter for Ahern, it was a matter for the Fianna Fáil parliamentary party, he was speaking the thoughts of most of the cabinet.

The satirical 'Diary of a Nortsoide Taoiseach' carried in *Phoenix* magazine may have made the best assessment of Ahern's move. The diary's author wrote: 'By naming Biffo publicly as me chosen heir, I'm buyin his future loyalty. He can't afford to shaft me anytime in the next five years. And as for de udders dat fancy de job, dey also know dat dere's no pointing tryin to get rid of me early, because Biffo is de real problem. By rewardin a loyal servant, derefore, I have also shifted all de heat onto him. I'm so devious, sometimes I scare meself.'

Similarly, several cabinet members were privately against constructing a coalition government with the Green Party. On numbers alone, Fianna Fáil didn't need them – they could maintain a Dáil majority with what was left of the Progressive Democrats and a few independent TDs – and on policy, on culture and on economics they were incompatible, several ministers thought. Privately, Cowen couldn't see the logic of it, but he didn't oppose Ahern's plans.

In a private lunch during the negotiations with one of his

senior ministers, Ahern explained his decision to seek an accord with the Greens. 'Why did you ask us to do this with these guys?' the minister asked. 'All you need is enough votes for the fourteenth. When we're in we'll stay in. Nobody will want an election.'

'Ah, you know, if we did that,' Ahern replied, 'the next election would be Fianna Fáil versus the rest again. We've spent two terms trying to get rid of that.' The PDs were doomed, he thought. Another alliance solely with them would sooner or later be effectively a single-party government. They would be back to Fianna Fáil against the rest. If they brought in the Greens, it would give the coalition model new life.

'If we do this,' he concluded, 'we'll have three options the next time – Labour, Sinn Féin and the Greens.' He was reinforcing the model of Fianna Fáil having most of the power all the time rather than all the power most of the time. It also meant that any part of the coalition could depart without bringing it down – an important consideration given his future at the tribunal. And with the ink hardly dry on the returning officer's signature, he was also thinking of the next election. It wasn't just about using power: more importantly, it was about keeping it.

The election result was hardly announced when Ahern had asked his ministers to seek negotiations with the Greens. Seamus Brennan had been texting Green TD John Gormley since the Thursday polling day, sounding him out about negotiations. On Sunday, Noel Dempsey called one of Ahern's staff. 'Can you put some stuff together to see where we are with the Greens?' he asked. They were starting early, the exhausted staffer thought. The talks began a few days afterwards. Seamus Brennan insisted that Fair Trade coffee should be provided for the negotiators; the staff ribbed him mercilessly about it. But the Greens noticed.

As Brennan, Cowen and Dempsey continued their negotiations with the Greens – beginning with the immortal line from Brennan 'You're playing senior hurling now, lads, but ye're playing with lads with a few All-Ireland medals' – Ahern was nailing down a third coalition deal with Harney, now acting leader of the

Progressive Democrats since McDowell had lost his seat and emotionally announced his retirement from public life.

In fact, throughout the negotiation with the Greens, Ahern kept in constant contact with Harney himself, repeatedly assuring her that he wanted the PDs to be part of the coalition, and that he wanted her in cabinet with him. On Friday 8 June, whilst attending a dinner at the home of businessman Martin Naughten, Harney learned that the Green Party had pulled out of the negotiations to form a government. She wasn't enormously concerned; that afternoon she had agreed the outline of a deal to enter government with Bertie Ahern for the third time. She would remain, they agreed, as minister for health. Seamus Brennan emerged from the stalled negotiations to make emollient noises. The Greens too shied away from saying it was all over. Both sides figured they could get a deal; the Fianna Fáilers were relieved that the Greens never mentioned the Mahon Tribunal.

Contacts were renewed over the weekend and two days before the Dáil met, the two party leaders met in Drumcondra to agree government formation and seal the agreement. The agreement surprised many in Fianna Fáil; they were even more surprised when Green Party leader Trevor Sargent, having concluded the deal and secured his party's agreement, told colleagues that he didn't want to be a cabinet minister himself, and would be resigning as leader of the party. Though he obviously supported the coalition agreement, he had promised not to lead his party into government with Ahern's party, and he would honour that pledge. The Fianna Fáilers thought Sargent must be suffering from some sort of mental incapacity.

Even before the deal with the Greens was eventually done, Ahern had augmented the novel arrangement by securing the support of three independents – the still-faithful Jackie Healy-Rae, the ex-Fine Gael TD Michael Lowry and the left-wing Dublin independent Finian McGrath – and one exile, Beverley Flynn, whom he indicated could once again rejoin Fianna Fáil in another phase of her Lanigan's Ball relationship with the party.

His final government was a curious beast, but it had a hefty Dáil majority of thirteen votes. As events would transpire, it would need them.

The new Dáil met on Thursday 14 June, a day after the Green Party's special conference had approved the recommendation of the leadership to enter coalition. The party's active membership shared the leadership's hunger for office: the deal was approved by nearly 90 per cent of the delegates. The first day of any Dáil tends to be restrained and congratulatory, with such partisanship as is on offer cloaked in relative good humour. The Fine Gael leader drew laughter from his own benches when he recalled the attitude of the two main coalition parties to one another in the campaign just past:

The Green Party said that the issue of the Taoiseach's finances made him 'a dead man walking'. Its members said that Fianna Fáil 'needs to go into opposition and radically change itself before the Greens could even consider a coalition with it'. Fianna Fáil, as the Ceann Comhairle will be aware, said 'the Greens are a rabid crowd of tree-hugging muesli-eating wackos . . . Ireland needs Green economics like a lettuce needs slugs . . .' Others described the party as jihadists. Members of the Green Party said, 'If the PDs pull the plug, who exactly are they going to go into government with?' They said 'the Greens wouldn't touch those opportunists with a barge pole'. I suppose that is why they are cycling out to Áras an Uachtaráin as well. They also said that with Fianna Fáil it is a case of 'If you don't like our policies today, we can change them tomorrow' . . . I hate to disappoint the Green Party members, but Fianna Fáil did not change its policies at all.'

This was a bit unfair. The Greens had deliberately stayed out of the two alternative government blocs which had offered them-selves to the electorate and the only logic of this position could be that they were willing to join either if the circumstances allowed or demanded it. The Greens had secured as much as they might have hoped for in a programme for government negotiated between a party with 78 (soon to be 79 when Beverley Flynn rejoined) seats and one with 6. It was nonetheless a surprising arrangement. But John Gormley had been in the Dáil for a decade; Trevor Sargent for a decade and a half; they would always be negotiating minority positions and concessions from a larger right-wing party, and they had no great love for the big farmers of Fine Gael. If not now, when? The Irish people had decided that Bertie Ahern's financial entanglements shouldn't be enough to debar him from leading the government – who were they to gainsay that instruction?

There is a strong institutional memory in the Department of Finance of the perilous budgetary situation of the state for much of its existence, and the resulting culture is one which is instinctively opposed to any new spending plans and to the extension of existing programmes. Even throughout the years of spectacular economic growth of the late 1990s, finance continued to find pressing reasons for restricting spending. In the autumn of 1998, for instance, finance officials by turns exasperated and amused ministers when they asserted that the collapse of the rouble and Russia's default on its debt meant that despite booming tax revenues in Ireland, spending should not be increased at all the following year.

All proposals for cabinet decisions pass through the Department of Finance for evaluation and generally the department will object if the proposal involves additional spending. The relevant officials appraise the proposal and send a recommendation to the minister before cabinet. Though he expanded spending as tax revenues surged, McCreevy was instinctively a hawk on spending – and officials knew that they were assured of a sympathetic hearing for their recommendations to block any new spending proposals. They soon realized that he had an open door on these things – senior officials could call down to the minister's office before cabinet and warn him about particular spending proposals from other ministers. 'You need to watch this aspect of the proposal,' officials would caution him, before elaborating on their written

memos. 'We think you need to oppose this because …'
McCreevy lapped it up, revelling as he did in being as well or
better briefed on ministers' proposals than they were themselves.
When he departed, however, the practice fell largely into
abeyance, something senior officials remarked on among themselves. Cowen's different approach reflected the new policy
priorities of the government. McCreevy's exit cleared the way to
shower money on public services, expand things like medical card
entitlement and take those at the bottom end of the wage scale out
of the tax net. The minister for finance still had to say no a lot of
the time, but he was saying yes a lot more frequently.

One official puts it in terms of his colleagues' level of comfort with interest groups with which they had to deal: 'They
found themselves in a much less adversarial position with their
stakeholders.' Another translated: people who came looking for
money were more likely to get it. There was money to fix every
problem.

In 2001 and the first half of 2002, McCreevy had done much
the same thing. But after the election, he dropped the anchor and
called a halt to runaway spending growth. His fiscal discipline was
necessitated by his own earlier profligacy, but it left the public
finances in reasonable health when he left. That approach did
not recommend itself to the government after the 2007 general
election. There was not, it is true, a sudden fall-off in economic
growth, as the government had witnessed in 2001 and 2002.
But there were signs around, all the same. For one thing, the
spectacular growth in the property market had long since abated.
In an economy that depended so much on construction, it is
remarkable that policy-makers didn't make some provision for
this. And the international credit crunch began not in 2008 but
in the summer of 2007.

For every post-election political honeymoon, there are several
predictions that it will be the shortest in history. In June 2007,
following a series of conversations with senior officials, I duly
wrote:

The emerging problem is as simple as this – the money coming in is slowing down, and the money going out is accelerating ... The government finances can live with that for a while, but not indefinitely. The latest monthly exchequer returns, for the month of May, show the money paid to the government in tax fell below what was expected for the first time since 2003. The Department of Finance is notoriously conservative in its projections of tax revenues, and for years has cheerfully underestimated the money that profligate politicians – all politicians are by definition spendthrifts, in the view of the Department of Finance – would have at their disposal. If not even the conservative estimates of the finance mandarins are being met by tax receipts, and if that trend continues, then this will rapidly become a very serious problem for the new government ... It will put concerns about Ahern's domestic financing in 1994 or what kind of petrol should go into the tanks of the ministers' cars in sharp perspective.

In fact, throughout the election, the paper had warned that the projections for economic growth were optimistic. The final editorial before the general election ruefully observed: 'Last week, the *Sunday Business Post* sent the main parties a series of questions on their economic policies, and particularly on their plans to deal with, and priorities in the event of, a more pronounced than expected slowdown in our economy over the course of the next five years. The answers were not encouraging.'

There were more objective indications, too. A survey by the state employment and training agency Fás and the ESRI showed that more than one-third of the country's construction firms were expecting to cut their workforce that summer.

There was another, more piquant signal to the government that the growth in property values – and therefore, the growth in taxation revenues from that source – was at an end: the banks had started to sell off their property portfolios. AIB sold much of their headquarters to the then property mogul Sean Dunne and Hibernian Insurance, recording a €230 million profit on the transaction. In February 2007, the bank announced that it had entered sale and leaseback arrangements on twenty-five of its branches. The Bank of Ireland had already completed similar deals for many of its branches. In a typically perspicacious radio column, Olivia O'Leary observed, 'There's always one sure sign that the ship's about to go down, they say – when little furry animals start scuttling off the decks. Beware. The banks are selling their property.'

In fact, warnings about the public finances were everywhere in the summer and autumn of 2007. The real reason that the leadership of the government did not seek to address the slow-down in government revenues was the same reason that the election was a near-disaster. Under Bertie Ahern, Fianna Fáil had been more focused on fighting elections than on governing; now if the party only stuttered through election campaigns because of distractions elsewhere, it did not bode well for competent and efficient government. The distraction elsewhere was what would soon become the slow strangulation of the now three-term Taoiseach by the inquiries of the Mahon Tribunal.

On 28 May, the Tribunal of Inquiry into Certain Planning Matters and Payments resumed for its 725th day, having ad-journed for the period of the election campaign, at the request of Ahern's lawyers and with the expectation that had the tribunal not agreed to an adjournment for the election, Ahern's lawyers would have petitioned the High Court to direct them to do so. Relations between the two sides were already hostile. Ahern's lawyers were about to dial the tension up by several degrees.

The opening statement by the tribunal's lawyers – the one that Fianna Fáil had been so worried about before the election – was dynamite. It suggested there were contradictions between the account given to the tribunal by Ahern and the evidence from the banks that its investigations had uncovered. Tribunal counsel Des O'Neill, whose house style was an odd mixture of the laconic and the aggressive, suggested that one particular lodgement was more likely to be an exchange of $45,000 rather than the sterling and odd Irish cash amount that Ahern maintained it was. 'A cus-tomer presenting exactly $45,000 for exchange into Irish currency on December 5th, 1994 would have received exactly IR £28,772.90 in exchange applying the AIB rate appropriate to a US dollar transaction to a value of up to £2,500 with a deduction of the discretionary IR£5 commission,' O'Neill said. That Irish pounds amount was one of four lodgements that the tribunal was now going to tease out in public. It seemed that the tribunal's lawyers believed the Taoiseach had lied to them and was hiding the truth about sums of money that appeared in his accounts.

The tribunal presented its statement in painstaking detail and couched in cautious terms, explaining that these were matters it wished to investigate in its public hearings and warning against conclusions being drawn at this stage. Nobody heard that bit. Those watching – which included Fine Gael staffers, much to the chagrin of Fianna Fáil – knew that had the statement been made before the election, it could have changed everything.

Conor Maguire, senior counsel for Ahern, knew what was coming, and he knew how he wanted to respond. He took off the gloves, and lashed out.

The tribunal had treated his client unfairly, had protected Tom Gilmartin in making his allegations against Ahern, had invented hypotheses about dollars and had risked subverting the democratic process, he suggested. 'Let me be very clear about this. A similar approach will not suffice on this occasion.'

Maguire's pyrotechnics weren't just designed to deflect attention from the uncomfortable evidence in the bank records, though Ahern would hardly have complained when they achieved that. There was a genuine sense of grievance on the Taoiseach's side and a belief that the tribunal was out to get him. His aides told him that after ten years, the tribunal had to nail somebody, and he was the biggest target in their sights. He believed that the tribunal had been reckless in circulating documents that were likely be leaked and which would damage him. Some of his aides and friends believed that whoever was doing the leaking was deliberately trying to damage him. They responded by attacking the tribunal at any opportunity, and briefing savagely about it. It was a conflict in which legal weapons were only part of the armoury. As the evidence progressed, the *Sunday Business Post* noted that it was clear that 'the Taoiseach believes the tribunal is out to get him, and that the tribunal believes the Taoiseach is telling lies. These are not, of course, mutually exclusive propositions.'

The stout legal defence couldn't disguise the fact that politically, the experience could only be enormously damaging. The Taoiseach of the country was now in open conflict with a tribunal of inquiry set up by the Oireachtas under his direction. Before the election, the opposition had been wary of dwelling too much on the tribunal issues, conscious of how it had backfired so badly on them in the past. After the election, there was no such hesitation. Fine Gael TDs and senators openly accused him of lying. At a leadership level, Kenny's advisers had decided they should try to spread the political damage that Ahern was suffering among the ministers who would be there after he had gone. The opposition, too, were looking beyond Ahern.

Compounding the damage for Ahern was the fact that by now, he had become largely remote from his own ministers. He had long become removed from the back-benchers. When he first became Taoiseach he had promised an aide that he wouldn't allow what had happened to Jack Lynch to happen to him. As a young TD he believed Lynch had become remote from the parliamentary party, allowing Haughey to build his base of support, and he vowed he would always maintain contact with the parliamentary party. And he largely did. In his first term, he was always conscious of keeping in touch with the back-benchers. 'He would always compliment you on something you had done on television or whatever – I presume someone told him you had been on,' said one back-bencher.

Ahern once surprised Sean Ardagh, a member of the public accounts sub-committee which examined tax avoidance by banks, by telling him he had watched the videos of the committee's hearings and seen Ardagh perform capably (as he did). Few back-benchers believed that Bertie had bothered to watch tapes of their media appearances; but they were impressed that he took

the trouble to tell them he did, and they were flattered if someone had watched them on his behalf. 'Imagine your sense of
importance!' says one. But that connection was in the past. He
was becoming out of touch in other ways, too. Later that year
when the latest in a series of large pay rises was recommended
for senior public servants and politicians by a body selected and
supported by public servants and politicians, Ahern's reaction to
the predictable public outrage was indignant and bad-tempered,
pointing out that he didn't have half the perks that his counterparts in other countries had. By the time he entered his eleventh
year as Taoiseach he was a more solitary figure than ever. He had
had a unique relationship with McCreevy, but Ahern had never
really been close to anyone in the cabinet. Partly this was because
of the position, but mostly it was Ahern's own nature, and the
fact that his cabal wasn't in Leinster House but in Drumcondra. 'I
was always fearful that there was no group of supportive ministers
around him,' remembers one aide. 'I knew we'd end up asking
them to do favours.'

Privately ministers wondered where it was going to end;
most guessed that it wasn't going to be edifying. Few evinced
any belief at all in his story – 'I'd say he got oodles of cash,' one
former minister told me – though they didn't believe he was
corrupt, or had necessarily received any money from Owen
O'Callaghan. And if they didn't believe Ahern's story, then it was
pretty obvious that the Mahon Tribunal didn't. And with more
public hearings scheduled for the autumn, that did not bode well
for the Taoiseach. As his heir apparent, Cowen was in a pivotal
position. But Ahern's nomination of him as his successor had
blunted any likelihood of any push from that quarter. In fact,
Cowen and other ministers were in the habit of damping down
any unease among the parliamentary party. From the summer
after the electoral great escape, the clock was ticking on Ahern's
leadership. It was a matter not of if but when. But the last thing
Cowen wanted was a messy exit.

According to several ministers and officials, one of the results
of the situation was that the overwhelming sense in government

circles was one of drift. That was to have profound economic and political consequences.

By the September exchequer returns, it was already clear that the freezing up of the residential housing market was having an effect on tax revenues – revenue from stamp duty was now expected to undershoot its targets by half a billion euros. In fact, the eventual figure would be almost three quarters of a billion. The September returns for the first nine months of the year showed that capital gains tax, VAT, excise duty and stamp duty were all behind target, at €107 million, €132 million, €225 million and €401 million respectively. Other taxes continued to perform strongly, but there was clearly something going on. The government didn't seem greatly concerned; after all, only twelve months earlier Michael McDowell was proclaiming that the state didn't need the revenue from stamp duty anyway. As it would turn out, the stamp duty collapse was the canary in the coal mine.

Ahern thought that it was vital that people maintain confidence. But he seemed to think that signals from their leaders alone could do that. In July, in response to warnings from commentators and economists, he told reporters that 'Sitting on the sidelines, cribbing and moaning is a lost opportunity. I don't know how people who engage in that don't commit suicide because frankly the only thing that motivates me is being able to actively change something.'

By now, his spin doctors were translating his thoughts with the preface 'I think what he meant was . . .' The same month Ahern again pooh-poohed concerns about the economy: 'There is no place for negativity. No need for any pessimism. Above all, there is no place for politically motivated attempts to talk down the economy and the achievements of our people across all sectors.'

This was the Sean Dunne school of economics, where property values could only go up and politically connected developers could only get richer and super-richer. Dunne, a Carlow-born builder who had returned from London and made a fortune building new housing estates in the 1990s, became a sort of totem for the rise and rise of the Celtic Tiger's property developer nouveau riche. By 2005, he had acquired himself the reputation at least of billionaire status, a new, blonde former-gossip-columnist wife and trophy homes in the exclusive Kildare golf and country club, the K-Club, and on Shrewsbury Road, one of the capital's most sought-after addresses. He had also cultivated a much-advertised close personal friendship with the Taoiseach, who travelled in his jet to sports fixtures and who in turn invited him to sit with his distinguished guests for his addresses to the Westminster parliament and, later, the US Congress. He was lionized in the customary Technicolor of the *Sunday Independent* as Dunner, the Baron of Ballsbridge.

Having paid an eye-watering €379 million for a 7-acre site in Ballsbridge and watched his gamble fail because of planning decisions and a falling property market, the baron subsequently became a totem for the spectacular implosion of property-based wealth in 2007 and 2008. By December 2008, he was telling the *New York Times* that his company 'could be considered insolvent'; he was wailing to friends and acquaintances that the country had to 'bring back Bertie Ahern and Charlie McCreevy'. What he really wanted was to turn the clock back and undo his disastrous investments. One evening shortly before Christmas 2008, the baron and his wife – and the reporter from the *New York Times* – met broadcaster Eamon Dunphy in a new private members' club, Residence, on St Stephen's Green. The club was designed for the boom, and that evening in the club bar, among the braying pinstripes and perma-tanned socialites, it almost seemed that the worsening economic crisis could be kept at bay by the champagne. An exuberant Dunphy at once heightened the spirit but punctured the illusion. Reaching into his pockets, he drew out crumpled banknotes and threw them at Dunne, shouting, 'Here Dunner! Here Dunner! You need the money!'

If Ahern seemed irrationally exuberant himself in the summer of 2007 about the economy's prospects, it was in keeping with his general mood at the time. Those who dealt with him regularly thought he was sometimes unrealistically upbeat, almost euphoric.

They remembered the depressed state he had been in prior to the election, and contrasted it with his current upbeat mood. 'He seemed to believe he was invincible,' says one person who worked closely with Ahern throughout the period. Another person suggested that he was like someone who has survived a plane crash and afterwards believes that nothing can harm him. His comments on the state of the economy didn't disprove the theory.

By his own admission, Ahern was thinking about the need for remedial action on the economy that summer and autumn. But he appeared to believe that restarting activity in the residential housing market and the broader construction industry was the solution. The telling phrase of the economist and writer David McWilliams that the Irish had developed an economy based on selling houses to one another was lost on him. In a later interview with Aengus Fanning of the *Sunday Independent* the following spring, he reflected:

We built from a Fianna Fáil point of view. We built the construction industry up to a massive strength and it was playing a huge role in the economy. It really was the strong point, but not the only point in the economy, in the last 10 years, with the pharmaceutical industry, the medical appliance industry, the financial services, the whole information technology sector, but the residential construction has gone down.

There is a number of reasons for that; the international situation, the fact that we had built at such growth for 10 years that you do reach a saturation point, but we have to continue to try to stimulate the residential market. I think the changes we made in the last budget on stamp duty, the fact that the rise in interest rates has stopped, the fact that the US market in construction is beginning to lift. I think at this stage there is hope, it is an area to which I have been giving huge attention since last autumn ... Construction is hugely strong and hugely important for this country. Despite the fact that there are so many detractors about developers in the construction industry, they are wrong, in my view.

In the autumn after the election, Cowen introduced a significant reform of the budget system by abandoning the old budget and estimates distinction and instead instituting a pre-budget outlook in October, followed by combined budget and spending estimates in place of the traditional budget-day package. Under the new system, the October outlook would show what the costs of maintaining existing services would be the following year; the budget would contain any new spending plans.

The first pre-budget outlook, published in mid-October 2007, gave an indication of how the big spending increases of recent years had built massive rising costs into the system. The cost of running the state, Cowen's figures revealed, would increase by nearly 5 per cent, or €2.3 billion, without any new spending. Economic growth was slowing, and the budget would have to be tough, he repeatedly warned. But he still indicated that he was expecting to increase spending by somewhere in the region of 7 or 8 per cent – a huge increase by the standards of anywhere else. However, the minister was phlegmatic. 'No one is suggesting we're on our uppers,' he told a press conference.

This was the point where McCreevy had brought down the guillotine five years previously, stabilizing the state's finances after pre-election spending growth, and in doing so laying the foundations not just for the government's unpopularity but for his own departure. Since McCreevy had moved on, economic policy had been the joint preserve of the Taoiseach and the minister for finance. For different reasons, neither wanted a round of cutbacks and spending control. The world and the Irish economic reality were changing rapidly, but for the managers of the Irish economy, it was business as usual.

The approach was emphasized when Cowen presented his budget in December. Current spending would increase by over 8 per cent; capital spending was to increase by over 10 per cent. Despite the fact that tax receipts had fallen €2 billion below expectations in 2007, Cowen didn't appear unduly concerned. He predicted that the tax revenues to pay for his spending increases would increase – although by just 3.3 per cent. The rest he would make up in borrowing. In actual fact, tax revenues would contract by nearly 14 per cent. The forecasts that Cowen relied upon would turn out to be hopelessly optimistic. It wasn't so much that the country needed confidence, as Ahern insisted; it needed realism. It was getting neither.

From the point of view of many observers, there didn't appear to be much that was realistic in the evidence of Michael Wall, the Manchester bus company owner and sometime landlord of Bertie Ahern, either. The striking, bearded figure of Wall arrived in Dublin Castle to give his evidence when the Mahon Tribunal resumed its public sittings in mid-September. The hearings would shine an uncomfortable and unflattering light on the story that Bertie Ahern had told the electorate months earlier.

Wall explained how he had thought about establishing business in Dublin, decided to buy a house and sub-contracted that task to Celia Larkin, who identified a suitable property. He bought it and agreed to rent the house to Bertie Ahern with an option to purchase. This took place while Ahern was expecting to become Taoiseach in late 1994, when concerns about his domestic situation were first publicly aired. Striking this agreement, Ahern mentioned that the house might need a conservatory and some other alterations, so Wall brought a suitcase of cash containing some £30,000 and, having taken out a few thousand for himself, handed it over to Ahern and Larkin. Their reaction? 'No particular reaction whatsoever.' Wall would later decide not to set up in Dublin, and sell the house to Ahern – though he had already decided to leave it to Ahern in his will.

This, Ahern would contend, was the explanation for a sum of money which turned up in his bank accounts at the time. Despite the agreement of Wall's and Ahern's accounts of the matter, it did not meet with widespread belief. Celia Larkin, Ahern's former partner, reinforced Wall's account at the hearing the following day, though only after acknowledging that previous recollections on her part had been deficient.

For hundreds of years, Dublin Castle has loomed large in the psyche of the Irish people. The seat of British power, it was also the policing and security hub of the ruling administration, and its cells and dungeons had seen many a gruesome interrogation. The hangar-like room where the tribunal's hearings took place was more comfortable than the dungeons, but it must have aroused similar feelings in some of the witnesses.

On Thursday 13 September, Ahern followed Larkin and Wall into the witness box. It was a gala day at Dublin Castle. Crowds awaited Ahern's arrival and thronged the large hall where the hearings were conducted. They hung around afterwards to cheer and jeer him on the way out; the tribunal team was also cheered and applauded. The press benches overflowed, and journalists vied with one another to point out the significance of various statements.

Ahern insisted that he was glad that the day had finally arrived when he could face in public the accusations against him. 'It's the first opportunity in seven and half years of being tormented about these issues that I have had the chance to come before the justices,' he declared. This was a courageous claim, as the tribunal would establish quickly. After a few hours in the box, Ahern acknowledged that he had not supplied the tribunal with the information it had sought – to the extent that in March 2006, it had threatened him with a summons to a public sitting of the tribunal. In other words, they were saying it was Ahern who had been responsible for the delay. The tribunal seemed at least as concerned with this affront to its dignity and authority as it was with the import of Ahern's evidence. On that Thursday, he conceded that his earlier evidence might have been incorrect. The tribunal was also anxious to point out that Ahern's earlier, incomplete accounts effectively left a 'hole' in the money trail.

Ahern's spin doctors and aides briefed assiduously while simultaneously complaining that the event had turned into a media circus. His press secretary, Eoghan Ó Neachtain, complained to RTÉ that he had counted nineteen staff from the national broadcaster in the press section, not counting technical people. Will ye get a grip, he advised. He was right – it was a media circus. It was a media circus because the tribunal was destroying Ahern in full public view.

Ahern spent four days in the witness box in late September, and the tribunal indicated that several more sessions would be required. The day after he left the box, the Dáil resumed after its summer break. The Ceann Comhairle, John O'Donoghue, who had been dropped by Ahern from the cabinet after the election, set the tone for the forthcoming term when he told deputies that they must realize that the Dáil had effectively delegated its function to hold the Taoiseach accountable for certain matters to the tribunal. 'However, we must be realistic. I understand that in the political domain there may be a wish by the party leaders to question the Taoiseach on the Mahon Tribunal. Therefore, it would be nonsensical of me to refuse that political imperative.'

Ahern had answered questions in the house before, of course, but O'Donoghue was almost sanctioning the opening of another front on Ahern. In doing so, he may have been affording a neat payback for his demotion: but he was also quite properly fulfilling his constitutional responsibilities, which are to the entire Dáil, not to the leader of his party. It was a new and dangerous development for Ahern; the judgements of politics are sometimes rougher and readier than those of law. They are certainly less governed by the rules of logic and evidence. That evening, Fine Gael gave concrete parliamentary form to its new aggressiveness on tribunal matters, forcing a debate on a motion of no confidence in the Taoiseach. Often a government welcomes a motion of no confidence as a means of rallying support among its own waverers. Not this time.

Ahern gave a lengthy speech. 'To many my affairs are unorthodox. That is because my lifestyle in that dark period was unorthodox. Many who have gone through the trauma of marital separation and legal proceedings will feel empathy with me. Mine was not a perfect life, nor a perfect family and matrimonial environment, but as I emerged from that period I was assisted by friends and my affairs were regularized over a short period.

'I have always been consistent in this one, fundamental matter.

I did not receive any payments from Mr O'Callaghan,' he said. This was true. But there were other parts of his story that hadn't been consistent, and this was becoming plain, too. In response, the Fine Gael leader was blunt in his assessment of Ahern's account. 'Most of the events we were discussing never happened. In my view, they are fictitious. They are complicated stories, part of a web of complicated stories designed to mask hard facts, and constructed stories to fit known facts ... We became besotted with stories about whip-arounds, after-dinner presentations and, more recently, a bag of sterling to refurbish a virtually new house.'

The Fianna Fáil speeches were combative, but awkward: they dwelt on Ahern's achievements and the need for due process to take its course. They steered away from the detail of the explanations offered by Ahern, though a new note was introduced by Cowen. 'I believe political loyalty is a virtue and that loyalty will be maintained by the government for the Taoiseach on the basis of his achievements and what he has to offer which is far greater than anything that Deputy Kenny could even contemplate.' There was no endorsement of the Taoiseach's evidence. It was a deeply uncomfortable episode for many ministers.

There were several contradictions and admissions of strangeness by Ahern and friendly witnesses during those fevered days of autumn 2008. Often, entering Dublin Castle required almost a suspension of disbelief in two areas. One required the listener to enter the odd world of Bertie Ahern's personal relationships and finances in the early to mid-1990s, a world in which the man who regularly proclaimed his lack of interest in money and possessions was in receipt of large sums from a variety of sources. The second strange presumption was to accept it was necessary and appropriate and fitting that the Taoiseach should be brought through his financial dealings in such minute detail on the hearsay suggestion of Tom Gilmartin, an unreliable witness.

The process ground grimly onwards. The close friends who had lent him money followed him into the witness box, when it transpired that some of them were neither close nor friends of him at the time. But with the exception of stockbroker Padraic O'Connor – whose account of matters differed substantially from Ahern's and revealed the important role that Des Richardson had played in the affair – they largely supported Ahern's account of the dig-outs and the Christmas donations. In the days before Christmas, Ahern returned to the witness box. He was no longer the battling figure intent on clearing his name; now he was a hunted figure, trying to stay ahead of the pursuing pack. In further cross-examination about the fundraising on his behalf in 1993 and 1994, he sustained more damage to the credibility of his story. He publicly railed against the inquiry now, accusing it from the witness box of trying to 'stitch me up'; but it proceeded with its relentless work, detailing another £5,000 lodgement that it was inquiring about in the minutes before it rose for the Christmas holidays. In his office on the Saturday before Christmas, while his staff detailed the list of Christmas presents that they had purchased on his behalf, he complained that the tribunal was managing the news cycles, bringing up issues just before adjournments so that they would be featured prominently in reports.

The new year dawned with the government facing the same two pressing problems that it had when it had taken office the previous June: the rapidly deteriorating economy and the question of its leader's future. Neither issue had been productively or conclusively addressed – in fact, the uncertainty over the leadership was actively militating against action on the economy. Heads had been in the sand for six months now, but neither issue would go away.

Full-year exchequer figures published in January confirmed the slide in many areas of revenue, with tax revenues coming in at nearly €2 billion below what was expected. Department of Finance officials began to worry that the deterioration had been accelerating in the last part of the previous year, as the contagion in property and construction fed into the rest of the economy.

In February, ministers received a briefing about the declining state of the exchequer finances. One minister recalls it being especially stark. It was clear to many of them that the situation was likely to deteriorate further and that measures to restrict spending could be necessary before the end of the year. Nothing was done. 'Look,' says one aide, 'there was very little being done in government by the Bert – apart from the elephant in the room.'

'The government was paralysed at the centre,' says one official who held a number of urgent and increasingly pessimistic conversations with his colleagues, who despaired of getting decisions taken and the normal work of government processed. 'Some of his advisers were concentrating wholly on the tribunal; there were rows internally when Ó Neachtain couldn't get them to go out and defend him.' Another insider concurs. 'A huge amount of time and effort and political capital was going in to defending him,' he told me. Even one of his most loyal staffers acknowledged that it was becoming impossible for the government to function properly. 'We couldn't get anything else done. It just sucked up all the oxygen.' Senior figures across government have all attested to this fact that dominated Ahern's final months. Handlers and spin doctors complained that every time their minister faced the media, he or she faced questions about the tribunal. As the evidence progressed and the outlook for the Taoiseach deteriorated, the questions were getting harder to answer.

Individual ministers recognized the emerging difficulties in the public finances, but the system appeared incapable of adjusting to it, much less taking early remedial steps. When one senior minister's adviser relayed the day's news to him after another bruising day at the tribunal for Ahern – 'Jesus, have you seen this Gráinne Carruth stuff?' – he replied: 'Fuck the Carruth stuff,' pointing to a brief from the minister for finance. 'This is really serious.'

At an Ogra–Fianna Fáil conference in Tullamore, Cowen sought to focus the message on the Lisbon Treaty. One aide remembers that Cowen did three interviews; in every one of them, Bertie Ahern's finances were the principal topic. Reflecting afterwards, the aide thought, This just can't go on.

The definitively final phase began when Ahern returned to the witness box on 21 February. Amid fractious exchanges between Ahern's legal team and a defensive and agitated tribunal, Ahern was grilled about lodgements from accounts in the Irish Permanent that he had not originally disclosed to the tribunal. Some of the money may have come from his late father's estate, he thought; he wasn't sure. Some of it may have come from 'personal donations for my personal use'; we had now gone well beyond innocent dig-outs and surprise whip-arounds. Now we were in the Ray Burke territory of 'walking around money' for buying raffle tickets and suchlike. He was bleeding now, but there was worse, much worse, to come.

One of the accounts showed a withdrawal of £30,000. This, Ahern explained, was for a staff member in St Luke's, whose elderly relatives faced a difficulty when their landlord died, and they faced possible eviction. The money went towards the purchase of the house, which was now owned by the staff member.

The following day, after some hours of re-examination, tribunal counsel, with the air of a poker player who knows he has a winning hand and is enjoying the wait to reveal it, asked: who was the staff member? Ahern, hunched and defensive, answered quietly but clearly: 'Celia Larkin.'

There was an intake of breath in the public gallery. The press benches paused, then scribbled and typed furiously. Radio reporters jumped out of their seats and left the hall to phone in the bombshell to their newsrooms.

It was clear that the revelation that Celia Larkin had bought a house with money which came from an account that the Taoiseach was saying was a Fianna Fáil account was dynamite, whatever way you looked at it. The explanation that the money was a loan and had been repaid didn't make it look any better – it had only been repaid a few weeks previously when the tribunal had started asking questions about the account. It changed the context of the entire encounter. Few people had the time or the inclination to follow the detail of the tribunal inquiries, but here was something they could easily understand. It was simple and it was devastating. For Fianna Fáil people up and down the country, who stood on church gate collections and dipped into their wallets and purses for raffle tickets, a Rubicon had been crossed. As Miriam Lord concluded the following day in one of her riveting accounts of days at the tribunal, 'This is not good. Not good at all.'

It was unclear what it had to do with the tribunal's legally proper inquiries into the allegation that Ahern had received bribes from Owen O'Callaghan. If the tribunal believed that some O'Callaghan money had been channelled to Ahern through a labyrinthine web that implicated virtually his entire network of friends and contacts, they had yet to produce the evidence for this suspicion. But they had shown that many of Ahern's explanations of his finances were inconsistent. The official explanation was that the tribunal had to ascertain that the considerable sums in Ahern's accounts did not come from O'Callaghan. Ahern was perhaps entitled to feel that there was no necessity to prove that their inquiries were not relevant to their terms of reference by means of extended public hearings that revealed facts about his finances that could only be politically ruinous. The legal consequences of all this were unclear, and would be the subject of much future wrangling. But the political consequences were quickly taking shape.

Ahern's lack of credibility on the tribunal's inquiries had severely undermined him among the public. In early March, a *Sunday Business Post*/Red C tracking poll only underlined the widespread disbelief of his story, though support for Fianna Fáil was holding up. Crucially, the poll showed that the credibility gap had been growing over the previous weeks. Reflecting on the results, the paper suggested the numbers offered 'further evidence that the fortunes of the party and its current leader are diverging.

The tide of public opinion continues to move against Bertie Ahern with regard to his evidence to the tribunal, and the corrosive effect it is having on his political reputation continues. This is a very dangerous trend for Ahern.' It was more than that.

More than half of all voters said they didn't believe his evidence to the tribunal, while exactly half of all voters said they no longer trusted him to run the country following his appearances at Dublin Castle. Almost 70 per cent of voters said he should resign if he was found to have misled the tribunal.

If the revelations about Larkin's gift/loan diminished Ahern amongst his own, the evidence of Gráinne Carruth would belittle him further among ordinary people, and particularly women.

Carruth had been a secretary in St Luke's from 1987 to 1999, and had lodged money on Ahern's behalf to an account in the Irish Permanent branch across the road. She had previously given evidence that she had not made particular lodgements and never dealt in sterling. That story was now coming apart, and Carruth appeared terrified by that realization.

Over two days, Carruth endured an uncomfortable cross-examination from Des O'Neill, the tribunal counsel, during which she was forced to admit that her earlier evidence was incorrect. She was warned that the consequences of lying to the tribunal could include massive fines and jail. Accepting 'as a matter of probability' that she had lodged sterling to Ahern's account, she repeatedly broke down in tears and told the tribunal at one stage, 'I just want to go home.'

The reaction was savage – not towards the witness who had revised her evidence, not to the tribunal counsel who had leaned on her, but towards the man many believed had sent her down to the tribunal to cover for him. Ahern was incensed at her treatment, but he could hardly escape the implications of it: in any case, the *Irish Independent* spelled them out for him the following day on page one: 'Taoiseach Bertie Ahern's entire credibility as a tribunal witness was in tatters last night after his former secretary flatly contradicted his explanation of the latest tranche of cash to appear in his accounts.'

The Fianna Fáil organization was hardly immune to the constant drip-drip of revelations. One of the failings of the Irish political system is that TDs are so close to their electorates; but one of its strengths is also that they are so close to them. TDs were hearing the grassroots' rumblings, and they were bringing them back to Dublin. One person with a valid claim to know the mind of ordinary members is blunt: 'He had lost the confidence of the organization ... After Celia and Gráinne Carruth, it was all over.' The same sentiment that was spreading throughout the Fianna Fáil organization was also feeding into a media climate that was increasingly hostile. It was given regular outings to Dublin Castle to exercise its feelings.

The twin forces of the media – some of which pursued Ahern with an almost feral bloodlust – and the organization's growing unease were prompting a round of what-are-we-going-to-do, something-has-to-be-done phone conversations between ministers. Ministerial responses to the effect that Ahern's finances, albeit messy, had nothing whatsoever to do with the tribunal's Quarryvale investigations, and that all questions should be answered at the tribunal, were growing thin, even to their ears. The Larkin house revelation and the Carruth evidence had blown that sort of response out of the water. A fear of going out to defend him was developing, not just because they didn't believe him, but because they didn't know if what he was going to say next might make them look stupid. Cowen and Micheál Martin were fire-fighting, telling people to back off, warning them not to do anything rash. They all knew Cowen would succeed him, and nobody wanted to be in a new Taoiseach's black books. But politicians can be impulsive sorts, and it wouldn't hold for ever.

In the last week of March, a Green councillor, Niall Ó Brolcháin, surfaced and said that Ahern should resign. Ó Brolcháin wasn't just some obscure county councillor: he was a former mayor of Galway and had been tipped for the Dáil seat the previous year. He was then working for the party leadership in Dublin, though his comments were a solo run. More tellingly, though, he indicated that the issue was likely to be discussed at the party's conference, due a fortnight later. Most people in the Green Party thought the Taoiseach should resign, he added.

A day later, another wound. Fiona O'Malley, who was in the midst of a leadership election in the Progressive Democrats, earned herself a front-page story in the *Irish Times* with a call on Ahern to clarify contradictions on his evidence. He was, she said, bringing the profession of politics into disrepute.

The following day, asked by reporters to respond to O'Malley's concerns, Harney came out and conceded there was 'considerable public disquiet' about the Taoiseach's evidence.

Momentum was building now. The laws of coalition politics dictated that if the Progressive Democrats were concerned, the Greens had to be even more concerned. John Gormley was attending a meeting in Lucan when his press officer, Liam Reid, joined him, holding a copy of the morning paper. 'Take a look at this,' he told him. 'What? What is it?' Gormley replied. 'That's the break,' Reid said. 'There's no way you can't come out and match that.' Soon, their phones started to ring with news of Harney's comments. Reporters wanted to know where Gormley would be later. He would have to have a line by the time they reached him. The arrangements were duly made and when Gormley later found himself in front of a TV3 microphone, he conceded there was a 'growing public interest in this issue and there are concerns'. It was in 'his best interest and that of his party and the country that a clarifying statement is made'.

A day later, a Fianna Fáil TD, Bobby Aylward, told reporters that the Taoiseach should clarify his evidence in the light of Carruth's testimony. Batt O'Keeffe, a junior minister and close friend of Cowen, merely reflected that Ahern 'knows best what to do'. But he added 'and will know the appropriate time'.

This was a new type of pressure, and Ahern knew it wouldn't go away. When Cowen returned from an official St Patrick's Day visit to Malaysia and a short family holiday in Vietnam, he went to St Luke's on Thursday 27 March to meet Ahern. The fact of the meeting itself was a sign. According to someone with knowledge of the encounter, there was no ultimatum from Cowen, but both men acknowledged the reality of the situation. The following Wednesday, 2 April, he was due to attend yet another Dáil session to answer opposition questions, the latest of a series of encounters he had already stumbled through. It made sense to go before then. Cowen and Ahern spoke by phone again a few times in the intervening days. Ahern was concerned that Cowen understood that he was actually going to go through with his resignation, at one stage calling him to say, 'You do know what I said?' By Saturday, he began to think about making the arrangements. Early on Sunday morning, he called his special adviser and principal speechwriter, Brian Murphy, and asked him to come to St Luke's. They chatted aimlessly about a few things while Murphy wondered what it was all about. Ahern disappeared upstairs and returned with a notepad, and suddenly said: 'It's like this – I'm going to jack it in!' 'What?!' Murphy was dumbfounded. 'I'm going to jack it in,' Ahern repeated.

Murphy was stunned, and tried to talk him out of it. Hang on, even until the summer. Go in your own time. Ahern advanced his reasons; there were several. Eventually, he said, 'Listen, let's do the speech and talk about what we'll say, and then we can come back and talk about it.' He produced some notes he had scribbled on a pad. Murphy understood: that was it. There would be no going back. This was one Bertie Ahern decision that wasn't open to revision.

Later that evening, agriculture minister Mary Coughlan appeared on RTÉ's *The Week in Politics* programme. Repeatedly asked by presenter Sean O'Rourke, she declined to say that she personally believed the Taoiseach's version of events. Five times she dodged the question. 'It's not a matter for me to believe or otherwise,' she insisted. Her evasions prompted a flurry of late-night calls and texts among ministers and advisers. Was there a push on? Coughlan was very close to Cowen. If not, should there be? And what was Ahern going to do? They didn't know that the decision had already been made.

With utmost secrecy, the arrangements were put together

over the following two days in St Luke's. Mandy Johnston had been among those Ahern had consulted and informed over the weekend and she planned the choreography of the final days.

Cowen came in on Tuesday and Rory Brady, who remained close to Ahern although he was no longer attorney general, reviewed his speech and recommended the inclusion of the line 'I have done no wrong and wronged no one.' That evening a small group including Brady, Johnston, Cyprian Brady, Sandra Cullough, Murphy and Dermot Carew gathered to make the final arrangements. In sombre mood, they adjourned across the road to Fagan's for a few drinks. They watched Manchester United defeat Roma 2–0 in a Champions League game. Business as usual. But not for Ahern. 'It'll be bedlam in here tomorrow night,' he told them.

Gormley received a message that Ahern wanted to speak to him. 'I have a way out of all this,' the Taoiseach told him. 'And I think you'll be happy with it.' They arranged to meet earlier than usual before cabinet the following day. Gormley didn't know what Ahern intended to do. What do you think? he asked his staff. No idea, they replied.

The same evening, Harney was in l'Ecrivain, the Michelin-starred restaurant on Baggot Street, when her phone rang. Normally in such circumstances, she wouldn't take the call but would return it later. However, when she saw the number flashing, she immediately excused herself and went outside to take the call. It was Ahern. The two spoke briefly. Harney had become very fond of Ahern since she had joined him in government in 1997, and she was immensely saddened by the way he was leaving. But she knew there was no choice.

On Wednesday morning, 2 April, ministers assembled for the weekly cabinet meeting. Mobile phones began to beep. Journalists had been summoned to an unscheduled and immediate press conference, and press officers and advisers were being asked: what's going on? Is he really—?

He was.

When I get back from the US, he told ministers, I will resign.

Now I'd like if you would come down with me to make the announcement.

His advisers milled around outside; they recorded that several members of the cabinet were emotional. Moving downstairs for the announcement, ministers saw the journalists around the marble steps of the entrance hall in Government Buildings in a state of nervous excitement. Some were quieter, absorbing the historic nature of what they were about to witness. Staff crowded around the balcony overlooking the hall. As Ahern spoke, many were in tears.

He had never, he said, put his own interests before the interests of the Irish people. He had done no wrong, and wronged no one. But the time had come. He would tender his resignation on 6 May, but in the meantime, he would continue to 'work hard'.

The Bertie Ahern era was over.

Epilogue

'Fianna Fáil is back in power!' the Fianna Fáil spin doctor exclaimed as the obsequies over the career of the now-departed Bertie Ahern were completed and Brian Cowen installed in his place. He was only half-joking. Though Ahern was rapturously acclaimed by the party grassroots, there was always something almost distant about the relationship, and it was more than just the distance of leadership. To those on the outside, this was preposterous. Ahern was the quintessential Fianna Fáiler: non-ideological, pragmatic, appearing to believe in nothing sufficiently strongly to negate any deal to his advantage – and now, in his final incarnation, the recipient of money in envelopes. Dedicated throughout to the retention of power, above all.

But to those who knew the soul of the organization, Bertie Ahern's relationship with Fianna Fáil was more ambiguous. When one of his constituency generals told the makers of the documentary about Ahern that they weren't really Fianna Fáil people at all, they were 'Bertie people', the suggestion appeared nonsensical to many. But Fianna Fáilers understood it immediately. He was lauded more than loved. Ahern's real love affair was not with the Fianna Fáil party, it was with the Irish people – who knew less of him, despite the man-of-the-people schtick. His relationship with Fianna Fáil was a politician's relationship; utilitarian, almost. Ahern had done more for the party than any one of its modern leaders; his unifying leadership had saved the party from itself. Yet he was, in a sense, not of them. Heresies like this were rarely uttered during the years of his ascendancy. But when his descent came, they were on the lips of many in the party. Ahern was never, they said, 'real Fianna Fáil' – whatever that meant. But it meant something to them. Probably it meant that they were moving on.

Ahern had restored the party to its pomp, the presumptive wielders of power and the font of patronage; he had given most of his life to the party and his role within it. But there was something in the mutterings, all the same. Because with Cowen it was different, viscerally so. Cowen was one of them. They loved him; they knew him; he was sprung from them. He had Fianna Fáil written in his DNA; in a get-to-know-each-other briefing with political correspondents, he told them without a hint of self-consciousness, 'I love this party.'

There was never a doubt that Cowen would succeed Ahern after his resignation; the only question was: would there be a futile challenge? None materialized. One by one, the cabinet ministers lined up to support him, and at the close of nominations on 12 April, there was only one candidate. The organization was exultant, the parliamentary party delighted, the cabinet relieved. Even those who harboured leadership ambitions themselves – and, as Noel Dempsey honestly acknowledged, they all entertained these thoughts, however fleetingly – were happy that a messy extraction and a bloody succession battle had been avoided. With the difficulties of Ahern's departure behind them their troubles were over, surely. In fact, they were just beginning.

Even as the former Taoiseach departed, the problems in the country's economy and the emerging calamity in the public finances were becoming evident. It would quickly become clear that no satisfactory evaluation of Ahern's two-and-a-bit terms of office could be possible until the financial crisis – only partly a product of his economic policies but worsened by the neglect of his final year – had played itself out. In other words, Ahern's legacy would be intricately bound up with the performance of the successor and his government. The ease of the handover of power and the warmth of the tributes to Ahern on his departure were genuine but they masked the wrench for the outgoing Taoiseach and the anger of many of those he left behind about his behaviour since the stories about his personal finances first came to dominate Irish politics. Those feelings would grow, not diminish in the year after Ahern resigned. He has let his friends know that he is not pleased with the performance of his successors in their first year, and this opinion has been echoed loudly among many of his supporters. Ahern's utterly disparaging view of the performance of Cowen's government is formed in the knowledge that its failures damage his legacy.

It was not the case, as many subsequently suggested, that Ahern's departure was perfectly timed, so that he left in a blaze of glory before the economic crash that was to define the leadership of his successor and, perhaps, the entire political generation that followed him. The precipitous decline of the Irish economy had been in progress for much of the previous year, and the months preceding Ahern's resignation saw that economic decline enter a new, more rapid and more dangerous phase – a fact evidenced in the month-by-month decline in taxation revenues. The crash was already happening but Ahern's third government – and his finance minister and successor – were unable or unwilling to face up to it. Nor did Ahern depart before the tribunal inquiries reached a critical stage – his credibility was already in shreds after the evidence of Gráinne Carruth. Several senior party figures are in little doubt: he waited until the last minute before he resigned. Had he tried to hang on, he would have been pushed. Cowen was loyal, certainly; but his greatest loyalty was to the party, not to the party leader. Ahern might have made it to the summer of 2008, but not beyond it.

Nor was Ahern's departure quite a clean break. He did not resign his office until 6 May, following an historic address to the United States Congress, and a valedictory meeting with Ian Paisley at Farmleigh. Few begrudged Ahern the space to go in his own time in the flurry of tributes that greeted his decision to step down, but by the time it concluded, the lengthy goodbye seemed indulgent to some. RTÉ's political correspondent, David McCullagh, memorably remarked when reporting on one of Ahern's final engagements, 'As laps of honour go, this isn't a sprint – it's a marathon!'

Ahern's staff and the friends who attended various events with him enjoyed themselves greatly. 'We should have resigned more often,' remarked Rory Brady. Ahern's speech in Washington was well received, but his guests as well as his words described his tenure. Among his party in the US Capitol for the address to Congress were Sean Dunne and Des Richardson. Property developers, and the fundraiser who brought them into the tent at the Galway Races, were part of the story, too.

The post-Ahern cabinet marked a generational change in the leadership of the party. The cabinet heavyweights who entered government with Ahern in 1997 and were obviously the senior members of the cabinet – Micheál Martin, Noel Dempsey and Dermot Ahern – were overlooked for the leadership positions of minister for finance and tánaiste. Instead, Cowen chose Brian Lenihan and Mary Coughlan – both, like himself, 'dynasty' politicians, who had inherited their seats from their fathers, both what the purists would call 'real Fianna Fáil'. Coughlan told friends that she did not want to be made finance minister; similarly Lenihan told people he wanted to stay in the Department of Justice, even if few of them believed him. He knew the finance ministry would position him in the front rank of possible successors to Cowen.

Both ministers were to face widespread questioning about their suitability for their jobs soon after being appointed. Cowen's political logic was compelling: the moves reinforced his dominance of the cabinet. But putting inexperienced hands into both the finance and the employment ministry during the greatest economic crisis in the history of the state was also a huge gamble. Just as it had been with his predecessor, the new Taoiseach was putting politics first and everything else second. Some things would change with the new administration; but not all.

Cowen's new government enjoyed a brief astral moment. As the new Taoiseach gave himself over to a weekend of revelry in his rejoicing, native Offaly, clambering on to the backs of lorries to belt out repeated monsterings of the worst county song in Ireland, 'The Offaly Rover', and further, a balladic tribute to his late father ('Ber Cowen, he is a TD, me boys, Ber Cowen he is a TD/He got Clara a swimming pool, 'coz it isn't near the sea'), voters around the country looked on more in amusement than anything else. There was a widespread relief that the unfortunate tawdriness of the final part of Bertie Ahern's public life was past now, and a hope that a new government could tackle the emerging economic crisis.

In an opinion poll in *The Sunday Business Post*, almost three-quarters of voters surveyed said that Cowen would 'make a good Taoiseach' and was 'a safe pair of hands'. Almost two-thirds of voters said that Cowen would make the best Taoiseach; fewer than 25 per cent preferred Enda Kenny. Fianna Fáil support jumped by five points in a week. Kenny had called for an election. 'I wonder does the opposition want an election now?' texted one senior government adviser when he learned of the poll result. Inevitably, it was termed 'the Biffo Bounce'.

The Biffo Bounce didn't last long: the new government flunked all its early tests. The first was the referendum on the Lisbon Treaty, held just a month after Cowen was elected Taoiseach by the Dáil on 7 May. A poor campaign by the government and the other parties which concentrated at least as much on promoting themselves as explaining the Lisbon Treaty was blown out of the water by a slick and sometimes misleading campaign by Libertas, the vehicle of multi-millionaire businessman Declan Ganley. Ganley, who grew up in England and the west of Ireland, had made his fortune in a variety of exotic enterprises including investment schemes in Albania and the forestry business in the former Soviet Union. He was now determined to spend some of his wealth opposing the Lisbon Treaty. During the referendum his organization was unable or unwilling to answer satisfactorily the most basic questions about itself and its funding, but Ganley's clever campaign, combined with considerable opposition to the treaty among the farming community, which feared a loss of agricultural subsidies, succeeded in bringing opposition to a European treaty to the political mainstream.

The failures of the Yes campaign worked at several levels. At the most basic level, the government and the broader Yes campaign allowed the No activists to define the question of the campaign: can the Lisbon Treaty protect us from unwelcome encroachments by Europe? Amazingly, the Yes campaign never managed to challenge successfully the fundamental premise of the question: that Europe wanted to do nasty things to Ireland. Despite its advantage in men and materiel, a flabby Yes campaign conceded this vital early ground to a No campaign whose occasionally contradictory diversity wasn't a handicap; in fact, it was a very great strength.

Politicians could not comprehend that for many people, having all the political parties in favour of a measure was itself enough to persuade them to vote against it. Perhaps politicians can't be expected to sympathize with this point of view; but they simply refused to believe it when it was demonstrated to them. In any event, the parties never mobilized for a ground war – subsequent research showed that fewer than 10 per cent of voters had actually been canvassed.

Other failures were just political gaffes; both Cowen and European Commissioner Charlie McCreevy admitted that they hadn't read the treaty. Their admissions were seized on by its opponents, particularly Ganley, who professed to have read the treaty, cover to cover. A Ganley supporter, the aviation tycoon and sometime holiday host of McCreevy and Mary Harney, Ulick McEvaddy, claimed he had read it twice. Writing in the *Sunday Tribune*, Michael Clifford dubbed Ganley 'The Man Who Has Read The Treaty'. Following Ganley on a canvass, Clifford described him handing out copies of the treaty in Sligo in the company of anti-abortion campaigners. '"Read it ... *They* haven't read it,"' says The Man Who Has Read The Treaty.'

As polling day approached, polls showed the contest tightening, and it was clear that a late swing either way would be decisive. It was also clear that the momentum was with the opponents of the treaty. When the votes were counted, the No side had an indisputable majority on a strong turnout – 53 to 47 per cent on a turnout of over 53 per cent. As RTÉ's Charlie

Bird declared with uncharacteristic understatement, 'This was not in the script for the government . . .'

The Lisbon result was decisive, crushing, embarrassing for the new government. Acclaimed both by those who simply sought a referendum on the treaty in their own countries and by traditional opponents of the EU, the Irish vote reverberated around the political and media élites of Europe as a deliberate and conscious rejection of Europe by one of the great beneficiaries of the EU project. For ministers attending meetings in Brussels, there was sympathy from their European peers at a troublesome constitution and a recalcitrant electorate; but also an unspoken question: when are you going to fix this?

It was the worst possible start for the new administration. A belated campaign postponed by Bertie Ahern's tribunal agonies and then his prolonged departure, a bungled strategy and the inability of the new Taoiseach to communicate effectively with voters meant that the government had played a significant role in its own defeat. Worse was to come.

The folly – and, post-election, the complete pointlessness – of the budgetary looseness of Bertie Ahern's final year in power was evident to those who cared to look long before the government declared that a round of mid-year cutbacks in spending would be necessary in July. Ministers had been briefed for months past about it, but the political imperatives of first changing the leader and then fighting the Lisbon campaign meant that addressing the growing gap between what the state raised in taxation and what it was spending day-to-day was pushed way down the agenda. In June, a report from the ESRI, the economic think-tank, predicted that the Irish economy would contract for the first time since the early 1980s; despite the obvious signs all around it, the country appeared unable to process the news. The tone of many public discussions was incredulous. How could we be in recession? How? How?

In truth, the government was not far ahead of the public in its incomprehension and denial. The new finance minister, having

light-heartedly decried his own misfortune at ascending to the
position, instituted a mid-year programme of spending controls
and savings, though his colleagues scrambled to protect their own
budgets. Lenihan promised to save €500 million in 2008 and a
further billion in 2009. It would be only a fraction of what was
needed, but even much of this was illusory. Lenihan pledged to
save 3 per cent of the public sector pay bill in the remainder
of 2008; however, his officials conceded that he was committed
to paying increases of 2.5 per cent to public servants under
the national wage agreements a few weeks later at the start of
September. His projected savings on the pay bill were wiped out
by agreed pay increases which he was unable or unwilling to
cancel. As the crisis would demonstrate again and again, the
politics couldn't keep pace with the economics.

In September the government finally realized that its financial
position wasn't a problem: it was a massive crisis. At the start
of the month, Lenihan announced that he would bring forward
the budget from early December to mid-October, though it
was unclear if this would achieve anything other than making it
look as though the government was doing something. Because
November is the biggest month for taxation receipts, his officials
would plan the spending for 2009 with only the haziest idea of
how much they would be short for 2008, and no reliable estimate
of how much revenue would be collected in taxation. This was
the economics of a banana republic.

Despite growing tensions between them about the need to cut
public spending – Lenihan favoured earlier and deeper cuts; the
Taoiseach didn't like the politics of it – the two men worked
hard at the Fianna Fáil parliamentary party's autumn get-together
to prepare government TDs for a rocky road ahead. Yet the
mood among TDs was unworried, jaunty almost. After some
pain, things would be all right, they thought. In the *Irish Times*,
Mark Hennessy reported from the meeting: 'The back-benchers'
calm is based on a simple premise. Tough decisions taken
quickly will right the ship in time for the next general election, if
not next year's local elections. The confidence is based on the

belief an upturn will come, if not quickly, then at least by 2010.'

They had been through an economic slowdown before, hadn't they? Not like this they hadn't.

The collapse of Lehman Brothers, a massive Wall Street investment bank, on 15 September 2008 changed the face of the global economic crisis. Suddenly, banks all over the world were potentially vulnerable. For the Irish banks, dependent on securing funding from other banks to finance their bloated loan-books, troubles came quickly. On the evening of Monday 29 September, a fortnight after Lehman's death-dive, the Irish banking system reached the brink.

Cowen and Lenihan had been receiving updates all day as the stock market savaged the banks' share prices. Since the Lehman collapse, the international credit markets had frozen up as banks, fearful of lending to the next casualty, and losing their money, became unwilling to lend to one another. For the Irish banks, this presented a deadly threat. Rumours had buzzed through London's financial circles over the weekend about imminent events with the Irish banks; traders began to take positions in anticipation. The market's sharks had smelled blood in the water. All day Monday, Anglo-Irish Bank shares were sold at lower and lower prices; by the time the Stock Exchange closed for business, the bank had lost half its value.

The falling share price wasn't the principal problem – the banks had already lost some 80 per cent of the 2007 highs – but it was what the falls represented that was concerning the ministers. The markets were anticipating that an Irish bank was going down, and that belief would sooner or later precipitate a run on one of them, possibly all of them. No bank, however healthy, can survive a run on deposits. A bank collapse would have ruinous effects on the economy and on the social order – at the first sign of any collapse, queues would form outside every bank to withdraw funds.

As soon as the Dublin market closed, Cowen and Lenihan, along with their secretaries-general Dermot McCarthy and David Doyle, met in the Department of the Taoiseach. Central Bank governor John Hurley and financial regulator Pat Neary joined them and later the attorney general Paul Gallagher sat in. Senior officials came and went during a rolling series of meetings that lasted all evening and into the early hours of the morning. They discussed nationalizing one of the banks, but concluded that to do so would put the others under probably fatal strain. They immediately dismissed doing nothing and allowing the markets to decide – at least some of the banks would soon fail. So they concluded that some form of state underwriting of the entire system would have to take place.

According to people who were involved in the process, this decision was reached relatively early in the evening. Senior banking executives were spirited in and out of the Department of Finance and the adjacent Government Buildings all evening. One civil servant, seeing a senior bank executive entering the building, enquired what was going on. 'For God's sake, don't say anything,' she was told. 'You'll have a run on the banks!' The chairmen and chief executives of the two biggest banks, Allied Irish Bank and Bank of Ireland, slipped into Government Buildings at about 9.30 that evening. Dermot Gleeson and Eugene Sheehy of AIB and Richard Burrows and Brian Goggin of Bank of Ireland were led in to the Sycamore Room and asked to wait. After two hours they were led in to see Cowen and Lenihan. Among the bankers' suggestions was that Anglo-Irish Bank could be nationalized. Cowen's response was, 'We're not fucking nationalizing Anglo.'

Having listened to the bankers, the Taoiseach and his finance minister made their decision. The state would guarantee the deposits, loans and obligations of the six Irish banks – a total sum under guarantee of some €400 billion, more than twice the country's GNP. Even if the men had felt they had no option, it was still a breathtakingly bold move.

Several ministers were put on notice that an incorporeal cabinet meeting would take place to approve the measure, and officials prepared briefings for them. Some ministers were easier to contact than others. When the formal telephone calls took place between

3.00 and 5.00 a.m., officials couldn't contact the Green party leader and environment minister John Gormley. His mobile phone was either switched off or powered down. Eventually, officials rang the gardaí at Irishtown. Gormley was woken by a garda at his door, asking him to ring the Taoiseach's office. In fact, Gormley had discussed the possibility of such a move with Cowen over the previous days. He had been heavily influenced by conversations he had had with the economist and columnist David McWilliams, who had advocated a government guarantee of bank deposits in the previous week's *Sunday Business Post*.

Later on the Tuesday morning, Lenihan, Cowen and some senior officials engaged in a round of telephone contacts with key European policy-makers to inform them what they planned, including the French finance minister, Christine Lagarde, Jean-Claude Juncker in Luxembourg (chair of the Eurozone group of finance ministers) and the European Central Bank chief, Jean-Claude Trichet. On the face of it, the move looked like favouring some banks to the exclusion of the others, contrary to European regulations. But they knew that the politics of the situation meant that some rules were more important than others. The British government was furious, and there were a number of testy telephone conversations between Dublin and London, involving Lenihan and Chancellor of the Exchequer Alastair Darling, and Cowen and Prime Minister Gordon Brown. Eventually, British-owned banks operating in Ireland were offered admittance to the scheme.

The government press secretary, Eoghan Ó Neachtain, had been swapping drafts of statements with the Department of Finance press office since the previous evening. Now, they formulated a rushed media timetable, tipping off the morning bulletins and arranging briefings. By the time reporters began to gather in the Department of Finance on Tuesday morning following a rushed summons, the magnitude of the threat was becoming clearer. 'We're in the eye of the storm here,' Lenihan told the hastily arranged press conference. 'It's time for action, swift and decisive.'

The reaction to the bank guarantee was broadly positive, despite the massive potential burden that the state had taken on, though some international media decried the Irish for a 'beggar-my-neighbour' approach. An *Irish Times* editorial observed, 'The government has acted decisively to underpin the banking system. Its response is not perfect but to date appears to have worked and few can argue that it was not justified by the circumstances.' The *Independent*'s Brendan Keenan was cautiously optimistic, suggesting that it might restore confidence in Irish banks. Many economists and commentators reserved judgement: they had no idea whether it would work or not. In truth, the government wasn't sure either.

In the Dáil, Fine Gael supported the move, though Labour opposed it. The political kudos for Lenihan, though, would not last long. Two weeks later, when the finance minister introduced his first budget, it blew up in his face.

If Charlie McCreevy had demonstrated that even budgets that give away billions can contain political landmines which detonate under government's feet, Lenihan demonstrated that they can surface in a hair-shirt budget, too. Though all welfare rates were substantially increased, the decision to scrap the automatic entitlement to a medical card for the over-seventies would excite furious opposition from those affected. The introduction of the universal entitlement to a card had been a last-minute political wheeze by Charlie McCreevy before the 2002 general election; the government did not even conduct serious costings. On a purely rational policy level, there was little justification for continuing with a universal scheme; but many pensioners had grown very attached to free medical care, and even for those who seldom used it, it was a pleasant comfort blanket.

The primary parliamentary duty of Fine Gael's Michael Ring, it often seems, is to shout hyperbolic observations about the depravity of Fianna Fáil and the sorry plight of the west of Ireland. But he spotted his opening straight away when Lenihan announced the medical card cut. 'That's an attack on the elderly!'

he roared. Over the coming days, it would become clear that the elderly were very much in agreement. Lenihan's ill-judged peroration, in which he described the budget as a 'call to patriotic action', compounded the damage.

The airwaves were flooded with fear and outrage. 'Elderly lobby groups yesterday reported receiving a flood of calls from confused pensioners in the wake of the Budget announcement,' reported the *Irish Independent*. '"People are very frightened about the future. One lady whose father is in hospital is very concerned about the bills he will face from January," a spokesman for Age Action said.' The fact that groups like St Vincent de Paul supported the move cut no ice with the outraged.

Media at all levels fanned the flames. Even by the standards of the medium, the reaction of callers to RTÉ's *Liveline* programme was hysterical. 'Mother of God above tonight, we'll be left with not even a shilling to be giving to the church gate collection – as a matter of fact we could be having the collections ourselves!' wailed one caller. Joe soothed them – 'OK, OK ... Yeah, yeah, yeah' – but he stoked them up, too; 'It's seen as an attack on the elderly!' he summed up.

Taking their cue, Fianna Fáil TDs began to agitate for the measure to be amended. Even as Cowen's spin doctors were writing a newspaper article to be published under his name defending the measure, the inevitability of a climb-down was already in the air. A stormy Fianna Fáil parliamentary party meeting showed the absent Taoiseach that he had a bona fide back-bench revolt on his hands; several TDs threatened to vote against the measure. Two days after the budget the government announced that it would alter the eligibility criteria, making the cards much more broadly available for pensioners. They were on the run now. One back-bencher, Joe Behan from Wicklow, resigned from the party, and others threatened to follow. On the Friday night after the budget, Cowen went on RTÉ's television news and promised to review the decision, though he insisted that the savings would still have to be made. The independent TD Finian McGrath, who had voted with the government after he had been promised some government spending for projects in his constituency, sniffed the political wind and announced he was rejoining the opposition. After a week of political chaos in which the fall of the government looked a very real possibility, Cowen announced a U-turn on the medical cards and on the extension of a 1 per cent income levy to the low-paid.

When thousands of pensioners assembled outside Leinster House anyway, several Fianna Fáil TDs watched, horrified, from the plinth. Dozens of gardaí attended at the front gate in case the pensioners stormed the parliament building. What would the gardaí have done? Baton them? As the mob hooted their derision at the unfortunate government representatives who tried to address them, the back-benchers could feel their seats ebbing away from them.

The government looked as though it was losing the authority to govern; privately, its own members despaired of their leader. After six months in office, his government had made its first serious and substantial effort to address the calamitous crisis in the public finances. It had failed spectacularly.

The new year, 2009, dawned with predictions of political strife and economic turmoil. They were not wrong. In an early January interview with Stephen Collins of the *Irish Times*, Cowen rejected the charge that he was failing to provide leadership at this critical juncture in the state's fortunes. 'I don't accept that, obviously. Where we are at really at the moment is trying to bring public opinion with us on the size of the problem facing us and on the method we are using to address it.'

But Cowen had demonstrated that he had a very substantial problem in communicating anything to the public. Partially that was because of the cack-handed way that the government had approached both the substantive issues of budgetary management and the task of communicating its actions to the public. But it was also because there was a fundamental contradiction between portraying the government as a victim of international events and presenting themselves as the only people who could get the voters out of this mess.

Cowen and Lenihan had three huge problems. They had limited control over two of them. Firstly they had a gaping €20 billion-plus hole in the state's finances, a 2009 deficit projected – at more than 10 per cent of GDP – to be over three times the EU's agreed limit for members of the Eurozone. Ireland was sheltering behind the protection of the euro, but smashing the rules for membership. The cost of running the state was not even approached by revenues raised from taxation. A revised plan to bring down the deficit was agreed by the European Commission in January; it would involve slashing public spending and increasing taxation over four years.

Secondly there was a very severe recession in the real economy with business failures, rising joblessness and falling standards of living an everyday reality. In the month of February alone, nearly 30,000 people lost their jobs; an epidemic of unemployment was spreading across the country.

Finally, there was a crisis in the country's banks, which were now guaranteed by the taxpayer but facing the dire consequences of reckless loans that would never be repaid. In the week before Christmas, the government had announced it would plough €5.5 billion from the National Pension Reserve Fund, the state's rainy-day money, into Bank of Ireland, AIB and Anglo-Irish Bank in an effort to recapitalize them; few thought it would be sufficient.

All three problems had the capacity certainly to derail the government and, potentially, to cause the economic collapse of the state. Together, they were a perfect storm, politically and economically. But the storm had been brewing when Cowen succeeded to the Taoiseach's office, even if he had chosen to ignore the weather forecast. Now after his first eight months, he had made little progress in plotting a course through the tempest.

By mid-January, another sudden and far-reaching decision was made by means of an incorporeal cabinet meeting. The Taoiseach was in Tokyo; Anglo-Irish Bank was on the edge of a cliff. On the evening of 15 January, at a hastily arranged press conference, Lenihan announced that the bank would be nationalized immediately. Revelations that the bank's former chief executive Sean Fitzpatrick had arranged nearly €90 million in loans for himself and then connived with other bankers – notably Irish Nationwide's Michael Fingleton – to hide that fact from his own auditors had destroyed whatever reputation and creditworthiness the bank retained. 'The government must move to the final and decisive step of public ownership,' Lenihan told journalists, announcing the move. The *Financial Times*, not unreasonably, lectured Ireland about 'crony capitalism'.

That the government was forced to nationalize having previously set its face against such a course not only emphasized how quickly and dangerously financial and economic events were moving; it also underlined how the government appeared to be constantly chasing events rather than leading them.

Two months after Lenihan declared that there was 'no question' of an emergency budget, Cowen told the Dáil that further measures to control public spending and raise revenues would be brought to the Dáil in a supplementary budget in early April. The taxation revenues expected by the government in the opening two months of the year had not materialized, and a further disastrous shortfall in the public finances was opening up. The government had made some progress in fixing its finances, implementing a pension levy on public-sector workers – which infuriated them, but which hardly replaced the lost revenue. Without further action, the country was facing insolvency. Comparing the Irish public finances to a car careering down a hill, Dan O'Brien of *The Economist* said that the government had two choices: slam on the brakes or hit a wall at full speed. Both involved a very sudden jolt.

Despite earlier commitments that there was no room for further tax increases, Lenihan's emergency budget on 7 April introduced a round of whopping tax hikes on income earners at all levels, At the highest levels, Lenihan had increased taxes by an eye-watering 9 per cent in his two budgets. The twenty-year commitment of Fianna Fáil to low personal taxation as an engine of economic growth seemed to have disappeared in the space of a few months. Its demise was strangely unremarked upon, as if ministers didn't want to believe it was really happening. On the other side of the ledger, cuts in public spending were kept to a minimum in the April budget; the government had decided that the public sector had been hit hard enough with the pension levy, and it was afraid of the political impact of cutting non-pay spending in areas like health and education.

Cowen had blamed himself for the debacle of the October budget and resolved that there would be no landmines to detonate underneath him on this occasion. For weeks before the budget ministers had closeted themselves away in a seemingly endless series of cabinet meetings, going through the budget proposals line by line to politically proof them. This resulted in a piecemeal, sectionalized approach that risked missing the bigger picture. The need for political survival – and there was a very real threat that the government could fall on the budget – resulted in the possible cutbacks to spending being watered down and the tax increases being moved up in importance. Ministers dedicated almost a dozen meetings – often lasting four or five hours – to agreeing the package of measures. It was a far cry from when Charlie McCreevy wouldn't even tell the Taoiseach what was in his budgets.

Nonetheless, the widespread leaking of several budgetary measures in advance had softened up the ground, preparing the public and government TDs for the severity of the harshest budget in living memory. A plan to establish a national assets management agency to relieve the banks of all development property debt was the subject of some furious debate, but for perhaps the first time, it suggested that the government could get to grips with the banking crisis, even if it was at the cost of tens of billions to the taxpayer.

As he passed the milestone of a year in office, Cowen was a political leader struggling to retain his authority. On becoming leader, he had been faced with as daunting a set of economic and political circumstances as any leader of the independent Irish state had encountered since de Valera. On those sunny days in May 2008, he had spoken – in the Dáil chamber and from the backs of lorries in Offaly villages – with a rhetorical fluency and intellectual consistency that few of his predecessors possessed. But when it came to political action, he had stumbled at almost every turn. Finance minister when the country's finances grew unsustainable, Cowen was now the Taoiseach of the bust. Though he had latterly displayed some signs that he was coming to grips with the problem – the public-sector pension levy and the asset management agency plan won some praise – for every one step his government took forward, it seemed to take two back. Fianna Fáil had played the politics of the boom for all it was worth; it seemed incapable of managing the bust.

In early June 2009, the politics of the bust came home to roost for Fianna Fáil. The local and European elections and two Dáil by-elections brought by far the worst results in the party's history. A chaotic and ineffectual campaign emphasized Cowen's clumsiness at modern political communications, while Fianna Fáil canvassers were taken aback at the scale of anger and hostility they encountered on the doorsteps. When the votes were counted on the weekend of 5–6 June, Fianna Fáil won just over 25 per cent of the local election vote, trailing Fine Gael by seven points and more than a hundred councillors. For the first time in the history of the state, Fine Gael was the largest party of local government. Association with the now toxic Fianna Fáil brand was fatal for its coalition partners: the Green Party was decimated, losing all but three of its councillors nationwide.

In the European elections, Fianna Fáil lost its seat in Dublin, and the son of the late Seamus Brennan crashed in the Dublin South by-election. But it was the Dublin Central by-election result that spoke loudest about the voters' verdict on Fianna Fáil's years in power. Maurice Ahern, elder brother of the former taoiseach, won just 12 per cent of the vote, and was relegated to fifth place on the first count. The humiliation was complete when the elder Ahern also lost his council seat. It was an astonishing rejection of Bertie Ahern by his own people. *Sic transit gloria mundi*. Showtime politics was buried in a Dublin Central grave.

As the American writer Joe Klein has observed, politics in a time of plenty is a subtle art, of balancing the needs of various constituencies and placating the different interest groups, convincing voters of their good fortune, and yet managing their expectations of national and personal advancement. Bertie Ahern used the bulging exchequer balances of the boom years to buy his popularity, but there was great political skill involved in the way he manoeuvred himself to face all ways at once, too. When the money runs out, it is very different: a time for hard choices and unpopular decisions. If to govern is to choose, the choices had become much more difficult for Brian Cowen than they had been for his predecessor. A year into the job, he looked no more capable of mastering those decisions than Ahern did of reaching easier ones.

The great change that has been wrought on the government and on the country is exemplified in the contrast between the two men. Ahern was a consensualist by nature and by politics, a man whose mission in life often appeared to be simply to avoid offending anyone. Politics elevated his personal inclination to avoid conflict into a political philosophy, though Ahern never felt the need to spell out his beliefs in those terms. Cowen is a more cerebral character, but also more temperamental than the Ahern. Ahern could compartmentalize his life, dealing dispassionately with mundane politics while he was being destroyed at the Mahon Tribunal. He was famously cool. Cowen can blow hot and cold, by turns reducing his officials to hysterics of laughter and then roaring abuse at them if he feels a speech or briefing paper is inadequate.

Ahern circumvented parliament and frequently moaned about the amount of time he was forced to spend there; it was his unlikely contention that his fellow European leaders were forever begging him to detain himself there less frequently. Cowen emphasizes its importance and regards it as a means of communicating with the Irish people. Both men generally dislike the media, but Ahern was better at hiding it. Ahern was his own best press officer, conducting, through his constant doorstep interviews, a rolling press conference that lasted for eleven years; Cowen eschews political communication as an occasional inconvenience. Ahern was a master of backroom deals with business leaders and trade union barons; Cowen thinks elected politicians should be the decision-makers, and on taking over as Taoiseach excluded advisers from meetings of cabinet sub-committees. And the most obvious difference: Ahern was emollient, Cowen is abrasive. Ahern hated to say no to people and was a master at achieving consensus; Cowen is often a take-it-or-leave-it man. Perhaps the country might have been better off if Cowen had been Taoiseach during the boom, and Ahern during the slump.

The transition did no favours for either man. At home, the focus on Ahern's departure and the eventual handover of power to Brian Cowen did immense damage to the campaign to pass the Lisbon Treaty, already suffering from leadership neglect in the months preceding Ahern's announcement. The ignoring of the scale of the emerging crisis in the state's finances, passed on to his successor, would do lasting damage to the economy and the country. The man who had negotiated a European constitution and welcomed more than anyone the ex-Soviet satellites into the until-then western European Union undermined his own country's place in the union; the leader who had presided over an economic miracle contributed mightily to its undoing.

The contributions of Ahern's administrations to Northern Ireland are incontestable, effecting a relatively stable and peaceful society with a functioning if contrived local politics. Across the border, in the state he presided over for a decade, his ultimate legacy – and the future of the party he dominated – will depend on how his successors deal with the unresolved problems they inherited from him.

Nonetheless, by any objective standards, the governments led by Bertie Ahern achieved a very great measure of success.

The two great failures of the independent Irish state, an economy that could not support its people and the unresolved conflict in Northern Ireland, were reversed. The position of Ireland was greatly enhanced within the European Union, and internationally. Even in the midst of a recession, the Ireland of today has made many advances since 1997.

But Ahern's governments were also afflicted by a terrible short-sightedness, an inability to act strategically, to plan wisely for the future. Ultimately, this has had profoundly damaging economic consequences. All politicians think of elections all the time; that much is hardly in dispute. But not all are willing to direct all the resources and priorities of government towards compliance with an election cycle. Ahern once told the Dáil that the real code of conduct in the House was to get in, and to try to stay in. So it became with his governments: being in power and staying there was an end in itself. So colossal amounts of government spending were decided with elections in mind and subsequently wasted; economics was shoehorned into the political cycle. A fearsome political machine played the you-never-had-it-so-good card with ruthless, overwhelming efficiency, but its governing was often fractured and confused. It delivered power, certainly. But it also contained the seeds of its own demise. The election packages and the giveaway budgets had to get bigger and bigger. The ever-growing demands of a public who have been told that they could have their cake and eat it – huge public spending *and* tax cuts – have become impossible to meet. And a financial crisis was ignored for too long because it didn't suit the politics to face up to it. Now the resolution of that crisis will define the legacy of the good times, and of those who led them.

In reality, the public's default position is that it has a pretty low expectation of politicians. Voters just want their governments to run the country, and not make an obvious mess of it. But that was never enough for Ahern and Fianna Fáil; they didn't trust themselves and their achievements. That's the irony of it all. For all the irresistible electoral success of Showtime politics, it was no way to run a country.

Index

He just wanted a decent book to read ...

Not too much to ask, is it? It was in 1935 when Allen Lane, Managing Director of Bodley Head Publishers, stood on a platform at Exeter railway station looking for something good to read on his journey back to London. His choice was limited to popular magazines and poor-quality paperbacks – the same choice faced every day by the vast majority of readers, few of whom could afford hardbacks. Lane's disappointment and subsequent anger at the range of books generally available led him to found a company – and change the world.

'We believed in the existence in this country of a vast reading public for intelligent books at a low price, and staked everything on it'
Sir Allen Lane, 1902–1970, founder of Penguin Books

The quality paperback had arrived – and not just in bookshops. Lane was adamant that his Penguins should appear in chain stores and tobacconists, and should cost no more than a packet of cigarettes.

Reading habits (and cigarette prices) have changed since 1935, but Penguin still believes in publishing the best books for everybody to enjoy. We still believe that good design costs no more than bad design, and we still believe that quality books published passionately and responsibly make the world a better place.

So wherever you see the little bird – whether it's on a piece of prize-winning literary fiction or a celebrity autobiography, political tour de force or historical masterpiece, a serial-killer thriller, reference book, world classic or a piece of pure escapism – you can bet that it represents the very best that the genre has to offer.

Whatever you like to read – trust Penguin.